Land of sport and glory

Sport and British society, 1887–1910

Sir Derek Birley

MANCHESTER UNIVERSITY PRESS
Manchester and New York

Distributed exclusively in the USA and Canada by St. Martin's Press

Copyright © Derek Birley 1995

Published by Manchester University Press
Oxford Road, Manchester M13 9NR, UK
and Room 400, 175 Fifth Avenue, New York, NY 10010, USA

Distributed exclusively in the USA and Canada
by St. Martin's Press, Inc., 175 Fifth Avenue, New York, NY 10010, USA

British Library cataloguing in publication data
A catalogue record for this book is available from the British Library

Library of Congress cataloguing in publication data
Birley, Derek.
    Land of sport and glory : sport and British society, 1887–1910 /
Derek Birley.
        p.   cm. — (International studies in the history of sport)
    Includes index.
    ISBN 0–7190–4494–4. — ISBN 0–7190–4495–2 (pbk.)
    1. Sports—Great Britain—History. 2. Sports—Social aspects–
–Great Britain—History.   I. Title.   II. Series.
    GV605.B55   1994
    796'.0941—dc20   94–26264
                                                                CIP

ISBN 0 7190 4494 4 *hardback*
      0 7190 4495 2 *paperback*

Photoset in Linotron Palatino by
Northern Phototypesetting Co Ltd, Bolton
Printed in Great Britain by
Redwood Books, Trowbridge

CONTENTS

LIST OF ILLUSTRATIONS

SERIES EDITOR'S FOREWORD

This is the second volume of Sir Derek Birley's trilogy on the evolution of sport in Britain. It covers the late Victorian and Edwardian eras. With its emphasis more on adults than adolescents and more on privilege and its defence than morality and its diffusion, mature years are given precedence over formative years which makes for a distinctively personal perspective.

The story of sport told here is very much one of distance, division and confrontation – socially, sexually, geographically and politically, and this volume, as delightfully readable as the first, is as much a social as a sporting commentary which, in my view, is just as it should be.

It is a sorry tale of double-standards, self-interest, hypocrisy, games-manship and snobbery. Even the Corinthians fail to come up to scratch. It should be required reading for idealistic politicians.

J.A. Mangan

ACKNOWLEDGEMENTS

As before my principal debts are to the authors, scholarly and sporting, whose work I have drawn upon – for inspiration as well as information and apt quotation. I have tried to acknowledge them all in the notes, and to indicate where pursuivant readers can find more treasure. Librarians, courteous members of an invaluable but often undervalued profession, have once again been supportive, especially, this time, those of the universities of Coventry and Warwick.

I owe particular thanks to three individuals. Tony Mangan's obstetric and analgesic skills greatly eased the birth-pangs of this second triplet. Frank Cass showed a generosity and chivalry unmatched even amongst Glamorgan supporters. My wife Norma gave sound advice on important issues, and never once looked as though she thought I ought to be doing something more functional.

For Robert and David –
half each, as always

INTRODUCTION

During the slow and erratic progress from her days as a remote and trouble-some outpost of the Roman Empire to the time when she became a great imperial power herself Britain had developed a taste for sport that bordered on obsession. For the confident middle classes it was a secular religion, and for the entrepreneurs a potential goldmine. For the aristocracy and gentry, who had once seen it as vocational training, sport had become a dream world, a refuge from the harsh pressures of the real one, in which first capitalism and then its accidental by-product democracy were gradually undermining the old order. On the other hand the dream-world was open to all, and sporting values, especially when gambling was involved, were potentially anarchical: given the chance Jack often turned out to be not merely as good as but better than his master. Beyond all this, however, people of all classes saw the sporting spirit as a vital ingredient in the British make-up, fostering qualities of character that fitted them uniquely well for the task of governing the vast empire they had acquired, and for defending it against lesser nations. The Establishment looked to the public schools, which set great store by team games, often at the expense of intellectual and cultural activities, to inculcate the qualities required for leadership at home and abroad.

The pure doctrines of muscular Christianity, team spirit and character-building enunciated so fervently in the re-organised public schools of the nineteenth century were alloyed by the hierarchical assumptions of the past. Leadership, for instance, was thought to be the prerogative of the well born, and the new rule-makers spent much time trying to equate the old notion of the gentleman with the new one of the amateur. By the late nineteenth century the old ascendancy was crumbling and the aristocracy were beginning a long, slow decline. The basis of their prosperity and social status was land and throughout Europe land values had plummeted, partly because American and Australasian big-scale agriculture and American mass-production flooded the market with cheap goods, and partly because of Europe's own increasing emphasis on industry. The consequences went beyond the economic. Competition not only brought international friction, but intensified the pressure for social change.

One of the principal causes of this pressure, commercialisation, was an inevitable result of the aristocracy's own descent into mercantilism. The distinctive ethos of Britain as a trading nation had long been accepted (with greater or lesser degrees of enthusiasm) as a source of strength. Free trade had been elevated into a philosophy, complementing the prevailing trickle-down theories of Adam Smith and reconciling idealists like Gladstone to the responsibilities of Empire. But industrialisation, in which Britain had initially taken the lead, proved a bigger challenge than she had bargained for. The railways, living emblems of the insistent new age, had thrust themselves into previously remote and unsullied areas. Trains, like factory chimneys and back-to-back houses in the towns and mining villages, belched forth smoke, blackening the brick and dulling the ironwork that characterised the age – an outward and visible sign, so writers, artists and preachers proclaimed, of an inward and spiritual decay. The new forces in politics, from the collective civic movements for better public health to the trades union leaders who broadened their concern from wages to social conditions, posed a similar threat to the old order.

All of this meant that the way forward signalled so optimistically by the Great Exhibition of 1851, the hope of ordered progress through the application of science, no longer seemed so clear. This book, continuing the story begun in *Sport and the Making of Britain*, tells how the games-playing British faced the challenges that lay ahead – Irish nationalism, democracy, urbanisation, commercialism, technology, foreign competition, and, not least, the first glimmerings of feminism. A 'new woman' was beginning to emerge. Her intellectual potential had already found recognition in the early girls' public schools. A daring few were seeking social and political equality. The dream-world of sport they now threatened to invade was one that reflected men's primeval role as hunters and their dominance as warriors, traders, priests and rulers in later, civilised societies. Except for a few Amazonian idiosyncrasies amongst governing elites women had been type-cast as chattels, prizes to be won or spoils to be seized in war, and as emblem-wearers, handkerchief-waving spectators and brow-soothers in sport.

The unconscious fears of their menfolk apart, it was not easy for Victorian women to change their own self-image and win a measure of public acceptance that they might begin to use their bodies as well as their minds more fully. Women's right to control the destinies of their bodies is the central issue in the struggle for a new relationship between the sexes that is still going on today. An early consequence of that struggle was that for middle-class women towards the end of the last century marriage was no longer always and inevitably seen as consignment to a life of large-scale child-bearing and disability for other pursuits. The trend towards smaller families that began in these circles as contraception became more widely practised, liberated women, physically and psychologically. It was hardly to be expected that they would have much influence on the male domination of the dream-world of sport (any more than they did in the real one) but at least they could play a

2

part.

Indeed such was the profusion of sports, games and recreations of all kinds that everyone could play a part. The British tried their hands at everything, and prided themselves on inventing, improving or at least bringing a sense of order into most of the world's athletic pleasures. There were many novelties but also many revivals. The old field sports tended to be frowned upon by the more moralistic amongst the urban middle classes, but hunting, shooting and fishing, each in a somewhat different fashion and with many social variants, continued to exercise a hold on the British imagination, which was heavily infused with reverence for the past. Horse-racing, on the Flat and over the sticks, was a favourite with all classes especially those who liked a flutter, and as the horse lost its place as a work animal it acquired added status for leisure purposes. The team games of the public schools were held in highest esteem, cricket most of all, and football reached new heights of popularity, but so did new suburban delights, such as lawn tennis and golf. The girls' public schools gave a new standing to hockey and lacrosse, and lesser schools prompted the discovery of netball. Cycling came into fashion and went out again. The islanders made for water whenever they could, besporting themselves on its surface in yachts and rowing boats, and millions took to swimming in it, overcoming an age-old aversion from immersion. Athletics and boxing lived down unsavoury reputations with some success.

This profusion of riches made things easy for contemporary participants but makes them correspondingly difficult for the present-day historian. Since the very range and multiplicity of what was on offer were essential characteristics of the British experience during the Glory Years it has seemed important to try to cover most of them, even offering a respectful salute in passing to such things as motor racing, winter sports and roller-skating. But it would be impossible, in the interests of coherence as well as digestibility, to give them all as much attention as they doubtless deserve. There are plenty of histories of particular sports, many of them very good and almost all produced with loving care, and I have referred to many that I have enjoyed or found useful in the notes. This book looks at the British sporting scene as a whole and in its social context.

It has two parts. The first deals with the late Victorian era up to the Boer War and the 'imperial lesson' that Kipling hoped had been learnt. The second covers the Edwardian heyday, the golden age. Within each part, as nearly chronologically as is practical, chapters are devoted to groups of sports, illustrative of various themes. Games, it is now widely accepted, are a serious business and I have approached the task of expounding their efflorescence over these years of British glory with what I trust will be regarded as due respect. But there is a difference between seriousness and solemnity and I hope that as well as casting light on a few dark corners the book may offer a little entertainment along the way.

PART I

Utopia limited
1887–1901

CHAPTER ONE

Grace and favour

Amid the cheers for Queen Victoria's Golden Jubilee a few discordant noises could be heard. Most of them came from Ireland – but that was to be expected. The Irish were a troublesome lot as everyone knew. The Queen herself despaired of them and they were by far the biggest threat to the complacency of her ministers. The Liberals should have strengthened their hold on power when they extended the franchise in 1885 but within a year they had split apart, mainly through the insistence of 'the Irish question', and the Conservatives were thrust into office. The decisive factor was Gladstone's conversion to the cause of Home Rule. Almost all the Whig peers deserted him: so did most of their counterparts in the Commons. From then on the Liberals found themselves heavily dependent on the Celtic fringe, an electoral hazard that helped to deny them power for all but three of the next twenty years.

The two leading defectors from the old Liberal ranks were strikingly different. One was Joseph Chamberlain, the reforming Birmingham industrialist who had seemed Gladstone's natural successor. The other was Lord Hartington, son of the Duke of Devonshire. What they had in common was a conviction that Home Rule was a threat to the Empire, and they now came together to form the Liberal Unionists, pledged like the Tories to uphold the sanctity of the Union. For all right-thinking Britishers belief in Queen and Empire was no mere political option but an obligatory hall-mark of moral rectitude. The Tories, led by the distinctly unprogressive Lord Salisbury, won the 1886 election and the Liberal Unionists, led by the sporting heir to the Cavendish estates, Lord Hartington, held the balance of power.

Gladstone's surrender to the clamour for Irish Home Rule raised further doubts amongst the electorate about whether the Liberals could really be trusted. Their image was already tarnished by the disruptive tendencies of the radical wing of the Party and its undesirable associates. Irish nationalism was a recurrent theme of the open-air meetings staged by socialists and anarchists in Trafalgar Square. Jubilee year was also the year of 'Bloody Sunday' when a meeting called to demand the release of a jailed Nationalist MP erupted into riots that had to be quelled by force. Party politics aside, there was growing anxiety amongst the older generation that social progress was not being achieved in quite the ordered fashion they had expected. The emergent working classes, so far from being content with the advances they had achieved, appeared only to want more. Uncontrolled and possibly uncontrollable forces were at work. Salisbury had struck a chord by his gloomy analysis of the disruptive tendencies in modern life in 1883, and three years later the revered Poet Laureate, Tennyson, to his admirer Gladstone's manifest dismay, had published a sensational recantation of his youthful liberal ideals.[1] Gladstone had replied with a recital of the benefits brought by Free Trade,[2] but this doctrine, once an article of faith for Tories and Whigs alike, was now being assailed from every side.

The most dangerous sign was that working men, coming more into the political reckoning, were beginning to find leaders of distinctly socialistic hue to speak for them in Parliament and outside. Reformers at mass meetings were clamouring for state intervention: in 1886, for instance, the Fair Trade League called on the government to 'start useful public works for the unemployed'. But it was not only the workers who were disaffected: some amongst the middle class, who were inclined to think themselves the hardest hit by the 'Great Depression', sought an answer in protectionism. The same meeting resolved that 'Parliament should. . .take measures to relieve our distressed agricultural interest;. . .fair play should be given to British industry, against the disastrous effects of hostile foreign tariffs and of foreign State bounties on products imported into the British market.'[3]

Certainly the cunning foreigners, who seemed to have fewer misgivings about mechanisation, were putting formidable obstacles in the path of economic progress. It was agriculture, for so long the staple, that first found itself painfully squeezed as British manufactured goods were sold abroad in return for cheap, imported food. Then, as industrial competition increased, the compensatory advantage in manufacture grew less and the balance of trade deteriorated. In 1870 the value of British exports had roughly equalled that of France, Germany and the USA combined. Twenty years later it was less than three-quarters.

The clash of past and present

But there was no turning back. The stark fact was that Britain, for all her lingering rural myths and remaining tracts of picturesque countryside, was now a heavily industrialised and urbanised country. The 1881 census had shown that over three-quarters of the 35 million inhabitants of the United Kingdom lived in and around towns and the proportion increased as the total grew to 41 million by 1901, 33 million of them in England and Wales. Britain had 24 towns with more than 50,000 inhabitants, but the most striking feature was the growth of conurbations, spectacularly in Greater London where over 7 million now lived, but also in Clydeside and in the English north and midlands. Even in Ireland (where the population, largely through emigration, fell from 5.4 million in 1881 to 4.3 million in 1901) urban concentration was a problem. Dublin's slums had long been notorious. Belfast, no more than 100,000 strong in 1851, had 350,000 people by 1891 and was still growing.

Belfast's prosperity, which was in marked contrast to the rest of Ireland, was based on the engineering, shipbuilding and linen trades. The new, largely Protestant industrial classes were the chief beneficiaries, adding fresh complexity to the social, ethnic and religious tensions that shaped Ireland's version of Britain's 'north–south divide'. This divide was not so much a geographical separation as a handy shorthand description of the social effects of the spread of settlement and conquest from the south of England under the Normans and their aristocratic successors. It had originally stemmed from the mal-distribution of land and that was still the basis of most discontent. The divide was complicated but not lessened by industrialisation, for, though it was 'northerners' that characteristically engaged in manufacture it was 'southern' landlords who had made most of the profits from the exploitation of mineral resources and rental of property in the early stages of the industrial revolution. The manufacturers, furthermore, might be capitalists but it was they who largely accounted for such spread of prosperity as there was and provided employment for the masses. So it was landlords rather than capitalists who faced the fiercest criticism as the recession hit agriculture.[4]

The worst agitation was in rural Ireland where the Land League's prolonged campaign against the most insensitive landlords, often absentees, was sharpened by ethnic and religious divisions. But there had been outbursts in the Highlands of Scotland, which the Irish nationalist Michael Davitt toured in 1887 urging the crofters to organised rebellion The traditional dislike of the Welsh for their landlords was also intensified by religious and ethnic tensions. In England it was more of a straight socio-economic issue: was it right that a few thousand people should own three-quarters of the land, growing rich on the profits?[5] There were few egalitarians but many admirers of the radical American economist, Henry George, whose catch-phrase 'unearned increment' had more impact on British socialists than Marxist notions of the overthrow of capitalism.

Consequently while landowners moaned about declining rents as land values fell under the pressure of international competition, they got little sympathy, for high rents were widely believed to be the main cause of agricultural decline. Farmers also complained about the rates they paid to the new county councils, which seemed to spend most of their funds on amenities for the small towns within the county boundaries and the spreading suburbs of the bigger ones. Country squires persuaded Tory Party conferences to pass resolutions demanding tariff restrictions to protect agriculture, but this was not a serious starter politically. Quite apart from the likelihood of repercussions and residual belief in Free Trade, too many grandees were doing remarkably well out of the new situation. Though the industrial revolution Britain had started was to be carried on better elsewhere, there were more congenial pickings to be had by politer methods than manufacture.

There were also plenty of excuses for complacency, for looking on the bright side. British trade was still expanding at a healthy rate, her capital investments brought in revenue from all parts of the globe and the great safeguard was the colonies, not only as receptive markets but as sources of cheap raw materials. It was the invisible exports, services such as banking and shipping, always the socially superior end of trade, that were expanding fastest, but that was a problem for the future. Similarly the inflow of imported commodities, often mass produced, not only benefited the consumers but opened new commercial possibilities for distributors. The fast-growing lower middle class was an obvious target. New popular newspapers showed that through mass circulation, advertising revenue could more than compensate for a reduced price; both the *Evening News* (1894) and the *Daily Mail* (1896) sold for a half penny. Democratic Tory aristocrats saw the political implications: 'We live in an age of advertisement,' Lord Randolph Churchill reminded Parliament, 'the age of Holloway's Pills, of Colman's Mustard and of Horniman's Pure Tea'.[6] Old-established grocers like Harrods became palatial department stores: Marshall and Snelgrove, Peter Robinson, John Lewis, Barker's and their provincial equivalents were *the* places to shop. Chain stores sprang up all over the country: Home and Colonial, Maypole, Lipton's, Boots, Freeman, Hardy and Willis, Hepworth's, Eastman's, Singer Sewing machines, and, of course, W.H. Smith, who had the railway bookstall monopoly. Collective purchasing associations from the original Co-operative Wholesale Society, compromising its socialist principles but thriving, to the Army & Navy Co-operative, formed to buy wine at advantageous rates, set up retail outlets.

If the proliferating middle classes did best in the consumer revolution wage-earners did surprisingly well. Even temporary set-backs in the economy had their good side. Recession led to falling prices, and increased competition amongst employers meant that workers were better able to fend off wage cuts in bad times and drive harder bargains in good. Finding and getting to work was made easier by the railways, the London underground, the electric tramways of provincial cities and, in town or country, the bicycle. Employability was also helped by the expanding public education system, particularly in the clerkly occupations that now abounded. The corresponding neglect of science and technology was almost as marked at lower levels of school and society as in the older universities and the public schools that set the tone.

The bias towards the humanities at Oxford and Cambridge, though widely held to be a spiritual shield against machine-age materialism, conferred no rich cultural benefits on the nation at large. The universities had caught the spirit of the public schools, forged in a pre-industrial atmosphere, and joined them in producing the colonial administrators, civil servants, churchmen, politicians and headmasters the country needed, a process in which character-building was deemed as important as scholarship, and games-playing was given a key role. The ossified curricula not only lacked relevance to modern industrial needs but seriously neglected creativity.

The older universities, in consequence, produced many influential critics and literati but few creative writers of any standing.[7] Oscar Wilde, the greatest, was also thought the most degenerate. The true literary giants of the age, Yeats, Shaw, Conrad, Kipling, Hardy – and such gifted innovators as H.G. Wells, R. L. Stevenson and Conan Doyle – came from outside the Oxbridge tradition. Tennyson died in 1892 and the popular choice to succeed him as Poet Laureate would undoubtedly have been Kipling, but Lord Salisbury eventually[8] picked Alfred Austin, best known for a prose work, The Garden that I love. Austin traded in nostalgia for the vanishing rural past of 'home-made jams, lavender bags, recitation of Gray's Elegy, and morning and evening prayers. One is offered, in place of them', he complained, 'ungraceful hurry and worry, perpetual postmen's knocks, an intermittent shower of telegrams'.[9] Not many telegrams, one imagines, rained on the back-streets of London, Birmingham or Austin's native Leeds.

In the other arts the strongest creative influences often came not only from outside the universities but outside the country. In painting the foremost British school was led by an American, John Singer Sargent, following French Impressionist models. Britain was fortunate in that amongst the many men with great new wealth, were some, unburdened by present-day levels of taxation, who sought memorials of a cultural nature, and the age was marked by the opening of the National Portrait Gallery, the Tate, the Wallace Collection and a major extension of the National Gallery. These and corresponding developments in the provinces all helped bring art within the ambit of ordinary people as the Carnegie libraries did for books. However the art establishment, like that of literature, was steeped in past values and rural myths: the anti-industrial views of John Ruskin, emeritus professor of Fine Art at Oxford, still prevailed.

Looking backwards was even more marked in architecture where public buildings retained the ornate trappings of earlier continental tradition and most admiration was reserved for the evocation of past ages. Towns, if they had to exist, ought to look old like Winchester, Exeter, Norwich and York. Similarly, although there was some improvement in domestic design, especially in the houses of the well-to-do, the inspiration tended to come from the past: the most celebrated interior designer was William Morris, an Oxford medievalist who sought to revive the idea of the artist-craftsman that had been submerged by capitalism. Morris was also a socialist and a noted writer of Utopias. His mantle fell upon Robert Blatchford, founder of *The Clarion*, the outstanding popular socialist publication of the time. Blatchford was also a lover of cricket and of all things rural. His book, *Merrie England*, which sold a million copies within a short time of its publication in 1894, fiercely denounced the notion that Britain should become 'the workshop of the world' and looked for a sweeter, agricultural existence free of the disfiguring factories and the greedy quest for material possessions.

Music was equally in need of innovation. The gap between popular and classical music had grown wider since Purcell, Britain's last native composer of note. Educated Victorian taste extended little further than oratorio and the religiosity of Handel's *Messiah* and Mendelssohn's *Elijah*. Foreign-born performers like the violinist Joachim, the pianist Clara Schumann and the conductors Charles Hallé and Hans Richter helped to leaven the mixture. The leading British composer, Sir Hubert Parry, of Eton, Oxford, Lloyds and the Royal Yacht Squadron, had Wagnerian leanings, and considerably raised the social tone, but made no lasting musical mark. At the other end of the spectrum, meanwhile, traditional folk-song was giving way to a new, urban variety. The songs of the music hall – bouncy numbers like 'Ta-ra-ra – Boom-de-ay' and 'Any Old Iron', flag-wavers like 'The Soldiers of the Queen', modern moralities like 'She was a sweet little Dicky Bird' and 'Oh, Oh, Antonio', and the serenade to the female cyclist, 'Daisy Bell' – were designed for the growing popular market.

Market forces

Market forces helped to bridge the gap. The early celebrity of Sir Arthur Sullivan came from his oratorio, *The Prodigal Son*, and he was much admired by Queen Victoria for this and other churchified works. Many thought he lowered himself when he began to write operettas in collaboration with the comic verse dramatist W.S. Gilbert. But for all his lofty ambitions and academic training Sullivan, the son of an Irish military bandsman, had a chronic need of money to fund his expensive tastes, and his superior light music not only matched that of Offenbach but perfectly presented Gilbert's clever lyrics and topical satire.

Gilbert had guyed everything in the early 1880s, from the modern Major-General and W.H. Smith, the businessman First Lord of the Admiralty, to the House of Lords. By 1893 in *Utopia Limited* there were some new targets like the bold and athletic Girton girl and the County Councillor, the product of the 1888 Local Government Act, whose antics seemed irresistibly funny to metropolitan taste:

> Great Britain's latest toy –
> On anything you like to name
> His talents he'll employ

But he also, and more sharply, attacked the degeneration of the aristocracy. When the King of Utopia decides to reform on British lines, prominent amongst the 'Flowers of Progress' is Mr Goldbury, a company promoter –

> No schemes too great and none too small
> For companification! –

and his scheme to make Utopia a limited company follows the British pattern:

> Some seven men form an Association
> (If possible all Peers and Baronets.)

Britain had the most permissive company laws in Europe: seven shareholders could constitute themselves into a company simply by signing a memorandum of association. Successive governments had tried to tighten things up, but without success – too many people found it profitable. The result was a gradual but relentless spread of the company system throughout British industry. As Ensor put it: 'Patriarchalism disappeared. The owner-entrepreneur disappeared also. Property passed to shareholders concerned only for dividends; control was exercised on the shareholders' behalf by boards of directors nominally elected by them, but in fact mainly co-opted, often representing only financial, social or personal "pulls" and devoid of any specialized understanding of the firm or even of the industry.'[10]

Social "pull" was often provided by the aristocracy. Of course there was nothing new in aristocratic involvement with companies; but until lately their interest had usually been limited to canal and railway companies or other developments on their own lands: now, however, the sharper ones began to engage in the affairs of public companies in the City, often withdrawing from local enterprises to do so. Impoverished landowners found the idea particularly attractive, and the boards of many highly speculative ventures into mining and ranching in America or Australia were adorned by men with high-sounding titles, as if to guarantee success. The expatriate Cecil Rhodes, who subsequently made a fortune in the diamond mines of Kimberley, went back to England in 1889 seeking impressive names to bolster the reputation of his British South Africa Company, and landed the Dukes of Abercorn and Fife who were selling off estates in Ireland and Scotland respectively.[11]

Gilbert was unusually acerbic in that year's operetta. To the mellifluous music of *The Gondoliers*: the Duke of Plaza-Toro sang:

> I sit, by selection,
> Upon the direction
>   Of several Companies bubble ——
>
> As soon as they're floated
> I'm freely bank-noted ——
>   I'm pretty well paid for my trouble,

and

> In short if you'd kindle
> The spark of a swindle
>   Lure simpletons into your clutches ——
>
> Or hoodwink a debtor,
> You cannot do better
>   Than trot out a duke or a duchess.

But ridicule was a small price to pay for society's acceptance of a departure from dignified earlier ideals of service. The middle classes might laugh at Gilbert's sallies but they were deeply impressed by titles and by pomp and ceremony, and looked down on less fortunate nations that lacked tradition. And the new commercialism was but a new variant of the old favourite Adam Smith philosophy of the invisible force benignly working its way down the social pyramid.

Nor for all the occasional rumblings of discontent was there any danger of egalitarian revolt. Most Britons, however lowly, accepted inequality as part of the price of living in a free society. As a result the plight of the poor, a mounting problem for the future, got less attention than it deserved not only because of upper-class insensitivity and middle-class complacency but also because the working class was itself stratified. The more skilled artisans were constantly being bought off by unspoken agreement between management and trades unions. Strikes were not part of some collective uprising against oppression and exploitation but separate battles between employers and the most powerful groups of workers seeking to improve their own selective lot. Though ideologically suspect this worked better than unfocused resentment, and if it pandered too much to the trickle-down theory of economics at least some were better off. The London dock strike of 1889, successful and non-violent, was a reminder of British realities to Marxists and others who harboured revolutionary thoughts.

The era of collective bargaining that followed not only improved and helped stabilise wages for those in favoured industries but institutionalised and sidelined protest. The independence of individual unions, born of medieval craft traditions, gave the movement a hierarchical character and relegated the Trades Union Congress, which had been around since 1868, to a minor role for many more years. Similarly, the unions were chary of throwing in their lot with political ventures like Keir Hardie's Independent Labour Party of 1893. Hardie was one of the rare few working-class members of Parliament, even rarer because he won his seat without the sponsorship of the Liberals. He soon lost it, for he was ahead of his time.

Whatever their political timidity – or perhaps because of it – Britain's unionised workers, skilled and semi-skilled, were economically the envy of Europe. By the end of the century a highly skilled craftsman, especially in London, might get as much as £2 a week, which was more than the majority of elementary school teachers were paid and as much as many heads. At the other end of the scale came the agricultural workers, who had a struggle to achieve an increase from 14s to 15s a week. In between there came the great mass for whom 25s was a good wage and 30s a princely sum. There were wide variations and many fluctuations, and the city slums were a standing reproach but, given the generally falling prices as a result of competition, most unionised workers did pretty well out of industrialisation and capitalism.

Collective bargaining also profoundly influenced the widening provision of leisure, which was itself a source of envy to less favoured nations. In their early days the unions had been concerned chiefly with wages, and shorter hours meant less money. The better-off workers soon reached a point where they could afford to work shorter hours and they enjoyed the experience. The Nine Hour Day had been a great landmark of the 1870s, for it extended benefits to trades hitherto unable to win the concession for themselves. The Eight Hour Day, approved by a thinly attended House of Commons in 1883, was largely ignored by employers until the Gasworkers' strike of 1889 made them start to toe the line.

Greater leisure meant more time for sport, for long a British addiction, and working class influence, however fitfully, gradually began to be felt. This again was not the result of egalitarian agitation, but rather the continuation of a historical process. The social conventions of the older sports had been set in earlier centuries by the aristocracy and gentry, often as an adjunct to gambling. There had always been professional sportsmen, from huntsmen and other skilled retainers to the footmen employed to run ahead of carriages, and the great men had always bestowed favours on talented performers. In eighteenth-century Britain the passion for gambling made these haphazard arrangements into a formalised system of patronage. Despite criticism from the strait-laced, young bloods rubbed shoulders with pugilists and grooms, and sometimes, especially in the fashionable game of cricket, even competed against them.

By the early nineteenth century gambling and commercialism had opened up social and economic avenues to shrewd or skilful vulgarians though without loosing such a fearful tide of democracy as to threaten the acknowledged barriers imposed by birth, breeding and education. Similarly the middle-class inheritors of Britain's sporting legacy, imbued with a new idealism – of which muscular Christianity was an important ingredient – sought to extend its benefits without shaking the foundations of the ordered society that the team games they so fervently espoused were supposed to help to build. Hence a great deal of time was spent by the administrators of emerging sports, and of modernised old ones, in trying to equate the established notion of the gentleman with the new concept of the amateur.

There were a few problems. Unfortunately the increasing commercialism of the age aroused the acquisitive instincts of some gentlemen sportsmen as much as those of their working-class counterparts. Sadly, too, artisans were not always welcome even if they were amateur. Different sports took different lines and there were often marked differences in attitude on the two sides of the north–south divide. The tensions were worst in the team games devised by public schoolboys in the recent past, notably football. Things were better in sports like horse-racing and pugilism where aristocratic patronage had set the tone. But there were peculiar difficulties in cricket where aristocratic and public school traditions had merged.

Cricket: years of Grace

Cricket was the citadel of true sporting values. It occupied the foremost place in the hierarchy of team sports cherished by the public schools for their character-building qualities and training in leadership. It baffled foreigners: indeed, though the English had taken it, in missionary spirit, to other parts of the British Isles, they regarded themselves, and were regarded, as the holders of the copyright. Its supreme authority, the Marylebone Cricket Club, was no recently concocted overseeing committee but a gentlemen's club founded in 1787, which had gradually and sometimes reluctantly widened its responsibilities with the consent of the other leading clubs. Its membership, originally entirely aristocrats, squires and young men about town, had remained exclusive, numbering only some 600 by the 1860s. More recently it had expanded to over 2000, but the social composition of its governing committee stayed much the same. As the popularity of cricket had grown so had the desire for membership of MCC. It had a long waiting list which meant that admission could be controlled – by 'blackballing' to keep out 'the wrong sort', and by judicious fixing of the membership fee, high enough to maintain proper standards but not too high to exclude the parsons and schoolmasters who did so much for the game or the well-connected but modestly provided. It still became very rich in the affluent 1890s: its revenue rose from £15,065 in 1884 to £21,632 in 1890, and a remarkable £82,565 in 1898.[12]

MCC and its powerful committee not only determined the rules of the game (characteristically known as 'laws') but set the tone for its conduct at the highest levels, notably in preserving a near-feudal relationship between amateurs and professionals. For a time in the 1850s and 1860s its authority had been threatened by groups of professionals who met the growth in popular demand for first-class cricket as a spectator sport by staging matches all over the country on a profit-sharing basis. But this professional 'circus' had long faded into the background, and the county clubs, also gentlemanly founda-tions, had become the mainstay of the first-class game. They were also the main employers of professional cricketers and they worked hand-in-hand with MCC to keep them in line.

One of the threats to this cosy state of affairs was, ironically, the spread of the game to the colonies. This otherwise pleasing indication that the finest of British flowers could be transplanted to distant parts was marred somewhat by the Australians, who not only proved irritatingly good at the game but seemed to care little about social distinctions. Cricket had been played in the colonies since the first British settlements; and crack British teams had been attracting colonial crowds since 1859 when a group of professionals visited Canada, where for some years cricket was popular enough to have claims to be the national sport. It took firmer root in sunny Australia, which the first English team had been persuaded to visit two years later. This and most of the frequent subsequent tours had been undertaken by professionals under the auspices of commercial sponsors or leading Australian clubs. A few amateurs, suitably recompensed, had also responded to colonial calls. Their aims were usually hedonistic – and in the case of W.G. Grace, the 'Champion', also mercenary – but one or two were more conscious of the potential of cricket as an imperially educative force. Chief amongst these was the young Lord Harris, a future colonial administrator, who took both cricket and the Empire very seriously indeed. The indignities he suffered at the hands of Australian crowds during a tour in 1878–79 had for a time cast a cloud over relations between the Australians and MCC, of which Harris was a leading light.[13] The colonists' cricket and its commercial possibilities were too good to be ignored, however, and in the competitive atmosphere of the times the so-called 'Test matches'[14] had caught the public imagination.

There was growing concern in MCC circles about the entrepreneurial activities of the Nottinghamshire professionals Alfred Shaw and Arthur Shrewsbury who were regularly mounting Antipodean tours for profit – and even more concern at the regular Australian tours of England. They were becoming too frequent, interfering with the domestic pattern in which the established programme of county matches was enhanced by such traditional fixtures as Eton v. Harrow, Oxford v. Cambridge and Gentlemen v. Players in a short season that allowed the gentlemen to be on the moors for the 'glorious twelfth' of August when grouse-shooting began. Furthermore these obtrusive Australians undertook their tours on a profit-sharing basis. Australian cricket was not hampered by the distinction between gentlemen and players, for apart from a few English immigrants who had gone out there as coaches, there were no full-time professionals. So despite their blatantly commercial outlook the Australians who came to England were technically amateurs, since they did not play the game for a living, and this was upsetting to the English order of things.

In England amateur cricketers were officially known as Gentlemen and were entitled to be called Mr and to have their initials before their surnames on scorecards and in Press reports. The professionals, by contrast, collectively known as Players, were called by their surnames alone. They also had to use separate dressing rooms and sometimes even different routes to and from the pavilion to the playing area from those used by the Gentlemen (to whom they had to show proper respect, addressing them as Sir and referring to them as Mr So-and-so). These badges of servitude were worn with philosophical calm by most English professionals, who likewise accepted without question that they must be led by amateurs in county and Test matches, but the ambivalent status of the visiting Australians and the fees they earned caused much resentment. It did not help that the sympathies of most of the visitors were with the English professionals. Indeed some were appalled at the feudal behaviour of the Gentlemen: one Australian captain, Joe Darling, recalled in his memoirs how certain English captains spoke to their professionals like dogs.[15]

For MCC and their supporters the observance of proper distinctions was essential to the true spirit of the game – anything else was just not cricket. The double standards that permeated their conduct of affairs flowed ineluctably from this conviction. For example the Gentlemen felt themselves free, and were felt to *be* free, from any obligation to put patriotic considerations above their own personal interests. Thus in 1890 A.E. Stoddart, the Middlesex amateur, twice declined to play for England because he preferred to assist his county in important championship matches. Yet he went on to become England's captain. By contrast the professionals had no choice in such matters: on the second of Stoddart's defections, when Yorkshire were Middlesex's opponents, Lord Hawke, the Yorkshire captain, refused permission to 'his' professionals, Ulyett and Peel, to accept the England selectors' invitation. The irony was that a number of leading amateurs, not least Stoddart himself, made a good deal of money – and certainly more than many run-of-the mill professionals – out of their cricket.

This is very clear from the undercover dealings several of them had with the dreaded Arthur Shrewsbury. Highly successful at first, by 1887–78 Shrewsbury's mainly professional tours had ceased to excite the Australian public or to attract the best Australian players as opponents. They had earned the implacable hostility of the Melbourne Club, which had social aspirations, and they faced competition from a rival English touring team assembled at Melbourne's invitation by G.F. Vernon, the Middlesex amateur. Though both teams contained a mixture of amateurs and professionals, Vernon's team, to Shrewsbury's chagrin, were billed by Melbourne and described by the Press as 'the English amateurs'. His annoyance was no mere class envy. The amateurs had a strong snob appeal and he wanted to cash in on it, as he explained in a letter home to his partner, Alfred Shaw. Vernon's team had made much more money from a game in Sydney than Shrewsbury's: 'People here think they are all amateurs – Gentlemen of England – and that is the reason they get patronage.'[16] He gave instructions for similar billing for his own team in the next match.

Shrewsbury's annoyance was no doubt increased by the heavy price he had had to pay for his own amateurs. At the end of the season, with cash flow problems, he sent Shaw a list of the amounts owed to the players. It read: 'Newham £146 16s 3d; Brann £189 17s 6d; Lohmann £80; Read £100; Briggs £60; Pilling £55; Preston £45; Pougher £75; Ulyett £130 less £57 4s 2d.' Newham and Brann were amateurs; which accounts for Shrewsbury's instructions that in the event of difficulties 'you must make Newham and Brann wait until the others are paid'. They were in no position to make a fuss.[17]

The ultimate irony of the situation was that it had been the amateur reaction to the professional revolt that had created county cricket in its modern form, turning entrepreneurial nomads into resident gladiators and making profits essential to survival. The resulting system with its excessive emphasis on competition had shocked the purists. One of the fiercest opponents was the Wykehamist sporting journalist, Frederick Gale, 'The Old Buffer', who had inveighed against the very idea at its inception and who was deeply distressed at the latest developments, notably the publication of primitive league tables according to schemes devised by the daily newspapers. In a long leading article in 1887 *The Times* answered his criticisms, concluding 'It would be more healthy if there were more love of cricket itself and less excitement about "results" . . . But the emulative spirit of our countrymen will not have it so . . . the intense spirit of competition which is the chief feature of modern cricket precipitates itself in the worship of success.' The Press were merely meeting a public demand and since these appetites were not to be denied they had better be fed with 'the whole truth'. Gale could be assured that there was no danger of 'the advent of the betting ring' as a result.[18]

Nevertheless the cricket establishment was alive to the dangers: did not disaster threaten both codes of football? In soccer[19] indeed, what had once been a matter of friendly rivalry amongst the public schools and their Old Boys had now degenerated into leagues, commercialism, professionalism and gambling. C.W. Alcock, the honorary secretary of the Football Association, had seen his harmless suggestion of a Challenge cup on the lines of the Cock House competition of his old school, Harrow, turn into a monster. Significantly in his other capacity as (paid) secretary of Surrey CCC, Alcock had advised MCC against introducing a similar cup in cricket, lest it breed an unhealthy spirit of emulation. The methods of cricket were better suited to keeping professionals in their proper place. The RFU, the custodians of the other football code, were desperately anxious to preserve its pristine amateur purity despite the spread of the game amongst the working classes of Wales and the North of England. It did not require the same commitment of time as first-class cricket so its gentlemanly amateurs could more easily afford to play without resort to payments of 'expenses'. Even so the temptations were there, especially, not surprisingly, amongst those who were also cricketers. The opportunist Shrewsbury, considering arrangements for a football tour at the end of the 1887–88 Australian cricket season instructed his partner Shaw, back in England, to try to sign a number of amateurs in order, as he put it, to 'raise the tone of the team'. He also tried to persuade some of the football playing amateurs amongst his touring cricketers to stay on in Australia, thus reducing the costs of passages out. Two of them, George Brann and C. Aubrey Smith[20] agreed, but later withdrew under pressure from C.W. Alcock who advised Smith's father that they would run the risk of being declared professionals by the RFU.

Shrewsbury was by that time relieved that the pair, after much shilly-shallying, were going home, for they were not renowned rugby players[21] and they had asked £200 each in expenses. But he had also signed Stoddart, a distinguished player with Blackheath, the senior rugby club, who was touring with Vernon's 'Gentlemen of England', and was most concerned that he might get cold feet. As he told Shaw, 'The only thing we are afraid of just now is that, should Stoddart hear they are not staying, he will want to go home as well. However . . . we sent him a cheque for £50 a few days since, which should bind him'.[22] His fears were groundless. Stoddart stayed on, and even became captain when the original choice was killed in a drowning accident.

The cricket establishment did not think Stoddart's financial arrangements whilst on tour had any bearing on his amateur status. (Nor, as will appear later, did the RFU.) Stoddart and Shrewsbury had opened the batting together when the two rival touring cricket teams had sunk their differences to salvage a little profit from the tour and formed a combined England XI to play a Test match. But when they returned to England after the rugby tour Shrewsbury was severely criticised for leaving Nottinghamshire in the lurch during the 1888 cricket season, whilst Stoddart's absence from Middlesex was accepted as a matter of course.

The moral climate was changing. There was soon a name for the dubious amateurs and they came in for some criticism. As the *Badminton Magazine* put it 'For frank and open professionalism there may be a good deal to be said, but nothing can make . . . the "shamateur" attractive.'[23] In fact the biggest 'shamateur' of all was the greatest cricketer, W.G. Grace himself. It was W.G. who had done most to popularise county cricket, raising the standard of batting to new heights. Crowds flocked to see him play and his utterances were received like gospel messages. Purists nodded their heads in heartfelt agreement when in a speech in 1891 he expressed his fears lest cricket should become 'too much of a business, like football'. Yet the amateur W.G., who had already been rewarded by a handsome testimonial, £1,400 towards the cost of buying himself a medical practice, earned £3,000 that very winter (and generous expenses for himself, his wife and daughter) from an Australian tour sponsored by the munificent Lord Sheffield.[24] Another testimonial in 1895 brought him £9,073.

For *The Times* the event was of sufficient moment to warrant a leading article – not about the amateur principle but about the timeliness of the gesture – illustrating another aspect of the changing moral climate. The testimonial, the writer reckoned, signified the collapse of ancient inhibitions: 'Fifty or even thirty years ago the British middle class, speaking generally, was still half-consciously ruled by a survival of the old Puritan idea that amusements as such were morally wrong.' The 'popular love of national games, and especially cricket', had now grown to 'a positive passion, thanks to the publicity given by the sporting Press'. This made it 'perfectly natural that when England happens to possess a cricketer alike unrivalled for his perform-ances and his staying power, the country should wish to do him honour'. A testimonial was 'the practical English variety of the honour which many nations have conferred, not only upon their warriors, but upon such of their sons as have distinguished themselves in the contests of peace'. It was to be hoped that it would cause W.G. 'not to regret that he sacrificed, during the years of his prime, his profession to the national game, and was content to be, instead of a busy country doctor, the greatest cricketer in the world'.[25]

There had been other compensations, less easy to explain away. There had been a great scandal in 1879 over his undercover payments from Gloucester-shire.[26] The gossip had continued, off and on, ever since and it surfaced again with the threatened strike a week before the Oval Test Match of 1896 when five professionals wrote to the Surrey Committee (who, according to the custom of the day, were responsible for picking the team for matches taking place on their ground) demanding a fee of twenty pounds instead of the ten they had been offered. They got short shrift: the Committee, feeling 'greatly aggrieved . . . did not hesitate for a moment as to the course to be pursued, at once taking steps to secure the best possible substitutes for the revolting players', and the mutiny was quickly quelled.[27] The matter did not end there, however, because the root cause of their dissatisfaction was the allowances paid to the amateurs chosen, notably W.G.: there was much publicity in the popular newspapers and in the end the committee were obliged to make a public statement about their financial relations with the great man, claiming that he was only to be paid £10. (Stoddart, also under criticism but presumably more sensitive than W.G., withdrew from the team just before the game.) The true nature of Grace's amateurism was revealed three years later, when he agreed to manage and lead a new team, London County, a commercial venture based at Crystal Palace and operating outside the county championship, at a salary of £600 a year and expenses. W.G. was surprised to find that Gloucestershire, who had themselves treated him not ungenerously, found this incompatible with his duties as their captain. He took the job anyway.

None of this may seem remarkable by modern standards, but in the context of Victorian attitudes towards cricket and its reputation for character-building it indicates an extraordinary capacity for self-deception. Cricket was thought to confer a special nobility on those who played it. To call something 'not cricket' was the sternest moral condemnation. It had passionate adherents like Edward Cracroft Lefroy, who wrote sonnets about the game: 'The whole edifice of the Christian virtues', he wrote in a letter to a friend,[28] 'could be raised on the basis of good cricket.' Grace was a particular object of reverence. A rhapsodical purveyor of cricketing whimsy, the playwright Herbert Farjeon, cited him forty-odd years later as a chivalric hero of his boyhood: 'Our father contended that we thought too much of cricket. It became, in fact, a vexed question in the house and we can think of moments which we would prefer not to live over again. We think our father to have been wrong, for cricket was the romance of our childhood, and childhood must have its romance. Lancelot or W.G. – What does it matter?'[29] It should have mattered, for only the most besotted partisan could regard W.G. as a chivalric figure.

For one thing he violated cricket's pious convention that umpires' decisions are sacrosanct, never to be challenged. These humble professionals, at the mercy of the amateur captains who controlled the county game according to the honour code of their public schools, had advanced little in status from their origins as servants of the early patrons of cricket and were still often in terror at the prospect of offending the great. Joe Darling reckoned it was a well-known fact that English umpires were reluctant to give W.G. and other amateurs out – the celebrated Bob Thoms was just about the only one who was not afraid to stand up to them. The public enjoyed the Great Cricketer's reputation for brushing them aside: a favourite joke was of W.G., bowled first ball in an exhibition match, replacing the bails and saying, 'People have come to see me bat, not you umpire.' F.B. Wilson, Cambridge Blue and sporting journalist, recalled in an article in *The Cricketer* in 1921 how he could intimidate them: 'I was allowed to bowl against W.G. Grace at the Crystal Palace once, and had him out! . . . He missed the ball entirely – so we thought – but hooked it round to short leg with his foot, and ran down the wicket shouting, "Out if I hadn't hit it, well bowled, out if I hadn't hit it" . . . the umpire's hand was up. But he put it down again and signalled a "hit".'

The Australians, having endured Grace's gamesmanship over the years, tended to be less amused by it. The most serious instance occurred in the famous Test match of 1882 when England first lost the mythical "Ashes". W.G., having fielded the ball, had pretended to throw it back to the bowler, and then, when the batsman, thinking the ball was 'dead', walked out of his ground to repair the pitch, threw down his wicket leaving the umpire no alternative but to give him out.[30] That kind of thing rankled. The British on the other hand, theoretically so fastidious about what was and was not 'cricket', were apt to chuckle over such antics as amiable foibles arising from W.G.'s boyish enthusiasm. As Lord Harris explained, 'W.G. was desperately keen for his side to win, and consequently was led, in his excitement, to be occasionally very rigid in demanding his full rights, but he was so popular, and had the game so thoroughly at heart that such slight incidents were readily forgiven him and indeed more often than not added to the fund of humorous stories about him.'[31]

The sanctimony was the greater for its double standards. A periodical publication of the time devoted an issue to '*The Religion of Cricket*'.[32] The author acknowledged that there was some heresy and backsliding, but he was inclined to blame 'the sordid side' on 'the professional element'. The professionals were, of course, capable of sordid behaviour. It often stemmed from drunkenness, as it did in 1896 when Bobby Peel, of Yorkshire and England, urinated on the side of the pitch in full view of the spectators, obliging his captain, Lord Hawke, to sack him on the spot. (Lord Hawke, as stern and pompous a martinet as Lord Harris was in Kent, was known to the wits as

Archbishop of York to Harris's Archbishop of Canterbury.) No such blatant vulgarities were recorded of the well-bred amateurs, though there were instances of manifest lack of good manners and even breaches of the code of honour amongst the finest exemplars of the gentlemanly tradition. In the 'Varsity matches of 1893 and 1896, for instance, the spirit of fair play was not much in evidence.

On the first occasion the principal offender was F.S. Jackson, captain of Cambridge, and generally regarded as the very model of amateur integrity.[33] Oxford, well behind towards the end of their first innings, would have been allowed by the laws of the time to follow on had the deficit remained more than 80. This at one time would not have bothered their opponents, but with improved pitches there was a risk that tired bowlers would come in for heavy punishment, so Oxford's last wicket batsmen tried to throw their wickets away. Jackson thereupon instructed his team to bowl wide of the wicket to frustrate Oxford's efforts and to try to give away runs by no-balling. There was fierce debate about the propriety of these events, but even more about the need to change the laws and MCC increased the required margin to 120. Nevertheless, in a similar situation three years later, Cambridge did precisely the same thing. This time the caddish action of the Cambridge captain, Frank Mitchell, caused pandemonium amongst the spectators. When the Cambridge team returned to the pavilion they were hooted at by the members, and there followed angry scenes in which many MCC members lost control of themselves, one of them throwing his field glasses at Mitchell.[34]

As a result MCC felt obliged to review the situation again, but the most fitting comment came from F. R. Spofforth, a great Australian bowler of the past, then settled in England. In a letter to the *Sporting Life* he wrote: 'I scarcely think, no matter how this rule is changed, it will have much effect on the game, seeing that in the annals of first-class cricket it has only been "infringed" twice, and that by a body of cricketers anyone would have least expected it from.

In the first instance there may have been an excuse, but when a conservative body like the MCC thought it so serious as to alter the rule, it showed the worst possible taste to breach it again.'[35]

County cricket and the Leagues

Like it or not the grip of competition had English cricket by the throat, and there were addicts in all walks of life who were prepared to go to any lengths to put it across their opponents, just as there were opportunists, amateur as well as professional, who had an eye to the main chance. The county championship, which was the crucible for these turbulent forces, lost a little more of its erstwhile innocence when the 'first-class' counties adopted an unofficial points system in 1888, finally making it official in 1890. A rebel County Cricket Council briefly appeared, calling for a league system with three divisions, but this was far too radical and the existing arrangements continued with an 'in' group determining its own membership. The glory had departed from Nottinghamshire by then and the dominant counties in the next decade were Surrey, Lancashire and Yorkshire. Kent, Middlesex, Gloucestershire and Sussex were the other members of the elite, joined in 1891 by Somerset to the displeasure of Derbyshire who had been dropped from the magic circle. There was much wrangling over membership, and in 1895 MCC were asked to define first-class status. As a result Derbyshire were re-admitted, along with Essex, Hampshire, Leicestershire and Warwickshire. Worcestershire made the grade four years later.

The founder members continued to dominate, and there were wide variations in the clubs' prosperity. Surrey, under Alcock's shrewd leadership, made the most of their London setting: in 1889 they already had a credit balance of £7,203, and ten years later their income from cricket was £13,593 and they had over 4,000 members: Yorkshire, who used grounds in various parts of the county, did almost as well. By contrast in 1894 a Derbyshire supporter ruefully commented that Derby County Football Club 'often took more in one match than the Cricket Club did during a whole season'.[36] Both professionals' wages and amateurs' expenses went up in the new, competitive atmosphere, and as few clubs had any reserves most of them lived pre-cariously. Apart from members' subscriptions they were largely dependent on gate-money from home games, no share of which went to opponents. Crowds in the 1880s and 1890s were almost double those of the 1870s, but they were mostly attracted to key matches or those involving the leading counties or star players. The stars – most of the England team, for instance – tended to come from the three leading counties.

In such circumstances movement of players between counties increased. A proposal to reduce the period required for residential qualification was defeated, the Middlesex representative remarking on the danger that other-wise 'the county with the largest purse would win the honour of first position'. The danger was not entirely averted, however, and by the end of the century only Kent and Yorkshire, the bastions of Lord Harris and Lord Hawke, did not select outsiders. There were no transfer fees, as in the infamous soccer system, and no cup-ties to help the weaker teams. Until 1899 the profits from Test matches went to MCC and the favoured few counties who staged them: afterwards a proportion was shared around but this did not go far. The struggling clubs were not immune from the lure of 'companification', but the few that succumbed did so for specific purposes, notably acquiring and improving grounds, and their shareholders were not seeking profit. Sir Thomas Martineau, seeking funds for the Cricket Ground Company formed by Warwickshire when creating their Edgbaston headquarters in 1885, stated that 'gentlemen who advanced the money needed were entitled to expect a fair return but the main object should be 'not to make dividends but to advance the interests and the position of the county club'.[37]

Similarly the counties' gentlemanly preference for members' subscriptions rather than gate-money as a source of finance, not only impoverished them but preserved the three-day match which was quite unsuited to a mass spectatorship. Membership, furthermore, was a great bargain compared with daily admission charges, for those who could afford both the fee and the time, but the very scarcity of these latter made it both necessary to keep fees down and difficult to recruit new members. Consequently club incomes remained low. Nevertheless the pattern of weekday cricket, with almost nobody there to see it, survived virtually unchallenged. It was considered a negation of the amateur spirit to adapt the game to suit the needs of paying spectators as some northern rugby clubs were beginning to do; and above all the gentlemanly elite who controlled county cricket wanted no truck with the cups and leagues that beset soccer.

There were, of course, already local cricket cups in the north of England. One of these, the Heavy Woollen Cup, launched in 1873, had developed into the Central Yorkshire League, and the Lamb Trophy, inaugurated in 1887, gave a fillip to the founding clubs of the Huddersfield Association. Soon leagues were proliferating in industrial districts, meeting the demands of working-class players and spectators with their new-found leisure. The Birmingham and District (1888) was closely followed by the North Staffordshire (1889), the North-East Lancashire (1890) and the Central Lancashire (1892). By the turn of the century there were a host of others – the Bradford, Leeds, Bolton, Northern, Ribblesdale and Yorkshire Leagues and the Yorkshire Council.

For spectators league cricket offered the attraction of Saturday afternoon matches played to a finish. Amateur players needed little if any time off, and for professionals, one or two of whom were usually allowed to each club, the appeal was obvious. Saturday play could be combined with a weekday job, rates of pay were reasonable and good performances were rewarded by collections. The county players benefited to some extent, for the counter-attraction obliged committees to offer better terms – not only in match pay but in security and in winter retainers to compensate for not having a year-round job. But generally it was only star players who got such concessions, particularly from the poorer counties. It was a big event when, in 1898, even lowly Warwickshire felt obliged to offer W.G. Quaife, a Test player, a five-year contract when he threatened to go into the Leagues.

That the county game was not affected more by the rival attractions of League cricket stemmed partly from its entrenched position as the custodian of established tradition and partly from the glamour it exuded as part of the myth of rural England, a touch of magic in an industrial age. Both gentlemen and players liked the aura of county cricket and fancied themselves a cut above their counterparts in the leagues. In county cricket the 'north–south divide' was not quite so evident either: true values were to be found even in the rough wastes of Yorkshire and Lancashire: Lord Hawke had his (slightly more modern) counterparts in Lancashire in fellow-Harrovians A.N. Hornby, son of a Blackburn mill-owner, and A.C. MacLaren, son of a Manchester business man, and the neo-feudal spirit flourished everywhere.

Below county level the divide stuck more closely to its geographical description. League cricket was essentially a phenomenon of the North and Midlands industrial conurbations. Serious one-day cricket in the South kept to the old pattern of a hierarchy of clubs playing annual fixtures against traditional rivals. Leading clubs like Hampstead could rely on the presence of dashing amateurs like Stoddart to attract the crowds without the vulgar intrusion of cups and leagues or the need to allow avowed professionals. Some of the southern clubs were well placed financially. Wimbledon CC, for instance, managed to buy its ground outright in 1889 for £3,612 and to improve its facilities in the next few years without incurring debt.

There were some gentlemanly outposts even in the north. At Liverpool – always more of a commercial than an industrial city, and grown rich from its shipping and mercantile interests – the Cricket Club had over 500 paid-up members in 1894 and could show a profit of £282 in spite of an expenditure of more than £1500.[38] But the general picture was less cheerful. When in 1887 the North Lancashire League Read CC made a profit of £25 compared with a loss of £9 by its footballing section the *Athletic News* pointed out that 'in 99 cases out of 100 it is the other way about . . . football helps cricket over the stile of financial embarrassment'.[39] This was all very well at club level. Indeed it was often a convenient arrangement when much the same players and officials were involved in summer as in winter. But those concerned with cricket in schools or in the counties saw great danger of contamination by the commercialism and excessive competition that afflicted football, a phenomenon to which we should now turn.

Notes

1 Lord Salisbury, 'Disintegration', *Quarterly Review*, January, 1883: Lord Tennyson, *Locksley Hall Sixty Years After*, 1886.
2 'Locksley Hall and the Jubilee', *Nineteenth Century*, October, 1887.

3 *The Illustrated London News*, 2 February, 1886.

4 An official inquiry in the 70s, designed to give the lie to the assertion of the radical John Bright that the whole of England was owned by fewer than 30,000 people, had drawn unwelcome attention to the true position. There were in fact nearly a million landowners in England and Wales but nearly 75 per cent of the land was owned by fewer than 5,000 people. Their income – unearned – was even more startling for several were drawing over £100,000 a year in this way This, furthermore, did not include the enormous sums some were getting from the leasing of their urban holdings. See D. Cannadine, *The Decline and Fall of the British Aristocracy*, London, 1992, pp 54–6.

5 *Ibid.*, p. 59.

6 R. Shannon, *The Crisis of Imperialism, 1865–1915*, St Albans, 1976, p. 206.

7 Of the poets A.E. Housman, an Oxford man and a professor of Latin at Cambridge, was a modest exception with his *A Shropshire Lad* (1896). Gerard Manley Hopkins, a Balliol man, who died in 1889, was later discovered by revisionist critics like F.R. Leavis, and was undoubtedly an original talent, but his poems were not published until 1918. Robert Bridges was scarcely known to the public when he became Poet Laureate in 1913.

8 In 1896, after a four-year interval for reflection, Austin at once confirmed the popular judgement by writing a set of idiotic verses about the Jameson raid.

9 *Haunts of Ancient Peace*, 1901, quoted in M.J. Wiener, *English Culture and the Decline of the Industrial Spirit, 1850–1980*, Cambridge, 1981, p. 45.

10 R.C.K. Ensor, *England 1870–1914*, Oxford, 1936, p. 113.

11 Cannadine, *Decline*, pp. 406–16.

12 This included £37,200 in once-for-all life membership fees. See K. Sandiford and W. Vamplew, 'The Peculiar Economics of English Cricket before 1914', *British Journal of Sports History*, December, 1986, p. 312.

13 Harris's largely amateur tour had been ruined when the crowd swarmed on the pitch in a match against New South Wales in protest at the decision of an umpire (a man from Victoria, NSW's traditional rivals, appointed by Lord Harris). See D. Birley, *Sport and the Making of Britain*, Manchester, 1993, Chapter 15.

14 The term had first been used to describe the matches against the Australian colonies played by the professional side led by H.H. Stephenson in 1861–2, and it was picked up again by the English Press in the 1880s and applied retrospectively to the two games against Combined XIs from Melbourne and Sydney played by James Lillywhite's professionals at the end of their 1876–7 tour. Matches were played with increasing frequency thereafter against teams called Australia, before the actual creation of the Commonwealth in 1902. MCC did not accept responsibility for tours until 1903–4.

15 Joe Darling, captain from 1899–1905, in D.K. Darling, *Test Tussles on and off the Field*, Hobart, 1970.

16 P. Wynne-Thomas, '*Give Me Arthur*', London, 1985, p. 83.

17 *Ibid.*, p. 91.

18 5 September, 1887, quoted in M Williams (ed.), *Double Century*, London, 1985 pp 93–6.

19 The colloquial terms soccer for Association Football and rugger for Rugby [Union] Football are late Victorian public school and undergraduate elaborations of an earlier abbreviation, 'footer' meaning football generally: (*OED* cites the *Boys Own Paper*, 1869. in which 'footer' is described as a term peculiar to Harrow but it spread with the game.) It was still used to mean either Rugby or Association football in the early part of the twentieth century. When P.G. Wodehouse used it, for instance, he meant

rugby, the game played at his old school, Dulwich. If the now archaic 'footer' were ever used at all these days by the general public, however, it would be taken to mean soccer, just as most people who say 'football' mean soccer. Football by the late 1880s was widely used to mean soccer – especially by the soccer men themselves – and rugby had to be specified for the other, less popular code. In this book football normally means football generally and soccer is used to mean the Association game. Soccer, spelt socca' (1889) and socker (1893 and 1894) in the earliest OED references, is now standard English and is used here for clarity. By contrast rugger, first recorded in 1893, still has an air of informality, and when used in this book instead of 'rugby' is intended to distinguish the determinedly amateur game of the Rugby Football Union from that of the breakaway Northern Union, which became the. Rugby League in 1921.

20 Smith, of Charterhouse and Cambridge University, was Shrewsbury's front man as captain of the 1887–8 tourists. After touring South Africa the following winter he remained there to set up a business. He afterwards became a well known actor, was knighted, and went to Hollywood where he specialised in parts as defenders of the British Raj.

21 They were better known as soccer players (Brann was a member of Corinthians FC) but the code did not worry Shrewsbury, who appeared to regard the difference as insignificant. Rugby apart, he planned to have the players coming from England learn the rules for a game to be played in Victoria under the local code during fitness training on the boat. Newham and Stoddart were well known Rugby players.

22 Wynne-Thomas, 'Give Me Arthur', pp. 89–90.

23 Vol. II 1896, p. 533, quoted in OED.

24 Henry North Holroyd, third Earl of Sheffield, earned the distinction of inclusion in the Dictionary of National Biography, under the description 'patron of cricket'. He spent his life playing (badly) and watching cricket. President of Sussex CCC for many years he took the team (starring W.G. Grace and managed by Alfred Shaw) to Australia in 1891–92. His interest in Australian cricket was lifelong: the Sheffield Shield he presented is still the trophy for interstate competition.

25 17 June 1895, quoted in Williams, Double Century, pp. 104–5.

26 See Birley, Sport, p. 333, and Williams, Double Century, pp. 75–6. See also, amongst the voluminous literature on the great man, A.G. Powell and S. Canynge Caple, The Graces, Hunstanton, 1948, B. Benison, Giants on Parade, London, 1936, and D. Birley, The Willow Wand, London, 1979.

27 Wisden, 1897, quoted in B. Green, (ed.), Wisden Anthology (1864–1900), London, 1979, pp 752–3. Wisden acknowledged that W.G.'s position was 'anomalous', but added sententiously 'nice customs curtsey to great kings'.

28 Quoted in an anthology (containing many other gems) The English Game, ed. G. Brodribb, London, 1948.

29 H. Farjeon, 'When Cricket Was Cricket' , in Herbert Farjeon's Cricket Bag, London, 1946, p. 50.

30 The testimony of F.R. Spofforth, who was playing in the game but authorised publication of his views only after his death, is referred to in a letter to The Times on 17 August 1926 by E.C. Sewell (reprinted in M. Williams (ed.), The Way to Lords, London, 1983, pp. 41–2).

31 Obituary, Wisden Cricketers' Almanack 1915, reprinted in B. Green (ed.), Wisden Anthology (1900–1940), London, 1980, pp. 442–5. Harris, unlike W.G., was a public school man, but like him was apt to depart on occasion from the canons of chivalry: he had indeed been involved in a controversial incident as captain of Eton in 1870. When, bowling, he had stopped in his run up and run the batsman out – within the

rules but 'not cricket'.

32 Reprinted in P.C. Standing, *Cricket of To-day and Tomorrow*, Edinburgh, 1902.

33 An accomplished all-rounder, Jackson – later Sir Stanley – was a distinguished soldier in the Boer War and a model public servant. No one better exemplified the virtues of a healthy mind in a healthy body.

34 For a participant observer's account see P.F. Warner, *Lord's 1787–1945*, London, 1974. Mitchell was to win international caps for Rugby as well as cricket, and, after serving in the Boer War, stayed on in South Africa, becoming their cricket captain. See also Chapter 13 below.

35 25 January, 1897.

36 Sandiford and Vamplew, 'Economics', p. 313.

37 *Ibid.*, pp. 320–1. In fact they were soon able to pay a regular 6 per cent dividend, a satisfactory enough return but hardly enough to offset the risk. Hampshire CC only managed 3.5 per cent.

38 *Ibid.*, p. 312.

39 *Ibid.*

CHAPTER TWO

The perils of success

Must more mean worse? Gladstone thought not. In 1886, indeed, he had criticised 'the classes' for consistently and erroneously aligning themselves against 'the masses' on great issues.[1] Now the extension of the electorate had begun to put the question to the test, and it was manifestly in the interests of 'the classes' to hope that he was right. For the confident and rising middle class the trick was to raise the standards of 'the masses' without lowering their own. In economic terms they had managed it fairly well so far through free trade and the expansive phase of the industrial revolution, and, though there were worries about controlling the turbulent social forces they had unleashed, by no means all was gloom. Their growing prosperity had given them more time to consider the finer things of life and the public schools they had created had evolved an ethos that had replaced the old feudal ideals or suffused them with new concepts of civic virtue.

Sport, these schools and their products believed, was undoubtedly one of the finer things of life. A healthy mind in a healthy body was the watchword and the Christianity of the establishment took on a distinctly muscular tinge. Hence many of the most fervent advocates of ball games and other athletic activities believed that they could and should be enjoyed by all. Indeed getting 'the masses' engaged in sport seemed a logical extension of the burgeoning belief in the power of games-playing as a character-building force. If leadership qualities were best fostered in the public schools nevertheless healthy-minded and healthy-bodied followers were needed too. Indeed it now seemed that games could play a useful part in solving the age-old problem of what the working class did with their leisure. It would keep them out of public houses and out of mischief generally, improve their physique and their morals, and help them to become truly worthy of the great nation to which they belonged.

The force of this logic did not yet extend to installing games in the curricula of the public elementary schools, where the debased form of gymnastics known as drill was usually all that could be managed, but this was by no means the only deficiency of education for the masses. The principle at least was established, after centuries of hostility and suspicion, that sport was a virtuous activity for working men in their spare time; an extension of 'rational recreation', the reforming movement that had led to the provision of public libraries, museums, baths and parks in congested urban areas. This was not entirely a collapse of the selective Puritanism to which the British were prone. Sport in its new form, shaking off the old trappings of decadence, was seen as a kind of medicine, and it was one that could be doled out to the general benefit and at little cost.[2]

A less moralistic reason for the encouragement of games-playing amongst the working class was middle-class keenness to see their own favourite sports expand. Some enthusiasts simply wanted their own sport or their own team to do well. Others had a professional stake in expansion: gentlemanly journalist-organisers like C.W. Alcock had played a leading part in shaping modern sports. Alcock himself, in addition to his posts with the FA and Surrey, had developed the Oval as the early venue of both rugby and soccer internationals as well as Test matches and was a prolific and influential writer on both cricket and soccer. Such men were deeply committed to the advance of their chosen sports. Their efforts had begun amongst 'the classes' but the quest had led them farther and farther afield.

Unfortunately both missionary zeal and partisanship took the expansionists into very marshy territory. They quickly found that working-class sport had a momentum of its own with fierce local loyalties and an uninhibited zest for competition, which led inexorably to leagues, cups, the cult of the spectator, gate-money and professionalism. Working-class participation was one thing but accepting working-class morality was quite another. When such values began to obtrude the only recourse seemed to be either to try to resist such undesirable forms of expansion or to go along with them, supplementing the honour code by greater regulation and industrial models of government. The first approach was favoured by the RFU: the second had to be adopted, *faute de mieux*, in the Association game because of its vastly greater popular appeal.

Soccer: Pandora's box

The lure of competition had been undermining amateur soccer ever since the launch of Alcock's all-too-successful FA Cup. The battle against professionalism had been fought and lost by the gentlemen of the Football Association. In the early 1880s Alcock had argued for moderation during the increasingly gloomy discussions about undercover payments to players in the up-and-coming northern, industrial teams. Attempts to restrict these payments to bona fide expenses and compensation for lost wages had failed miserably and the time had clearly come when the FA had to decide whether to sink its principles or to see control of the game slipping into other hands. In 1885 they had reluctantly accepted professionalism, creating deep internal divisions, only to find that the delay had been fatal and although they remained in nominal control of soccer at all levels, at the top its destiny lay with the League clubs.

The top was no longer the preserve of the 'southern' teams – public school Old Boys, Army officers, Civil servants and the like – that had once dominated the scene. Blackburn Rovers, one of several rival clubs in the north and midlands in which local youths played alongside professional imports, had won the FA Cup three times running in the 1880s. In urging toleration of professionalism, however, the Harrovian Alcock had had the support of established gentry from the better public schools, notably the Etonian Lord Kinnaird, a fervent muscular Christian.[3] Greater hostility had come from men slightly lower down the social scale in industrial cities where the amateur cause seemed not yet so entirely lost as in the little Lancashire towns – men like J.C. Clegg, a Sheffield solicitor, and Charles Crump of Birmingham, a regional manager on the Great Western Railway, who thought that the introduction of professionalism would be 'the ruin of the pastime'.[4] Even more fiercely opposed were their southern counterparts who looked down their noses at anything remotely connected with trade and who wore their amateurism like a badge of gentility. The most prominent of these was N.L. Jackson, an entrepreneurial journalist who made a very good living out of organising, as well as writing about amateur sport, notably those favoured by the better sort, such as lawn tennis and golf, and who, in 1883 had founded the Corinthian Football Club. Unlike Alcock, Jackson was not quite out of the top drawer (for a man who made so much of public school traditions he was remarkably coy about his own schooling, for instance) and he was correspondingly more insistent on preserving the gulf between amateurs and professionals. His ostensible aim in founding the Corinthians had been to give the public school and university men who filled most of the places in the English international side an opportunity to play together and thus improve their chances against Scotland. It certainly helped in this, but it also assisted the less noble purpose of demonstrating the intrinsic superiority of the amateur cause. In Blackburn's cup-winning run the Corinthians took them on and beat them each year.

Jackson still hoped that what he took to be the moral of this would be heeded, but the professionals were only just beginning. In 1888 William McGregor, an immigrant Scottish draper who had won local renown on the board of directors of Aston Villa, one of the less respectable Birmingham clubs, found like-minded souls in Blackburn, Bolton, Preston and West Bromwich to support his idea of a Football League for selected clubs playing each other 'home and home' on a regular basis. Accrington, Burnley, Everton, Wolverhampton, Derby, Notts County and Stoke also joined in. The success of the new League was immediate. Unlike cricket the League clubs had no established county system to contend with and they quickly rose to a new kind of elitism based on professional skill. In its industrial heartland the League's unambiguously competitive ethos was obviously more to the liking of working-class crowds than the Corinthians' laid-back approach. During one of their Northern tours a local newspaper noted with amusement how those Corinthians who were not playing 'viewed the game from the stand, gently clapping their kid-gloved hands when applauding the team, or encouraging (them) with a "Well played, old chappie," uttered in a listless drawling style'.[5]

Other northern critics found this something of a veneer. On the same tour a Lancashire paper complained that the Corinthians systematically indulged in rough play and were the most dangerously cruel team that ever opposed provincial footballers.[6] Yet the prevailing view in reputable circles was that league and cup football had debased soccer, on and off the field. As early as 1889 a *Birmingham Daily Mail* sports reporter was noting, 'The lower element of partisans of the Small Heath Football Club are a particularly objectionable lot. Not content with resorting to disgusting expletives, they not infrequently molest strangers when the chances of (their) team are vanishing.'[7] And by 1895 an editorial in the same newspaper was regretfully declaring, 'the professional game has not only greatly lowered (soccer's) tone, but has led to frequent discreditable scenes of violence . . . The fierce and unruly partisanship of the spectators has on several occasions been stimulated to a dangerous extent by the example of the contending players on the field itself'.[8]

Professional football offered other temptations for the notoriously vulnerable lower orders. In 1892, for instance, an intellectual critic, E.C. Edwardes, complained that the 'popular adulation' given to footballers was 'enough to turn the head of a Prime Minister': there were street ovations, photographs in shop windows, glowing newspaper articles, civic receptions and banquets, with Mayors and MPs performing ceremonial kick-offs 'to show their sympathy with the popular ferment'.[9] Gambling was also a source of concern. The FA banned bookmakers and betting from their grounds, and many of the directors of the clubs themselves strongly supported this, but the ban gave rise to an ingenious evasion. It began, modestly enough, in the new football periodicals that sprang up in the northern strongholds of League football. In 1886 the Bolton weekly, *The Football Field*, offered £1 2s 6d to any reader who could predict the winners of the first round ties in the Lancashire Cup. By 1890 the *Athletic News* was offering £5 for forecasting the winner of the FA Cup and soon there were regular competitions of this kind based on the regular League fixtures. A Blackburn bookmaker began to offer prizes for successful predictions from a penny stake: as the number of entries increased, the prize

money went up from £12 to £37. The Anti-Gambling League brought prosecutions against several promoters charging them with running a lottery, but
the element of skill involved was judged a defence.

Urban soccer, amateur or professional, with its leagues and cups, had also
quickly established a reputation for encouraging drinking. Landlords made
rooms available for players to change and for committees to pick the teams:
even church clubs made pubs their headquarters. In 1889 a correspondent of a
north-eastern newspaper complained that 'the headquarters of the game are
generally at a public house, the play-up cards in the hats of the partisans bear
the name of some public house or hotel, players and patrons meet after a
match in tap-room, bar parlour and vault, then make a night of it as they
discuss the details of the play and the prospects of the team'.[10] There were
counter-arguments. The *Athletic News* reckoned that watching a match helped
many a working man to tide over 'that most dangerous part of the week-end
afternoon' and the Secretary of the Sunderland Branch of the Church of
England Temperance Society went so far as to say that it would be 'a serious
blow to the work of temperance . . . if the great counter-attraction of the
Saturday afternoon were discontinued'.[11] Nevertheless the atmosphere of
high excitement offered temptations, not least for the players, for whom
public admiration was often expressed in liquid form. In 1891 the Aston Villa
Committee attributed their team's poor performance during Christmas and
New Year to over-indulgence, and the following year the President of Darwen
FC, which had suffered a series of heavy defeats, appealed to supporters not
to treat the players to drinks.

All of this was a considerable disappointment both for those reformers who
sought to include soccer in the scope of 'rational recreation' and for the
ordinary middle-class enthusiasts for the game who were seeing it transformed by working-class partisanship of a kind they found abhorrent. Hence
the anxious letters to the *Newcastle Daily Chronicle* in 1889 complaining of
'demoralising tendencies' in what was intrinsically a source of 'healthy amusement and exercise' brought about by the 'introduction of cups which stopped
men playing the game simply for the love of it'.[12] The clash of values even
between local committee members, who tended to be middle-class, and the
rank-and-file supporters of their own team is well illustrated by the goings-on
at a special meeting of the Middlesborough Club that same year. The members
were split over a motion of censure on the club secretary, 'who while acting as
umpire had disallowed a Middlesborough goal which had "cost them the
match". Committee members praised the way he had "acted as an honourable
gentleman", but the hissing and booing which met the chairman's claim that
the motion was not carried, despite the "very large number of hands" in
favour, clearly reflected the feeling of many of the audience that he should not

have disallowed the goal'.[13]

The divisions within the Football Association as they contemplated the darkening national scene grew steadily worse. Some of the founding fathers withdrew at once when the implications of League soccer became clear. The Old Etonian Major (later Sir Francis) Marindin, a leading player and referee in the old amateur days, resigned as President in 1890 when the regulations regarding registration of players were relaxed. Lord Kinnaird, true to his Christian principles, agreed to succeed him but no fewer than five Vice-Presidents, all from southern amateur clubs, resigned in quick succession. One who stayed to continue the fight from within was N.L. Jackson, who in 1890 proposed that the Association should be divided into two more or less autonomous sections, one amateur, one professional. He was unsuccessful but he kept up his rearguard action.

The following year Jackson strongly opposed the introduction of the penalty kick, on the grounds that it was an insult to the honour of a gentleman to suggest that he would either deliberately commit a foul or stoop to take advantage of an opponent's transgression. He was again unsuccessful but it was some years before not only his Corinthians but many other Old Boys and public school teams would play the new rule. C.B. Fry, the most illustrious advertisement for the doctrine of 'a healthy mind in a healthy body' in the coming decade, was to pronounce it 'a standing insult to sportsmen to have to play under a rule which assumes that players intend to trip, hack and push into opponents and to behave like cads of the most unscrupulous kidney'.[14] The amateurs still retained one privilege – captaincy, as in cricket, was thought to be their preserve; but the dwindling number of top-class amateurs made this a lonely and demanding task. In 1891 only one was selected to play for England against Scotland. He was made captain, of course, and Jackson, who took charge of the team for the FA, wrote an article in his magazine, *Pastime*, musing on the experience. He expressed himself agreeably surprised: 'Paid football players are supposed to be inferior in manners and breeding to the average run of cricket professionals, and it might be supposed that the solitary amateur in the English team, who, as captain, was called upon to associate to some extent with his men, would have found his position more or less irksome. As it happened, however, these particular professionals turned out to be men of easy and gentlemanly demeanour, and they found their captain a very sociable companion'.

This might indeed have been the case, the Manchester-based *Athletic News* scornfully retorted, had the gentleman in question actually exposed himself to their company, 'but it hardly seems the right thing to our unsophisticated minds for a captain of an international team not to recognise his men on a long railway journey, not to speak to them in any way, to travel in a separate compartment, to dine away from them at the hotel, to leave them severely alone until driving off to the match, and generally to behave as if he were a superior sort of being . . . Sport levels all classes . . . It is a rare good text, Mr Jackson'.[15] Jackson's defence was that he had consulted the professionals and that they had preferred the separate arrangement, first because they wanted to dine earlier than the gentlemanly hour so that they could go to a music-hall, and second because they would have felt inhibited in their conversation by the presence of gentlemen.

Jackson's snobbish approach irritated not only the northern press but north country bourgeoises who had now come to the fore in the FA, men like J.C. Clegg who had adapted their moral indignation and were prepared to defend professionalism provided it stayed under the control of the FA. Clegg, Jackson wrote in his memoirs, 'always appeared to be hostile to the public school and university element', with rancour surprising 'in one who was a perfervid radical, Methodist and teetotaller'. It was a further blow that when an Amateur Challenge Cup was started in 1893 the committee of amateurs chosen to run it were men acceptable to Clegg and the growing number of League club representatives on the FA (and, it followed, did not include Jackson). Three years later Jackson was so sure that the FA's decision to require prior application from organisers of certain friendly matches was directed insultingly at him personally, and that Clegg was behind it, that he resigned as Vice-President and left the main Council. 'The episode further awakened the amateurs to a sense of the inferior position in which they had been placed by the predominance of the professional element in the Council', he recalled.[16] Thereafter he devoted his energies to agitating for a separate Amateur Association and to preserving the purity of his own London region.

Apart from these internal disputes the FA was frequently at odds with the Football League, the two main sources of disagreement being the League's failure to limit players' wages and their practice of restricting movement between clubs by the 'retain and transfer' system. The League clubs were ambivalent on the wages question. It was obviously in the general interest to keep wage levels down, but the richer clubs, who could afford it, paid whatever it took to hire the best players. The inflationary trend was first apparent with regard to signing-on fees: the official limit was £10 but soon £50 to £75 was the going rate for the bigger clubs. Wages themselves spiralled. By 1893, according to the *Athletic News*, the twenty-four clubs paid an average of £3 a week in the season and £2 in the summer whereas a typical club, Burnley, had paid, before the coming of the League, only £1 5s in winter and 10s in summer. Yet the clubs voted by 14 votes to 10 that year against a proposal to impose a maximum wage of £4. Wages were, in any event, not negotiated by collective bargaining, even within the individual clubs: each transaction was a separate, secret deal. During the deliberations over the proposed maximum wage W.G. Rose, the Wolverhampton goalkeeper, tried to organise a Players' Union to combat the idea, but once the threat receded the scheme fizzled out. Though working class, the players were entrepreneurial rather than union-minded – and, of course, those who made the grade were already considerably better off than other skilled workers.

This system suited club managements for they were paying for results and if they did not get them they could simply not renew a player's contract. They also hit upon a splendid method of protection against being held to ransom by star players. The system, which began in 1892, became a kind of annual cattle-market. The League Management Committee published at the end of each season a list of the players each club wanted to keep and the prices they expected to get for those they were willing to release. The FA disapproved strongly of this. In 1899 a committee chaired by J.C. Clegg declared the system unsportsmanlike, criticising in particular the practice of smaller clubs discovering and bringing on young players with the object of selling them to wealthier rivals. However, the economics of League football, competitive but requiring enough thriving clubs to make the matches interesting to spectators, demanded some method of redistributing resources. Thus began the tail-chasing process, still surviving, in which gate-money went to buy better players in order to attract bigger crowds and so on, whilst clubs unable to attract big crowds had to sell their best players in order to pay the wages of those they kept.

Star players increasingly dictated their own terms. In 1899, for instance, Atherstone demanded £4 a week and a £120 signing-on fee to join Aston Villa. That same year the League President mooted the idea of a £5 maximum wage but even this was rejected by the bigger clubs. The following year the FA, seeking to assert their authority, introduced a £4 maximum, which was accepted in theory but in practice merely encouraged under-the-counter payments. Success was what brought in the crowds, so that in addition winning bonuses, attractive to all types of club, rose to as much as £2 for an away win. No one could have foreseen how far beyond this the logic of the system was to take the Football League, but already it had made professional soccer a commodity and the players wage-slaves.

'Little shopkeepers'

The players' new masters were not Gradgrinds, for with rare exceptions they were not seeking material gain from their involvement with their local clubs but rather a kind of reflected glory. Nevertheless they lacked something of grace and style, finding it difficult to reconcile sporting and commercial values, and all too often relishing the social distinctions that set them above their talented hirelings. A modern critic, himself a former professional, has contested the conventional wisdom of later, disillusioned times 'that money has ruined soccer, that the greed of contemporary players and their agents is a cancer that is destroying the game', believing rather 'that professional football was deformed at birth. The game was never honourable, never decent, never rational or just. Class was the root of all professional football's evils: those who played the game for money, the heroes who drew the crowds, were working class; those who administered the game, the directors and football club shareholders, were, as the greatest player of the age, Billy Meredith, contemptuously described them, "little shopkeepers who governed our destiny" '.[17]

The process of 'companification' went further and with more unfortunate consequences in professional soccer than the limited gentlemanly efforts of the county cricket clubs or the superior rugger clubs like the Blackheath Cricket, Football and Lawn Tennis Club, who in 1885 issued a prospectus offering £1 shares to raise capital of £3,000 in order to lease 'land known as the Rectory Field, Charlton'. With such reputable models in mind the *Athletic News* in 1888 felt able to recommend soccer clubs with an annual turnover of £1,000 to take advantage of the Companies Act. A few were hesitant. In 1889 a sub-committee advised the Aston Villa board that the notion was 'against true sport'; but the practice spread and within a few years Villa was following the majority, not only of clubs within the League but of all those with ambition.

The FA were alive to the dangers from the start, restricting shareholders' profits to 5 per cent (determinedly holding to it until the First World War) and forbidding directors from receiving fees. So this was no opportunity to get rich quick. It was more often civic pride, particularly in smaller towns, and the desire to be someone in a local community, that led people to take shares in a soccer club. That there was kudos to be gained was evident from the importance local politicians attached to supporting individual clubs and the care many national ones took to appear sympathetic to the game. Some aspirant politicians became chairmen of clubs. Other chairmen tended to be brewers, caterers or property developers, and they sometimes found it a lucrative hobby. For the most part, however, being on a board of directors was not so much a matter of collecting rich pickings as of helping to stave off bankruptcy in the early days of many clubs. Newton Heath, for instance, went bankrupt in the 1890s before re-appearing as Manchester United in 1902.

There were, nevertheless, a number of smart operators who managed to make a little profit on the side – 'King John' Houlding, President of Everton FC, for instance. Houlding, a brewer and a leading Tory, was part-owner of the club's ground at Anfield as well as proprietor of the nearby Sandon Hotel and he held the refreshments concession at the club. This was all well and good, but when he tried to award himself a higher rent, leading shareholders, including Hartley the jam-maker and Hudson the soap-manufacturer, took exception and it was decided to acquire a new ground at nearby Goodison Park. Houlding started a new club at the old ground and tried to keep the name Everton for it, but the FA ruled against him so he was obliged to call his new venture Liverpool FC. This was an exceptional case, but everywhere the soccer club directors brought a business ethos: the only question was whether it was an honest or a corrupt one.

One striking feature of the way companification worked out in soccer was the dearth of high-level playing experience amongst the directors. This was largely a function of the game's professionalisation; there were few retired club captains or similar custodians of true sporting values on the boards. And the fact that the FA forbade professionals to become directors not only deprived the boards of technical know-how but further widened the social gap between those who played and those who ran the game at its highest levels. The result, as Billy Meredith showed, was often a mutual loathing. All they had in common was a desire that their team should be a playing and financial success. Similarly their only interest in spectators was as a source of vocal support and of revenue. There was a world of difference between being a member of a county cricket club and a soccer season-ticket holder.

The money that came through the turnstiles might perhaps, in a different society, have gone towards creating something more like a genuine club atmosphere rather than in transfer fees and illegal payments, and much subsequent trouble would have been avoided. But in truth such an idealistic solution to the problems of emergent urban democracy was neither practical nor foremost in the thoughts of either the directors or their principal hirelings. Shareholding proved a singularly inappropriate method of determining control of League soccer. Gentlemen, already repelled by the professional ethos, stayed aloof. At the other extreme the workers, from whose ranks the players came, did not take up share-ownership, either from ideological or economic reasons, even in the rare cases where clubs encouraged small investors. Blackburn Rovers, early champions of northern workers, sold most of their shares to manufacturers, managers and publicans. Three brewers and two publicans between them owned most of Manchester City's shares. When Aston Villa finally overcame their scruples they did the job thoroughly, offering shares at £5 rather than the usual £1. Sheffield United (£10 ordinary, £20 preference) went even further up market. It followed that most boards of directors were dominated by tradespeople and businessmen who saw themselves as a cut above the players and the general run of spectators.

Very few clubs were, of course, actually of working-class origin. One of the exceptions, Arsenal, had great difficulty in retaining its orientation. It had been founded in 1886 by a few soccer players who took up jobs at the Royal Arsenal munitions factory at Woolwich, a predominantly rugger-playing area. They formed a team, called at first Dial Square, to play matches on the local common: sixteen workers scraped together 10s 6d to buy their first football. The factory management showed no interest in the club but sympathisers at foreman level soon earned Arsenal a reputation for finding good jobs for promising players. In 1891, playing on a rented ground, they were expelled from N.L. Jackson's London FA for professionalism. They became part of a new Woolwich League but needed stronger competition than they could find locally. They tried to form a Southern League with a few other outcasts but professional clubs were scarce in the south. Then in 1893 the Football League, seeking to extend its empire, formed a Second Division and invited Arsenal to join.

This put their costs up yet again: for one thing, as the only southern club in the division they faced even longer and more expensive journeys. When on top of this their landlord asked them for another £150 rent their committee reluctantly accepted the inevitable and formed themselves into a limited company in order to buy a ground of their own. They still tried to fend off the evils of capitalism by encouraging working-class share-holding. Of the 4,000 £1 shares 1,552 went to 886 small investors and the biggest holding was 50 by a local coffee-shop owner. They were on a slippery slope nevertheless. Mortgage repayments and meagre gates consigned them to penury, and then the Boer War precipitated a crisis: armaments workers were given overtime for Saturday afternoon shifts and the club's main source of support dwindled away. By 1900 the committee, £3,400 in debt, had to turn to a clothier for help and from then on the businessmen took over.[18]

Regional variants

Professional football had made little headway in the metropolis. After dominating the first, amateur decade London teams had failed to reach the FA Cup Final since 1882–83. It had been held since the beginning at the Oval, but with Surrey CC increasingly worried about the damage the crowds might do to their pitch it was moved to a northern ground – Fallowfield, Manchester, in 1893 and Everton in 1894. The FA's decision to return to the capital the following year was partly a restatement of ownership, partly a commercial decision and in no way a reflection of the geographical balance of power. Of the 45,000 who went to Crystal Palace to see Aston Villa play Wolverhampton Wanderers many were home supporters making a day's outing of it.

Midland and northern clubs from the Football League continued to sweep the board until the turn of the century. The London FA's implacable opposition meant that professional clubs in the capital were slower to emerge, more isolated and more dependent on outside talent than elsewhere. The Southern League, founded in 1894, too late to recruit Arsenal, attracted enough clubs to form two divisions, but was distinctly inferior to the Football League. Its first member to achieve distinction was Southampton from the more tolerant Hampshire FA which had allowed professionalism for some years. The Southampton team that reached the FA Cup Final in 1900 consequently had a good share of local shipyard workers and other artisans.[19] In London, by contrast, the board of West Ham United, born of the philanthropic ideals of an Oxonian heir to an ironworks, sadly concluded in 1895 that what the community wanted 'was not local representatives on the field but the chance to participate in a vicarious battle that would end in victory for their gladiator'.[20] The following year Tottenham Hotspurs, formed in 1882 as the winter branch of a cricket club, turned professional and joined the Southern League. When they won the FA Cup in 1901 their side consisted of three northerners, two Welshmen, an Irishman. and no fewer than five Scots.

Professionalism had by then taken firm hold in Scotland itself despite the resistance of the Scottish FA. The amateur glory ended with the decline of Queen's Park, Glasgow, after two appearances in the English FA Cup Final in the mid-1880s. Glasgow Rangers with gentlemanly intentions on its foundation in 1873, had quickly attracted a popular following and soon had an income of some £1,500 a year and a core of professionals. Glasgow Celtic, formed in 1888 to raise money for Irish Catholic charities, clearly felt that the end justified the means, and found the means highly lucrative. These two clubs were the twin pillars of the Scottish League, formed in 1891. Queen's Park, fearful of the effects of this organised invitation to professionalism, led the opposition, but by 1900 were themselves obliged to join for lack of alternative fixtures of any quality. Meanwhile sectarian rivalry fanned the flames of competition: 30,000 watched Rangers v. Celtic in 1896 and both persuasions benefited financially if not in Christian charity. Rangers' income that year reached £5,000, but in 1897 Celtic paid £10,000 for a splendid new ground, the finest in Britain.

They could well afford it for their income was also the highest in Britain, £16,000 a year. Celtic players were obviously well rewarded, not only in wages but in presents such as new suits and, more substantially, by the tenancy of choice public houses. Glasgow also led the way in developing the notion of management as something beyond simply coaching the players. When Celtic's manager Willie Maley was made a lucrative offer to join Sheffield United he was persuaded to stay by a five-year contract at £150 a year, and when the club became a limited liability company in 1897 he became its secretary. Maley was also able to exploit his local celebrity through his sideline as 'Hosier, Hatter, Glover and Athletic Outfitter'. Similarly his counterpart at

Rangers, Tom Vallance, advertised his splendid facilities at the "Club" Res-
taurant in the *Scottish Football Annual* of 1895–96, commending them to
'Football, Cricket, Volunteer and every other form of Club'.[21]

As in England the game for amateurs in Scotland increasingly became
rugger, a middle-class preserve except in the market towns of the border area,
and strongest in the Edinburgh district with its fervent public school tradition.
Rugby had an even bigger following in Wales. Public school men had brought
the game there, too, and were still highly influential, but the proximity of west
of England clubs and the spread of English business interests had helped it
take hold not only in Cardiff but in the smaller towns of the prosperous
southern industrial belt whose teams were perforce less socially exclusive.
There were many junior soccer clubs in Wales, but the attraction of rugby in
the most populous districts made a separate senior soccer League impractical.
When Cardiff FC eventually reached a high enough standard in 1899 they
sought their fortunes in the Second Division of the Football League. Similarly
many of the best Welsh soccer players, especially from the smaller towns,
went from minor local football to English senior clubs. In North Wales,
relatively untouched by both industry and rugby, there was a cluster of clubs
around Wrexham, some of which played in the Shropshire and District
League, and it was there that Billy Meredith, perhaps the greatest soccer
player of his day, was discovered by the scouts of the Ardwick club, which
later became Manchester City.

The scouts of the other Manchester club, United, found their happy hunting
ground in Northern Ireland where the English League could offer relief from
sectarian as well as economic pressures. Irish soccer faced not only the challenge of rugger, the game of the Anglo-Irish ascendancy, but of Gaelic
football, the game of the nationalists, and it was controlled by the Belfast-
based Irish FA, a middle-class largely Protestant foundation inspired by the
Scottish, Queen's Park tradition and intent on maintaining gentlemanly
values. However, the Irish Cup, started in 1881, had been growing both in
popularity and in scope with teams from Dublin and Banbridge joining the
much stronger contingents from Belfast, Londonderry and Monaghan in
1885–86, and gate receipts from the Cup Final in 1888 exceeded those from the
two internationals played that season. The cup helped soccer to spread
throughout the country and there was soon a strong following in the south,
especially in the working-class parts of Dublin, and the smaller towns everywhere. But it also, as it had done in England, unleashed the forces of competition and all that went with it.

The pressure on the Irish FA to legalise professionalism increased when an
Irish League was founded in 1890, largely on the initiative of the Belfast clubs,
Linfield and Glentoran. The IFA stood firm and English and Scottish clubs

were quick to take advantage. The first of many signings by Manchester United – still Newton Heath – was John Peden from Linfield. Eventually, in 1894, evidence of falling standards and fear of further English depredations led the clubs to vote by a large majority to allow professionalism (ironically, the resolution was moved by the ultra-amateur Cliftonville) but it was five more years before professionals were allowed to play for the national team. Even then it was only after a succession of humiliating defeats, culminating in a 13–2 rout by England, and bitter accusations by southern clubs of northern prejudice that the Irish FA relented. Thus in 1899 Peden was accorded the honour of being the first professional to play for Ireland. He scored the only goal, giving Ireland her first international victory, against Wales, including the great Meredith. There was a social price to pay for this improvement in standards. Economic circumstances meant that professionalism was never to be on anything like the scale of England and Scotland, whose clubs continued to attract the best Irish professionals. But the change was enough to increase the attraction of the rugger code for the middle classes and the better schools.

Rugby: towards the Northern Union

The Rugby Union's amateur purity had only been preserved in England after great travail. As with soccer the trouble stemmed from the north of England, though in this case the difficulties lay to the east of the Pennines. In Yorkshire, with its broader acres and smaller leading towns, the social composition of rugby teams was less select than in the two great conurbations of Lancashire, where the prestigious Manchester and Liverpool clubs set the tone and soccer held the attention of the populace. Small Yorkshire towns and 'obscure villages whose names we cannot discover in Bradshaw'[22] were achieving great rugby success not only by training and coaching, themselves anathema to the gentlemanly ideal, but by finding jobs for promising working-class players and offering inducements such as 'broken time' compensation for lost wages.

The RFU's opposition to Shrewsbury's 1888 tour of Australia, because it was 'organised for the benefit of individual promoters', was stiffened by the fact that 18 of the 21 chosen for the tour were from northern clubs. And whereas A.E. Stoddart and the other amateur cricketers who were thinking of staying on to play Rugby had been able to discuss financial matters privately with Shrewsbury himself in Antipodean obscurity, the rest were recruited through an agent in England whose very furtiveness made him conspicuous. There were soon well-founded rumours of his approaches to players with offers of expenses and such inducements as £15 to buy clothes. It was bitter rivalry between two Yorkshire clubs, Dewsbury and Halifax, that brought the story to light. Shrewsbury's agent had made offers to three Dewsbury players and one from Halifax. All but one signed: this purist, a Welshman playing for Dewsbury, reported the offer to the club. Dewsbury, drawn against Halifax in the Yorkshire Cup, decided to set a trap for their opponents. One of their fallen men had second thoughts and withdrew from the tour, and they dropped their other defaulter for the Cup-tie. Halifax, however, unaware of what was going on, picked their own transgressor, J.P. Clowes, and when Halifax won the match Dewsbury reported them to the Rugby Union for playing a professional.

The RFU found that Clowes was indeed a professional, adding that they had 'formed a very strong opinion that others composing the Australian team had also infringed these laws', and would require explanations from them when they got back. In the event, all that happened was that each player was required to make an affidavit that he had received no pecuniary benefit from the tour; all did so, leaving poor Clowes as the only sufferer.[23] The most fortunate to survive with reputation intact was Stoddart, whose stock-broking activities were apparently lucrative and undemanding enough to allow him freedom to exist on expenses while he played cricket and football in Australia for a year. The RFU undoubtedly regarded wage-earners as most unreasonable in seeking compensation for lost earnings: to compare this with amateurs claiming 'expenses' seemed to them irrelevant and unfair. As Dr Arthur Budd, RFU President in 1888, later explained, 'If AB of the Stock Exchange were to ask for compensation for loss of time for a two days' football tour, such compensation to be fixed on a scale commensurate with his earnings, the football community would denounce it as a scandal. AB, the stockbroker, has to stop at his desk because he cannot afford to play, but CD, the working man, is to be allowed his outing and compensation for leaving his work, which in other circumstances he could not afford to abandon.'[24]

By this time Yorkshire clubs, fortified by the 'gate-money' that enabled them to employ such discriminatory practices, were sweeping all before them. The county championship had evolved from early rivalry between Yorkshire and Lancashire, but neither Lancashire nor anyone else could hold a candle to Yorkshire by the late 1880s. As the official history of the RFU put it, 'In 1889 and 1890 Yorkshire were unbeaten in county matches and the Rugby Union declared them champions, but such a state of affairs was unsatisfactory.'[25] Not all Yorkshire clubs were in favour of broken time. The opposition was led by the Revd Frank Marshall, a prominent member of both the Yorkshire Union and the RFU itself and a highly regarded writer on rugby, who campaigned ceaselessly for the cause of true amateurism. But there were others of weaker flesh. A sorrowful chronicler of later decades recalled that the Yorkshire Union 'included members . . . tainted with professionalism' and 'even those of Marshall's colleagues . . . who were amateur at heart' yielded to the pressure from their constituents and supported the clubs' proposal to legitimise broken time payments.[26]

For the southerners and their allies the game's very survival depended on withstanding such inroads into amateurism. In 1892 Dr Budd went so far as to claim that 'no professional sport under its own government and independently of amateur supervision' had ever thrived or could ever 'permanently prosper'. If the 'blind enthusiasts of working men's clubs' insisted on introducing professionalism the amateur 'must refuse to submit to the process of slow extinction' that had been going on in soccer 'and say at once that henceforth he will play and compete with his own class alone' without waiting 'to see the whole of the North and part of the South given up to subsidized players'.[27] Many feared not merely a loss of social tone but a deterioration in sportsmanship. E.C. Edwardes, arguing that monetary rewards inevitably led to unscrupulousness and corruption, described the indignities, abuse and threats of violence offered by an angry crowd to a soccer referee.[28] H.H. Almond,[29] Headmaster of Loretto, foremost of the group of Edinburgh schools that formed the core of Scottish rugby, feared that refereeing[30] would become impossible if the game became professionalised. Rugby referees could not hope to see everything that was going on. This put an onus on the players: 'there has to be a certain amount of bona fides . . . or it soon becomes no game at all. But from the professional player we cannot expect this bona fides. His object is to win, no matter how, for his livelihood depends upon his success'.[31] Almond feared corruption of club managements as well as players. The cup-ties in Yorkshire were breeding 'a fictitious sort of keenness, which is only too apt to lead to tricks of all descriptions . . . The executives of clubs will, in the first instance, do anything lawful to win. Next they will do what is doubtfully lawful. They will use inducements to procure recruits wherever they can get them, and these inducements are apt very soon to pass the limits of fair persuasion'.[32]

Awkwardly for the RFU, Yorkshire accounted for 150 of the 350 or so rugger clubs under their banner. When the Yorkshire Union submitted their proposal to legalise broken-time to the AGM in 1893 the alarm bells rang, for it was obvious that they would attend in force. The signal went out for all who had the true interests of the game at heart to come to the aid of the Union. As the official history gleefully recorded nearly a century later, the barbarian hordes were outwitted. The ends were clearly thought to justify the means: 'The Northerners came down in two special trains to make sure of maximum possible representation (but fortunately) some of them got lost in the metropolis as country bumpkins used to do, even in those days . . . (Better still) they were up against the brilliant organising genius of H.E. Steer'[33] Steer's brilliance included collecting the proxy votes of 120 backwoodsmen who could not attend in person, and the university representatives did their bit by dubiously awarding themselves a vote for each constituent college.

But the southern victory did not end the matter. The corruption was spreading far beyond Yorkshire. 'Gate-money' clubs had for years been attracting working-class players from outside the county, notably from Wales. Lancashire clubs also began importing Welsh players as the competition from soccer drove them to seek greater success and bigger gates. In Wales public school influence, initially strong, had not manifested itself in dominance of the game's administration as competition developed.[34] Cup-ties and local derbies had produced 'gate-money' in plenty – the takings of Cardiff RFC, for instance, had risen from £364 in 1884–85 to £1,985 in 1890–91[35] – and the working-class players no doubt benefited from 'expenses' if not 'broken-time'. But it was a different matter when they deserted their local followers. Thus when, in 1893, it emerged that the James brothers, the idols of Swansea, had been attracted north by the prospect of jobs (at 25s a week, rising to £2), there was great dismay in the locality and the players were subjected to much criticism. Yet when the Rugby Union suspended them it was regarded as a slight on Welsh rugby and the newspapers predicted cheering crowds when the Jameses next appeared in Swansea.[36]

To the Rugby Union, however, the cause of amateur purity was all-important. In 1895 they produced definitive rules that thoroughly and com-prehensively prohibited all forms of remuneration to players, even extending the ban to writing about the game. That August representatives of the northern 'gate-money' clubs met at the George Hotel, Huddersfield, and decided to form their own Union. In the fierce controversy that followed the culture clash was strongly in evidence. How, one supporter of the rebel clubs asked, did 'the gentlemen of the Rugby Union' suppose that 'the class of men . . . now playing in the North . . . working men at an average wage . . . of not more than 27s a week' could afford to lose time and money playing football; it was far better for the northern clubs to belong honestly to a Union that allowed broken time than to continue making payments illicitly under the RFU.[37] For the purists on the other hand *Old Ebor* of the conservative *Yorkshire Post* argued that once the dissidents had gone the Yorkshire Rugby Union could 'stand before the country with clean hands' and would be spared the indignity of having some of its members "spotted" one by one for professionalism'. He was quite clear that the broken time issue was only the tip of the iceberg; 'the only possible justification for a Northern Union is professionalism'.[38]

Rugby, soccer and the great divide

This indeed was the general view even in the north. Those who thought they could contain the pressure for payment to players to broken time were simply deluding themselves, wrote one critic. The Northern Union might try to restrict their members, but 'the clubs were free to roam in search of players, far and near . . . Does anyone imagine that a man is coming, say, from Wales to Lancashire or Yorkshire for a miserable 6s a day for time broken when playing football?' It was 'excruciatingly funny' to think of the legislators of a breakaway Union at some time in the future trying to legislate against out-and-out professionalism. 'It would be a monumental example of Satan rebuking sin.'[39] Nevertheless the Northern Union fervently hoped professionalism would not automatically follow the split, and they did their best to prevent it. Their regulations not only restricted 'broken-time' to 6s a day for one day a week, but made having a job outside football compulsory and time off dependent on employers' permission.[40] They tried hard to enforce the regulations and went to inordinate lengths to see that the players did not neglect their outside jobs.

Their approach was thus quite different from that of the Football League, professional from the outset, which required its players *not* to take jobs outside football. Unlike the League the Northern Union was not an elite gathering. It included as well as the big clubs modest foundations like Melbourne, Fairburn, Ossett, Alverthorpe, Hebden Bridge, Doncaster, Kirkstall St Stephen's and Windhill, and it took in new recruits like Leeds Parish church, Millom, Ulverston, Barton and Altrincham. They were also remarkably unsuccessful in the early stages, basically because of competition from soccer itself. Already in 1896 the *Yorkshire Post* was claiming that the northern Union experiment had gone badly wrong: 'there is no use blinking facts . . . the game has dwindled in the very quarters where . . . it should be most expected to succeed'.[41] The few clubs that had done well out of the change could be numbered on the fingers of one hand, whilst others, such as Halifax and Bradford, which had previously made four-figure profits each year, had been brought to the verge of bankruptcy. The reason was competition from soccer. The situation was so bad that some clubs were trying to run soccer teams as well, and a few were even hiring out their grounds to soccer clubs. This amounted, the *Post* reckoned, to seeking 'to repair their Rugby weakness by killing it by the Association code'.[42]

Desperate measures were needed to bring back the crowds. This chiefly meant winning, but it also meant entertaining the spectators, which to the purists was almost as damaging morally as trying too hard to win. That autumn H.H. Almond warned against 'the prevalent tendency to care more about what interests spectators than what interests players', evidenced by the proposal amongst some northern clubs to reduce the size of teams. 'Let all who have (the main purpose of) games at heart . . . make Rugby Football as interesting as possible to all players . . . and let them treat the preferences of spectators as a very unimportant matter.'[43] That, however, was exactly what the Northern Union could not do, and they considered various eye-catching rule changes in the next few years.

The leading Northern Union clubs also continued their plundering raids on Wales. 'Llanelli in football' complained a supporter in 1897, 'has been to the Northern Union what Rayader is to Birmingham in the matter of water supply.'[44] The Welsh clubs obviously took what modest protective measures they could. These were normally invisible to the naked, London eye. However there was something of a stir in 1897 when Newport, one of the more gentlemanly clubs, decided, perhaps with the parallel of W.G. Grace in mind, to award a testimonial to A.J. Gould, an international of some renown. The Welsh RU not only approved the idea but sent a contribution, and were with some difficulty persuaded by the RFU that it would be more seemly if Gould were bought a house rather than given money. That same year Wales again attracted attention when the James brothers, sins apparently purged, appeared for Swansea: the crowds, as predicted, were vast. In 1899 the Welsh RU chose them to play for Wales in a game against England that drew 30,000 spectators – and that England lost by 26 points to 3. Twelve days later the pair became registered professionals with Broughton Rangers, Manchester, each receiving a generous signing-on fee, and the whole James family, sixteen strong, moved north. A few perceptive critics put England's thrashing down to the loss of Lancashire and Yorkshire forwards but respectable opinion, darkly observing the 'drill by experts' of the Welsh team – 'a departure in the methods of International procedure' – formed its own conclusions'.[45]

Things were much better ordered in Scotland. The soccer menace had consumed the working-classes especially in Glasgow, but rugby thrived in the better schools, the former pupils' clubs and the universities (though these last were creamed of their 'best' students by Oxford and Cambridge). As the Badminton Library volume on football put it in 1899, 'In Scotland Rugby is the game of the classes; the masses are devoted to Association, with the exception of one district, generally classed as the Borders, where . . . Rugby is the game of the people.'[46] This was only a minor difficulty. In the small market towns of the Border area circumstances, as in parts of Yorkshire, obliged a wider social mix than in more populated areas, encouraging both gate-money and un-Almond-like competition. There was, indeed a Border League and a Melrose seven-a-side knockout tournament.[47] Such things were looked at askance in Edinburgh, but it was a very local phenomenon and was free of the nastier elements to be found in industrial areas. The Almond philosophy was generally unquestioned and defectors to the Northern Union were almost unheard of.

So too in Ireland. Rugby there had begun, in its innocent infancy, at Trinity College, the ascendancy stronghold, and its club's first secretary had been from Rugby School itself. In Dublin it had grown up around a coterie of suburban clubs dominated by young professional and business people, inspired by those who had learned the game in English schools. In Belfast the leading club, North of Ireland, was an offshoot of a cricket club, and rugby was the favoured game of the better local schools and suburban area clubs. Links had been formed early with the leading centres across the water, the Dublin clubs with the emergent RFU and the Belfast ones with the Scots. Irish Rugby faced two problems: first, it did not take hold in rural areas, mostly Catholic, inclined to nationalism and tending to prefer Gaelic games; second, it had strong competition from soccer, the choice of the Protestant working classes of the urbanised north. But in Dublin, Cork, Limerick and Galway in the south, and in small market towns like Dungannon as well as Belfast in the north it became the middle-class game. The narrowness of its base ensured that it remained wholly amateur. Each of the four provinces formed its own branch of the Irish RFU – Leinster (1882), Ulster (1885), Munster (1886) and Connaught (1896) – and the annual encounters between them helped to institutionalise cup competition without fear of professional infiltration.[48]

Throughout the British Isles the divisions both in rugby and in soccer reflected perfectly the 'north–south divide'. How deep this divide was is clear from a vitriolic essay in 1898 by E.K. Ensor, who evidently saw what had happened to football as a case of savages eating the missionaries who had brought them the gospel. Rugby Football, he wrote

> began in the South. Enthusiasts who faced jeers and taunts had their reward and the game made its way northwards. There it was passionately adopted by that people whose warped sporting instincts are so difficult to understand, even when they are quite familiar.
>
> For a time it was played as a game, money was not a disturbing element; but the warped sporting instincts asserted themselves – the main chance is not ignored for long north of the Trent – and the clubs began to import players from all sides, in order to gratify the prevailing desire to get the better of one's neighbour.

Ensor went on to express relief that 'the contagion' had not so far spread to the south, where the influence of the public schools and universities was strongest. By contrast in soccer, which had 'touched pitch and been shockingly defiled' gentlemen could now only play against other gentlemen for fear of 'plunging into this moral slough'.[49]

The hopes of the soccer missionaries had indeed been dashed: the middle classes had passed on their game but not the values with which they had invested it. In 1889 it had been possible for a Scottish advocate of 'rational recreation' to argue that soccer 'shows by example the necessity of gentleness and fairness, the superiority of the mind over the body, temperance and humility . . . in every match these moral precepts are an example before the spectators, as well as the chance of condemning what is wrong in behaviour and conduct, and we like to believe that these short Saturday afternoon sermons are not without their effect on the reformation of the people'.[50] Even he had felt impelled to add, however, that soccer would 'never be worth the name of muscular Christianity until it devotes all its surplus funds for the purpose of open-handed charity'. By 1898 Ensor was complaining, 'Professional football is doing more harm every year . . . the system is bad for the players, worse for the spectators. The former learn improvident habits, become vastly conceited, whilst failing to see that they are treated like chattels and cannot help but be brutalised. The latter are injured physically and morally . . . The physique of the manufacturing population is bad enough already; it is rapidly growing worse under the pleasures no less than the pains of civilisation.' 'Fair play' survived only in 'thinly-populated' districts where sport could not be exploited for money.[51]

Earlier that year the Northern Union, in further demonstration of warped northern sporting instincts, had been obliged to agree to out-and-out professionalism. They still tried to avoid the abyss into which soccer had fallen, however, insisting that it should be part-time, not only retaining the 'work and play' rule but doing their earnest best to enforce it. Fitzgerald, the Batley centre-three-quarter, was suspended for almost two seasons for failing to find a job outside the game. Many supporting arguments were advanced in favour of this benevolent paternalism, from wanting the players to keep fit between matches to off-setting the insecurity and brevity of their sporting careers. An important factor was undoubtedly disapproval of the attitude of many Welshmen coming north who were paid so much for playing that they could not be bothered to work. This was felt to be a thoroughly bad influence on the game. In theory the Northern Union would now have much more control over what the players did during the week: 'It will be a treat to see some of those lovely Taffies work', commented *Old Ebor*.[52] But in practice it was not quite so simple. The better the players, the less willing *they* were to accept, and the less able the clubs were to impose, irksome conditions. The Welsh were again a particular threat to good order, and there were many jokes about their getting jobs shovelling steam at the gas works, keeping flies off newly painted pubs and so forth.[53] Another of the Union's concerns was to keep the players free of the malign influence of alcohol and gambling. They tried to insist on their having respectable jobs: bookies' runner, billiard marker or potman would not do. Booth of Radcliffe had his registration cancelled when he was found to be 'waiting on'.[54]

Despite these puritanical urges the Union found it increasingly necessary to follow the logic of commerce rather than amateur sport. The reduction in the number of players that Almond had forecast did not take place for a while yet, but between 1897 and 1901 there were various changes designed to appeal to spectators. But what supporters chiefly wanted was success in competition. This began, as in soccer, with a Challenge Cup. In 1901 30,000 people paid a total of £1650 to see Batley play Warrington. The Northern Union made contributions from the proceeds to clubs and to county organisations, which followed a similar policy of re-distribution of profits. Most senior clubs, however, found themselves unable to meet the costs of wages and upkeep of grounds: something was needed to arouse greater interest week by week. They came to the same conclusion as their soccer rivals – that the answer was to form a League. They were truly on the downward path, as the next era would show.

Notes

1 *Pall Mall Gazette*, vol. 11, p. 2, 3 May, 1886.
2 For the place of sport in the 'rational recreation' movement and the problems it encountered see R.J. Holt, *Sport and the British*, Oxford, 1989, pp. 136–8.
3 Kinnaird was also a supporter of the philanthropist Quintin Hogg's work in founding a 'ragged school' and a 'Youths' Christian Institute' in London.
4 An early England international, Clegg afterwards recalled being patronised on his first appearance by snobbish southern team-mates. He became Sir James Clegg and a pillar of the Football Association. Crump also stayed on to become a Vice-President.
5 N.L. Jackson, *Sporting Days and Sporting Ways*, London, 1932, p. 91.
6 *Ibid.*
7 6 May, 1889, quoted by J. Maguire, 'Images of Manliness', *BJSH*, December, 1986, pp. 278–9.
8 23 November, 1895, in Maguire, 'Images,' p. 275.
9 E.C. Edwardes, 'The New Football Mania', *Nineteenth Century*, 32, 1892.
10 M. Huggins, 'The Spread of Football in North-East England, 1876–90', *IJHS*, December, 1989, p. 312.
11 *Sunderland, Herald*, 14 July, 1896 quoted in T. Mason, *Association Football and English Society*, Brighton, 1980, p. 176. Mason's book is essential reading for students of the period.
12 Huggins, 'The Spread of Football', p. 313.
13 *Ibid.*
14 Quoted in P. McIntosh, *Ethics in Sport and Education*, London, p. 80.
15 *Athletic News*, 11 April, 1892, quoted in Mason, *Association Football*, p. 77.
16 Jackson, *Sporting Days*, pp. 152 and 175.
17 E. Dunphy, *A Strange Kind of Glory*, London, 1991, pp. 27–8.
18 See B Joy, *Forward Arsenal*, London, 1952, for a detailed account.

19 On its second appearance in the Final in 1902 it also included the illustrious amateur, C.B. Fry.
20 C.P. Korr, 'West Ham United Football Club and the Beginnings of Professional Football in East London, 1895–1914', *Journal of Contemporary History*, vol. 13, 1978, p. 228.
21 J. Hutchinson, *The Football Industry*, London, 1982, p. 90. This is a fascinating pictorial record of the game's swift transition from amateur pastime to big business.
22 The standard railway guide. Part of a warning about declining southern standards by 'A Londoner', 'Metropolitan Football' in F.P. Marshall (ed.), *Football: the Rugby Union Game*, London, 1892, p. 323.
23 E. Dunning and K. Sheard, *Barbarians, Gentlemen and Players*, Oxford, 1979, pp. 151–2, from which much of the illustrative material in this section is taken.
24 *Ibid.*, p. 158.
25 U.A. Titley and R. McWhirter, *Centenary History of the Rugby Football Union*, London, 1970, p. 108.
26 G.F. Berney, *Progress of the Rugby Football Union from 1892–3*, in L.R. Tosswill, (ed.), *Football: the Rugby Union Game*, London, 1925, p. 57.
27 Dunning and Sheard, *Barbarians*.
28 Edwardes, 'Football Mania'.
29 Hely Hutchinson Almond (1832–1903), Glaswegian descendant of a Provost of Trinity College, Dublin and classical scholar, had set the seal on his muscular Christian philosophy at Balliol College, Oxford. Frustrated in his ambition to become a colonial administrator, he had turned to schoolmastering and by his Spartan regime and encouragement of games (notably rugby but also cricket) had raised Loretto to public school status.
30 Unlike the older game, cricket, where the umpires were lowly professionals, the referees in football still reflected the public school origin of the game. They were much more authoritarian figures and, of course, amateurs. This tradition has persisted in the Rugby Union game, but soon disappeared in soccer as it became professionalised.
31 'Football as a Moral Agent', *Nineteenth Century*, December, 1893.
32 *Ibid.*
33 Titley and McWhirter, *Centenary History*, p. 203.
34 Dunning and Sheard, *Barbarians*, pp. 223–4.
35 *Ibid.*, p. 225, quoting from W.J. Morgan and G. Nicholson, London, 1959.
36 For the early history of Welsh rugby the standard work is D. Smith and G. Williams, *Fields of Praise*, Cardiff, 1980. See also J.B.G. Thomas, *The Men in Scarlet*, London, 1972, and G. Williams, 'Rugby Union' in T. Mason (ed.), *Sport in Britain*, Cambridge, 1989.
37 *Leeds Daily News*, 28 August, 1895.
38 30 August, 1895.
39 28 August, 1895.
40 P. Greenhalgh, ' "The Work and Play Principle": The Professional Regulations of the Northern Rugby Football Union, 1898–1905', *IJHS*, December 1992, p. 375. The regulations are printed in full on pp. 374–5.
41 'Stands Rugby Football Where It Did?', 22 April, 1896.
42 *Ibid.*
43 *The Field*, October, 1896.
44 *Llanelli Mercury*, quoted by G. Hughes, *The Scarlets*, Llanelli, 1986.
45 Smith and Williams, *Fields*, p. 118.
46 Quoted in J. Arlott (ed.), *The Oxford Companion to Sports and Games*, St Albans, 1977,

p. 784.

47 Introduced in 1883 by the Melrose captain and town butcher, Ned Haig, to solve the
    problem of chronic shortage of funds and a popular attraction ever since.

48 For early Scottish rugby see A.C.M. Thorburn, *The Scottish Rugby Union Official
    History*, Edinburgh, 1985, and A. Massie, *A Portrait of Scottish Rugby*, Edinburgh,.
    1984. For early Irish Rugby see J.J. McCarthy, 'International Football: Ireland', in
    Marshall, *Football*, E.E. Van Esbeck, *One Hundred Years of Irish Rugby*, Dublin, 1974,
    and S. Differy, *The Men in Green*, London, 1973.

49 E.K. Ensor, 'The Football Madness', *Contemporary Review*, November, 1898, pp.
    571–60.

50 G. Guthrie, *Scottish Football Annual, 1889–90*, quoted more fully in Maguire,
    'Images', p. 273.

51 Ensor, 'The Football Madness'.

52 *Athletic News*, 8 August, 1898.

53 Greenhalgh, 'Work and Play', p. 373.

54 Greenhalgh, p. 368. See also K. Macklin, *The History of Rugby League Football*,
    London, 1962, and T.R. Delaney, *The Roots of Rugby League*, Keighley, 1984.

CHAPTER THREE

True blues –
and a touch of green

The values of the public schools had been absorbed by the universities of Oxford and Cambridge.[1] They had come to see their main task as preparing the country's future leaders, less through some Socratic equation of virtue with knowledge than a sturdily British conviction that 'character' mattered more than brains. There was heated debate about the direction they had taken. At Oxford there had been a much-publicised set-to amongst the senior academics about the proper function of a university. The Rector of Lincoln College, Mark Pattison, had argued passionately that it should be a place of science and learning not a home for 'the foppish exquisite of the drawing room or the barbarised athlete of the arena'.[2] But he had lost the argument, hands down, and thirty years later neither university showed much interest, as *The Spectator* complained, in 'nominalism, idealism, realism and materialism in contrast to athleticism'.[3]

Their enthusiasm brought them to the forefront in the national organisation of various sports. Two in which they were particularly influential were rowing and athletics. The two had achieved very different positions in the sporting and social hierarchy. Rowing was the admired emblem of muscular Christianity: athletics, individualistic and undisciplined, was much less admired despite its Greek overtones. But the two had been closely related in their early Victorian emergence as organised sports and both had subsequently received the reforming attentions of university men.[4] And both were subjected to unwelcome American influence in violation of the amateur ideal.

Rowing: amateurism by exclusion

Jubilee year was a good one for true blue rowing men, particularly the paler shade. Cambridge won the Boat Race and Trinity Hall the Grand Challenge Cup at Henley. Concern about ill-bred American intrusions at the royal regatta was temporarily forgotten in the warm glow of admiration by more distinguished visitors: on the third day, *The Field* reported, 'the regatta was honoured by the Prince and Princess of Wales, the King of Denmark, the King of the Hellenes, the Princes Albert Victor and George of Wales, the Princesses Victoria, Sophie and Margaret of Prussia, the Hereditary Princess of Saxe-Meiningen, the Duke of Sparta, Prince George of Greece, the Duke of Cambridge and the Indian Princes staying in England'.[5]

A less welcome aspect of the regatta's celebrity was the carnival atmosphere it engendered: 'The curse of Henley', wrote The *Field*, 'is the picnicking – we care not a straw whether it is afloat on houseboats or ashore in the meadows . . . This picnicking, this ostentatious display of female finery, of flowers, of fruit, of wine, of viands, is a modern innovation and a sign of the luxurious selfishness of the times – a selfishness which is exampled by the total disregard of the competitors and in a bon mot uttered on a houseboat that the regatta would be perfect were it not for the horrid rowing men'.[6] In this regrettably licentious modern world, indeed, rowing and picnicking went hand in hand; it was for pleasure boating, not competitive rowing, that most people used the inland waterways of Britain. They were doing so in vast numbers: the Thames was now festooned each day by 'a brilliant tangle of bright blazers, and gay caps, and saucy hats, and many-coloured parasols'.[7] To make matters worse these merry-makers, many drawn from the clerk and small tradesman class, had no respect for the Sabbath: as the Bishop of Oxford complained, 'The idlers cannot omit one day in the week from their quest of pleasure.'[8]

The Bishop was a former college oar, part of the tradition of muscular Christianity, characterised, in Trollope's words, by such earnestness that 'men must row until there comes upon us a fear whether or not they are killing themselves – or they are nothing'.[9] Trollope had marvelled at the sophisticated coaching, considered anathema in other amateur sports, rowing required: young university men were put to the torture as if they were galley-slaves.[10] Discipline, in fact, was, an essential part of the rowing cult, for it emphasised team-work. (Eight-oared boats were thought to be by far the noblest part of rowing. Sculling, at the other extreme, was highly suspect not only because it was individualistic but because it lent itself more easily to betting and corruption.) In token of the purity of this concept, however, the professional watermen who had been an essential part of public school and university rowing in its unregenerate days were now entirely banished, even as coaches, because it was felt they degraded the discipline and made it a soul-destroying mechanical exercise.

Trollope, who was all for keeping professionals in their place,[11] had duly recognised the value of a sport in which 'true amateurs are not swamped in a crowd of noisy spectators' and give their all in concerted striving for excellence in bleak and lonely practice sessions. The crowds on the towpath for the

University Boat Race could be noisy enough, of course, for its appeal went far beyond university circles, but they were not paying crowds: rowing was untainted by the temptations of gate-money events. Indeed this and the banishment of the gladiatorial element from the upper reaches of the sport had almost killed off the professional side. Doggett's Cap and Badge, the traditional prize for newly qualified watermen, was virtually the only professional race of any standing left. The next task was to ensure that amateur rowing was not debased by working-class and other vulgar influences.

In the old days there had been no problem. There were three classes of club – for gentlemen, tradesmen and watermen. The former champion oarsman, W.B. Woodgate, now a judge, whose youthful evasions of the rules had caused the rowing authorities much grief, expressed the position with beguiling clarity in 1888: 'the old theory of an amateur was that he was a gentleman and the two were simply convertible terms'.[12] He was in a good position to know, for when he had been accused of professionalism the Henley Stewards had exonerated him on the grounds that since he was a member of the Kingston, a club for gentlemen, he must be an amateur.

The trouble had begun when Henley's rowing fame had started to attract entries from foreign, particularly American, clubs, which did not meet the Woodgate criterion – mostly college crews of dubious morality but even a set of Canadian lumberjacks on one occasion. The result had been a tightening of the rules, first by the Henley Stewards themselves and from 1882 by the Amateur Rowing Association (ARA). This was no reforming crusade. It had sprung from an elite group of clubs (led by Leander, restricted to select Oxbridge alumni) whose avowed object had been to form a national team able to beat off foreign challenge but in whose minds the laudable aim of 'raising the standards of British amateur rowing' had proved inseparable from that of preserving gentlemanly amateurism. The new Henley rules had excluded from competition not only persons 'employed in or about boats for money or wages' but any 'mechanic, artisan or labourer'. To this the zealots of the ARA added 'anyone engaged in menial duty.'

These clauses offended not only outside liberal opinion but some members of rowing clubs, gentlemen themselves who nevertheless wanted to extend the benefits of rowing to respectable working-class amateurs. The most outspoken reformer was Dr F.J. Furnivall, a former Cambridge oarsman and now a noted philologist and literary critic. He was a dedicated worker for the cause of working-class education, first as a Christian socialist and later independently. Like Quintin Hogg, patron of the Regent St Polytechnic, and his friend Lord Kinnaird, Furnivall believed that education for the workers must be recreational and cultural as well as vocational. In rowing his eccentricities included encouraging women, preferring sculling and enjoying the company of the lower orders who formed a large proportion of the members of the club he founded at Hammersmith. He also thought nothing of holding races on Sundays in marked contrast to the policy of the ARA.

Dr Furnivall was particularly scathing about the university influence on the ARA's social stance: 'for a University to send its earnest intellectual men into an East End or other settlement to live with and help working-men in their studies and sports, while it sends its rowing-men into the ARA to say to these working-men, "You're labourers; your work renders you unfit to associate and row with us", is . . . an inconsistency . . . which loyal sons of the University ought to avoid.'[13] In 1890 he joined with a group of like-minded people, including the Revd P.G.S. (later Prebendary) Probert, the Cambridge Blue S.E. Swann and R.C. Bourne of Oxford, to form the National Amateur Rowing Association (NARA). Hogg was an early supporter and the polytechnic provided its first honorary secretary.

The NARA's minute book recorded their concern that 'a large body of amateurs in the true sense of the term – men who row for the love of the sport and not for gain – had no definite status or organisation because they did not belong to the ARA on the one hand or the "Tradesmen" – a professional class – on the other'.[14] They differed from the ARA solely on this question of social class: their regulations made no concessions whatever to professionalism and they retained the prohibition of those employed in or about boats, instructors, coaches and so forth. They also disclaimed any disruptive intent, recording in their minutes their hope of working together with other amateur rowing associations 'for the general welfare of all'. With this in mind they met representatives of the ARA in April 1891 to try to reach a modus vivendi.

They did not go so far as to ask the ARA to remove the ban on mechanics. F.J. Vincent of the Falcon Club, Oxford, who was unable to attend personally, expressed his view in a letter: 'I do not ask the ARA to alter their amateur definition in regard to the exclusion of mechanics because I am open-minded enough to understand and appreciate the object of some such classes being barred; the condition of athletics and football form arguments which only those who are wilfully blind cannot see.' What he wanted was merely relaxation of the rule that debarred men solely because they had rowed with or against the mechanic classes. Vincent, indeed, was quite content with the hierarchical principle: 'I want the NARA to represent the "people" and the ARA the aristocracy.'[15]

Dr Furnivall, however, seems to have been less deferential: in any event the ARA declined to change their rules. This meant not only that NARA clubs could not take part in ARA regattas but neither could individual members whatever their personal social circumstances. Nor would the ARA recognise the NARA as having any standing as an organisation (which made co-operation impossible and caused difficulties about suspensions and disqualifications). They gave as reasons the undesirability of rival ruling bodies and the short time the NARA had been in existence, and their firm stance was warmly applauded by die-hards such as the editor of *The Field*. Indeed *The Field* called the Old Etonian W.P. Wetherell, captain of Marlow RC, a malcontent and a traitor when he asked the ARA to have another look at the amateur question in 1893.[16] On the other hand *Truth*, the creation of the radical Liberal MP Henry Labouchere, declared that 'the phrase "menial duty" is one that disgraces any sporting rule'.[17] That autumn the ARA themselves appointed a sub-committee to consider the rule and *The Field* invited comments from rowing clubs all over the country on the desirability of change.

There were few egalitarians. The secretary of the Irex club (on the Lea in north-east London) replied that his committee thought the ARA definition of an amateur too stringent: 'Not only are bricklayers, labourers and such like barred, but engineers, men who are in every way desirable members for amateur clubs, have either to join a working men's club, or not row at all.' Even he balked at admitting Tom, Dick or Harry, however. 'Whether the rule could be modified without going to the other extreme of allowing everyone who does not row for money, I do not presume to say, but . . . (the ARA) . . . could use such discretion as would prevent the social condition of the sport being lowered to any level not in accordance with the dignity of the body who rule the rowing world.' The Marlow club had no such inhibitions: 'It has proved detrimental to the encouragement of rowing throughout the country that such as gain their living by manual labour should be classed as professional oarsmen.' It took an unusually starry-eyed view of the general sporting scene: 'While a different spirit pervades all other English sports and pastimes without any damage whatsoever, the ARA still holds back and refuses to admit the great bulk of the people to the enjoyment of their sport.'[18]

Pressed for suggestions as to how new rules should be framed, Marlow proposed in effect that the NARA definition should be accepted, and this was supported by a handful of clubs, most of whom had fallen foul of either the Henley or ARA rules, such as Burton-on-Trent and Barry. The very idea was anathema to the purists, however, and most provincial clubs declared themselves against change for fear of contamination – Warwick, for instance, stated that 'considering the unsportsmanlike conditions to which other branches of athletics have degenerated where an extension of the amateur rule had been made, it does not appear that the time has yet arrived for any extension such as that suggested by Marlow'.[19] One of the most revealing examples of 'facing-both-ways', and of the ramifications of British snobbery, came from a cleric, a recent Oxford Blue, W.A. Hewett, who had worked at the university's mission in Bethnal Green.

He wrote movingly of the bewilderment and dismay of the decent working-class oarsmen on the river Lea at being excluded simply on social grounds. He pointed out that the lowest class of clerks, who just came within the ARA requirements, were associating in other sports with artisans, with good results. It was unnecessary and inexpedient, he suggested, to artificially keep up a barrier which was being broken down in other sports. He saw no danger from the usual objection – gambling. 'The basic anxiety about betting and consequently dishonest rowing is largely a bogey. Prizes are not large enough, and never could be, owing to lack of gate money, to induce men to take up amateur rowing as a veiled profession.' And, though sculling was obviously an exception, the danger of crews being 'bought' was 'extremely improbable'. But even so he did not ask for the ending of the 'menial' rule, merely that it be confined to first-class regattas. He added, lest this be misconstrued, 'I hope that the whole question will be discussed from the point of view of what is expedient for the best interests of rowing, and that the "heroics" of Dr Furnivall and the "brotherhood of man" sort of nonsense will be kept out.'[20] He need not have worried on that account. When the sub-committee's report came out in April 1894, it recommended no change.

Surprisingly, however, there was a minority report by none other than the ARA's honorary secretary, R.C. Lehmann. Lehmann, of independent means as well as opinions, though a Cambridge oarsman and a respected coach was a radical in politics who later opposed the Boer War. He now argued against the 'menial' clause on two grounds: first, that since rowing was as much about skill as muscularity he doubted whether working men had any intrinsic advantage; second, that justice, particularly towards the East End clubs attached to university missions, required their inclusion. *The Field* was not to be wrong-footed morally: 'we can appreciate the spirit of chivalry to the working classes which apparently prompts him to take what may be termed a wider view of the amateur question, but it is a moral duty to be just before being generous. Justice to the amateur competitor in a muscular exercise demands that his opponents, like himself, should have developed their skill and anatomy alike by labouring for love and not for money'.[21] Lehmann got nowhere with his main proposition, but it is a tribute to his diplomatic skills as well as his sincerity and manifest loyalty to the cause of amateurism that he did persuade the ARA to move a little on one small point. In defining precisely what a professional was, under his guidance, they also incidentally created a new category of 'non-amateurs' between them and the true-blue gentlemen of the ARA. These were the members of the NARA, who although still excluded from the inner circle of amateur competition could at least henceforth row together with the elite in private matches or for recreation.

And there the matter was to rest for over forty years. As the long interval before eventual change indicates, the rift between the ARA and the breakaway NARA fell some way short of a revolutionary rising on behalf of the workers. Quintin Hogg had given great delight to the NARA when he persuaded the Duke of Fife to become its president. The polytechnic itself, most of whose students were lower middle class rather than manual workers, maintained two clubs, an official one which belonged to the NARA, and another, known as the Quintin, which belonged to the ARA.[22] Indeed the differences between the two rival groups were much less than the points on which they agreed, and both were bitterly opposed to the kind of professionalism that had afflicted soccer. The dissident Lehmann continued as secretary of the ARA until 1901 in which year he joined with W.H. Grenfell, the future Lord Desborough, and Edmond Warre, Headmaster of Eton, in proposing that foreigners – notably the dreaded Americans – be banned from Henley. The move failed but the alternative was even stricter vigilance over the regulations concerning amateurism.

Athletics: slowly to Olympus

Athletics was an amalgam of traditional sports of mixed lineage, some Celtic, some militaristic, some *outré*, some plebeian, and all too individualistic to be readily susceptible to the reforming intentions of the Amateur Athletic Association formed at Oxford in 1880 by representatives of the universities and leading clubs.[23] These clubs themselves had been infected by the lure of open competition: the championships of the elite Amateur Athletic Club and the casual contests of its metropolitan imitators born in the 1860s around a nucleus of public school Old Boys – the City businessmen's club Mincing Lane, later London AC; and offshoots of clubs for other sports whose members wanted to keep fit in the off-season, such as West London Rowing Club and the Blackheath Harriers[24] – had given way to undue emphasis on performance and an inevitable lowering of the social tone. London AC had turned to invitation-only events, but tradesmen were admitted even there, and artisans were on the increase especially in the Harrier clubs. In the early 1880s there were complaints that allowing shopkeepers into 'the circle of Amateurism' had encouraged pot-hunting by 'athletic criminals'.[25]

And naturally things were much worse in the north and midlands where the threat of the Northern Counties Athletic Association, which opened the door to working-class athletes provided only that they had never run for money, had been a main reason for the foundation of the AAA. Birmingham clubs like Moseley and Birchfield Harriers were producing well-organised teams of artisans that systematically destroyed their social betters. Promoters, handicap races and bookmakers abounded. This encouragement of proletarian values was attributed by some gentlemanly critics to upstart bourgeois honorary club secretaries who made money out of judging and organising as well as writing in the newspapers. But the problem was deeper-seated. The AAC itself had borne the stamp of older traditions of foot-racing in clubs such as the MCC whose members liked to back their fancies with a bet. And 'pedestrianism'[26] had been the central feature of sports meetings long before the new clubs had arisen: for many decades the urban working classes had turned up in droves to watch their heroes. The uphill nature of the AAA's task was apparent from the burning down of the AAC's famous Lillie Bridge stadium in 1887 by a betting gang.

The AAA drew their committees from the educated, professional middle classes, the Oxbridge influence was strong and their orientation was metro-politan and 'public school'. But the circumstances made their stance on amateurism more like that of the NARA than the ARA. Like the NARA they sought added lustre from the patronage of the aristocracy. Their first President was the Earl of Jersey and their second Viscount Alverstone, Attorney-General when he first took office and later Lord Chief Justice. The fever for open competition and records, and the temptations of gate-money, meant, however, that their hold on the 'northern' element was tenuous and as the number of clubs in membership grew from 45 in 1880 to 185 in 1887 and 200 ten years later there was a clear division even within the Association between the superior few and the rest. The division was exemplified by London AC's substitution of gold watch-chain shields for the notorious 'pots'. Another manifestation was the withdrawal of the university athletes, partly at least from distaste for physical dressing-room contact with riff-raff.[27]

The public school preference for team games was another limiting factor. The universities' own athletic sports might be models of amateur perfection but they were things apart. At the universities team spirit was emphasised by holding inter-college and inter-'Varsity athletics matches and by giving promi-nence to relay races in these meetings.[28] Few Oxbridge men continued in athletics after university. There were occasional exceptions like Revd H.C. Lenox Tindall, also a fine rugby player and a Kent county cricketer, who in 1889 at the advanced age of twenty-six set a new world record for the 440 yards in the AAA sports. More typical was the approach of C.B. Fry, triple Blue and polymath, who almost casually equalled the world record for the long jump in the Oxford sports of 1894 but took no part in competitive athletics after he went down, preferring cricket and football.

University support for the AAA's championships at Stamford Bridge was therefore fitful to say the least and the high hopes entertained for this annual show-case were already dwindling by Jubilee year when the 100 yards was won by a black African with north-country connections.[29] London AC, once so prominent especially in the sprints, now, apart from a few 'shamateurs', began to fade into the background. Regional specialists dominated the field events, Lakelanders in the pole vault and Irishmen the weight and hammer-throwing and in part the high and long jumps. And there was real cause for concern, especially in the distance races, over the growing supremacy of Harrier clubs. Furthermore Americans had begun to appear, not many, but depressingly good and depressingly well and professionally coached.

The AAA's reaction was predictable, and in 1892 they took the bold but unrealistic step of banning the payment of expenses altogether. They also made other cosmetic moves. In 1893, for instance, they obliged the Blackley (Manchester) Cricket and Athletics Club to change the title of their Booth Hall Plate in the hope of keeping the bookmakers away. They had little chance. Not only bookmakers but promoters of professional events went the rounds of the amateur meetings looking for talent. Those recruited were not always from the artisan class of whom the purists were so suspicious. George Blennerhasset Tincler, for example, was the wayward son of the solicitor to the Irish Turf Club and a cousin of the celebrated Baddeley twins who were dazzling the world of fashionable lawn tennis in the early 1890s. An unintellectual schoolboy, Tincler won the Irish AAA mile and the GAA half-mile at the age of eighteen. Two years later, in 1894, he tried to cash in on his talents by attempting to pass himself off as 'J. Craig of Inverness'. As Craig he had been given a favourable handicap in a race at the Powderhall Grounds in Edinburgh, which had now taken the leadership in professional athletics from Sheffield and other earlier English centres.[30] The plot was discovered and Tincler, who was fortunate to escape prosecution for fraud, joined the professional circuit, first as J. Craig, and later, shockingly, under his own name.

By 1896 the AAA decided the time had come to crack down hard. Six athletes were declared professionals for taking appearance money. They included Charley Bradley of Huddersfield, four times winner of the AAA 100 yards title and Alf Downer, a Jamaican-Scot, one of a coterie known as the Scottish Pelicans, who had recently dead-heated with Bradley in world record time. The expulsion of these star performers, though deeply satisfying to the purists, only scratched the surface of the problem, and the AAA were confounded when Edgar Bredin of London AC, who had equalled the world 440 yards record in 1895, decided to join them. His defection, declared Montague Shearman, one of the founding fathers, 'was received with great surprise, as he was a gentleman by birth and education'.[31]

These events made a nonsense of the excuses given the previous year for London AC when they took a strong team, including Bredin and Bradley, to challenge New York AC, and lost every event. The complaints about American athletics, such as the professionalised coaching schemes in their universities and colleges, continued nevertheless. It did not help generate friendly feelings that many of the best athletes and coaches were Irish immigrants. One of the complaints of the nationalist Gaelic Athletic Association was the relative neglect of field events – as distinct from 'pedestrianism' – under the AAA, and Irish talents came to the fore in the throwing events when transatlantic opportunity presented itself. The Irish-American athletes were not merely strong men, however. They were unencumbered by English public school notions about the vulgarity of training and quick to embrace the 'professional' American philosophy that technique and innovation, coupled with systematic training programmes, were the key to success. High-jumper Mike Sweeney astonished British onlookers at Manhattan Field, not only by clearing 6 ft 5½ ins but by doing so in his new 'eastern cut-off' style instead of the conventional upright 'scissors', and it was another Irish-American, Mike Murphy, who introduced the crouch start in sprinting.[32]

The expulsion of the star amateur performers in 1894 gave a much-needed fillip to the professional circuit. In England it was largely a 'northern' phenomenon. There were major centres in Manchester and Newcastle and any amount of local meetings in such places as Rochdale, Ashton-under-Lyne, Bolton and Barrow. A number of football clubs, soccer and Northern Union, saw athletics meetings as a useful source of additional income. Even Sheffield, whose glory days as the leading pedestrian centre were long gone, showed signs of recovery: after two modest handicaps in 1897 the promoters were encouraged to stage a £100 event the following year. This proved a flash in the pan, but it was a sign of the times.

Professional athletics also enjoyed a boom in the Celtic fringe. There were regular meetings in Belfast, Dublin and South Wales, but Scotland was at the heart of the revival with Powderhall just one of several competing centres. The AAA were greatly encouraged when like-minded colleagues north of the Border began to take the situation in hand. The first blow for the cause was struck by the Highland Society who decided the time had come to clean up the Highland Games. The Braemar Royal Highland Gatherings, which had first been held, as modern versions of ancient ethnic contests, to raise money for victims of Waterloo and their dependants, had enjoyed a vogue in Victorian times, giving the lairds a chance to show off their tartan kilts and sporrans to the visiting English court. But the contestants, at these and its many imitators and at counterparts such as the Border Games and the English Lakeland Games, were plebeians increasingly interested in prize-money as well as honour, and the circuit had become a seedy affair, highly attractive to the bookmakers. Now it was decided that the Highland Society's events were to be truly amateur; indeed the pedestrian events were to be restricted to members of the Black Watch regiment. This worked quite well at Braemar and in 1896 some seven thousand respectable citizens attended a highly decorous affair. It was a different story, however, at many meetings, and the Scottish AAA had their work cut out.

They ran into trouble, for instance, in 1897 by trying to ban members of the Scottish Cyclists' Union from their meetings. Cycling events were a popular addition at many centres, but they were a frequent source of dispute about amateurism, and the AAA and their Scottish counterparts regarded racing cyclists with grave suspicion. They pulled in the spectators, however, and it was a setback to the Scottish amateur cause when a rival organisation calling itself the Scottish Amateur Athletics Union sprang up ready to accommodate the cyclists: innocent organisers of local meetings were sometimes deceived by the similarity of name – or insufficiently aware of the importance of the distinction.

Scottish track and field athletes themselves needed watching. In 1899 the Scottish AAA received complaints from organisers of amateur meetings at Whitehaven, Manchester (Blackley) and Belfast about a number of their runners. They had drawn attention to themselves by recording remarkably fast times and then not bothering to collect their prizes (not money but sets of cutlery, clocks, ornaments and so forth as permitted under amateur rules), making instead straight for the bookmakers, collecting their winnings and departing. It emerged that they were professionals running under false names. The Scottish AAA went to great lengths to track down offenders, prosecuting the professionals for fraud and expelling any amateurs who allowed their names to be used. Sometimes these amateurs were innocent victims – it was a relatively safe practice for unscrupulous professionals to pick an obscure name provided they did not record too startling times when using them. The danger arose when the competition was fierce: record times by unknowns might cause a sensation. One interloper at the West of Scotland Harriers meeting in 1900, seeking to guard against this, used the name of Hugh Welsh, the AAA mile champion, and ended up in prison.

None of this did much to enhance the image of the sport, especially in the public schools and amongst the earnest moralisers. The fearsome E.K. Ensor had reserved some of his harshest criticism of modern-day sporting standards for this kind of thing. 'The unutterable corruption of amateur athletics during the last few years need not be dwelt upon; the betting, the swindling, the feigned names, the selling of races, pace-making, that hateful travesty of sport, and many other abuses are notorious.' And to such as Ensor betting and corruption were inevitable consequences of encouraging working-class participation: 'The terms "gentleman" and "amateur" now have very different connotations, he complained. 'Gentlemen must not run foot-races or ride bicycle races in open company'.[33]

It was not surprising, therefore, that no-one of any importance had taken much notice of the obscure sports meeting that took place at Athens in 1896.[34] Nor did the man behind it loom large in British public awareness: he was, after all, a Frenchman, Baron Pierre de Coubertin. Yet his initial enthusiasm for what became a crusade had stemmed from England. Greatly taken with the idea of fair play and team spirit, in 1886 he had made a pilgrimage to Rugby School, the setting for *Tom Brown's Schooldays*, which had made a marked impression on him in his formative years. He also saw the potential importance of sport, of the right kind, to national pride. He had grown up in the humiliating aftermath of the Franco-Prussian War and he looked for an honourable role for France in creating a better world. By 1892 he was propounding to a distinguished Parisian audience a 'true Free trade of the future' in which the exports would be oarsmen, runners and fencers. One of his recurring dreams was of a revival of the ancient Olympic festival. German scholars had led the way in the re-discovery of the glories of ancient Greece and its games: why should not France take the lead in restoring them?

British athletics was not yet ready for life on such an elevated plane: establishing true amateurism at home was the main task in hand. De Coubertin had made several visits to England in pursuit of his dream, attending in 1890, for example, the Much Wenlock Games, established forty years earlier by another aspirant towards the Olympic ideal, Dr W. Brookes, who became his friend and ally. De Coubertin thought London the obvious place to stage a modern Olympiad. He was realistic enough, however, to hedge his bets by making contact with influential people in Greece itself.[35] This was just as well; the British who attended his International Athletic Congress in Paris in 1894 were mainly interested in discussing the question of amateurism. Preserving amateur purity was an essential part of de Coubertin's Olympian vision: earning money from sport, he believed, would make people narrow and oafish: they would tend to 'give up their whole existence to one particular sport, grow rich by practising it and thus deprive it of all nobility, and destroy the just equilibrium of man by making the muscles preponderate over the mind'.[36]

Whilst this won wholehearted support at the Paris meeting, the notion of reviving the Olympics itself aroused less enthusiasm. De Coubertin had privately solicited the backing of the Greek royal family and government for the idea – staging it in its original home had obvious attractions, and eventually Athens was chosen as the venue. Greece was thought out of the way and somewhat backward by the more sophisticated delegates and London would have been their first choice, but the selection of Athens brought manifest relief to the English delegate, Mr Herbert of the AAA.

Of the 311 athletes taking part in 1896 230 were from Greece, 19 each from

France and Germany, 14 from the USA, and only 8 from Britain, none very well known. The organisation was so casual that entries were accepted even from tourists. One such was John Pius Boland, a nationalistic Irish student at Oxford. Learning of the venture from a Greek fellow-student, who later became secretary of the organising committee, Boland travelled to Athens intending only to watch but on impulse entered the lawn tennis competition – and won. The inaugural Olympic festival is remembered chiefly for the victory in the Marathon of Louis Spiridon, the simple Greek rustic who salvaged the nation's honour by fending off the foreign athletes before returning to his village, declining all reward except a horse and cart that he put to communal use. This romantic myth helped to sustain the Olympic ideal through the many vicissitudes it suffered in the years to come. However, a more characteristic story was that of Edwin Flack, a 22-year-old Australian accountant with Price, Waterhouse in London who took a month's holiday to go to Athens and won both the 800 and 1500 metres. And most of the other events were dominated by American college students.

This haphazard affair made no perceptible impression on the AAA as they tried to come to terms with the realities of life in the new competitive age. Faced with declining crowds in 1896 and 1897 their outlook was grim. Their high-minded stance on amateurism clearly was not helping and in 1899 they relaxed the rules to allow payment of expenses. The die-hards were not pleased. The Paris Olympics of 1900 showed the perils of making concessions to commercialism. They were held, at de Coubertin's earnest entreaty, in Paris, but only at the price of their becoming part of the attractions of the Paris Exposition. Its organisers so detested de Coubertin and his associates that they kept him firmly in the background whilst its director, who despised sport, did everything he could to exploit its commercial possibilities.

Nor was there much attempt at Greek authenticity. Indeed many of the sports included – golf, rugby, lawn tennis, croquet and even cricket – were British. Soccer and polo were advertised but appear to have found no takers. There were numerous disputes, notably in the Marathon, in which the winner, a Parisian baker's roundsman, was accused of taking short cuts based on his specialised local knowledge. The swimming took place in the Seine and was ruined by competitors being driven off course by the currents. Most regrettably of all there were several private enterprise events of a professional nature and great confusion between them and the official Olympics. De Coubertin had clearly not found a solution to the problem of expanding without lowering standards and the AAA resumed the unequal struggle.

Ireland: a special case

The importation of the latest English fashions in recreation was a source of great irritation to Irish nationalists. The field sports of the landowners had long attracted hostile attention from the Land League, and the spread of new middle-class diversions was a fresh source of division. The background was of changing political attitudes as the successive attempts to achieve Home Rule came and went. Though technically legal and non-violent the Land League relied in practice on the implicit threat of violence, and when constitutional methods failed the violent elements were harder to control. The League was able to achieve success in the new county council elections, but the sharp edge of parliamentary protest had been blunted by the divisions arising from Parnell's downfall, and in Belfast, the only place in Ireland with 'modern' urban conditions, organised labour was committed to Unionism. The frustration encouraged more radical elements such as the Irish Revolutionary Brigade and in Ulster the Ancient Order of Hibernians, whose shadowy activities had hitherto provoked as much derision as apprehension, and increased the flow of funds from American Fenians. At the same time philosophical nationalism was gaining ground, inspired by the Gaelic League, which aimed at the revival of the Irish language, and by a new wave of Anglo-Irish writers, notably George Moore, J.M. Synge and W.B. Yeats, who gave Gaelic culture, history and myth a romantic cloak of modern texture. The same invocation of a pre-English and hence prelapsarian past had inspired the foundation of an organisation to foster native Irish sports, the Gaelic Athletic Association, with the support of the Land League leader, Michael Davitt.

The distinctiveness of Irish sport had hitherto lain in activities developed under ascendancy auspices. Much of the lengthy *Thoughts Upon Sport* (1896) of Harry R. Sargent, a Wexford man, was devoted to the field sports and other horsey activities of the old aristocracy and gentry; utterly loyalist, his nationalism went no further than pride in the recent Irish domination of the Grand National, the crowning glory of steeplechasing, a sport that originated in Ireland but had been developed by fashionable sweepstakes in England. As for games, for him polo came first 'for it is the game of games, the cream of the cream of summer amusement'.[37] It was also the epitome of the British Raj. Ordinary ball-games came much lower down in Sargent's hierarchy but he took their spread in Ireland under English auspices for granted. 'Cricket', he remarked with bizarre but loyal exaggeration, 'is now as great a favourite in Ireland as ever it was in England.'[38] He did not mention hurling, recently revived by the GAA, nor Gaelic football, which it had created. The football that won his admiration was imported from England: he commented approvingly on the spread of both codes, believing rugger in particular to embody the noble virtues of courage, endurance and self-discipline.

Irish rugby had been born at Trinity College, which was also a pillar of the ARA and of the elite Irish Champion Athletic Club and its offshoot the Irish AAA. It had been dissatisfaction with the importation of English rules – and bad habits such as 'pot-hunting' – in athletics and the snobberies of the Trinity set that had first aroused the indignation of the GAA's founder, Michael Cusack.[39] Begun in obscurity the GAA had been bedevilled from the start by political dissension and shortage of funds. In 1886, barely two years on, Cusack, who was stronger on rhetoric than organisation, had been ousted as executive secretary and had set up a weekly newspaper *The Celtic Times* in opposition to the official policy. There were also disputes between the leadership and influential member clubs, especially in Dublin, who saw nothing wrong in having their sports meetings conducted under Irish AAA rules. Gaelic football had had to face the challenges from soccer and rugger in their respective social spheres noted in the previous chapter. Hurling did best, but revival was not easy. And at headquarters there were years of tense struggle between the moderate nationalists like its president, the old AAA champion Maurice Davin, and the fire-eaters, mostly members of the Irish Republican Brotherhood (IRB), who did their best to have their own candidates elected to key posts.

Davin himself remained in office for a while, largely because there were more acute immediate sources of dissension. The year 1888 was given over to the excitement of an episode which revealed the mixture of Celtic twilight romanticism and modern politics that marked the early GAA. It started with an old idea of Cusack's that had been taken up by Michael Davitt – the revival of the ancient Tailtean Games. The first, planned for the summer of 1889, was estimated to cost £5,000 and when a local appeal for funds produced only a tiny fraction of that Davitt turned to another cherished idea – a Gaelic athletic tour of America. It was intended both as a goodwill mission and a fund-raising expedition, but it was markedly more successful socially than financially. The fifty athletes and officials were rapturously received in New York and in the initial sports meeting the Irishmen did remarkably well, setting up new records in many events. They continued in similar vein for five weeks. Their expenses were very heavy, however, and bad weather and relative lack of interest in hurling (everywhere but Boston) meant that so far from making money they had to borrow £400 from Davitt's scarce funds to pay their fares home. Furthermore some of the officials got themselves involved in the politics of American athletics, siding with the National Amateur Athletic Association who were in dispute with the dominant and subsequently all-important AAAA. And many of the Irish athletes, including the world champion weight-thrower, J.S. Mitchell, found America so congenial that they stayed there permanently. Three months later, with the IRB renewing its efforts at take-over and financial disaster imminent, Davin was forced to resign.

The GAA was saved, in spite of its leadership problems, by its gradual success at local level, where it filled a need for working-class sport, especially in the country's rural heartland. It also, as nationalist politics became keener with disillusionment about the prospects of Home Rule, gave the Fenians a fruitful source of recruitment. The connection aroused the interest of the Royal Irish Constabulary. Members of the RIC had been excluded from membership since 1887 but they evidently still had moles inside. A report headed 'Modus operandi of seducing one of the GAA into the IRB society', compiled by a divisional inspector of the South Western Division in 1890, included the less than astonishing revelation, 'He is treated to plenty of drink, & tested whether he can hold his tongue.'[40] However, as things quietened down politically as a result of the government's various placatory land measures, the police became less hostile, and the GAA, now desperately seeking members and pressed by the active sportsmen in the rank-and-file to keep out of the political limelight, removed the ban in 1893.

The Dublin Association, which had broken away at the height of the dissension, now came back into the fold, and Archbishop Croke, a distinguished early sympathiser who had withdrawn his skirts from the party political skirmishing, was persuaded to restore his support. In 1896 the Croke Cups, for inter-county competitions in hurling and Gaelic football, were introduced. Under the guidance of a less fervently political secretary, Dick Baker, of Navan farming stock, the GAA, still desperate for members, even relaxed its 'foreign rule'. This, which originated with Cusack's antipathy to the Irish Champion Athletic Club (ICAC), had excluded from membership anyone who competed in Ireland under the rules of any other organisation. Its relaxation made for better relationships with the Protestant IAAA and may have brought in a few members but it naturally upset many of the old ones. The gulf widened further with a bitter dispute amongst the leadership about whether to support the planned nationalist celebration in 1898 of the centenary of Wolfe Tone's rising. The 1898 men, who were in tune with popular sentiment, won and led the brief revival that followed. Even this was blighted by severe shortage of funds and the effects of near-famine in Munster and Connacht as the potato crop failed again. It needed the Boer War and a new wave of anti-imperialist feeling to regain momentum in the new century.

Notes

1 London and the English provincial universities are little mentioned in this book, mainly for reasons of space. This apart they were less distinguished and innovatory

in sport than in academic matters and much less influential in either than Oxford and Cambridge, Trinity, Dublin and the Scottish universities. Their chief problem in sport was the lack of facilities and of a residential tradition. For an account of the emergence of the newer universities and their relationship to the old see V.H.H. Green, *The Universities*, Harmondsworth, 1969, For a short survey of their role in sport see J. Lowerson, *Sport and the English Middle Classes, 1870–1914*, Manchester 1993, pp. 72–7. Note also the role of London colleges in women's sport in Chapter Four below and subsequent chapters.

2 M. Pattison, *Academical Organisation*, London, 1868, quoted in Green, *Universities*, p. 72.

3 *Spectator*, 30 March, 1896, quoted in J.A. Mangan, *Athleticism and the Victorian Public School*, Cambridge, 1981, pp. 124–5.

4 For their early history and relationship, see D. Birley, *Sport and the Making of Britain*, Manchester, 1993, esp. pp. 190–1, 236–9, 290–1 (rowing) and pp. 239–42, 276–82 (athletics).

5 *The Field*, June. 1887.

6 *Ibid*.

7 J.K. Jerome, *Three Men in a Boat*, London, 1889, p. 79.

8 Lowerson, *Sport and the English Middle Classes*, p. 275.

9 A. Trollope (ed.), *British Sports and Pastimes*, London, 1868, Preface p. 6.

10 *Ibid.*, pp. 227–56.

11 He was very critical of rebellious cricket professionals and idle yachting crews, for instance.

12 W.B. Woodgate, *Boating*, London, 1888, p. 192.

13 E. Halladay, 'Of Pride and Prejudice: the Amateur Question in English Nineteenth Century Rowing', *IJHS*, May, 1987, p. 50.

14 9 July 1891.

15 Halladay, 'Of Pride and Prejudice'.

16 *Ibid.*, p. 51.

17 *Truth*, 9 Dec., 1893.

18 *The Field*, 11 Nov., 1893.

19 *Ibid.*, 25 Nov., 1893.

20 H. Cleaver, *A History of Rowing*, London, 1957, pp. 131–2.

21 *The Field*, 5 May, 1894.

22 Cleaver, *History of Rowing*, pp. 139–40.

23 For the foundation and early years of the AAA see P. Lovesey, *The Official Centenary History of the AAA*, London, 1979. and the article by J. Crump in T. Mason, *Sport in Britain*, Cambridge, 1989, esp, pp. 44–52. For earlier traditions and the attitude of the GAA towards English Athletics see Birley, *Sport*, pp. 239–42, 276–82.

24 Hare-and-hounds was a jollier form of cross-country running popular in public schools as a training exercise.

25 *Sporting Mirror*, 1882, quoted in Lowerson, *Sport and the English Middle Classes*, p. 164.

26 The word, which originally had referred to long-distance walking, often for freakish bets, had become a portmanteau term covering running events from sprints to endurance contests,.

27 See Lowerson, *Sport and the English Middle Classes*, p. 166.

28 In 1894 Oxford and Cambridge combined to compete against Harvard and Yale, and despite the tendency for superior English lips to curl up at anything American, suspicion of the influence of coaching and disapproval of the organised inter-collegiate competition that had begun in New England, these events against 'ivy

league' universities became a regular thing, and a sporting thing at that.

29 Arthur Wharton, for the second consecutive year. See R. Jenkins, 'Salvation for the Fittest?', *IJHS*, May, 1990, pp. 23–51.

30 For the early 'pedestrian' scene, Powderhall and Tincler, see D.A. Jamieson, *Powderhall Grounds and Pedestrianism*, Edinburgh, 1943, esp. pp. 84–7.

31 Quoted in D. Wallechinsky, *The Complete Book of the Olympics*, London, 1988, p. 18. Not all Victorian gentlemen followed orthodox patterns of behaviour. Bredin, who was thirty years old at the time, had already tried his hand at tea-planting, fruit-farming and service in the Royal Canadian North West Mounted Police.

32 For Irish-American influence on early athletics see R.L. Quercetani, *World History of Track and Field Athletics,(1864–1964)*, London, 1964. The 'eastern cut-off' and its better-known rival the 'western roll' were being tentatively introduced into state grammar schools in England by progressive physical education teachers in the late 1930s.

33 E.K. Ensor, 'The Football Madness', *Contemporary Review*, November, 1898, pp. 571–600.

34 See R. Mandell, *The First Modern Olympics*, Berkeley, 1976; Lord Killanin and J. Rodda (eds.), *The Olympic Games*, London, 1984; J.J. MacAloon, *This Great Symbol: Pierre de Coubertin and the Origins of the Modern Olympic Games*, Chicago, 1981.

35 See D.C. Young, 'The Origins of the Modern Olympics: a New Version', *IJHS*, December 1987, pp. 271–88, for fresh light on a complicated story.

36 D. Cort, 'The Olympics: Myth of the Amateur', *The Nation*, April, 1964, p. 199.

37 H.R. Sargent, *Thoughts upon Sport*, London, 1896, p. 298.

38 *Ibid.*, p. 297.

39 For the full, and intricate, story of the early days of the GAA, see M de Burca, *The GAA: a History*, Dublin, 1980. Birley, *Sport*, pp. 276–282 misstates the time and causes of Davin's resignation but is otherwise a reliable short account.

40 14 April 1890 (State Paper Office, Dublin CBS 181/127 S). Extract circulated in facsimile by GAA. in 1984.

CHAPTER FOUR

New games: new players

Apart from rattling class barriers and widening the 'north–south divide' the expansion of sport also brought to the fore the insistent claims of the changing status of women. The changes had begun with a revaluation of women's intellectual capacity. This, though inescapable in a rational society, struck at the roots of the paternalism that preferred to regard women as delicate plants, more for ornament than use. Male die-hards were still inclined to conceal their fears by making fun of women writers and intellectuals, but rapid progress was now being made in girls' education especially in expensive fee-paying schools for the well-to-do. Where they most challenged male assumptions and threatened male security was in physical education. This, in moderation, was beginning to be accepted as desirable, even important, but so far as the official curriculum was concerned it had been largely confined at first to gymnastics.

British interest in gymnastics, never strong amongst chauvinistic followers of the *Tom Brown's Schooldays* tradition, had nevertheless been sharpened somewhat by continental advocates, notably refugees from the 1848 revolutions. There were two main strands. One was German, following the teachings of J.F.C. Guts Muth and Ludwig Jahn, involving marching, singing, free exercises to uplifting music, vaulting and rope-climbing, swinging clubs and dumbbells, and using ladders and wall-bars and so forth. Its citadel in London was Stempel's Physical Institute, Gymnasium and Academy (popularly called the German Gymnasium) in Regent's Park which also taught fencing, boxing and swimming. An English adherent was Archibald Alexander, who had a gymnasium in Oxford, and whose teachings strongly influenced the Army's developing interest in physical education. There was also a lady-like adaptation on offer at the Alexandra House Gymnasium, Kensington, run by the Misses Bear. The other strand, the Swedish, was, however, the one favoured by those who saw the need for a more fundamentally and specifically feminine approach.

Its inspiration was the doctrine of Per Hendrik Ling, an eighteenth-century innovator who emphasised style, grace and precision, devising individual exercises, progressing in difficulty, with the goal of harmony between mind and body. In its spread through Europe Ling's philosophy came to the notice of an influential member of the new London School Board, which took the bold step in 1879 of appointing a superintendent of physical education for its girls' schools with the brief of introducing the Ling system. The second holder of the post was the remarkable Madame Bergman-Osterberg, who fervently rejected the conventional notion that strenuous physical activity and femininity were incompatible, and equally fervently stressed the unsuitability for girls of the militaristic type of drill to which boys and men were subjected and of male teachers who could not hope to understand female physiology. In 1885 she left the LCC to put her ideas into practice amongst the influential middle classes, starting her own college in Hampstead with the aim of producing a select band of women physical education teachers.

Lawn tennis finds a niche

They were to become the prototypes of the 'games mistress'. In the early girls' schools, such as Miss Beale's Cheltenham College and Miss Buss's North London Collegiate School, games had come in only slowly, as improvised, informal activities arranged by the girls themselves. For older girls, to whom greater freedom was allowed in recreational matters, dignified and corseted dress was an essential prerequisite and croquet, badminton and lawn tennis were the earliest games to find favour. All three were played at Somerville College, Oxford from its opening in 1870. Lawn tennis, the most vigorous, yet still entirely ladylike, had quickly established itself as the favourite with students. At Lady Margaret Hall, Oxford, grass and hard courts were constructed soon after the first permanent buildings in the early 1880s. Competition, in-college only at first, soon spread, especially at Cambridge where Girton and Newnham rivalry even produced a silver Challenge Cup for the doubles' winners. (Doubles play was preferred as not only less gruelling but also more of a team effort than singles.) Inter – varsity matches began in 1883 and quickly became an established institution. They were private affairs, greatly enjoyed by enthusiastic if small crowds of past and present students, and because they were held on privately owned courts were not open to vulgar public gaze. The 1890 match was hosted by the Archbishop of Canterbury at Lambeth Palace in memory of his late daughter, a student at LMH.[1]

Much more was at stake than the colleges' reputations. Women moving into the masculine world of sport, a modern historian reckons, 'stood . . . on the threshold of definitions between male and female and between women of the past and future' symbolising 'the manifest changes affecting not only women but the value systems of societies as a whole.'[2] Nor was it only men who wanted to preserve the ordained order of things. Femininity was a precious gift that few women wanted to jeopardise. The muscles acquired by games-playing schoolgirls, declared Arabella Kenealy, were 'stigmata of abnormal sex-transformation'.[3] Another great issue was that of corsets. Some enthusiasts for women's physical education were known to favour abandoning them during play: Madame Bergman-Osterberg was one. There was growing medical opposition to the practice of tight-lacing (to achieve small waists as current fashion dictated) and in 1888 two doctors actually read a paper at the meeting of the British Association recommending 'moderate lacing'. But corsets of some kind were generally thought essential for health as well as aesthetic reasons.

This view was hotly contested by the members of the Rational Dress Society and their formidable President, Florence Pomeroy, Viscountess Harberton. The RDS were not impressed by even moderate medical opinion, and they were appalled by the attitude of Lydia Becker, veteran campaigner for women's rights and editor of *Women's Suffrage*. Miss Becker, like many prominent suffragists, was cautious in the matter of dress for fear of attracting unwelcome publicity for the suffragist cause. She had stood up at the British Association meeting to declare: 'Stick to your stays. They improve the form, give warmth and assist you. Stick to your stays, ladies, and triumph over the other sex.' Lady Harberton's reply was withering: 'One wonders to find such an argument proceeding from such a source.'[4] But most women games players, as we shall see, agreed with Miss Becker. Indeed they were for the most part utterly circumspect not least in the question of skirts, a much more visible sign of propriety.

This circumspection had served them well in securing the acceptance of lawn tennis, by all but the most antediluvian, as an entirely suitable recreation for young ladies. Indeed its garden party image had inhibited its acceptance as a serious, i.e. male, sport. However it had been taken up not only by men seeking mixed company but those who saw its possibilities as an outdoor alternative to real tennis and racquets, which had long been favourite individual games in the public schools and universities, the services and fashionable gentlemen's clubs. MCC, whilst manifestly more attuned to real tennis, had been amongst the first to provide lawn tennis courts for their members and had for a time lent their authority to its evolving national rules.[5] Nevertheless lawn tennis had made little headway in the public schools, which preferred team games and thought it lacked virility, and it was the universities and the entrepreneurial sporting journalists, not always in concert, that took it beyond the vicarage lawn.

The telling factor was that it proved suitable for competition as well as less formal knockabouts. The most important of the many tournaments that had sprung up was that of the All-England Lawn Tennis Club at Worple Road, Wimbledon, originally a Croquet Club but since 1884 disowning its parentage and reaping the benefits of the newer vogue. In its fervour for the cause, the All-England Club had been plunged into strife, both internal and external. Its current Secretary, Julian Marshall, an old Harrovian rackets and real tennis player, saw himself as the supreme authority on the game. He rode rough-shod over other clubs in the matter of arranging tournament dates and made many enemies in the process. One was N. Lane Jackson, who was not only a journalistic rival but a ubiquitous organiser of tournaments and handicapper.

Jackson had tried in the early 1880s to persuade the provincial clubs to break free of All-England, and he acquired powerful allies in 1887 when Marshall insulted H.S. Scrivener, the President of the Oxford University Club, who had asked for his match at Wimbledon to be postponed so that he could play in the 'Varsity match. Scrivener and his friend, George Hillyard, MCC member and all-round sportsman, took up Jackson's idea and despite Marshall's opposi-tion the Lawn Tennis Association was set up in 1888, with Willie Renshaw, seven times Wimbledon champion, as its first President.[6] After much back-biting, reduced when Marshall left his post in a hurry after summarily dismissing a gardener, a modus vivendi was established. The LTA, comprising representatives of all the leading clubs, was to become the governing body of the game nationally, but All-England, whilst reverting to simple club status, retained control over the championship – and its purse-strings – giving them far the best of the bargain in the long run.

Nevertheless the LTA were blithely confident. As their Chairman H.W.W. (later Sir Herbert) Wilberforce saw it in 1890, 'To that anomalous individual the thoughtful observer the success of lawn tennis, unprecedented alike in extent and rapidity, cannot have been a surprise. *A priori* it is just the game to fill a want in human nature, or at any rate in English men and women.'[7] Spencer Gore, the rackets player who had won the first Wimbledon championship, was not so sure: 'Whether anyone who has played really well at cricket, [real] tennis or even rackets will ever seriously give his attention to lawn tennis beyond showing himself to be a promising player is extremely doubtful, for in all probability the monotony of the game as compared with the others would choke him off before he had time to excel in it.'[8] It not only lacked subtlety, furthermore, but fell short in the manly vigour that really serious games were supposed to have. George Hillyard afterwards recalled that for most young men the summer game was cricket 'every time and all the time': lawn tennis not only seemed but *was* 'pat-ball'. Indeed a boys' encyclopaedia of 1892 suggested that it lent itself to ostentation, and that its encouragement of blatant competition was not the best way of producing 'the strong, erect, full-chested, broad-shouldered men of vigour, constitution, high animal spirits and dauntless courage . . . wanted by the Church to-day'.[9]

Blatant competition certainly needed to be explained away. Wilberforce did his best, implying that it was all in a good cause: 'Throughout the season there is a series of these [lawn tennis tournaments] at all the more important towns and watering-places: at the seaside the season is incomplete without one; and they are becoming as potent in the name of charity as bazaars and black bishops.' Yet, he assured his readers, professionalism was 'a taint from which the game (had) happily remained free', and would, he felt, 'prove a merely visionary danger'.[10] This was not one of the world's great prophecies. Indeed, even in that innocent dawn there were prizes to be won, of the ornamental kind like those in amateur athletics, and handicappers to be satisfied – and sometimes deceived. The Press were always on the look-out for a hint of scandal. N.L. Jackson recalled in his memoirs being summoned as a witness in a libel suit after the Macclesfield tournament in 1888. Two young ladies from the West Country had arrived in Macclesfield at the last moment and had entered the tournament under what turned out to be assumed names. This was an ambivalent but not necessarily sinister thing to do: pseudonyms were frequently used by the young to avoid parental disapproval. This time, however, when one of the two won both the Open and Handicap events, *The Sportsman* and *Athletic News* suggested that they had set out to deceive the handicapper. They won their case and were awarded £25 each in damages, but the lawn tennis circuit was obviously not entirely a round of charitable functions.[11]

Whatever went on in Macclesfield, however, there was no doubt of Wimbledon's social tone. Wilberforce also noted the progress of the game in fashionable circles in Ireland. With a revealing mixture of patronising banter and missionary pride he suggested some of the reasons for its popularity there: 'there is very little cricket, the rivers are unsuited to boating, and the roads generally too bad for bicycling'. He also, of course, paid tribute to the generous hospitality that ensured the success of Irish tournaments. The Fitzwilliam Club in Dublin was the acme of lawn tennis fashion and its Annual Meeting 'was almost, if not quite, as popular with Dublin society as the Horse Show'. Success in the Irish championships was 'looked upon as quite on a par with winning at Wimbledon' whilst 'the very jarveys of the jaunting cars took a keen interest in the proceedings, and made bets amongst themselves across the railings of Fitzwilliam Square'.[12] It aroused different passions amongst the leadership of the Gaelic Athletic Association and its fiercely nationalistic patron, Archbishop Croke, but lawn tennis was part of the other, ascendancy-dominated Ireland.

For a while, indeed, the Irish could fairly claim world supremacy. Willie

Renshaw lost his Wimbledon title to an Irishman in 1890, for seven years Irishmen won the championship and for the last six of them the final was an all-Irish affair. Sadly – and perhaps in consequence – this coincided with a decline in the game's fortunes. Wimbledon's attendances fell sharply, and so did the profits. Another reason was the departure of the remarkable Lottie Dod who had dominated women's lawn tennis since she first won the Wimbledon title in 1887 at the age of fifteen, serving underarm but employing the volley and the smash and hitting the ball almost as hard as if she were a man. Seven years later, after five championship wins (in spite of two years' absence whilst she went on a world cruise) she had retired to take up golf, leaving Wimbledon a much duller place. For one reason or another by 1894 the championships were running at a loss, and the prizes were reduced in value (£25 for men and £10 for ladies). At the same time admission charges were increased, after the first day, to 2s 6d (12½ pence) and the All-England Plate for those eliminated in the first round was introduced to try to sustain interest for a longer period.

Wheels of change

One of the contributory factors to lawn tennis's decline was the vogue for cycling that was sweeping fashionable circles. The bicycle, which had reached something like its present form by the 1880s and no longer required great athleticism simply to mount it, had long been socially suspect.[13] Part of the trouble was the unsavoury reputation of cycle-racing, which was even lower than that of athletics. Many fine purpose-built tracks were provided with the assistance of enterprising cycle manufacturers in the 1880s and places like Paddington, Herne Hill, Manchester and Coventry joined the older centres, Glasgow, Edinburgh and the Lansdowne complex in Dublin. The new bicycles allowed more speed and there was keen competition as more and more took up the sport. Equipment was readily supplied to promising riders by the manufacturers and, of course, the bookmakers also took a hand. In consequence it no longer attracted gentlemen.

Recreational cycling also had powerful enemies. One of the oldest class distinctions was between those who rode horses and those who were obliged to go on foot, and the new machines threatened to erode it. 'It is the "horsey" instinct, we take it,' commented *Cycling* in 1894, 'that has been the largest factor in barring the use of the cycle in the upper reaches.' Then, with dramatic suddenness, cycling became the latest fashionable craze. It began in 1895 and by the following year *The Hub* was speculating that the horsey interests had lost £5 million a year as a result. Certainly there were many redundancies on the staffs of the big houses as the younger set took up cycling. Equally

unfortunately the craze, like that for boating, encouraged further encroach-
ment of the Sabbath by those engaged in their shops and offices during the
week, and churchmen were divided between the optimistic liberals who saw
no harm, and indeed much good, in a healthy afternoon spin after worship
and the gloomier majority who recognised yet another secular alternative.

The most disturbing feature of the new vogue, however, was its appeal to
women. Like croquet before it – and lawn tennis more recently – cycling
offered opportunities for mixed sport and jolly flirtation, like an outdoor
version of ballroom dancing. But cycling was much more controversial. Its
image had been besmirched in earlier days by the unseemly spectacle of a few
daring female practitioners wearing bifurcated garments. They were mostly
French women or professionals. The British cycling press, highly conscious of
the sport's precarious reputation, had been as critical as everyone else, and the
much-respected columnist G. Lacy Hillier, had warned that such behaviour
was but the forerunner of a wider movement, heralding a storm of revolt
against the petticoat.[14] Now as the vogue reached its height Mrs Eliza Linton,
a renowned opponent of 'rational dress' issued a solemn warning. These
cycling creatures, she told the readers of the Lady's Realm in 1896, were entirely
lacking in 'that sweet spirit of allurement which, conscious or unconscious, is
woman's supreme attraction'. There was no telling where it would all lead:
'Chief among all dangers attending this new development of feminine freedom is the intoxication which comes with unfettered liberty'[15]

Lady Harberton, who was, of course, a cyclist, was absolutely opposed to
wearing skirts for the pastime. She began from the idealistic position that
dress in itself was neither masculine nor feminine 'as the idea of sex is entirely
conveyed by the association in our own mind'.[16] She believed the logical
garment for athletic exercise was the divided skirt. (This was in fact a pair of
long trousers, cunningly pleated to look like a skirt, but a pair of trousers
nevertheless.) At first even the RDS had fought shy of recommending such a
costume, recalling the ignominious fate of the 'bloomer' experiment of mid-
Victorian days, but they were carried along by Lady Harberton's enthusiasm
and earned more and more abuse.

Cycling, many thought, was dangerous enough without the added risks of
licentious costumes. The unfettered liberty Mrs Linton warned against looked
all very well in the bicycle advertisements showing young men and women
getting away from the smoky, overcrowded cities to the joys of the countryside, but it certainly had its perils. Apart from the risk of attack from vicious
tramps on lonely roads or ogling from the prurient, those who adopted
'rational' principles faced the jeers and taunts of the populace at large. A writer
in the socialist Clarion complained bitterly of the general attitude: 'Few would
believe how insulting and coarse the British public could be unless they had

ridden through a populated district with a lady wearing Rationals.'[17]

Most cycling enthusiasts, however, found association with extremist dress reformers distasteful and detrimental to the true interests of the pastime. And most lady cyclists wanted to preserve femininity and to conceal it artistically according to the historic destiny of womankind. 'What rationals! – save the mark', protested the fashion correspondent of a cycling magazine, 'Have some women no eyes, or sense of cut and fit?'[18] This view was shared by an aristocratic practitioner, Susan, Countess of Malmesbury – such a 'hideous, unpicturesque, inartistic costume was never produced or invented'.[19] Lady Malmesbury expressed herself more temperately in an authoritative ency-clopaedia of the time, but the message was the same. 'The wearing of the skirt', she wrote in 1897, was 'still a much debated question.' In England there had never been much encouragement for the 'extremely unbecoming attire worn by many French cycling women' and she hoped there never would be: 'the skirt, if properly cut, helps to conceal the ugly action of the knees and legs, and never need be a cause of danger if fastened down by elastic straps . . . (and it was unfortunate that) for the professional riders, and for women who could not afford a well-cut skirt, knickerbocker costumes are the only alter-native'.[20]

Skirts were certainly a requirement at the ladies' colleges where the students' enthusiasm for cycling presented great problems for their guardians. At Girton, remote from the centre of Cambridge, a club was permitted in 1894 and at once became popular, but the girls were not allowed to cycle into town. Nor, before 1900, could they cycle on Sundays.[21] The dangers, from traffic, molestation, public criticism and unfettered liberty, were even greater in London but the young ladies of Westfield College were allowed to ride in public in 1895 provided they observed strict rules: their dress had to be approved by the Mistress; they had to pass a test before venturing on public roads; they could not ride 'into or towards London' or beyond an area marked on a map; and they cold not 'go out alone or after dark'.[22]

Decorum established however, there were obviously great benefits to be had from cycling. As Lady Malmesbury pointed out, 'In the case of girls earning their own living and confined all the week in places of business, certain cycling clubs instituted on their behalf are a great boon. The members are taken in parties to various places of interest and during their holidays pleasant tours are arranged'. Lady Malmesbury also discounted the view that cycling was too strenuous an activity for women. (Conservative medical opinion held, for instance, that it might result in distortion of the pelvis with disastrous effects on child-bearing.) Amongst doctors, she declared, 'all but the obstinately blind' agreed with women's cycling – in moderation, of course. It was particularly good for the 'nervous, overwrought woman' helping with 'hysteria, sick headaches, anaemia and neuralgia, as well as imaginary ills'.[23]

Lawn tennis resurgent

The cycling craze had some surprising side-effects. As the appeal of lawn tennis fell away even the All-England Club lost its nerve. To offset its financial losses the club admitted thirty croquet players as 'season visitors' in 1896 and the following year allowed them to revive the croquet championship. Most poignant of all, the name 'croquet' was re-introduced into the club's title. For the re-entering croquet players this was a bitter-sweet moment. There was satisfaction at the volte-face by the ruling clique at All-England. But the croquet players had paid a price for their earlier association: croquet as practised by the Wimbledon 'cracks', with smaller hoops, had proved far too demanding for the vicarage lawn or for the thriving but socially inclined clubs at places like Cheltenham, Budleigh Salterton, Oxford and Brighton, and the return to Wimbledon was a sign, not a cause, of its revival as a competitive sport.

This revival had stemmed largely from the initiative of a Mrs Hill, a former Cheltenham member who had moved to Maidstone and arranged a tournament there in 1894. It became an annual event and by 1896 attracted sixty entries. Observing this success and noting its lessons an All-England member, B.C. Evelegh, champion before the Fall, and a couple of fellow spirits, Walter Peel and Captain Drummond, determined this time to use Wimbledon merely as a base from which to seek independence. Together they got up a United All-England Croquet Association, organising tournaments using larger hoops and a handicap system, with such effect that by 1900 they were able to leave Worple Road for a ground of their own. Croquet was never, of course, to regain its former glory, but it was firmly established as a pleasant suburban diversion for all ages and both sexes.[24]

Another such diversion was Badminton, once the rival and perhaps the inspiration of lawn tennis, with which it shared the original hour-glass court and beginnings as a military pastime in India.[25] It suffered by comparison with lawn tennis because of its unsuitability for the British outdoors, and indoors it could only be played in large high-ceilinged halls. With its exotic resonances and possibilities for elitist conviviality and healthy exercise it had, however, a following amongst retired Army officers and their ladies, and it thrived in the spas and watering places where they resided: the leading clubs were in towns like Folkestone, Teignmouth, Bognor Regis, Bath and Southsea as well as in the superior London suburbs. Local rules and conditions varied widely: at Ealing the court was 60 ft by 30 ft and at Guildford 44 ft by 20 ft. But it was not until 1893 that the need for standardisation was felt sufficiently to justify action: a meeting of fourteen clubs at Southsea agreed to form a Badminton Association. Several Scottish and Irish clubs joined it, and the game was sufficiently strong in Ireland for its own Badminton Union to be established in 1899.

Competition remained informal and fairly casual, anything more being regarded with some suspicion. Inter-club matches were preferred to tournaments, singles play was thought vulgarly individualistic and there were 3-, 4- and even 5-a-side matches as well as doubles. It was more than five years before championships were held, a private venture at Guildford, and the Association took it over with some reluctance in 1899. The All-England championships began as a doubles tournament and though singles came in the following year the purists still thought this a somewhat undesirable, individualistic departure from the true spirit of the game. Commercial interest was not encouraged. Racquets, which varied greatly in size and shape, mostly came from France though the game was almost unknown there. Shuttlecocks were hand made and differed considerably in weight and size. Sir George Thomas, a competitor in the 1890 championships afterwards recalled that at the start of the match the players were offered a choice between a 'rocket' and a 'slow wobbler'. Once issued the shuttles had to be used as long as feathers remained. In this particular stratum of society male players predominated. Most clubs had lady members, often quite a lot, but their talents were not highly regarded. At Ealing their encounters were known as 'Hit and Scream'.[26]

Lawn tennis, meanwhile, had recovered its lost ground. In 1897 Lottie Dod had been cautiously optimistic about its prospects in an encyclopaedia article: 'In spite of prognostications that it would die out entirely, which have persistently been made for the last twelve years, it still more than holds its own, and though it is not the fashionable craze it once was, and is not played as much at garden parties, there are still a vast number of enthusiastic adherents.'[27] Never one for the vicarage lawn approach herself Miss Dod marvelled that people should frequently ask her whether lawn tennis was an athletic game, advising doubters to watch 'a men's five setter played under a broiling sun'. 'For ladies, too', she added, 'it is decidedly a very athletic exercise, always supposing that they go in for it heartily and do not merely frivol at garden parties.'

Despite this seriousness of purpose, however, Lottie Dod, like most leading sportswomen, was no revolutionary. Her conservatism was apparent from her remarks on dress, which she admitted was a problem: 'the blessings of our sex would be heaped upon anyone who could invent a practical, comfortable and withal becoming costume. It must be becoming', she made clear, 'or very few of us would want to wear it'. Thus she accepted the necessity of a skirt, nuisance though this essential emblem of comeliness was, but she added a daring proviso: 'As the skirt must be endured, it is important to have it somewhat short, reaching to the ankles.'[28] It had, of course, been this kind of circumspection that had led to the widespread acceptance of lawn tennis as the premier women's game.

Even competition, though widely considered particularly harmful for the female constitution, was not likely to lead to excessive strain in lawn tennis, for it was not usually (Miss Dod notwithstanding) a matter of hard hitting. Grace and style were the desirable feminine qualities in a game which even de Coubertin, renowned for his opposition to women's sport, was able to accept for inclusion in the 1900 Olympics. By the same token the social dangers of competition, such as exposure to the public gaze, were lessened. The slightly dashing air about some of the early tournaments, as portrayed by N.L. Jackson, for instance, was more than offset by the thoroughly genteel family backgrounds, often clerical, of the contestants and the strict rules of conduct in the clubs that sponsored them.

The tone was set by Blanche Bingley, the upright and much-admired champion of 1886, temporarily displaced by the Dod phenomenon, who, after her marriage to George Hillyard, demonstrated that lawn tennis could be an entirely suitable game for a married woman and a dignified one at that. A leading player for twenty years – she won her sixth championship in 1900 and the (unofficial) doubles title in 1906 – her influence was profound in all aspects of the game. Another splendid example was Charlotte 'Chattie' Cooper, the winner in 1895, 1896 and 1898, who as Mrs Sterry continued playing with distinction for many years. Wimbledon's essential obscurity – and the status of women's sport – at this time, however, can be adduced from her experience in 1895. She had been staying with her brother, a doctor in Surbiton, during the tournament, cycling back and forth. On the day of her success she came home to find her brother pruning the roses. 'What have you been up to, Chattie?', he asked conversationally, and when she told him he went on pruning the roses!

It was on the men's game that the future of lawn tennis depended, and it, lacking support in the public schools because of its perceived lack of moral fibre and high seriousness compounded by its feminine associations, was languishing. Even the critical press began to take notice in 1897, however, with the arrival of a pair of brothers greater than the Renshaws and with impeccable credentials. These were Reggie and Laurie Doherty, 'Big Do' and 'Little Do', of Westminster and Cambridge. Between them they carried all before them, re-invigorating Wimbledon and bringing back the crowds. Reggie was the champion until the end of the century and Laurie for most of the next decade. They were models of sportsmanship. When they found themselves drawn to play against each other in the semi-finals of the Paris

Olympics they declined to do so, and Reggie courteously stood aside to allow his brother Laurie to go through, and, of course, win.[29]

The Press gradually became more supportive and stopped predicting demise. Under the stimulus of the Dohertys the Wimbledon championships began to make a profit and after 1898 never looked back. The Irish challenge was beaten off and no one paid much attention to the small but enthusiastic band of Americans who had begun to come to the championships. When in 1900 Dwight Davis presented a cup for international competition it was with the avowed hope that the game in the USA would take inspiration from contact with the British experts. It was a minor embarrassment when the pupils beat the masters in the very first Davis Cup match at Longwood, Boston. But the British had plenty of excuses – no Dohertys, long grass, atrocious nets held up by continually sagging guy ropes, and above all soft and 'mothery-looking' balls, which 'when served with the American twist came at you like an animated egg-plum.'[30]

Cycling steadily downhill

If the racquet and ball makers breathed a sigh of relief as lawn tennis survived its crisis the bicycle manufacturers were in despair, for cycling's fashionable phase ended as suddenly as it had begun. When the vogue was at its height Britain had some seven hundred factories producing three-quarters of a million machines a year, but the demand fell rapidly and recession overtook the industry.With the expansion bicycles had grown cheaper, and whereas this ensured their continued popularity as transport it accelerated their social decline. Whilst the all-pervading artisan took over cycle-racing the immediate future for recreational cycling lay with socialists and lower middle-class or health-conscious urbanites seeking escape. One of their main pre-occupations was convincing the authorities of their right to use the highway without interference from the law. The Cyclists' Touring Club, which built up to a membership of some sixty thousand by the end of the century, was the umbrella organisation for hundreds of the better local clubs who regularly filled the roads with their weekend tours, with social as much as sporting intent.

Their cause was not assisted by the enthusiasts for competition who thought the roads made a splendid race-track. The mildest form of road racing, individual striving after record times, upset the authorities only if there was crowd trouble. Road racing proper was not actually illegal either, but in 1895 after a series of prosecutions for 'furious riding' and the death of a woman whose horse had been frightened by cyclists, the National Cyclists' Union, the sport's governing body, reluctantly decided to ban racing on public roads.

Some established races, like the celebrated North Road 24-hour race, transferred to the track. However, one of the North Road Club members, F.T. Bidlake, devised an ingenious alternative, the time trial, in which road riders started at intervals and were separately timed. This, too, was banned by the NCU in 1897, but it caught on nevertheless, and the stealthy way in which it was practised added to the seedy image of the sport.[31]

For women cyclists there was a stern reminder of social realities in 1899 when Lady Harberton, still a leading member of the Cyclists' Touring Club, exposed herself to public view. On seeking refreshment during an excursion, she was refused entry to the parlour of a Surrey hotel because of her costume and directed to the men's bar. Her Ladyship took this as an insult and sued the landlady, Mrs Sprake, for failing to provide refreshment to a bona fide traveller. The court proceedings were enlivened by the production of photographs – by Lady Harberton to demonstrate the rational seemliness of her baggy pantaloons and long jacket and by Mrs Sprake to show the dignity of her establishment. Mrs Sprake, who expressed her abhorrence of the females that could be seen cycling on the Portsmouth road in tights, won her case to applause from the public gallery.[32]

More discreet – and younger – ladies, particularly in the environs of the schools and colleges, were to win the right to use such a handy and practical means of transport early in the new century. But cycling, as a fashionable craze, had had its day. It certainly no longer posed any social threat to the horse. Indeed almost before the battle between the cyclists and the horsey set had been joined, technology had brought a much more serious challenge. Horseless carriages had been talked about since Leonardo da Vinci and in the intervening years various air, clockwork, gas and steam machines had been invented. Now German technology, in the forefront of the accelerating industrial revolution, made the dreams a reality, harnessing the petrol-driven internal combustion engine to rubber-tyred road vehicles. The discoveries of Carl Benz and Gottfried Daimler in the 1880s led by 1895 to commercial production of Daimler-Benz motor cars. In France Panhard, De Dion-Bouton, Peugeot and Renault and in Italy Isotta-Frascini and Fiat quickly followed. In the USA, from the ruck of earlier competition, Olds and Packard were setting the pace by the 1890s.

The British were slow off the mark by comparison and their first petrol-driven cars came from the English subsidiary of Daimler. Consequently in motor sport, though individual Britons showed interest and aptitude, it was the Americans and the French who led the way. Both road-racing (1895) and the closed-circuit variety (1898) began in France and it was the American newspaper magnate Gordon Bennett[33] who offered the first international trophy in 1899. One reason for Britain's sluggish start was the resistance of those who might have afforded them to such noisy, smelly and altogether alarming contraptions. Country-dwellers were the loudest protesters and the horsey set thought them an abomination, worse, if possible than the railways: MFH were particularly disapproving and no true gentleman would have anything to do with them. It was the raffish or quirky and the vulgar newly-rich who first began to acquire them. Alfred Harmsworth, the future Lord Northcliffe, proprietor of the first cheap popular newspaper, the *Daily Mail*, was an early and typical motor-car owner. When he drove down to Sussex in it to persuade Rudyard Kipling to write some articles for the paper, Kipling – confirming the opinions of those who thought him a bit of a bounder – was so taken with the thing that he ordered one for himself.

'O ye Ice and Snow . . .'

The quest for novelty that had brought in new games like lawn tennis, the intrusive bicycle and the alarming motor car also took the British to foreign parts. To the old aristocratic tradition of the Grand Tour were now added or substituted round-the-world tours, explorations of the wilder shores of America and distant parts of the Empire. Europe, either for culture or sheer enjoyment, was well within range for regular visits, facilitated by the genteel precursors of package holidays pioneered by Thomas Cook. Everywhere they found climatic conditions and topographical features that enabled them to demonstrate the universal applicability of the national genius for sport and its organisation. One of the more outlandish examples was the fashion for winter sports.

It had begun with the accidental discovery by marooned British visitors of the unsuspected sporting potential of the Swiss Alps. What had chiefly taken them there earlier in the century had been the mountains themselves. Serious mountaineers, such as the members of the prestigious Alpine club, founded in 1857, tended to be geologists, botanists, ornithologists and artists, or at the very least people who published accounts of their visits and discoveries. There was also a distinctive strain of muscular Christians seeking to demonstrate the protective power of the Almighty by venturing unaided into hazardous situations.[34] The wider sporting possibilities of the Swiss winter were first exploited by enthusiastic skaters who began making regular visits to St Moritz in the 1870s. The weather was, of course, an inhibiting factor for skating in Britain, and the technological and social problems of artificially refrigerated rinks were considerable: pure air and exclusiveness were essential requirements. The best people – those, that is, who did not regard ice merely as an enemy of hunting – increasingly went to Switzerland to get them.

St Moritz was then a place of quiet dignity and the skating itself, under

British guidance, was also dignified.[35] 'The few habitués of the rink have taken the early teaching of the (London) Skating Club as their starting point', wrote T. Maxwell Witham approvingly.[36] By skating he meant figure-skating. Speed-skating in Britain, despite the democratising efforts of the National Skating Association,[37] still bore the stigma of its artisan Fenland origins and the heavy betting that had disfigured the sport in mid-century. Even in figure-skating free-style cavortings were not admired and the distinctive, somewhat statuesque, British style had to be protected from modern aberrations like bending the trailing leg and, worse, skating to music. This was less easy at nearby Davos where the club at the new Belvedere Hotel was swamped by continentals, but the British tended to keep themselves to themselves.

The dignified reputation of St Moritz was also kept up by its curling club, founded in 1880 by Scottish visitors. For the more boisterous clientèle of Davos, sledging became the latest vogue, again as a result of British initiative. The writer, John Addington Symonds, who had a chalet in the area, was one of a group, who, spotting the possibilities for sport in the luges the locals used as hand carts, began tobogganing down a path from the road to the Belvedere. From this, impromptu races against local families developed; then the men began to have special luges made for greater speed, and more serious races were held on the main road from Davos to Klosters. After a few accidents and near-misses a Major W.H. Bulpetts, assisted by a local youth, constructed a special course down from the Engadiner Kalm Hotel to the village of Cresta. The first organised race on it was, appropriately, called the Grand National. As the primitive track was gradually developed, timed descents and team competitions made the Cresta Run an increasingly popular attraction. St Moritz started its own Tobogganing Club in 1887. An improvisation, tying two sledges together, led to the creation of the bobsleigh and by 1897 a separate Bobsleigh Club had been formed. Two of the founder members were women: mixed racing, usually with two men and a woman to a team, was highly popular. Again the first enthusiasts began by racing down a road but when they started constructing banks to speed up the corners the local citizens objected, and another course was built in hotel grounds.[38]

At first only a few eccentrics, whom the skaters disparagingly described as 'plank-hoppers', tried to master the art of ski-ing. The Swiss themselves knew very little of this Scandinavian mystery and it was a Norwegian manservant of a Colonel Napier, the tenant of Robert Louis Stevenson's old chalet near Davos, who first demonstrated the art to astonished tourists by ski-ing down from the chalet to the hotel. When the colonel went home he left his skis behind and a little group of English men and women took to amusing themselves by trying to get the things to work. One of them, Sir Arthur Conan Doyle, was proficient enough by 1894 to cross the Malenfelder Farka from

Davos to Arosa with two local guides. It was an Austrian, Matthias Zdarsky, who led the way in ski instruction, both civil and military, and the first serious ski races were held in Austria in 1893 but the British as ever were at hand to enjoy and to organise ski-ing competitively and it soon became an established part of the Swiss winter sports scene.[39]

'Some recommend the Bowling Green'[40]

The quest for novelty also led to some surprising revivals of half-forgotten sports. Whilst the Renshaws were dazzling the crowds at Wimbledon a much greater sporting hero, W.G. Grace, seeking fresh attractions for his London Counties venture, decided to replace the tennis lawns at Crystal Palace by bowling greens. This, like most of W.G.'s decisions, was one which combined personal pleasure with commercial acumen. He himself like other leading cricketers, enjoyed the game, which was well suited to his age (fifty-two) and bulk (considerable) and he saw great scope for its development. So far from being a new game it was redolent of England's glorious past: everyone knew the story of Sir Francis Drake on Plymouth Hoe. But it had steadily fallen in social esteem since its Elizabethan hey-day: as well as the greens of great houses it had also been played in the alleys of public houses and had many times been prohibited because of its dissolute associations.[41] By Victorian times it had become a minor pleasure of a somewhat bucolic sort, played usually on rough ground. The potential for revival W.G. descried was more evident in Scotland.

There it had retained a higher reputation, had fewer dissolute connections, had never been subject to prohibition and had continued through the centuries as a pleasant feature of many villages and country towns. The Scots were renowned gardeners, and their bowlers took great trouble over their greens, employing experts and importing sea-washed turf, from the Cumberland coast if necessary. (The more reflective Scots had a penchant for rolling and aiming games. Curling, in season, was an established favourite. Amongst its leading adherents there had always been many clergymen – one of them wrote the first book on the subject – but there were more worldly players too, such as Tam Samson, whose death had been mourned in a poem by Burns.[42] In 1890 there were nearly a hundred clubs in the central area around Stirling alone, for example, and in 1900 the two most popular clubs were finding it necessary to turn down applicants for membership for lack of facilities.[43] Quoiting, another traditional medieval sport[44] for which enthusiasm had continued in Scotland as in the north of England, was a rough ground variant and hence attractive to the less privileged.[45]) If golf, which required more space and specialised terrain, had flourished on the eastern coastal strip near Edinburgh, bowls was the game of the professional and business classes of the Clydeside conurbation. The first modern rules had been drawn up in Glasgow in 1848 and the first book of instruction was written there sixteen years later. In the 1880s clubs sprang up all over the lowlands. 'Few towns or villages in Stirlingshire are without a club', commented a local newspaper in 1887.[46] Women were strongly represented in the membership (as they were in curling) though it was men who took the lead in decision-making and developed the 'serious', competitive side. In 1889 a letter to *The Scotsman* called for a single rule-making body to unite east and west Scotland, and after prolonged negotiations the Scottish Bowling Association was set up in 1892. Soon over 400 clubs were in membership.

Meanwhile there had been some revival of interest in England, but its organisation had not developed beyond a few regional associations, beginning in 1882 with Northumberland and Durham and the neighbouring border counties, and extending only in 1895 to the midlands and London and southern counties. (In Ireland, though a Belfast club had been formed in 1842, it remained the only one of note for thirty years, and still continued thereafter, under Scottish expatriate leadership, as by far the leading centre. In Wales, the two major clubs both in Cardiff had been founded as recently as 1878 and 1892, and the Welsh like the Irish took their inspiration from occasional visits to Glasgow.) The London and southern counties associations were also part of this informal circuit but showed no disposition towards creating more formal competition or – a necessary preliminary step – standardising the rules. This was the situation in 1899 when WG began to set out his stall at Crystal Palace.

His involvement in wider organisational matters arose in part from irritation at the lackadaisical existing arrangements and in part from the stimulus of a new initiative that threatened his own plans. This came from Australia, where bowls was extremely popular, not least because of the interest of Scottish immigrants. In 1899 two of the leading Australian administrators came to England to follow the fortunes of Joe Darling's touring cricket team which included a number of bowls-players. At the Oval match they met a fellow-enthusiast from Hove and the idea arose of a bowls 'Test' match between England and Australia. This grew into the noble concept of extending the game throughout the Empire – or at least the white sections of it – and later that year an Imperial Bowling Association was formed, under the presidency of the Earl of Jersey, and with the ostensible support of W.G.

By the time the first international match between England and Australia took place in June, 1901, at Brownswood, London, W.G. had formed his own strategy. When he started his own London Counties Association that year he applied for affiliation to the Scottish Bowling Association, thus astutely securing permission to use the Scottish laws and to share in their competitions. This allowed him to circumvent the English regions, with their half-baked ideas about co-ordination and to cut across the plans of the somewhat nebulous Imperial Association. There followed a series of matches at Crystal Palace and in Scotland at which the presence of the Great Cricketer brought hundreds of spectators and greatly boosted club membership. Here, perhaps, were new possibilities for exploitation in the next decade.[47]

Notes

1 K.E. McCrone, 'The Lady Blue: Sport at the Oxbridge Colleges from their Foundation to 1914', *The British Journal of Sports History*, September, 1986, pp. 191–211.
2 McCrone, 'Play Up! Play Up!' in J.B. Mangan and R.A. Park, *Fair Sex to Feminism*, p. 98.
3 Quoted in S. Fletcher, 'The Making and Breaking of a female Tradition: Women's Physical Education in England, 1880–1980' in Mangan and Park, *Fair Sex*, p. 145.
4 F. Pomeroy, 'On Dress Reform and Stays', *Sanitary Record*, 15 Dec. 1888, p. 254.
5 MCC's new real tennis court (1900) was one of several that were built between 1880 and the First World War. Cambridge, which had three, had produced the leading player of the late Victorian years, the all-round sportsman Alfred Lyttelton, who was English amateur champion twelve times. Oxford's leading player, Sir Edward Grey, amateur champion twice in the 1890s, was sent down for incorrigible idleness, no doubt much of it on the tennis courts, before turning his mind to affairs of state. (He became Viscount Grey of Falloden, Foreign Secretary – and Chancellor of the University of Oxford.)
6 The seventh came in 1889. William Renshaw and his twin brother Ernest had dominated the championship in the 1880s. They were Cheltenham College boys, but had learned and perfected the game outside the school. See D. Birley, *Sport and the Making of Britain*, Manchester, 1993, p. 317.
7 Reprinted as a chapter in G.W. Hillyard, *Forty Years of First-Class Lawn Tennis*, London, 1924.
8 A. Wallis Myers, *Fifty Years of Wimbledon*, London, 1926, p. 35.
9 G.A. Hutchinson, *Outdoor Games and Recreations: a Popular Encyclopaedia for Boys*, Religious Tract Society, 1892, quoted by H. Walker, 'Lawn Tennis', in T. Mason (ed.), *Sport in Britain*, Cambridge, 1989, p. 248.
10 Hillyard, *Forty Years*.
11 N.L. Jackson, *Sporting Days and Sporting Ways*, London, 1932.
12 Wilberforce in Hillyard, *Forty Years*.
13 See Birley, *Sport*, pp. 323–5.
14 For early cycling see A. Ritchie, *King of the Road*, London, 1975.
15 D. Rubinstein, 'Cycling in the 1890s', *Victorian Studies*, autumn 1977, pp. 66–8.
16 *Reasons for Reform in Dress*, London c.1885, p. 9, quoted in J. Park, 'Sport, Dress Reform and the Emancipation of Women in Victorian England', in *International Journal of the History of Sport*, May, 1989, pp. 11–27, a most valuable survey of events and opinions.
17 Founded in 1891 by Robert Blatchford, *The Clarion* was until the First World War the most influential socialist periodical. Blatchford himself was a keen cricketer – and a sturdy patriot – and the paper supported many healthy and virtuous sporting causes and founded a number of Clarion cycling clubs.
18 *The Hub*, 18 March, 1899.
19 *The Hub*, 29 August, 1896.

20 'Cycling' in H.C. Howard, Earl of Suffolk and Berkshire, and others (ed.), *The Encyclopaedia of Sport*, 2 vols. 1897–8, vol. 1.
21 K.E. McCrone, 'The Lady Blue', *IJHS*, September, 1986, p. 199.
22 K.E. McCrone, 'Women's Sport at the University of London', *IJHS*, September, 1990, p. 213.
23 Lady Malmesbury, 'Cycling', *The Hub*, 20 August, 1896.
24 For the ups-and-downs of croquet see D.C.M. Pritchard, *The History of Croquet*, London, 1981.
25 See Birley, *Sport*, p. 312.
26 See N. Radford, *Badminton*, London, 1954.
27 Suffolk, *Encyclopaedia*, vol. I.
28 *Ibid.*
29 They regarded the Olympics as a 'minor tournament'. They had little opposition, either numerically or in quality. The British provided all four semi-finalists in the singles. The Dohertys won the doubles from a mixed American-French pair. In the women's singles Charlotte Cooper, the winner, was the only British competitor. Women's doubles was not considered an interesting enough game for serious competition.
30 H. Roper Barratt, a member of the British team, quoted in A. Wallis Myers, *Fifty Years of Wimbledon*, All-England Club, Wimbledon, 1926, p. 35.
31 There was already much disquiet amongst the purists about the widespread practice of pacing, secret training sessions and under-the-counter payments. By the end of the century, when great strides were being made in the USA and continental Europe, where massed-start road racing was allowed and time trials were regarded as a British aberration, the leading cycling nations, France, Belgium, Switzerland and the USA, grew tired of British domination of the existing international body and started a new one, the Union Cycliste Internationale, with headquarters in Geneva, to which Britain eventually had to apply to join.
32 R. Watson and M. Gray, *The Penguin Book of the Bicycle*, London, 1978, p. 125.
33 Son of the pioneering editor of the *New York Herald*, Gordon Bennett achieved such celebrity in England that his name became a euphemistic Cockney slang way of invoking the Deity, as 'Gawd – on Bennett!'.
34 A. Trollope, *British Sports and Pastimes*, Chapter Seven, is highly critical both of the pretentiousness of the Alpine Club and of the willingness of the rasher muscular Christians to lure native guides into dangerous situations by the offer of a few francs, brought to light by the tragedy on the Matterhorn in 1865.
35 For early skating see Birley, *Sport*, pp. 321–2, and, for a fuller account, N. Brown, *Ice-skating: a History*, London. 1958.
36 In J.M. Heathcote *et al.*, *Skating, Curling, Tobogganing and Other Ice Sports*, Badminton Library, ed. A.E.T. Watson, 1892.
37 One of the few national organisations not to be based on London, the NSA was the brainchild of James Digby, a Cambridge (town) journalist and, remarkably, had both figure-skating and speed skating under its umbrella.
38 H. Bass, *Winter Sports*, London, 1968.
39 R. Flower, *The Story of Ski-ing*, London, 1978.
40 'To cure the mind's wrong bias, spleen/Some recommend the bowling green', Matthew Green, *The Grotto*, 1732.
41 See Birley, *Sport*, pp. 36–139 *passim*.
42 R. Burns, 'Tam Samson's Elegy', 1786. Tam walked with 'bottle-swagger'.
43 N. Tranter, 'The Chronology of Organised Sport in Nineteenth Century Scotland', *IJHS*, September, 1990, p. 189 and p. 195. There was one club for every 650 males in

the population. It should be noted, however, that there were over 500 soccer clubs.

44 Birley, *Sport*, p. 37.
45 Tranter, 'The Chronology', pp. 189–90. There were 87 curling clubs in central Scotland in the 1890s, 43 for bowling and 45 for quoits suggesting a social division in the summer season.
46 *Ibid.*, p. 197.
47 P. Sullivan, *Bowls: the Records*, London, 1986, pp. 19–20

CHAPTER FIVE

Striking out

It was one thing for women to frolic around on tennis courts. Storming male citadels was quite another matter. Their most remarkable achievement was in the 'mannish' game of hockey, which they not only took up with fervour but organised independently of their distinctly unsympathetic male counterparts.

Hockey: a virile game for ladies

There had been some striking developments in girls' physical education in the 1880s. The Misses Lawrence who founded the small but expensive Roedean at Brighton in 1885, overtly modelled it on the boys' public schools with two hours' physical exercise a day in winter and three in summer, and as well as running, swimming and gymnastics they encouraged the girls to play not merely lawn tennis but the more vigorous hockey and cricket. Hockey in particular was becoming popular with the pupils, if not the authorities, of a number of girls' schools and colleges. At Cheltenham, for instance, though the staff thought it a violent and unladylike pursuit, the girls played it with unpeeled ash sticks, like inverted walking sticks with curved handles, which they bought from a local supplier for fourpence each.[1] Madame Bergman-Osterberg soon came to see the educational possibilities of the games that the girls of her adopted country enjoyed, and by 1889 hockey had become part of her college's curriculum. The following year at Girton the Lawn Tennis Club, seeking a winter outlet, formed a hockey section and persuaded the college authorities to provide a pitch, amid much trepidation lest 'the revelation that "those Girton girls had actually taken to hockey"' would cause 'a national shudder'.[2]

Organised hockey was only just beginning even for men. Though of ancient origin it had had the sort of inglorious existence in Britain that kept it out of the written record except when it was being banned.[3] It had survived in various regional forms – shinty, bandy, hurling – and as an informal game for public schoolboys but despite a brief vogue at Cambridge had recently been quite overshadowed by football.[4] It was a suburban cricket club, Teddington, seeking a winter outlet of a compatible kind, that found a way of adapting hockey for modern tastes, using the smooth grass of the cricket field, playing with a cricket ball and putting a brake on indiscriminate swiping, and drew up rules for their matches with neighbouring Richmond, Wimbledon and Surbiton. By 1884 a hockey tournament was being advertised as part of a week's festivities in Bath[5] and two years later representatives of seven London clubs and Trinity College, Cambridge, formed a Hockey Association. In 1890 *Bell's Handbook of Athletic Sports* gave hockey 'a foremost place' amongst games that had 'come into fashion of late years'.

The Hockey Association neither sought nor achieved mass appeal, proceeding on a purely amateur course untroubled by questions of gate-money and professionalism. Oxford and Cambridge matches, which began in 1890, gave the sport a certain cachet but nothing like that of the cricketers and rugby players. In the regional encounters between north and south which also began in 1890 the south were completely dominant, the northerners achieving only one draw before their first victory in 1900. Five regional associations were eventually formed, the last, the west, in 1895. In that year, too, 'home internationals' began, with a 5–0 victory for England over Ireland.[6] It was 1900 before an International Hockey Board – confined to the British Isles – evolved. It had, however, also acquired a following in military circles (outside the cavalry elite) flourishing particularly in India where the hard, fast pitches and good light added to the pleasure. The first clubs were formed in Calcutta in the 1880s, and competitions such as the Beighton Cup and the Aga Khan Tournament which began locally were soon attracting entries from all over India, uncovering in the process a great natural aptitude for the game amongst the native population. Such trophies and competitions were not to the Hockey Association's taste, and any that crept into Britain – north of the divide, for instance – were regarded with a baleful eye.[7]

Hockey was thus free of the competitive vulgarities that rendered other games unsuited to ladies. It was, however, undoubtedly 'mannish' and it was specifically forbidden at Lady Margaret Hall, Oxford for that reason. The first adult club, at the west London suburb of Molesey in 1887, confined itself initially to internal matches, and neither it nor Ealing the following year made much impact. Two years later, however, Madame Bergman-Osterberg included hockey in her plan 'to combine (such) games with Swedish gymnastics and thus create a perfect training system for the English girl'[8] and, of more immediate impact, a new club was formed at Wimbledon. When Wimbledon played Molesey in the first season they found the experience 'disagreeable',[9] but they persisted, women's hockey caught a small current of fashion and never looked back. The formation of the Girton Hockey Club in 1890 had been the decisive factor. Girton were playing Newnham by 1892, in 1893 the ban at Lady Margaret Hall, Oxford, was lifted (subject to parental permission) and 'Varsity matches began in 1894.

Cambridge's narrow victory in the first of these encounters drew the satirical attention of *Punch*, which found the whole thing a great joke, warning the men of Oxford that this defeat far outweighed any of their own sporting victories. Such ribaldry notwithstanding, women were on the brink of their most significant achievement in the male-dominated world of sport. The immediate stimulus towards national organisation came from Ireland where hockey was a small but significant emblem of the ascendancy. Smart young Protestant males were taking up hockey rather than hurling and in 1894 an Irish Ladies Hockey Union was formed, almost all of them from the fashionable Alexandra College, Dublin. These enthusiasts invited friends from Newnham to bring a team over during the Christmas vacation, and ten past and present students made the trip. They played three matches, finding the pitches and the weather deplorable but greatly enjoying the 'crack'.

The leader of the party, Miss I. Jameson, found the experience so inspiring that she sounded out the leading clubs back home about the possibility of forming an English Ladies Union to play a return match. Some, like Wimbledon, declined. Students at Oxford and Cambridge were either not interested or wanted to make conditions. Her best support came from slightly lower down the social scale. The University of London was a relatively progressive but socially suspect institution in which organised sport, for men as well as women, suffered from the absence of a residential tradition. The Royal Holloway College, established seven years earlier from the bounty of a rich pill-manufacturer and by far the grandest and best-equipped of its small women's colleges, was doing its utmost to remedy the deficiency. Now a keen student, Miss Guinness, threw in her lot with Miss Jameson and together with a Miss Johnson of the Molesey Club they decided to get up their own England team.

They held a trial at Neasden on 30 March 1895, and the chosen XI met the Irish Ladies, all from Alexandra College, on 10 April at Brighton. The game was greatly enjoyed and in the after-glow of excitement the English ladies and their supporters met in a tea-shop and agreed to form a permanent Association. Miss Jameson became Vice-President, but a more senior figure was needed as President. They sought to interest the Principal of Newnham but she declined and they turned instead to Miss Lillian Faithfull, an Old Somervillian, formerly a lecturer at Royal Holloway and now Vice-Principal of King's College, London.[10]

By November when the first formal meeting took place, four of the ten representatives were from the Oxbridge colleges. This was no feminist group.

They applied to the Hockey Association, by whose rules they played, seeking affiliation, but they were coldly rebuffed. The Hockey Association, wrote its Honorary Secretary,[11] had been formed entirely in the interests of men's clubs and it could not officially recognise the existence of the new association. The ladies responded with proper spirit, resolving that henceforth no man should ever hold office in their Association, which they re-named the following year the All-England Women's Hockey Association. Nevertheless the spirit of emulation was kept within proper bounds and, though they called themselves 'Women' the members of the AEWHA never forgot that they were ladies.

This came out clearly in the lengthy consideration of the clothing that hockey players in membership should be required to wear. The claims of health as well as propriety were taken into account, and sometimes even prevailed, as in the hotly-debated decision in 1895 to ban 'hat-pins, or sailor or other hard-brimmed hats'. Skirt-length, too, was much discussed. Convention decreed that long skirts were essential, and Lottie Dod was amongst those who argued that they could be used to advantage, especially when mud-soaked and dragging at the back, as a safe way of stopping the ball. Sporting ethics apart, however, long and muddy skirts were certainly ungraceful and an impediment to running and in 1899 the AEWHA ruled that skirts must be six inches off the ground and the same length all round. Even this did not satisfy some. Amongst the dangerous libertarians were Madame Bergman-Osterberg's students. From the first they had worn functional rather than conventional garments for gymnastics – long-sleeved, knee-length, blue merino dresses over knickers and stockings – and in 1892 these were super-seded by a sleeveless knee-length tunic.[12] The students soon began to use their tunics for games as well. This often shocked the girls' parents and there was even more trouble if tunics were worn going to and from matches: a progressive student recalled the annoyance of being called 'those dreadful girls' both by 'men who don't know how troublesome skirts are and by women who don't know how delicious it is to be free of them'.[13] The physical educationists' tunic-wearing had little immediate impact on adult sportswear fashions, however. In 1898 the AEWHA authorised the raising of hemlines to eight inches, but the skirt remained firmly in place. The attitude of Madame Bergman-Osterberg and one or two other radicals in the matter of corsets (in any event a less ostentatiously feminist issue) also had relatively little influence. The dictates of fashion and fears of developing in unfeminine directions, as well as the requirements of seemliness, usually discouraged adults from throwing their stays away entirely; there were special sporting models on the market and this covert and largely unmentioned nuisance seems usually to have been endured in silence.

Seemliness also added an extra female dimension to the AEWHA's attitude to competition and publicity. In 1898 the *Ladies' Field*, a new venture based on the male original, offered the AEWHA a challenge cup worth 20 guineas for annual competition, and though some clubs were in favour the Association primly declined, considering the idea demeaning and likely to provoke resignations. This last was a very real danger as the AEWHA had already discovered in their early dabblings in the deep waters of publicity. A few years before, *The Field* itself had offered to print their fixture lists, and this dangerous practice became a matter of great controversy when their first home international in 1897 was not only advertised in advance but attracted paying spectators from the general public. The representative of Royal Holloway particularly deplored such publicity-seeking.

Playing hockey even in private was still thought very bold, and, as the Dartford girls had found, respectable citizens were apt to be affronted by the sight of 'unsexed creatures' on their way to and from matches: older women showing themselves off for money would be thought simply disgusting. This apart, it was important to keep the prurient out. The AEWHA, suitably abashed, declared that it did not 'countenance advertising by posters in public places, or in newspapers' and would take 'no further steps to facilitate particular journalists in writing about women's hockey'. This was still not enough for the ladies of Royal Holloway, and they resigned in the autumn of 1898. The result was a resolution of painstaking probity, that 'to protect the game from "roughs" and other undesirable spectators . . . tickets for international matches be obtained by members free beforehand from secretaries of clubs, non-members obtaining tickets before the day paying one shilling only if their application is accompanied by a member's card, and two shillings and sixpence at the gate only if accompanied by a ticket-holder or on the production of the card of a member'.[14]

This circumspection paid off. The lady hockey players won gradual acceptance in the best circles and the AEWHA made steady progress. The games cult was now firmly installed in girls' as well as boys' public schools. In 1898 Penelope Lawrence, Principal of Roedean – a founder-member of the AEWHA and already, after a mere dozen years of life, renowned for its quasi-masculine deployment of games as an educational instrument – had written a lengthy article for an official government Report: 'Games have an important advantage over drilling and dancing in that the movements are voluntary and not to command', it argued.[15] The AEWHA were fully aware of their distinctive place in the new national scheme of things. As their organ *The Hockey Field* declared in 1899, 'It has been said of us as a nation that we take our pleasures seriously. Whether or not this is true in every case, there can be no doubt that we have always approached our outdoor games in a spirit which is not wholly unbecoming in a religious rite. To this spirit may be credited the beneficial influence which games have exercised upon the national character and the national physique.'[16]

'Aren't women as good as men?'

Punch's wisecracks about the women's 'Varsity hockey match showed how precariously even the circumspect AEWHA's approach was balanced in public esteem. The British Ladies Football Club founded in 1890 was even less likely to find favour, not only because of the manifestly indelicate nature of soccer but because one of the Ladies Club's avowed objectives was to help destroy 'that hydra-headed monster, the present dress of women'. N.L. Jackson recalled a typical re-action:

> The good lady who is organizing the football teams which are to startle the world as representatives of 'the British Ladies' Football Club' – that is if the world cares to plank down its bawbees to see a feminine rendering of the Association game – has been interviewed and this is the way she justifies her somewhat startling departure: 'Aren't women as good as men? We ladies have too long borne the degradation of presumed inferiority to the other sex. If men can play football, so can women.' . . . We are not prudes, either on the prowl or on the growl, but there is a great deal of difference between a lot of schoolgirls romping after a ball in their field in their own way, and a promiscuously selected set trying to make money out of that which would be just as interesting as if a troupe of males attempted to exhibit themselves as champions at skipping rope.[17]

They went ahead, with predictable results. Though Alcock and his Committee were criticised as 'ungallant' by the more extreme feminists for refusing them permission to play at the Oval their judgement was vindicated by events. In central Scotland, for instance, a great football area and one which exhibited considerable enthusiasm for novelty and a more than usual encouragement to women to take part in sport, the Ladies' Football team were regarded as a spectacle for men to gawk at rather than a serious sporting activity. Their several visits to Falkirk and Stirling evoked no local upsurge of interest from potential female players and indeed their efforts were condemned by the local press as 'ludicrous'.[18] Everywhere the matches were criticised because the performers had little idea of how to play the game and it must be assumed that the sizeable crowds they attracted were due largely to male curiosity and prurience: the two teams wore 'blue serge knickers of the divided skirt pattern and cardinal and pale-blue blouses respectively'.

This apart, soccer had no appeal to fashionable young ladies and even informal skirmishing in the privacy of their own grounds was forbidden to them in the superior schools and colleges. Cricket, with fewer problems in the way of dress and a better history of women's participation in stoolball, rounders and family knockabouts, fared better.[19] As a serious sport, however, the claims of femininity were against it. Running between the wickets, encumbered by pads, for instance, presented an inelegant appearance. Cricket was not allowed at Lady Margaret Hall where the Principal considered it altogether 'too masculine'.[20] Nevertheless it was on offer at Roedean and it enjoyed something of a vogue amongst fashionable young adults. The most celebrated venture was the White Heather Club at Nun Appleton, Yorkshire, formed in 1887 to play country-house cricket, where the members included such notables as Lady Milner, the Hons M. and B. Brassey, Lady Idira and Lady Henry Nevill, the Hon. M.B. Lawrence and Miss Chandos-Pole. Dame Ethel Smyth, the composer and suffragette, afterwards recalled that in 1889 cricket mania gripped all the young women of her circle.[21]

But women players risked being labelled as feminists, not least by male cricketers: 'The New Woman is taking up cricket, evidently with the same energy which has characterised her in other and more important spheres of life', commented the journal *Cricket* in 1895.[22] At the very least they could expect jocularity like that of a Birmingham newspaper, which, having dismissed a local effort as a 'pretty little burlesque' went on to warn that if this sort of thing continued 'the man of the future' would become 'the stocking-mender, and the children's nurse'.[23] For various reasons, then, cricket appealed less to grown-up young ladies than the more graceful and feminine lawn tennis and its early vogue amongst the adventurous was brought to an end by the sudden craze for cycling.

The attempt by male entrepreneurs in 1890 to popularise women's cricket as a spectator sport, though markedly less daring than that in football, was not a success. The organisers' advertisements emphasised the purity of their motives: 'With the object of proving the suitability of the national game as a pastime for the fair sex in preference to Lawn tennis and other less scientific games the English Cricket and Athletics Association have organised two complete XIs of Female Players under the title of THE ORIGINAL ENGLISH LADY CRICKETERS.' They were to be 'elegantly and appropriately attired' and 'every effort' was to be made 'to keep the organisation select and refined'. With this in mind a matron was to accompany each eleven to all engagements.

The idea was to play exhibitions or challenge matches. 'Private engagements of one or both elevens can be arranged or a complete match or to meet lady amateurs.'[24] The teams, known as the Reds and the Blues because of their distinctive costumes (supplied by Lillywhite, Froude & Co.) played a number of matches, often before sizeable crowds – 15,000 people came to their Easter match at the Police Athletic Grounds in Liverpool – but the novelty soon wore off. The players, decent lower middle-class girls seeking a pleasant way to earn a few pounds, seem not to have been prepared for the commercial realities of the venture. A projected winter tour to Australia was abandoned because of parental objections and the teams disbanded at the end of the season amid dispute about the distribution of the profits.

Medical opinion was divided about women's cricket. In 1890 The *Lancet* warned of the dangers of sudden muscular strain, dislocated shoulders from throwing (female shoulder joints were shallower than men's) and malignancy caused by blows to the breast. This last, however, according to one doctor who thought cricket otherwise a sport well-suited to girls, could be obviated by the wearing of a well-padded corset.[25] In the great debates of the time about women's sport it is hard to separate true medical opinion, which was mostly male and often unscientifically based, from the more general concern for propriety and the need to ensure that women did not seek to emulate men or encroach on their preserves. The confusion was particularly marked in the girls' schools and women's colleges, so conscious of their reputation and that of their charges and yet anxious to demonstrate their awareness of the value of properly regulated physical education and recreation.

Rowing, or boating as it was usually called in its gentler feminine form, had such high status that the proximity of a river was a social asset not to be ignored. For once the ladies of Oxford were more active than those of Cambridge (where Newnham and Girton were physically less well placed). The authorities at Somerville had allowed boating since 1884 – incidentally bringing in a requirement that all prospective rowers must learn to swim, an activity that had no social prestige at all. A significant body of medical opinion held that strenuous rowing was bad for the heart, which was one reason why it was allowed only for recreational purposes, but there were others: boating was permitted only on the Cherwell when there were unlikely to be men around, and not at all on the Isis, lest they be thought to interfere in any way with the more serious male activities there: as an 1898 account explained, 'A Somerville boat would be very much disliked on the river, so, though the college owns five boats, two canoes and a punt these are kept on the Cherwell.'[26] A similar policy was in force at Lady Margaret Hall, where in 1885 the authorities, unable to find a site for a rackets court, used the money to buy a boat and boat-house instead. At St Hilda's, adjoining the river, a boat club was formed that soon owned an eight-oared boat as well as a four. But the eight, emblematic of the male side of the sport with its emphasis on team contests, was only used on a secluded part of the river. The ladies, instructed by a waterman, were scrupulous in their dress, encircling their skirts with elastic bands to avoid entanglement with the sliding seats and similar embarrassments.[27]

The ladies of the London University colleges were a good deal less inhibited, not so much in the matter of dress as in the nature of the boating allowed. There were no male students in close proximity whose sensitivities might be upset. At Bedford College the Boat Club, started in 1889, was holding competitive races by 1892. Furthermore these included sculling contests, considered dangerously individualistic in purist rowing circles. The ladies of King's College also began sculling in 1899, using the boats of Dr Furnivall's Hammersmith Rowing and Sculling Club. Women's rowing was one of the many enthusiasms of that idiosyncratic scholar, and he was given to encouraging not only his own students but also the waitresses in his local ABC café to join the club and share in their picnic expeditions from Hammersmith to Canvey Island.[28]

Another intrinsically masculine sport taken up by superior girls' schools and colleges was lacrosse.[29] This North American game had acquired a certain cachet amongst men in mid-century and in the 1880s an adapted version began to be played in schools like Roedean that believed in female games-playing on masculine lines. It was girls from one such school, St Leonard's in St Andrews, Scotland, who formed the nucleus of a Lacrosse Club at Girton in 1899. The club did not last long because of the greater popularity of hockey, and lacrosse remained an exclusive somewhat exotic pursuit. One American importation, much less outlandish and requiring much less space, came to Britain through Madame Bergman-Osterberg's academy. In 1891 Dr James Naismith, Professor of Physical Education at the University of Kansas, had introduced a game of his own invention, basketball, at the International YMCA Training School at Springfield Mass. A women's version was devised, the YWCA also took it up and it was soon highly popular in both forms at schools and colleges throughout America. In 1895 an American visiting professor introduced the women's version to Madame's students – then still at Hampstead – and two years later another American visitor to the college's well-appointed new home at Dartford demonstrated the latest outdoor version. It had an obvious appeal in the schools – the pupils at North London Collegiate were playing an improvised version in 1899, using waste-paper baskets on top of high jump supports as targets – and the authorities liked it because it was simple and because it involved no bodily contact.

Formalising a modified version of the new game, netball, was one of the first projects of the Ling Association, started in 1899 by and for Dartford graduates 'to unite trained gymnastics teachers' and to protect their interests in salaries and conditions of service. Madame disapproved of this new body fearing that it would lower standards and forbade her instructors to join, preferring to start her own Bergman-Osterberg Association. The Ling Association's version of basketball, netball, for which they published rules and regulations in 1901, shrewdly prescribing a standard-sized football (smaller than the American original) to make the game even more accessible, was, despite Madame's disapproval of its authors, a success, and it was this rather than the parent game that first became popular in England. What it lacked, however, was prestige, and under the auspices of popularisers like the Ling Association it soon lacked any social pretensions.

For similar elitist reasons Madame disapproved of the other women's colleges of physical education that followed her own. One of these, Chelsea College of Physical Training, which opened in 1898, was started by a young Bavarian woman, Dorette Wilke, who had trained at Stempel's Gymnasium, and its curriculum was based on German gymnastics and hence ideologically suspect. Furthermore as it was under the auspices of the South Western Polytechnic and its students played their games in Battersea Park and swam in Chelsea Public Baths, it catered for a lower stratum of society. Nor did Madame like it when her own old pupils began to spread the word in the provinces. One of them, Rhoda Anstey, incurred severe displeasure when in 1897 she started her own college, first in rural Worcestershire, then in sub-urban Birmingham. Nevertheless, the impetus given to the cause of women's physical education by Madame Bergman-Osterberg started a new profession for women and put it far ahead of the system for men, in which physical training remained in the hands of drill instructors and the like and the more prestigious teaching of games was left to amateurs – university graduates in other subjects.

Golf in the ascendant[30]

Golf, for various reasons, lay outside the main stream of public school sports. Apart from its Scottish ancestry it was not a team game, it needed no great athleticism – indeed it was much favoured by those of riper years – and it required a great deal of space. Lack of space also inhibited its development as an adult game, particularly in London, whence fashions in sport, as in every-thing else, tended to spring. Furthermore, in its original, 'natural' form golf needed a special kind of land that had restricted its progress even in Scotland. The links land between sea and shore on the coastal strip from Edinburgh to St Andrews and beyond – springy turf, few trees, sandy sub-soil and natural sand bunkers was the ideal. In England the few Scottish-exile clubs at places like Manchester, Blackheath and Wimbledon, making do on crowded inland commons, had been the standard-bearers until the 1860s when the members of the North Devon and Hoylake clubs, exploiting the natural terrain, had brought down professionals from St Andrews to lay out their courses.

The expansion that followed can be – and often is – explained as an English take-over. Certainly there was a marked shift in geographical distribution of clubs. Ten years after Hoylake's foundation there were still only 72 golf clubs, 52 of which were in Scotland: by 1888 the *Golfing Annual* listed 57 in England alone. But by then there were also 73 in Scotland, 6 in Ireland and 2 in Wales. The initial growth reflected the discovery of golf by a particular class, throughout the British Isles, often under Scottish auspices, and the development of courses was almost always under Scottish guidance. The English predominance that was to come, as a result of her greater population and wealth, was more a matter of infiltration than take-over.

To join a golf club in England in those early days was not just to take up a sport but to be accepted into an exclusive social circle. Golfers needed a good deal of time and money. Common land was much less readily available and more heavily used than in Scotland. Equipment was not cheap. Golfers were expected to hire caddies, make use of the professional's services as teacher or playing partner, pay substantial membership fees or take shareholdings, and to play a part in the social side, including keeping their end up at the 'nineteenth hole'. The neophytes were also supremely conscious of the game's etiquette and traditions. These were already well-established on gentlemanly Scottish lines, for although Scottish golfers might play on common land their clubs were socially select and the members had a neo-feudal relationship with the professionals. These clubs, though fiercely proud of their independence, had a reverence for the traditions of their game, and the Royal and Ancient club at St Andrews was first amongst equals in the control of it. The R&A's own inclinations, which were deeply conservative, not to say fastidious, kept it from seeking domination.

For decades the R&A had been jealously regarded by the Honourable Company of Edinburgh golfers which was always ready to point to its earlier date of foundation[31] and its authorship of the original rules on which St Andrews had based theirs. The Honourable Company finally gave up their claims to independence in 1895, however, and a Rules of Golf Committee consisting entirely of R&A members was established. The new English clubs, deeply conscious of entering a hierarchical tradition, were usually more than anxious to have the approval and imprimatur of St Andrews in the hope that some of the aura of antiquity might rub off on them.

Here, then, was an interesting variant on the north–south divide. The vulgarisation of their game that Scottish golfers were soon to complain about was not a matter of plebeian invasion but of the conspicuous expenditure through which superior new English clubs made it into a stock-brokers' paradise. The Scots, whose claims to a democratic tradition of the Burnsian type need not be taken at face value, could nevertheless fairly point out that it was the upstart English clubs, with their private inland courses – not even proper links – that stiffened the social barriers of golf in the later part of the century. Club membership was an essential part of English golf, and it was more than the working man could afford even if he found some way of gaining access to this esoteric world. The English had also made their distinctive contribution to the competitive side of golf when in 1885 the Hoylake club, soon to be the Royal Liverpool,[32] had devised an Amateur championship with suitably discriminatory rules to keep out artisans.[33] Thereafter the influx of new, wealthy young English players, augmented by the introduction of the game to Oxford and Cambridge, had added to golf's glamour. But it remained firmly under R&A auspices, with only Hoylake and the even grander Sandwich admitted to the tiny circle who staged this and the Open Championship.[34]

The new clubs were financed by every conceivable means from 'companification' to municipal enterprise. The Lancashire coast had been the earliest to be exploited, in the interests of the business and professional men of the Liverpool and Manchester conurbations, culminating in Birkdale (1889). Declining land values found more and more aristocrats eager to exchange agricultural tenants for sporting ones. Eastbourne (1887) was the first of the southern watering-places to form a club, aided by its patron the Duke of Devonshire, who leased it some of his downland sheep pastures. At Bournemouth (1893), the Corporation itself sponsored a golf club in order to keep up with the fashion. Meanwhile Hunstanton (1891) and Brancaster, later the Royal West Norfolk (1892), showed the possibilities of the east coast. Seacroft (1900) at Skegness, Lincolnshire, arose from the enterprise of Lord Scarborough, developing the new resort as a rival to Scarborough itself where golfers had to travel inland to Ganton (1891).

Harlech (Royal St David's) in 1894 and (Royal) Porthcawl in 1896 brought Wales into belated reckoning. In Ireland, mainly through Scottish and military influence, the golf mania had come much earlier, and Royal Belfast was an admired model.[35] The inland Phoenix Park course in Dublin gained lustre from the patronage of the Anglo-Scottish aristocrat, A.J. Balfour, Lord Salisbury's nephew, who played there during his time as Secretary for Ireland between 1887 and 1891. His sharp reaction to the disorders that marred Jubilee year, with the jailing of Nationalist MPs and three rioters killed by police, earned him the title of 'Bloody Balfour'. He showed a proper British insouciance, writing to a friend: 'I am taking great care of myself, golf or real tennis 12 to 2, the Castle 2 to 7.' The golf required special precautions: he needed 'two caddies, one for carrying the clubs and the other to act as fore-caddie, both being trusted (and fully armed) members of the famous G Division of the DMP'.[36]

In the north, after sectarian riots in Belfast in 1886, a calmer atmosphere prevailed. The seaside venture at Portrush (1888) was assisted by the Northern

Counties Railway Company, which offered free passes to members of the Belfast Club (now Royal) who turned up in force for its inaugural competition, won by Mr Tom Gilroy, a St Andrews' University man coached by a brother of the legendary 'Old Tom' Morris who had laid out the course.[37] *The Field* predicted an illustrious future for Portrush's 'unrivalled links': 'it is not difficult to surmise where the future St Andrews of Ireland is destined to be'.[38] In 1889 Tom Morris also gave his imprimatur to the superb links at Newcastle, County Down (where Lord Annesley, ADC to the Earl of Eglinton, a former Lord Lieutenant, had leased the club some of his land and became its President) and another Royal Club was in the making. Scottish exiles were the nucleus of the new club formed at Portmarnock further down the coast in 1892, under the presidency of Mr John Jameson, the whiskey manufacturer, who leased the club some of his family land. For their first greenkeeper they poached Mungo Park, the celebrated Musselburgh professional from nearby Foxrock, formed the previous year.[39] Under Park's grooming the course so impressed the Golfing Union of Ireland, started in 1891 by a group of northern clubs, that it soon joined Portrush and Newcastle as the venue for championship matches.

With the Land League around there were, not surprisingly, one or two setbacks. The Killymoon club started at Cookstown, County Tyrone, in 1889 by a Royal Portrush member intent on missionary work, took two changes of course and the lapse of thirty years before it reached stability. Tom Gilroy fared even worse. He had laid out a fourteen hole course on his estate near Drogheda, locating the first hole about two hundred yards from the entrance gates of his residence, Mornington Hall. The terrain, according to a local newspaper, was 'the nearest approach to that of St Andrews'. However 'local opposition' forced Mr Gilroy to abandon not only this but a new course on the other side of the Boyne and the Gilroys departed for England in 1895.[40]

In English golf land was also an issue, and if not a republican cause, one that touched on ancient manorial rights. In Lincoln in the 1890s a guild of freemen drove cattle on the course during the matches of clubs using common land, and at Ipswich in 1895 a gentlemen's club was incommoded 'by the refusal of the commoners to permit the furze to be sufficiently cut away'.[41] The Home Counties were particularly vulnerable. At Chorley Wood on the Herts-Bucks border the highly exclusive club started on the common in 1890, with such superior members as A.J. Balfour, the Marquess of Granby and Earl Wemyss, soon were complaining that 'it was used indiscriminately by the public who ignored the course rules'. In London itself the early courses had been bedevilled by the Municipal Commons Act, which meant shared use and constant battles with other users. One way round the problem emerged at Mitcham where Henry Deeley, later Mallaby-Deeley MP, was both Chairman of the Common Conservators' Committee, and promoter of the Prince's Golf Club which began in 1892 with A.J. Balfour as President. The railway station a few yards from the club-house made it less than half-an-hour's journey from Victoria, and Prince's, Mitcham, quickly became an oasis for the residents of Mayfair and Belgravia as well as leading members of Parliament. Less-elevated citizens of Tooting and Mitcham were not so happy about it, but an attempt to make it an issue in the 1894 Conservators' elections came to nothing.[42]

Meanwhile the railway companies were collaborating with property developers to exploit the possibilities of the 'stockbroker belt'. The problem was finding land that was not only private but suitable. The West Middlesex acquired a gravel soil site at Hamwell in 1891, but the great discovery was the heathland of Surrey, with a sandy sub-soil ideal for golf. That same year Richmond, later Royal Mid-Surrey, found a secluded park near the former Thames-side village of Ham and a string of new clubs followed. (An interesting one was Woking where in 1893 a group of golfing lawyers were able to lease land from the London Necropolis and Mausoleum Company reviewing their requirements in the light of the falling death-rate.) In 1889 there had been only 10 clubs within 15 miles of Charing Cross: by 1899 there were 49. The following year came a distinguished 50th, the superb Sunningdale just across the Berkshire border.

The increased number of clubs and the greater emphasis on landscaping especially in the manufactured inland courses also greatly enlarged the opportunities for Scottish professionals. Green-keeping had always been a highly-regarded if ill-rewarded part of their job and the 1888 *Golfing Annual* still described most professionals as greenkeepers. Club-making, which in the days of hickory shafts called for highly specialised craftsmanship, was also a valued service. Willie Fernie of Troon had the grandest title, in proper hierarchical order: 'Greenkeeper, Club-maker and Professional'. Many sprang from the despised juvenile or idler sub-trade of caddying, which seems to have been regarded as an outdoor version of billiard-marking. Horace Hutchinson of Royal North Devon and Oxford University, who turned his own golfing talent to rich profit through books and journalism, was acerbic about the species.

'The professional, as we are now chiefly acquainted with him,' he wrote, 'is a "feckless", reckless creature. In the golfing season in Scotland he makes his money all the day and spends it all the night. His sole loves are golf and whisky. He works at odd times (repairing clubs); but he only does it when reduced to an extremity . . . He can lightly earn seven and sixpence a day by playing two rounds of golf (with members); or, if he does not get an engagement, three and sixpence a day by carrying clubs. These are about the fees paid at St Andrews and Musselburgh, Scotland, which are the great manufactories of the professionals who go forth to so many links as green-keepers . . . In the medal weeks they pick up a little more, and an extra shilling or two comes into their pockets from bets . . . They often sell with great advantage clubs to young players, who fondly imagine magic properties to dwell in the wand itself, rather than in the hands of the sorcerers who wield it.'

Hutchinson went on: 'Occasionally they combine with golf-playing more general branches of industry, which they pursue in a spasmodic fashion. Thus when we asked of one of them whether a brother professional had no other trade but that of golf, he replied, "Ou aye! he has that – he breaks stanes." '[43] In the early days, indeed, the parents of youthful golf addicts had often made them take up apprenticeships in the building trade as some kind of security. And there were undoubtedly plenty who were not only rough but feckless. But there were others who rose above the temptations. The Open Champion of 1887 and 1889, Willie Park, junior, was a good example. Better educated than most, and with a good head for business, he was frugal in his habits and like Hutchinson he used his fame and skills as a player to launch out into profitable sidelines. Park was the first professional to put his name to a book of instruction[44] and also one of the first golf architects much in demand for designing and supervising the construction of new courses. Hutchinson, who shared the common view that these were activities requiring amateur flair and perspective, nevertheless saw useful and appropriate new avenues for the industrious artisan: 'now that so many more openings are occurring for green-keepers, in the increase in the number of links all over England (one) may hope to see these further inducements developing better habits in the professional class'.

With these new openings, in fact Hutchinson's racist Scottish stereotype gave way to a cherished English one – the outstanding player who, though of humble origin, was also a man of character and natural dignity, the serf who rose to yeoman rank but posed no threat to the established hierarchy. This model professional was J.H. Taylor, son of a Northam labourer who had started out as a houseboy in a golfing household, caddying in his spare time for, amongst others, Hutchinson himself. Taylor was fortunate in that the Royal North Devon, who played on what had originally been common land, sponsored a Working Men's Golf Club, operating unobtrusively at unsocial hours in return for services to the gentlemen's club, and he soon became its best player. He got a job as an assistant greenkeeper at Royal North Devon and in 1891, aged twenty, went to Burnham-on-Sea as a fully fledged greenkeeper and professional.

Another product of the English golfing boom, perhaps even greater, was Harry Vardon, a year older than Taylor, who also began as a caddie. One of six sons of a Jersey gardener, he and his brothers augmented the family income by carrying clubs for the English gentry, who had brought the game to the island. Between rounds these lads competed with each other on the common land near the course. On leaving school at the age of thirteen Vardon took up his father's trade of gardener, but his employer, Major Spofforth, an enthusiastic golfer, encouraged him to follow his older brother, Tom, who had already gone to the mainland as an assistant professional. Harry became greenkeeper at the age of twenty at a nine-hole course at Ripon, before moving first to a Lancashire businessmen's club at Bury and then to Scarborough's Ganton, from which base he won his first Open Championship in 1896. The Scottish monopoly on this oldest but thoroughly professionalised championship had already been broken six years earlier by one of the new-style full-time English amateurs, John Ball, of Royal Liverpool (who had also taken the Amateur title from Horace Hutchinson in 1888). The Scottish pros had regained the Open in 1891, but then Mr Harold Hilton, also of Royal Liverpool, had taken it, and after another Scottish victory J.H. Taylor, by then at (Royal) Winchester, had demonstrated the advance of the new English professionals by winning it in 1894 at Sandwich. (The recognition of Royal St George's, Sandwich, was itself an indication of the opulent 'English' direction the game was taking: it inherited the mantle of Mallaby-Deeley's resplendent Prince's Club.) Taylor repeated his success in 1895 in the Scottish citadel of St Andrews. Then came Vardon at Muirfield. Harold Hilton won again on his home course at Hoylake in 1897, after which came Vardon twice more (first at Prestwick, then at Sandwich) and Taylor, now elevated to the superior Royal Mid-Surrey (Richmond), at St Andrews. Even when the Scot James Braid won at Muirfield in 1901 his professional base was Romford in Essex.

These new trends, ending Scottish dominance, made the Open in particular, and competitive golf in general, a topic of absorbing interest to the English Press and public. They also raised the spectre of professional entrepreneurism. Golf clubs, unlike those in football or even cricket, were not in competition with each other for gate-money, and they had been able to demand a neo-feudal allegiance from their servants. The first ripple of discontent came on the eve of the 1899 Open when a few malcontents staged a strike for more prize-money. This, raised to £100 in total in 1893 (£30 for the winner), they now considered inadequate in view of the event's growing success. The strike fizzled out, principally because none of the leading players wanted anything to do with it. For them the actual prize-money was not the main consideration. Vardon, for instance, was able to cash in on his success by making lucrative tours of America and Taylor was a renowned golf architect. The more far sighted amongst the average club professionals were also more interested in the indirect effects of the Open's success, notably in attracting more members to their clubs, which increased the demand for their services as teachers and the sales of equipment of the type used by the tournament heroes.

Making clubs was an ancient Scottish art, first practised by diversifying bowyers, and selling them to members was one of the perquisites of the club professional's job. James Braid, fortunate in being prudentially apprenticed to a joiner, had played as an amateur until he felt able to set up as a club-maker to augment his income as a pro. £1 a week or less was what many clubs offered as a basic wage: green-keeping might add a few more shillings, and the top men could earn an occasional fee as a golf architect, but club-making was potentially a bigger money-spinner for the ambitious pro. Even before winning the first of his five Open Championships Braid had become club-maker to the Army and Navy Stores. Good hand-made hickory shafted clubs cost around five shillings and purchasers were not satisfied by a mediocre product even if it bore a famous name. Ben Sayers of the fashionable North Berwick, which boasted Balfour as a member, was no more than a good player but he was a first-rate club-maker and his firm, built up from small beginnings, soon had a reputation all over the golfing world.

This by the end of the century included not only the Empire, but America, potentially a huge market. The Americans, still learning the game, needed instructors as well as equipment, and it was there that many of the more adventurous young professionals, particularly Scottish ones, went to make a new life when times were hard at home, much as the Irish did in athletics but with much greater financial reward. For a long time, too, American tournaments offered easy pickings. The first winner of the US Open, in 1895, was an obscure young English assistant professional called Rawlins, of whom nothing was afterwards heard, and British players, notably immigrant Scots, won it for the next fifteen years. Harry Vardon's tour in 1899 was a triumphal procession and he duly won the US Open in 1900.

In spite of the growing public interest in competition, however, British golf remained primarily a social, club activity for people with plenty of money but no particular skill or competitive ambition The leading English amateurs, caught in the honey-trap of exclusiveness, thereafter struggled to reach the standards of the professionals. There were those, indeed, who felt that amateurs should be debarred from the Open lest, touching pitch, they were defiled. At club level the quest for sylvan seclusion that characterised the game helped to keep up membership fees and so further restrict it socially. Achieving club membership was not always the easiest matter, even for those who could afford it, for the better clubs took care, by judicious use of the black-balling system, to keep out 'the wrong sort'. It was best not to be a Jew, for instance, and small traders and the like were often looked at askance.

Golf club secretaries, though increasingly paid for their services, also had to be of the right sort. For the managerial assistance they required committees turned not to out-and-out professionals, either from sport or commerce, but to men of their own class, often retired officers and the like. They serviced the committees, organised medal competitions and supervised both the domestic staff and the golf professionals. They were not members but they enjoyed the social and playing privileges, and, of course, retained their amateur status. Other non-members of a less desirable kind might sometimes be found particularly when the temptation to increase revenue could not be resisted. An important caste mark was whether a club allowed unrestricted access by payment of a green fee, a common practice at seaside courses, but fraught with social hazard.

Clubs which idealistically sought to enlarge their social range were few indeed. Artisan golfers could sometimes take advantage of arrangements, originally inspired by the need for appeasement on courses taken out of common land, which allowed them to play at unfashionable hours in return for green-keeping and similar tasks. Earlier informal agreements, like those at Northam which produced J.H. Taylor, and Royal Liverpool's Hoylake Village Play Committee, were followed by a variety of schemes such as Great Yarmouth's Workmen's Golf Club in 1892 and the more famous and more resonantly feudal Royal Ashdown Forest's Cantelupe Club of 1897. This gradually modulated into more overtly commercial arrangements: at Redhill, Surrey, for instance there was an annual fee for artisans of four shillings compared with full membership at two guineas.[45] In Scotland, as in rural England, such arrangements could be a stepping-stone from caddying to professional status but were unlikely to lead to recognition as leading amateurs.

For those who satisfied the social criteria, however, golf was a splendid game. It could be played by people of all ages, it was physically and mentally refreshing and it offered an infinitely variable mix of recreation, competition and personal challenge to suit individual needs. It was helped in this by an ingenious handicapping system that could be applied to any player in any club, allowing performers of very different standards to play together with enjoyment, and, not least, to pit themselves constantly against their own previous best standards. Its early advocates humanised it by postulating a mythical opponent, called Colonel Bogey, who always posted a perfect score.[46]

Choleric colonels, throwing mashie-niblicks around in fury, were amongst the earliest golfing jokes. They were also, in the *Punch* tradition, highly impatient of women on the links, regarding them as incapable of keeping quiet as spectators let alone of playing the game. Such extremists apart, most members regarded golf clubs as a male preserve and many saw them as a refuge from women, particularly wives. It was enough to invite them into the club house on special occasions. Still there had been, first of all at St Andrews, no less, and also at North Devon, ladies golf clubs as early as the 1860s. They went no further than putting, but it was only a question of time, in this new libertarian era, before women were golfing in earnest.

Indeed, fatally for its male chauvinists, golf had outstanding advantages as a ladies' pastime, not least its relatively unathletic nature, which also helped them meet conventional requirements with regard to dress. Mabel Stringer, one of the early stalwarts, later wondered 'how on earth any one of us ever managed to hit a ball, or get along at all in the outrageous garments with which fashion decreed we were to cover ourselves'.[47] The handicapping system also made mixed golf a realistic proposition sometimes with remarkable results. There was, for example, Mrs Wright, wife of a Scottish army officer stationed in Belfast. On 1 October 1887 *The Field* reported on a novel competition at Royal Belfast: 'Mr Gregg, Captain of the club, and Mrs Wright played in a foursome against Col Lyon Campbell RE and Capt Wright, Gordon Highlanders. The match attracted quite a turn-out of ladies. At the end of the first round the former were four up, the lady having played particularly well. In the second round, however, the Colonel and his partner pulled the game down to all even and one to play. The last hole was keenly contested and was won by a long and well-laid put (sic) of Capt Wright.'[48]

Nor was that all. Amongst the admiring spectators was Miss C.E. McGee, who was visiting the club as a guest of Mr Gregg and who asked to meet Mrs Wright: 'We were introduced and she inspired me with a wish to play the game.'[49] The inspiration was not towards mixed golf, which was not to everyone's taste, particularly men who did not like losing or took the contest with Colonel Bogey too seriously to want distractions, but to the segregated variety, a radical enough notion for the Belfast male. The following autumn Miss McGee and some fellow-enthusiasts enlisted the help of Mr Gregg and one or two other liberal members in founding the Holywood Ladies Golf Club to play on the Royal Belfast links. Miss McGee afterwards recalled that 'it was uphill work, as there were many prejudices in those days regarding "petticoats on the links" as we were dubbed by some opposing members'. She gave sound advice to aspirant lady golfers: 'Club rules, of which we were ignorant, had to be studied, and I always think it was the strict observance of these rules which contributed to the success of our undertaking and to the winning over of those who thought a ladies' club impossible.'[50]

Similar ventures, undertaken in a similar spirit, were soon under way all over Britain. In the Stirling region of Scotland, for instance, of the 31 golf clubs active in the 1890s 13 had a significant number of lady members. Almost a third of the Aberfoyle Golf Club's members in 1894 were ladies; this was 60 per cent of the upper- and middle-class female population.[51] Some clubs, like Formby, were able to provide a separate small ladies' course inside the main links. Usually women were allowed on the main course, playing off greatly shortened tees, at times and places where they did not disturb the male members. Women's dependence on the men for a course on which to play generally reflected their general economic dependence, but also had social connotations. In 1892 the Brighton & Hove Ladies formed a separate club when the established male club refused to admit women members; but this was fairly rare. Women tended, if they were allowed, to begin as members of a men's club and not all of them wanted to go on to join separate women's clubs even when they were formed. In 1894 the Stirling Golf Club had 80 women members: a Ladies' Club was formed in 1897 but by 1900 still had only 70 members.[52]

Lady golfers who aspired to more than local friendly competition faced similar inhibitions to those of the hockey players, but this was lessened by the greater exclusiveness of the game and consequent decreased anxiety about prurient spectators. The greater conformity with male expectations and the claims of femininity in the matter of dress that golf allowed also helped. Photographs of the first British champion, Lady Margaret Scott, give more evidence of her sartorial dignity, straw boater, voluminous skirts and all, than of her much-admired 'classical swing'. Lady Margaret was a member of the Ranelagh Club, near Barnes Common. Ranelagh was chiefly known for its polo and for the opulence and elegance of the men who played and those who came to see them perform, but it also had croquet and tennis lawns – and a small golf course, flat and ornamental but entirely suitable to young ladies of fashion. Golf in 1892 was latest thing amongst the sort of adventurous trend-setters who a few years before had begun the brief vogue for cricket and three years later were to take up cycling. Lady Margaret's title and Ranelagh membership put her in the forefront of fashion and like a true thoroughbred she retired whilst still very young, but she was no mere ornament.

Representing Ranelagh, she was the most illustrious of the select group that in 1893 responded to the call of Miss Lisette Pearson, who proposed with the help of Mr Laidlaw Purves of Wimbledon to form a Ladies' Golfing Union. Twenty clubs joined in, from Scotland and Ireland as well as England. Lady Margaret Scott won the Union's first three championships before her swift retirement. The first was held at Lytham St Anne's Ladies Golf club in April 1893. That December a group of Irish ladies, all from the North, met to form an Irish Union. Their early influence on the standard of the women's game was quite out of proportion to Ireland's population. The third Ladies' Championship, held at Portrush in recognition of Irish enthusiasm, was duly won by Lady Margaret Scott, but four years later, at Newcastle, County Down, the title was taken by a 17-year old, Miss May Hezlet from Portrush, and the following year by the 18-year-old Miss Rhona Adair from Killymoon, daughter of the Portrush member who had implanted the game there.

Their prowess and influence appears to have impressed even their own entrenched males. An editorial in *The Irish Golfer* in 1899, protesting 'on behalf of lady golfers at the treatment they too often receive at the hands of *gentlemen* both on the green and off it', reckoned that so far from being a nuisance women's presence on the links had great advantages, sporting, social and intellectual: 'Many conscientious fathers of families can now take their families to the sea-side and enjoy their rounds of golf because their women-folk also pursue the game, instead of boring themselves to death in sea-side lodgings talking scandal or reading trashy novels. Women can now also take an intelligent part in golf conversation and their knowledge of the game and its terms has rendered golf a topic of conversation between the sexes, which until lately it has not been.'[53]

Notes

1 F.C. Steadman, *In the Days of Miss Beale*, London, 1931.
2 K. Waldron, Hockey for Ladies', *Lady's Realm*, 1898, quoted in K.E. McCrone, 'The Lady Blue', *IJHS*, September, 1986, p. 197.
3 See D. Birley, *Sport and the Making of Britain*, Manchester, 1993, pp. 309–10.
4 There had been a similar split led by Blackheath who had formed a Hockey Union which favoured a rough-ground, free-ranging version with crude sticks, a hard rubber puck and much wild hitting , but this had given way to the Hockey Association's politer version and wound up in 1895.
5 *Bath Journal*, 16 February, 1884 (*OED*).
6 It was 1904 before England were beaten in the Irish matches. Wales, who were accorded matches in 1898 did not achieve so much as a draw until the 1930s. Scotland did not enter the scene until 1903.
7 Calcutta needed watching in the matter of cups. It had been the disbanding Calcutta Rugby Club in 1877 that offered the balance of its funds to the RFU for a trophy to be competed for on the lines of the FA Cup. Fortunately they had left it open to the RFU to choose an alternative use and they had preferred the much more gentlemanly option of putting it up as a trophy for the winners of the annual England v. Scotland match.
8 Quoted in S. Fletcher, *Women First, The Female Tradition in English Physical Education, 1880–1980*, London, 1984. See also J. May, *Madame Bergman-Osterberg*, London, 1969.
9 J. Arlott (ed.), *The Oxford Companion to Sports and Games*, Oxford, 1976, p. 431.
10 For Miss Faithfull, a leading figure in the development of women's sport, not only an enthusiast but a fine teacher and administrator and a person of great charm and diplomatic skills, see K .E. McCrone, 'Emancipation or Recreation? The Development of Women's Sport at the University of London', *IJHS*, September, 1990, p. 211. For early women's hockey generally see M. Pollard, *Fifty Years of Women's Hockey*, London, 1946.
11 Stanley Christopherson of Uppingham who played cricket for Kent and (once)

for England and later became President of MCC.

12 This was part of a uniform one of the students had devised: knee length tunic with box pleats front and back, over knickers and stockings below and a jersey or cotton blouse according to season above.

13 Ann Pagan, *St George's Chronicle*, May, 1894, quoted in K.E. McCrone, *Sport and the Physical Emancipation of Women, 1870–1914*, London, 1988, p. 223.

14 AEWHA minutes 4 November, 1898, quoted in McCrone, *Physical Emancipation*, p. 132.

15 P. Lawrence, 'Games and Athletics in Secondary Schools for Girls', *Education Department: Special Reports on Educational Subjects*, London, 1898, vol. II, pp. 145–58.

16 Quoted in Foreword to Pollard, *Fifty Years*.

17 Quoted in N.L. Jackson, *Sporting Days and Sporting Ways*, London, 1932, pp. 134–5.

18 N.L. Tranter, 'Sport and the Middle Class Woman in Scotland', *IJHS*, May, 1989 p. 44.

19 Sir Philip Sidney had celebrated rustic female stoolball in his pastoral *Dialogue between Two Shepherdesses* in 1586. In the early nineteenth century Miss Christina Willes was said to have shown the possibilities of round-arm bowling, introduced controversially by her brother John, by her bowling action in their family games, necessitated by her crinoline skirt. W.G. Grace himself paid tribute to his mother's wise counsel and encouragement in his childhood days, and his daughter Bessie was a celebrated woman player.

20 McCrone, 'Lady Blue", p. 203.

21 J. Park 'Sport, Dress Reform and the Emancipation of Women in Victorian England', *International Journal of the History of Sport*, May, 1989, p. 17.

22 Quoted in K.E. McCrone, *Physical Emancipation*, p. 144.

23 *Ibid.*, p. 144.

24 Advertisement in *Lillywhite's Cricketers' Annual*, 1892, quoted in R. Hayhoe-Flint and N. Rheinberg, *Fair Play: the Story of Women's Cricket*, London, 1976, p. 25.

25 McCrone, pp. 144 and 200.

26 McCrone, 'Lady Blue', pp. 204–5.

27 *Ibid.*, p. 205.

28 C. Dodd, 'Rowing' in T. Mason (ed.), *Sport in Britain*, Cambridge, 1989, p. 298.

29 Originally a North American Indian game, baggattaway, it had acquired its cachet in Victorian England from exhibition matches one of which had been watched by the Prince of Wales. The men's game had taken root chiefly in the area round Manchester where school and Old Boy clubs were its mainstay, but exhibitions and visits from American and Canadian clubs helped to keep it alive in London and elsewhere in the south. There were also Scottish and Irish Unions and 'home internationals' were played from 1875.

30 This section draws on a variety of sources, including as well as those specifically noted, B. Darwin *et al*, *A History of Golf in Britain*, London, 1952: R. Browning, *A History of Golf*, London, 1955: G. Cousins, *Golfers at Law*, London, 1958, *Golf in Britain*, London, 1958, and *Lords of the Links*, London, 1977; J. Lowerson, 'Golf' in Mason, *Sport*, and *Sport and the English Middle Classes, 1870–1914*, Manchester, 1993, pp. 187–214.

31 1744 compared with St Andrews' mere 1754 .

32 The epithet 'Royal' had been freely bestowed on elite sporting clubs since William IV had honoured St Andrews in 1834: the Prince of Wales was always ready to extend his patronage for a good cause. But it was a highly valued caste-mark.

33 There had, of course, been earlier competitions for gentlemen: see Birley, *Sport*, pp. 249–50, and, for the case of Douglas Rolland and Mr John Ball jnr, p. 320.

34 The Open Championship (started by the West of Scotland innovators, Prestwick, in 1860) had alternated between there, St Andrews and the Honourable Company's links at Musselburgh since 1872 . The Amateur Championship moved sedately between St Andrews, Prestwick, the Honourable Company's splendid new Muirfield course, Hoylake and Sandwich, which were also, in the 1890s, given the honour of staging the Open.

35 See Birley, *Sport*, p. 321.

36 Irish Field, 29 July, 1922, quoted in W.H. Gibson, *Early Irish Golf*, Naas, 1988, p. 55.

37 Tom Morris, Senior, first greenkeeper and professional golfer at the R&A, won the Open Championship Belt three times before 1868 when he was surpassed by his son, 'Young Tom' who won the Belt outright. Tom junior had died, aged 25, in 1875, but Tom Senior, who outlived him by many years, became the doyen of the old school of golf professionals. His advice was much sought after in the construction of new courses in England, notably North Devon. His brother George laid out the course and George's son Jack was the first professional at Hoylake, which produced the phenomenal young English amateur, John Ball.

38 19 April, 1890, quoted by Gibson, p. 31.

39 Gibson, *Irish Golf*, pp. 226–7.

40 *Ibid.*, pp. 212–13.

41 Lowerson, *Sport and the English Middle Classes*, pp. 145–6.

42 Commoners' rights came to the fore again in the slightly changed social circumstances and greater over-crowding of the Edwardian era, and there were some long drawn out legal battles (notably at Mitcham where assertive local golfers were a problem) but the issues were gradually resolved largely in the golf clubs' favour with the aid of sympathetic magistrates, socially conscious councils, a few concessions and some hefty legal fees. For a fuller account see Lowerson, *Sport and the English Middle Classes*, pp. 144–131.

43 P. Dobereiner, *The Glorious World of Golf*, New York, 1973, pp. 167–8, gives the date as 1900.

44 W. Park, *The Game of Golf*, London, 1896.

45 Lowerson, *Sport and the English Middle Classes*, p. 143.

46 The most popular of the several explanations of the name is given in *OED*, 2nd edition, 1989. The term is still used, but as standards have risen the value of a bogey score has diminished.

47 M. Stringer, *Golfing Reminiscences*, London, 1926, quoted in Park, 'Sport, Dress reform', p. 20.

48 Gibson, *Irish Golf*, p. 105.

49 *Ibid.*, p. 179.

50 *Ibid.*

51 Tranter, 'Sport and Middle Class Women', p. 37.

52 *Ibid.*

53 Gibson, *Irish Golf*, p. 117.

CHAPTER SIX

The old order

For all the advance of the middle classes and the mutterings of democracy some things had not changed. 'In those days', wrote Winston Churchill recalling the spring of 1896, 'English society still existed in its old form. It was a brilliant and powerful body, with standards of conduct and methods of enforcing them now altogether forgotten. In a very large degree everyone knew everyone else and who they were. The few hundred great families who had governed England for so many generations and had seen her rise to the pinnacle of her glory, were inter-related to an enormous extent by marriage . . . The leading figures of Society were in many cases the leading statesmen in Parliament, and also the leading sportsmen on the Turf. Lord Salisbury was accustomed scrupulously to avoid calling a Cabinet when there was racing at Newmarket, and the House of Commons made a practice of adjourning for the Derby'.[1] This elite remained a powerful and cohesive group regardless of the swings of party political fortunes.

Social continuities

The point had been brought home during the Liberals' return to power after the General Election of 1892. Gladstone, by then eighty-two, made one more assault on the Irish question, but retired two years later when the House of Lords rejected his second Home Rule Bill. He was succeeded by the 5th Earl of Rosebery, chosen by Queen Victoria over the heads of senior but more radical Liberals. Not that she admired him personally, for he was a member of the Prince of Wales's raffish Marlborough Club circle of which she strongly dis-approved, but he was sound on the things that mattered, Ireland and the Empire. Indeed his out-and-out imperialism and thorough-going dedication to establishment values were a great embarrassment to the Liberals. Invited to leave Oxford because of his activities on the Turf, he joined the Jockey Club at 23 and his principal achievement as Prime Minister was that in those brief sixteen months his horses won the Derby twice. This made him immensely popular with the sporting public but less so with his Cabinet colleagues, many of whom shared the Queen's belief that the Turf was corrupt.

The Liberals' only success was achieved in spite of their leader. The Anglo-Scottish patrician Rosebery, his vast estates secured by marriage to a Rothschild heiress, opposed the party's proposal to introduce death duties. It was steered through the House of Lords nevertheless by Hartington, now the eighth Duke of Devonshire, Lord-Lieutenant of Derbyshire and of County Waterford, a landed Liberal Unionist whose self-interest was more enlightened. This 'punitive measure' – a mild 8 per cent – and Gladstone's earlier palliatives, allaying rural discontent even on the Celtic fringes, proved a helpful legacy to Lord Salisbury's Tories when in alliance with Devonshire and Chamberlain they took office in 1895. The alliance was sustained by the swelling tide of imperialism, the claim of Queen and country that grew stronger than ever as the indomitable old lady approached her Diamond Jubilee.

There were some superficial paradoxes. Balfour, Salisbury's heir apparent, liked modern games (lawn tennis, cycling and, of course, golf) and, unlike the departed Rosebery, his contemporary at Eton, who hated games, had no taste for traditional aristocratic sports. Yet Balfour, also an Anglo-Scottish patrician and an intellectual opponent of science, was modern only in his sporting tastes. It was the older Devonshire, a hunting man in his youth, still fond of shooting and fishing, and addicted to the turf, who strongly supported Cambridge University's awakening interest in applied science, who had first made common cause with the modernist provincial Chamberlain and who balanced the feudal responsibility of land ownership by keen interest in his urban properties in both Eastbourne and industrial Barrow. So unimpressed by the trappings of political power as to refuse the premiership three times, the Duke's reputation for lavish entertainment, at his house in Newmarket as well as Chatsworth and in town, was enhanced by marriage late in life to the flamboyant widow of the Duke of Manchester. The Duchess's fancy-dress party in July 1897 was the highlight of the Diamond Jubilee season. The brilliant array of distinguished guests, dressed up as the great figures of history, represented the social forces, above and beyond party politics, that really mattered. Foremost amongst them was the heir to the throne, the ultimate symbol of unity, waiting impatiently in the wings.

The Prince of Wales found it easy to rise above party politics of so convoluted a nature, particularly since his mother had always steadfastly refused to allow him any responsibility or authority. Rosebery had, as Foreign Secretary in earlier times surreptitiously showed him a few documents, but he was too indiscreet and lacking in seriousness to become involved in affairs of state. In an important sense this made his social influence so much the greater, leaving him free to undertake the role he so much loved, of arbiter of fashion and custodian of the code of honour. His spiritual level was that of the Jockey Club, the Royal Yacht Squadron, the shooting box, the salon and the card-table. If he fell short of the expectations of the aristocratic elite it was because his expensive tastes and inadequate income had driven him into the company of the Jews and *nouveaux riches* who were insidiously creeping into the inner circle.

Hunting feels the pinch

The Prince was not a hunting man, partly because he had grown too fat, but partly because of his leaning towards the faster pleasures. Deer-hunting, once the royal sport, had dwindled with the supply of game. Wild red deer were hunted only in Devon and Somerset, and even there the supply was fitful and uncertain. The sport was chiefly continued by carting captured deer to convenient locations and releasing them a few minutes before the hounds. There were a score of such de-natured hunts, mostly in the Home Counties, including the much-derided Royal Buck Hounds, maintained by the public purse at a cost of £6,000 a year and favoured by undiscriminating social climbers. By far the best was the Vale of Aylesbury, where the Rothschilds provided lavish entertainment entirely at their own expense. *The Field* greatly perturbed its readers in 1892 when it inadvertently included an article which equated hunting carted deer with bull-baiting and badger-hunting,[2] but it amply made amends by printing many glowing accounts of 'grand runs' by fashionable groups like the Dragoon Guards Stag Hounds.

Hare-hunting, the gentlemanly as opposed to the truly noble sport in the medieval hierarchy, survived rather better. Its social prestige was assured as long as the hunting was done on horse-back and the quarry was indeed a hare not a rabbit. The Royal Harriers, unlike the Buckhounds, had interested Prince Albert and the young Prince of Wales. This had given the sport a certain cachet, especially amongst the well-born but indigent, and a fair number of new packs had been started. An Association of Masters of Harriers and Beagles was formed in 1891 and by the turn of the century there were nearly a hundred packs in membership, all of them riding to hounds. Beagling on foot, an even more economical alternative, was much less prestigious, but there were packs in the leading Oxbridge colleges and, notoriously, at Eton, not yet wholly converted to muscular Christianity. Edmond Warre, the headmaster, in fact managed to reconcile support for beagling with membership of the Windsor branch of the RSPCA, somewhat to the embarrassment of their national headquarters.

The RSPCA, the emblem of bourgeois morality, felt itself on firmer ground in condoning fox-hunting. Though opposed to hunting on ethical grounds, the Society was not prepared to condemn chasing foxes until some less cruel alternative form of controlling these vermin was devised. This was just as well, for the once-despised fox was, *faute de mieux*, what the best people now chased.[3] For the true aristocrat, fox-hunting had come to symbolise a way of life, an important but costly tradition that it was their duty to maintain. The nineteenth Lord Willoughby de Broke, who had followed his father and grandfather as Master of the North Warwickshire, afterwards recalled the county hierarchy in the 1890s. The Master of Foxhounds was second only to the Lord-Lieutenant and ranked above his fellow-landowners, the Bishop, the chairman of the quarter sessions, the Colonel of the Yeomanry, the MPs, the Dean, the Archdeacons, the Justices of the Peace, the lesser clergy and the bigger farmers.[4] The fifth Earl Spencer, a pillar of the Liberal Party and a member of every Gladstone government, was himself Lord-Lieutenant of Northamptonshire when he returned for a third spell as Master of the Pytchley from 1890 to 1894. (He was also Chairman of the County Council, an additional task that many aristocrats nowadays felt it their public duty to undertake.)

It says much for the powerful grip of the old order that the nostalgic appeal of the countryside and its traditions noted in Chapter One helped the late Victorian aristocracy to save their own 'field sports' – hunting, shooting and fishing – from the fate of the common people's 'blood sports' – cock-fighting, animal baiting and the modern urban pleasures of dog-fighting and ratting – which had been suppressed or driven underground earlier in the century under the pressure of middle-class morality. For decades now, however, this neo-feudal style had been threatened. Good hunting country was fast being eroded by urbanisation. London, Bristol and Birmingham had taken huge bites out of Hertfordshire, Surrey, Gloucestershire and Warwickshire; North Durham, South Yorkshire and Lanarkshire were on their way to destruction.

The sport had survived only at some social sacrifice. As a modern chronicler put it, 'hunting on balance benefited greatly from the growth of towns and their wealth: if the South Notts and Warwickshire fields were sometimes unmanageably swollen, subscriptions were plumper too'.[5] But the tone had deteriorated badly, and the wealthy vulgarians, commuting by rail, exemplified by Surtees' fictional London grocer, Jorrocks, had taken their place in the demonology of the chase. With the supply of 'old money' that had sustained the family packs of the past rapidly drying up, few could afford to reject the opportunity of the new. Even the superior Quorn had acknowledged this: 'The sporting proclivities of the city of Leicester are increasing in proportion as its hosiery and elastic web manufactures grow in importance', as a contemporary put it.[6]

The real problem came indeed when there was no convenient supply of new money. Whole districts, with perfectly good hunting territory, sometimes dropped out of the reckoning. This was especially true of Scotland where Aberdeenshire, Perthshire, Forfar and later the Lothians had lost interest. East Somerset was the greatest and least explicable loss – 'rural, rideable, with the right amount of covert, and with a long and lively fox-hunting tradition' – yet neither the gentry nor the farmers now showed any interest.[7] The farmers' support was everywhere hard to come by: now that times were hard they had every excuse to express their social resentment. Being patronised by the aristocracy and gentry had been tolerable in the old days when the great landowners had offered free sport to their friends, neighbours and favoured tenants, but the subscription pack whose members were required to contribute to the master's expenses were now the norm.

Another threat to the hunt was the vogue for shooting. Its popularity with the plutocratic infiltrators of high society, enhanced by the early nineteenth century introduction of the battue, intensified the historic antipathy between hunters and shooters.[8] Parvenus apart, shooting landowners' gamekeepers were not always above poisoning or even shooting foxes in their zeal to protect game birds and their eggs. For one reason or another, though they were often forced into uneasy alliance in fending off the moralistic criticisms of bourgeois town-dwellers, there was rarely entire goodwill between hunting and shooting devotees. Norfolk was a notable exception, probably because of the generally unspoiled nature of the terrain which left plenty of room for both: certainly relationships were worst where industry and urbanisation had made the biggest inroads.

Farmers who did not hunt could be a fearful nuisance. In extreme cases they might commit the unpardonable offence of shooting foxes. More frequently they annoyed the hunters by the growing practice of using wire for fencing. Ordinary wire, which had been in use since the 1850s was bad enough: barbed wire, which came in from America in the 1880s, was worse. In the best hunting country, given reasonable goodwill towards the master, farmers might set it out in full view with posts; elsewhere it might be entwined through the tops of thorns, hard to see and very dangerous. Many small tenant farmers genuinely could not afford to ignore such a cheap new aid. But there were other reasons, rarely openly stated. One was 'pure bloody-mindedness' on the part of the 'socially resentful or personally vengeful' farmer. Another, even less talked about, was that 'large landowners, pretending to be friends of fox-hunting in order to retain local popularity, used it or allowed it to be used so that they could save money to spend on their race-horses, their pheasant shoots, or, worst their hunting establishments in other (hunting) countries'.[9] At first Masters of Hounds had tried to persuade farmers to build fences or plant hedges instead, and they enjoyed some success. 'But by 1900 money talked louder than Masters of Hounds.'

The hunts were fortunate indeed if they had an old-style magnate who could still afford to keep up the traditional standards like the hunting dynasties of the Dukes of Beaufort at Badminton and the Dukes of Rutland at Belvoir. Their despotic power could cheerfully be borne in return for free sport. But even they had been obliged eventually to ask for subscriptions and Rutland was forced in 1891 to cut down his hunting from five to four days a week: when he retired in 1896 the sporting press described it as 'a national calamity'. That same year the archetypal Anglo-Irish loyalist, Harry R. Sargent, published his tribute to this vanishing breed.[10] In an impassioned passage he urged Radicals and Socialists to 'ponder well before they strive to injure the classes who maintain our sports. Let them recognise the fact that, as a universal benefactor in bringing to the poor the rich man's money, A SUBSTITUTE FOR SPORT CAN NEVER BE FOUND'.[11]

His argument was based on returns collected from over 300 hunts of all types throughout the United Kingdom. There were by then 16 packs of staghounds (three in Ireland) and 128 harriers (25 in Ireland) but the great majority in numbers and importance were foxhounds. The bulk of the expense was borne by the master, especially in the fashionable hunts: 'To fox-hunt a country in the style Lord Waterford did the Curraghmore, or as his father-in-law, the Duke of Beaufort, does the Badminton, would cost annually, at the least, a thousand pounds . . . for each day a week they hunt.'[12] Most hunts did not manage more than three days a week but even so Sargent reckoned the average annual cost of the packs, some 9.000 couple of hounds in total, ranged from £650 a year for foxhounds to a mere £200 for harriers, an aggregate total of £414,850. Then came the cost to the hunt members:

> Each Hunt has an average field of, say, 100 hunting men, each of whom has, say, three horses in his stable. That gives us 99,000 hunters. These cost fifteen shillings a week per annum to keep, which amounts to a total of £3,861,000 . . . We can, therefore, put down the bare cost of maintaining the Hunts and keeping the hunters of the United Kingdom at over four millions and a quarter per annum; and this prodigious sum includes none of the 'extras' contingent upon hunting, such as mansions and houses taken for the hunting season, entertaining friends, covert hacks and carriage horses, travelling expenses, red coat, top boots and breeches, or the many gratuities which render the hospitality of hunting men proverbial.'[13]

Nevertheless the ungrateful peasantry continued to show their resentment, especially on the Celtic fringes. Ireland was, of course, the worst affected. Most hunts had suffered first from the backlash of the famine and then the Land League agitation. In Scotland, where unsuitable terrain, urbanisation the claims of shooting and deer-stalking, and general loss of interest were bigger problems, the opulent Eglinton traditions of eccentric tyranny continued but the Duke of Buccleuch's vast territory was eaten into by less fashionable hunts. The context was, however, one in which such hereditary lowland Parliamentarians as Lord Haddo were defeated at the polls and crofter candidates ousted landowners throughout the Highlands. Similar changes occurred in Wales, where the Williams-Wynn family were thrown out of their Denbighshire stronghold after two hundred years and, unable to win the seat back, eventually retired from politics. Sir Watkin Williams-Wynn, whose uncle, the sixth baronet, had started the first pack to be taken seriously in England, was indefatigable in the pursuit of excellence but the other historic family packs suffered changes. Their efforts at recovery were recorded with some facetiousness by a modern English chronicler: 'The Flint and Denbigh (Puleston family) was re-established as an independent hunt, at first with names of great length and strangeness. The efforts of the Ynysfor (Jones family) were supplemented by professional fox-catchers, of whom the most famous were women.'[14] The Pryse family's vast Goggerdan in Cardiganshire, known for its rough-coated Welsh hounds, hunted otter as well as fox and its Plâs Maccynlleth off-shoot started with harriers.

In England some of the rich new masters who came in had more money than breeding. Sir Bache Cunard of the Liverpool shipping family was a notable example. Hence the Earl of Lonsdale, a fervent hunter of distinguished lineage, seemed heaven-sent when the Mastership of the Quorn became vacant in 1893. "It is an open secret', declared *The Country Gentleman*, 'that there is in our midst the ideal man, a good sportsman, a fine horseman, of a personal popularity with all classes – the farmers especially – to give fox-hunting a new lease of life.'[15] Unmentioned but undoubtedly the main attraction was his money. The £3,000 a year the Quorn guaranteed him in subscriptions was only a fraction of what he spent. His huntsman, Tom Firr, and the hunt servants were the best turned out in the country in their white leather breeches and dark red coats, mounted on long-tailed, long-maned chestnut thoroughbreds. The farmers certainly loved Lonsdale, but his tyrannical methods pleased no one else: as *The Field* put it in April, 1894, 'Men and women obey Lord Lonsdale as well as trained wolves obey their instructors, going only at the word of command.' His sharp tongue and humourless insistence on perfection soon wore out his welcome with the members. For his part Lonsdale, too, was growing disenchanted and in 1896 only a petition from the farmers induced him to stay on. (He lasted only two more seasons: in 1898 he was obliged to resign when, with his iron-ore mines beginning to peter out, the trustees of his estate grew alarmed at the enormous expense, much of it in farmers' damages and poultry claims.)

Though hunting remained a man's world its elevated social status had meant that historically women, or at least some of them, had featured from time to time in the annals of the sport. For the most part, despite occasional aberrations,[16] they had ridden in long skirts and side-saddle. As hunting had become faster and more dangerous technical improvements to saddles, riding habits and girths had made it possible for this decorous practice to continue. They still nevertheless encountered male hostility to the invasion of their territory but this had been gradually lessened by a slight but perceptible softening of male hunting manners. Circumspection was always required, not only to overcome male prejudice but to avoid the trap of unfemininity – as Trollope shrewdly observed, 'the young lady who has become of the horse horsey has made a fearful, almost fatal mistake'.[17] But riding was not restricted to the young: 'A middle-aged woman of fortune can do anything she likes without exciting the anxious sympathies of lookers-on, whether she is ducked in a brook or rides home in a fly *tête-à-tête* with a horse-breaker.'[18] Ladies of all ages continued to 'ride jealous and to over-ride hounds: and they were far harder to stop than men, especially if their husbands or fathers were big subscribers'.[19] One thing none of them was yet allowed to do, however, was to ride astride, still less to flaunt themselves in breeches.

The shooting set

Queen Victoria had shared her late husband's distaste for the horsey set and was indignant on his behalf at the opposition to his free-trading ideas by 'gentlemen who did nothing but hunt all day, drank Claret or Port Wine in the evening and never studied or read about any of these questions'.[20] The Prince of Wales, in his younger days, had enjoyed an occasional day out with Lord Macclesfield's South Oxfordshire, Henry Chaplin's Blankney, the Pytchley or the Belvoir. His mother did not entirely approve, though she much preferred fox-hunting to the extravagant cruelty of pheasant-shooting, to which he was addicted. There was more to the Prince's addiction than simply blood-lust. Shooting parties were one of the best settings for the discreet extra-marital sexual liaisons in which the Victorians specialised. The Earl of Lonsdale, one of the rare breed who both hunted and shot with equal seriousness, also enjoyed this aspect of the sport.

The Prince of Wales rarely went to the same parties as Lonsdale, however. This was partly because he could not afford to risk further censure from his mother and the serious newspapers by being seen too often in the circles frequented by the impious Lonsdale. (In 1884, for instance, Lonsdale had been involved in an unseemly public brawl in Hyde Park with Sir George Chetwynd, another horsey type, over Lillie Langtry, the Prince's former mistress.) The heir to the throne, who handled his own sexual affairs more discreetly, had aroused public scandal in 1890 when his involvement in a case of suspected cheating in a game of baccarat led to his appearance in the witness box in a libel suit. The following year when Lonsdale invited him to a pheasant shoot the Press were quick to criticise: 'The announcement that the Prince of Wales intends to pay a long visit to the notorious Lord Lonsdale at Lowther Castle serves to set wagging again the tongues of scandal.'[21] The visit was cancelled.

The Prince had other reasons for staying away. Lonsdale was a friend of the German Kaiser Wilhelm II, of whom the Prince was extremely jealous. For some years Britain and Germany had enjoyed peaceful relations, fostered latterly by the prudent German Chancellor, Bismarck, and Victoria herself was an admirer of anything that reminded her of her beloved Albert. For his part the young Wilhelm had assiduously courted her favour. Lonsdale and the Kaiser had much in common, including love of display and a strong sense of their own importance. Lonsdale was very proud of holding the honorary post of Master of the Horse at the German court, to which he paid frequent visits. The full effects of the Kaiser's dismissal of Bismarck in 1890, in pursuit of his aggressive new policy of attempting to re-capture former German glories, had not yet become apparent. So when Lonsdale entertained the Kaiser at Lowther Castle in 1891, although there were some snide press remarks about 'Wilhelm's English pal' and the like, there were also some sycophantic comments: 'Lord Lonsdale is in very truth a Prince in his own county' was one that cannot have been well received in Marlborough House.[22] The entertainment was certainly on a princely scale. Deciding that his own moors were unworthy of the occasion, Lonsdale hired the Earl of Strathmore's Wemmergill for the 'glorious Twelfth'. Five hundred brace of grouse were shot in four drives. Lonsdale also thoughtfully arranged for a little wood to be stocked with rabbits which could be released at a strategic moment during a short stroll through the grounds.

Anything more strenuous, such as tramping the estate on foot, shooting at wild birds in the old fashion, was distinctly out of favour. The shooters' code of honour, never an impressive affair, had long since extended to include blazing away at a succession of specially reared game birds driven overhead by beaters. Socially, it was much easier for would-be country gentlemen to learn than hunting and far easier to gain acceptance by offering the prospect of huge bags of game to influential friends and neighbours. Yet some of the most fervent shots were aristocrats, notably Lord de Grey and his kinsman, Lord Walsingham, two of the deadliest performers in England. One of de Grey's numerous records was shooting 920 rabbits in a day out of a total of 5,086 killed at Rhiwlas, North Wales, in 1885. Rabbits were not the serious end of the sport, however. In 1888 Walsingham accomplished a remarkable feat described in admiring detail by Harry R. Sargent: 'On his Blubberhouse moor, in Yorkshire, on August 30, 1888, Lord Walsingham made the largest bag of game ever made in a day to one gun. It totalled 1,058 birds and was made between 5.15 am and 7.30 pm. He had twenty drives, which occupied seven hours and twenty-nine minutes, the rest of the time being spent in waiting for the drivers or in picking up the birds. From 7 to 7.30 was spent in walking home, during which fourteen birds were shot . . . Four guns were used, and two loaders employed. Not a shot was fired by anyone but Lord Walsingham.'[23]

The justification for this mayhem, according to its supporters, was in the economic benefits it bestowed. The Highlands of Scotland, already enjoying the touristic advantages conferred by the coming of the railway and the fashion set earlier in the century by the visits to Balmoral by Victoria and Albert, now experienced an unprecedented vogue. Deer-stalking, stylised in the same way as game-shooting, had its own devotees, for whom the competition lay in the size, symmetry and number of points on the antlered heads they displayed. But the grouse moors were even more sought after. The sporting brewers Guinness, Bass and Whitbread had all purchased estates in Scotland in 1885, and not long afterwards Cecil Rhodes rented a shot on Rannoch Moor for two months at a cost of £2,000. Harry R. Sargent regarded this too as a kind of social service. Though the capital investment was a good deal less than hunting (£4.5 million compared with over £11 million) this was still substantial, and the annual turnover, £6 million, was much the same. Scotland alone had some 3,300 shoots, either let to tenants or used by their owners. Each employed a keeper at about £1 a week and two assistants at 15s, not to mention two additional gillies at 25s a week during the six-week season. The rental yield of these moors, at 3s 6d a week for the season, which averaged out at about 7.5d a week over the year, left little if any margin. The chief beneficiaries, he reckoned, were the crofters and labourers, followed by the tradesmen and their employees.

Even so, we might add, the Duke of Sutherland could well afford to set aside 212,658 acres of his 1,358,000-acre estates (rental income £141,000 a year) for grouse-shooting. The Duke of Buccleuch, who drew £217,000 from his 460,000 acres, was even better placed. And, as Sargent himself noted, a laird could get a return per acre about twice what could be expected from a sheep-farm 'without any trouble to himself, besides being able to sell off the sheep at the price he paid for them'.[24] Grouse, unlike pheasant, cost nothing to rear. Still, it was undoubtedly an expensive business. Dogs had to be bought, or bred and reared, and fed. Sargent reckoned that some £42,000 a year was spent on cartridges (at 1½d each) in Scotland alone, and perhaps three times that amount in England.[25]

Pheasant shooting was a particular cause of annoyance to many farmers, especially when the landlords sold their surplus. One of Gladstone's modest concessions to the farmers had been the Ground Game Act, 1880, which gave them the right to shoot hares and rabbits, but they were still not allowed to kill any of the winged game that gorged their crops. Some went to law over it, and in one or two cases shooters had had to pay damages for keeping an 'excessive' amount of game. A writer in *Land and Water* summed up the situation judiciously. 'Before the Ground Game Act was passed, we have heard occupiers cry out if there were half-a-dozen rabbits. Now as they have an equal right to the rabbits and hares, the complaint is as to winged game.' Pheasants were the problem – 'We have never heard yet of an action where it was sought to recover damages for partridges or grouse' – and then only when bred to excess. 'The reasons are obvious when we hear that an exalted personage is going to honour Lord A. by shooting with him . . . We confess to having very little sympathy with the man, whether the great landowner or the rich sporting tenant, who, to enable him to swagger as to having had the largest bag of the season at his shoots, gets up an abnormal head of pheasants.'[26]

The great landowners were less given to swaggering than the rich sporting tenants, for economic as well as social reasons. Game-dealers frequently made arrangements with landowners to dispose of what they and their guests shot but could not eat. Nevertheless Lord Walsingham, who overdid things somewhat, eventually had to sell up his estates and spend the last seven years of his life abroad. Hence the increasing preponderance of brewers like Sir Edward Guinness (later Lord Iveagh) and wealthy Jews like Sir Ernest Cassel in the best shooting circles. Lord Winterton complained in his memoirs that shooting meant 'eating too many big dinners, meeting too many rich Jews, and shooting too many fat pheasants.'[27] Sargent's analysis omitted, indeed, an essential factor in the increase in costs – the element of competition, not only in the pursuit of game but in the ostentatious display of hospitality, between these plutocratic sportsmen.

Even the Prince of Wales, who relied greatly on the hospitality of others, spent three times the £7,000 annual rental from his Sandringham estate in making a show of reciprocation. Consequently he was intent on making the most of the pheasant and partridge for which the estate was renowned. Sandringham clocks were kept half-an-hour fast to squeeze in more daylight for shooting. Under his watchful eye the annual bag of game rose from seven thousand to thirty thousand birds – and still he never seemed satisfied. He was not a first-rate shot, nor did those who were first-rate feel comfortable shooting alongside him, for whilst he would allow difficult targets to whizz past he would afterwards claim all the fallen birds in his vicinity if he could get away with it. He felt truly proprietorial, wanting to offer good sport to his cronies but determined to get his share of the credit.[28] Nevertheless, he passed the acid test amongst the sport-loving public. As Sargent admiringly declared, 'HRH the Prince of Wales, than whom there is not a better sportsman in Great Britain . . . gives away, mostly to his tenants, all the game which is shot in his preserves except what is used in the Royal Household.'[29]

In cold blood

Fishing, the third of the traditional triad of field sports, had a much better chance of commending itself to urban moralists. It was by common consent a 'gentle' sport, its image enshrined by literary associations, from the legendary Dame Juliana Berners' medieval treatise[30] through Izaac Walton (whose *The Compleat Angler* (1654) was one of those classics held in reverence even by those who had never read it) to nineteenth century scholars like Sir Humphry Davy[31] and statesmen like Viscount Grey of Falloden.[32] It was as much a part of the mythology of rural England as dancing round the maypole or watching cricket on the village green. Anglers were thought to be a contemplative, mildly eccentric set inclined to exaggerating the size of fish that got away but benignly throwing little ones back in the water unharmed. And they aroused less antagonism than the practitioners of other field sports, because fish, being cold-blooded, were deemed to feel no pain.

Though it held little appeal for the more ostentatious, or for party-going, restless types like the Prince of Wales, fly fishing was, nevertheless an elitist sport, refined from its rustic origins by improved equipment and accessories, special clothing and elaborating mystiques, and protected from vulgar invasion by the creation of a category of game fish (salmon and trout) which frequented the pure, swift-running chalk-streams of the great estates, as distinct from coarse fishing in the more sluggish canals and waterways of the flatter, industrialised regions. Urbanisation had enhanced the social status of 'getting away from it all', not least to Scotland and Ireland, where game fish abounded; but this was for most a holiday expedition and the pressure on game waters within weekend striking distance of the great cities of England and Wales mounted in the last quarter of the nineteenth century. Landowners put up their rents accordingly, and in 1879 the government began to take its cut by introducing game rod licensing. Still the demand grew. By 1900 the *Fishing Gazette* was reporting that the cost of a season's fishing on the preserved waters of the Hampshire Meon was £50.[33] Pisciculture became a thriving, minor industry.

According to Harry R. Sargent fishing was putting some £500,000 annually into circulation to the great benefit of the poorer classes, particularly in

Scotland and Ireland where the need was greatest and the sport best found. English equipment-makers did not do badly either. Hardy Brothers of Alnwick, previously gun-makers, had begun to develop their rod, reel and tackle business in the 1870s, and by the 1890s they were inviting comparison with the leading American firms. An article in a local newspaper at the time recalled the boldness of their innovation in opening their new factory 'thus introducing to that neighbourhood an entirely new industry. They had an up hill task to begin with, but north-country determination, a prolific inventive faculty and sound workmanship carried them through.'[34] Their customers soon included not only leading anglers, but persons of social distinction at home and abroad, including Prince Albert Victor, King of the Belgians and the ubiquitous German Kaiser.

Their annual catalogues were treasure-houses of anecdote, instruction and entertainment as well as mere advertisement.[35] The classic rods of 1888 were the Alnwick Greenhearts (from 9 ft to 30 ft in length and costing from 30s to £5 7s 6d), the Perfect Test, the telescopic Red Spinner and the General Rod 'made to the order of H. Cholmondely-Pennell Esq. and approved by him as the best for general work'. Ten years later came The Ideal, a trout rod 'fitted with Cork Handle, Patent "Universal" Winch Fittings and Bridge Rings, Five Guineas. If with Steel Centre, Six Guineas'. Esoteric trout flies were offered at 2s a dozen. Testimonials to favourite rods provided an excuse for boasting of a kind that might otherwise have been thought unseemly, and sometimes, contrary to the general perception, revealed a willingness to let blood as fierce as that of the hunters and shooters. Thus 'M B' wrote in 1887, 'My take this year has been 506. I credit the rod with 1,226 deaths since it has been in my possession.' And another grateful correspondent – evidently not above a spot of coarse fishing, too – looked back from 1902 on a gory record lovingly kept: 'The number of the slain appears from my angling record to be as follows:

> 560 salmon up to 32 pounds
> 275 white trout up to 5¾ pounds
> 20,066 brown trout up to 4 pounds 14 ounces
> 1,040 perch up to 1¾ pounds
> 15 pike up to 10¼ pounds
> 56 eels up to 5½ pounds, or a total of 22,157 fish.

Of the other coarse fish I have kept no record, but had I done so the total would have been considerably increased.'

Sporting criteria were much discussed, not least the use of tackle that was not too heavy for the particular fish. This sin was amongst the many attributed to lower-class despoilers of the fly fishers' sylvan idyll. Andrew Lang, the Anglo-Scottish 'man of letters', returned to Scotland in the 1890s and was distressed at what he found: 'The Glenaber burn is about 20 miles from any railway station, but on the last occasion when I visited it, three louts were worming their way up it, within twenty yards of each other, each lout, with his huge rod, showing himself wholly to any trout that might be left in the water.'[36] For resident Scots, in fact, salmon-fishing was another mixed blessing conferred by the railways, romanticised images of Highland mythology and lowland Tartanism. To the celebrated stereotypes – Queen Victoria's outspoken retainer John Brown, monosyllabic golf professionals, and gardeners who tersely kept their masters and mistresses in line – was added the canny gillie. All were dependent on English patronage and suffered from English humour only slightly less crude than that directed at the Irish.

In England meanwhile the new urban lower middle class, and, increasingly the working class, found coarse-fishing the best possible escape into rural bliss. They were to be seen in increasing numbers on the banks of canals, reservoirs and slow-moving rivers of the plains near the great industrial centres. Many were members of angling clubs, started in the 1870s in London and the great northern centre Sheffield (where the particular industrial structure of the cutlery and other steel trades gave skilled workers an unusual degree of independence in the matter of taking time off). These clubs were often adjuncts of friendly societies and either thus or independently frequenters of sympathetic, entrepreneurial public houses where they were welcomed as convivial but respectable customers. Angling clubs formed themselves into larger associations, initially to negotiate access to rivers at reasonable rates and to arrange cheap day excursions into the countryside, and afterwards to organise competitions. These last, which were anathema to the fly fishers, helped to widen the social gulf between the two main angling factions, and to extend the 'north–south divide', as the Sheffield pattern of development was copied in other industrial conurbations.

The basic division between coarse and game fishermen both symbolised and helped to explain why working-class angling developed separately and was more free of the inhibitions and hypocrisies of the fly fishermen. Similarly coarse-fishing became a favourite target for the moralists who complained of its associations with drink, with Sabbath-breaking and with gambling. Idealists on the other hand pointed to its ameliorating effect on the uncouth habits of the urban artisan, though in fact this might have been greater but for the almost complete absence of women from this end of the sport. Whereas fly-fishing attracted quite a few ladies from the upper reaches of society, working class women had neither the leisure nor the support of their husbands to join in their jaunts. Working class angling succeeded without the benefit of tutelage in organising skills from the middle classes, and without aping their values, largely because of the powerful attraction of competition, which brought professionalism (albeit of a minor kind) and gambling in its wake.

The Turf

A much greater source of concern for the working-classes' improvident habits lay in the oldest and most prestigious aristocratic competitive sport, horse-racing.[37] The great summer folk-festival on Epsom Downs, the Derby, and the springtime excitements of the Grand National were accidental by-products of an elite tradition which pervaded even the common passion for gambling that sustained it. The gaming laws had always been selective and the reforming Act of 1853 which distinguished between 'the legitimate species of betting' at the actual races and off-course betting had reflected the fear that 'working men, induced by the temptation of receiving a large sum for a small one' might be 'driven into robbing . . . their employers',[38] and whilst hundreds of betting shops catering for small 'investors' had been closed down, the Jockey Club, the alliance of powerful owners who governed racing, had had sufficient members in the House of Lords to secure exemption for private transactions like those conducted at Tattersall's subscription rooms in London and Newmarket, which were for vastly greater sums. The Act, furthermore, did not stamp out the little man's off-course betting, but simply drove it under-ground – or rather round the street corner where the bookies' runners lurked and betting slips furtively changed hands. And, whilst backstreet bookmakers hired look-out men to warn them of police approach, their on-course colleagues sought official protection from the race-gangs who preyed on them. In 1892 a group of leading bookmakers approached the Jockey Club for protection, offering funds for the 'raising and maintenance of a body of detective police' to control these 'desperadoes'.[39] The Jockey Club declined the responsibility.

Aristocratic disdain for the bookies extended also to the public who made use of them. Crowds were a nuisance that could be tolerated once a year at Epsom but were distinctly unwelcome at the Jockey Club's headquarters at Newmarket. At less fastidious centres the clientèle were often an unrefined and unruly bunch especially since charging admission, which meant enclosure, was thought impractical. Urbanisation, the railways and greater working-class leisure had increased the perils. Government action in concert with Jockey Club licensing had led to the closure of the worst metropolitan tracks which had been run on starkly commercial lines. They had been replaced however by more respectable but distinctly unaristocratic enclosed suburban courses first at Sandown Park and later Kempton Park, Gatwick, Hurst Park and Lingfield which offered Saturday afternoon meetings. The syndicates which ran them followed Sandown's lead (1886) into 'companification'. The Jockey Club set a dividend limitation of 10 per cent but this was still a healthy enough return.

Income from admission charges meant that the promoters could provide bigger prizes and thus attract the best horses. They offered programmes that were interesting to spectators – short distances, handicaps and races for two year-olds – with an element of genuine uncertainty and a lively betting market correspondingly less open to the sharp practices that characterised many of the older races. Though lacking tradition and social prestige the new-style race-meetings soon put some of the old open courses out of business and jolted the complacency of the committees who controlled the destinies of celebrated ones like Goodwood, Doncaster and York and even Ascot. Enclosure also assisted control over those admitted and allowed the exclusion of the old cock-fights, and stricter control over the activities of card-sharps, tricksters and operators of gaming booths.

As the atmosphere grew politer the proportion of respectable women amongst the spectators gradually increased. The older courses had always been patronised by ladies of fashion and some of loose morals. Both required seclusion. A private carriage was needed at Newmarket. There were private stands and boxes at Epsom, Goodwood and Ascot – a box at Ascot cost ten guineas. The Park courses began to change these mores somewhat by starting race-clubs, with carefully scrutinised admission, whose members could buy ladies' badges for a small extra charge. The members themselves were, of course, exclusively male, as were those of the Jockey Club itself. Convention required horses racing under Jockey Club rules to be owned by men. This was something of a charade. Everyone knew, for instance, that Caroline, widow of the fourth Duke of Montrose, kept horses in training, and ran them under the name of 'Mr Manton'. Lillie Langtry, whose profitable liaisons had made her into a race-horse owner, raced as 'Mr Jersey'. These subterfuges were well known and well publicised in the sporting press, but for the Victorian Turf appearances were all that mattered.

The greater emphasis the new courses placed on prize-money was a trend the older ones were obliged to follow. In 1886 Sandown Park had offered the largest prize for a single race so far known – £10,000 added – and this started a steady spiral amongst its rivals, first the new ones, then the old. By the turn of the century the total value of prize money on the English Turf had risen to £450,000. This in turn gave added incentive to owners to keep horses in training – the numbers went up from about 2,500 in 1869 to nearly 4,000 in 1902. More importantly for the aristocratic owner-breeders, the value of horses went up even more dramatically, and the cost of stud fees, which had been 40 or 50 guineas in the 1870s became anything from 200 to 300 guineas. Breeding, the gentlemanly end of the business, was a marked impediment to Harry R. Sargent's trickle-down theories. Xenophobia came to his rescue. The British, he reckoned, had been lamentably foolish in failing to take advantage of their opportunities and were being out-manoeuvred by 'wily foreigners'. Honest Britishers put a lot of money and effort into breeding the best horses and then, when they had taken all the risks, foreign investors came along and took their pick of the crop. But in fact some British breeders did well out of foreign sales. When the Earl of Lonsdale left the Quorn in 1898 he sold his hunters for no less than 18,000 guineas, many of the best going to the Kaiser. And race-horse breeding was vastly more profitable.

The bloodline was considered all-important, and careful note was taken of the success of progeny of great horses, particularly stallions. Hence the great reputation of St Simon, who had never been entered for the classic three-year-old races, but was leading sire nine times between 1890 and 1901 – measured by the value of prizes won by his off-spring. It cost 500 guineas a time to secure his services. The sixth Duke of Portland, St Simon's owner, had thus secured a great bargain when he bought him as an unconsidered two-year old for 1,600 guineas. Portland was himself leading owner in 1888, 1889, and 1890, winning prizes amounting to around £125,000 in those years alone, and though there were some successful owners of less blue blood, notably those associated with the bookmaking profession, generally speaking the aristocracy, given reasonable prudence and the wherewithal for initial capital investment, could hope at least to offset most of the costs of their sport.

Bigger prize money also meant a bigger share for successful trainers. John Porter, who trained his seventh Derby winner in 1899 (his third for the Duke of Westminster) won £56,546 for his owners that year and they were no doubt suitably grateful. Though trainers were still, in the peculiar neo-feudal hierarchy of the Turf, regarded as tradesmen, they were often very substantial tradesmen indeed. The best usually came from the ranks of successful and intelligent jockeys, who often had family connections with the leading stables. They less frequently nowadays served their apprenticeship on the Flat, where light weight had become an all-important consideration, but both Richard Marsh, leading trainer in 1897, 1898 and 1900 and Porter himself were amongst the many who had gained their experience in National Hunt racing, which still offered an outlet – at heavier weights – for the 'gentleman rider'.

Such recruits from the ambivalent social milieu of steeplechasing helped the gradual rise in status of the trainers many of whom had originally been former grooms and the like, mere horse-keepers. But there was a vast gulf between them and the racing managers and advisers of the great, drawn from the scions of noble families like Lord Arthur Somerset and his successor Lord Marcus Beresford, equerries to the Prince of Wales. The Hon. George Lambton, brother of Lord Durham, a member of the Jockey Club, was the first to cross the social gulf. When his career as a gentleman steeplechase rider was brought to a premature end by a fall he became a trainer – not a racing manager but an out-and-out trainer. He was the first of such elevated rank to take up this socially suspect but highly lucrative trade, but he paved the way for others. It was an ideal occupation for unintellectual sprigs of the nobility. Some knowledge of horseflesh, a little capital, a little luck and – perhaps above all – the right connections were all that was required.

Lambton himself never looked back after the sixteenth Earl of Derby sent him his horses to be trained. Furthermore he retained his social standing: he hunted all winter, usually with the Grafton or the Pytchley, sharing a hunting box near Market Harborough with Count Charles Kinsky, and, in summer, as the gossip columnists, ever mindful of social niceties, were fond of pointing out, would go round his racing stables in a faultlessly cut Saville Row suit, with a flower in his button hole and wearing brown and white buckskin shoes. He was, they made clear, a 'gentleman trainer', not to be confused with his humbler brethren. Even the training reports in the sporting prints referred to him as *Mr* Lambton: the rest were, like professional cricketers, thought unworthy of such a prefix.[40]

There were more harmful snobberies. A feudal facade concealed a situation in which professional jockeys (of whom the leading group of eight or ten were probably making £5,000 and more in a season, from riding fees alone) and the bookmakers and betting syndicates with whom many of them worked, ran a modern version of the old aristocratic 'system of plunder'.[41] The Jockey Club was greatly handicapped in its occasional attempts at reform by reliance on a code of honour which assumed, against the evidence, that a gentleman's word was his bond and that he would not stoop to sordid behaviour with persons of inferior social status. These assumptions were rudely shattered by Sir George Chetwynd, a Steward of the Jockey Club and a crony of the Prince of Wales. It was common gossip that Chetwynd's horses were not to be relied upon, especially when ridden by Charles Wood, champion jockey in 1887. At the annual Gimcrack dinner that December the guest speaker, Lord Durham confirmed the family reputation for unorthodox integrity[42] by speaking critically of the in-and-out running of 'a certain stable', adding that had he been the owner of the horses concerned he would have insisted upon an enquiry into their performance. Chetwynd, recognisably the owner concerned, protested at this caddish attack from a fellow-member and the Jockey Club set up a quasi-legal tribunal to investigate the matter.

It revealed a situation far worse than Lord Durham had hinted at. The trainer's role had been insignificant, Chetwynd and Wood had been fixing things between them, and Wood, furthermore, was the real owner of some of the horses, whilst Chetwynd, the pillar of the Jockey Club, was in effect a professional gambler aiding and abetting Wood in a racket. The result was characteristic of the Jockey Club's approach. The actual allegations made by

Lord Durham were deemed to be unfounded – as indeed technically they were – but the tribunal awarded Chetwynd only a farthing damages, a mark of censure that obliged him to leave the Turf. Disgrace and social ostracism were, so the code of honour deemed, sufficient punishment for gentlemanly transgressors. Wood, treated according to his rank, was struck off the list.

It was a sign of the times, many felt, that Wood was allowed to return to riding in 1897, celebrating his return by winning the Derby once more and eventually dying a rich man. In 1901 the Earl of Ellesmere, a former Jockey Club Steward, complained of the great pressure that was often exerted by owners to have such transgressors re-instated.[43] The fact was that little fellows of seven or eight stones with the necessary skill and experience were in very short supply, which in a competitive business meant that deviation from the highest moral standards was easily tolerated and sometimes encouraged. The leading jockeys, technically mere underlings, were not only very rich but often in effect the masters not the servants of the owners. If the traditional hierarchy of the Turf had been undermined by capitalistic values, the root cause was the venality of the owners themselves.[44]

The invasion

It was more usual to blame the influx of plutocratic newcomers who were diluting the old aristocracy. The Prince of Wales was a prime cause. His chronic shortage of money had been greatly eased by association with ultra-rich acquaintances whom he in turn helped to gain an entrée to all but the most select circles. When his exotic Jewish protégé Baron Hirsch, unable to buy his way into German society, came to England, rented a town house in London, a country house near Sandringham and a shoot near Newmarket, the Prince, as his sponsor, was chagrined that Queen Victoria declined to invite him to the Palace. The Jockey Club were more amenable. (Baron Meyer Rothschild, an earlier protégé, had made the grade in 1871.) Hirsch was an almost immediate success as an owner and HRH was able for the first time to take up racing seriously himself. Previously unable to afford little more than a few steeplechasers he now began to build up a stable on the Flat. Unlike those of Hirsch most of his horses turned out to be modest performers, however. The Prince's first trainer, the veteran John Porter, was unable to work the desired miracle quickly enough and HRH had no hesitation in awarding his custom instead to Richard Marsh, who had just removed to magnificent new stables reputedly costing £13,000 a year in upkeep. The change did the trick. In 1896 HRH's Persimmon won the Derby. There was no surer way for a public figure to gain popularity, and the vast crowd at Epsom swarmed on to the course, cheering and shouting. Even the Queen, no doubt relieved to find Bertie receiving favourable publicity at last, sent him a congratulatory telegram. Persimmon went on to win the St Leger, the Jockey Club Stakes, the Ascot Gold Cup and Sandown's opulent Eclipse Stakes and thereafter the Prince was a celebrated and successful owner. He was not an ungenerous one. His prize-money in 1896 totalled £26,819. Out of the £5,450 prize for the Derby he sent Richard Marsh £800: £500 for himself, £100 for the lad who 'did' Persimmon, £50 for the head lad, £50 for the travelling head lad and £100 to be shared amongst the other stable lads. At the end of the season Marsh received another £1,000 present. And in the following year, which brought Royal victories in the Ascot Gold Cup and Eclipse Stakes, he got another £1,000 bonus.

An increasing amount of the new money circulating in the upper reaches of British society came across the Atlantic. American plutocrats regularly visited Europe with their socially conscious wives and well-endowed daughters. Impoverished British aristocrats responded to the opportunity: one in ten fashionable marriages featured American brides. HRH courted the fathers. His circle of rich friends, like the Rothschilds, the Sassoons, Sir Ernest Cassel and Baron Hirsch, easily accommodated William Waldorf Astor who became a naturalised British citizen in 1891, and, on his way to a Viscountcy, sent his sons to Eton and Oxford. It was Astor's purchase of the Duke of Westminster's Cliveden estate in 1893 that led the *Estates Gazette* to comment, 'The American invasion of England has begun with a vengeance.'[45] Racing men were particularly apprehensive about the results.

The English Turf was in fact greatly assisted by the phenomenon. For most visiting American owners the appeal of tradition, aristocratic connections, display and pageantry was irresistible. And since their aim was amusement and cutting a social dash rather than seeking to make money the influence of men like J.B. Kane, August Belmont and the Whitneys, W.C. and J.B., was beneficial not only to the prosperity but to the integrity of the Turf. Nevertheless they were much resented, and there was an even more hostile attitude to the trainers and jockeys who came over in search of profit. One trainer who attracted spiteful comment from the anti-American lobby was the highly successful Enoch Wishard. To some extent their criticisms were based on envy and prejudice. The British had antiquated ideas about health matters: they had always worn too much clothing themselves, they lived in badly ventilated houses and they applied the same principles to training horses. They could not understand how Wishard's horses could look so well when he exercised them without swathing them in greatcoats and blankets. He was also known, however, to make liberal use of drugs. This was the practice in the States where distance made ten-day meetings a common feature: in England it was not illegal, but it was frowned upon and was usually associated with underhand dealings to achieve betting coups. There is no doubt that Wishard and his partner, Duke, found profit in losing as well as winning races, and in concealing the true form of their horses. These were, of course, age-old features of the English scene, but that did not excuse the incursion of these crafty foreigners. And since they tended to avoid the big races and to restrict their operations to the less fashionable courses they were better able to evade the attentions of the Jockey Club.

The Jockey Club were in any event inept and unscientific in their efforts to curb doping. They were more successful in combating the menace of the American jockeys who began to strut the scene adding to the problems caused by the increasing bumptiousness and doubtful methods of some of the home-grown breed. Lester and Johnny Reiff, brought over by Wishard, were highly suspect and they were watched very carefully indeed. But it was the brash and independent-minded Tod Sloan, immortalised in the musical 'Yankee-Doodle-Dandy', who first hit serious trouble. He had attracted attention, and some derision from envious rivals and other patriotic Britishers for the 'monkey-on-a-stick' style of riding he introduced. This technique, which involved standing up in the stirrups crouched over the horse's neck instead of the traditional method of sitting upright in the saddle with legs gripping its belly, proved annoyingly effective. On his first brief reconnoitring visit in 1897 Sloan cleared £2,000 over and above his expenses, which included considerable outlay on his much-publicised taste for wine, women and song. He did even better in 1898 and came over for the whole season in 1899. His compatriot Lester Rieff became champion jockey in 1900 by which time, as a contemporary observer noted, 'English jockeys had become exceedingly doleful that they were to be swept practically out of existence' by the Americans.[46] It was even rumoured that the Prince of Wales, putting patriotic considerations aside, had offered Sloan a 6,000 guinea retainer to ride for him in 1901.

Before that could happen Sloan had been told not to bother re-applying for a licence. He had been found guilty of placing a bet, which, since 1883, following an episode involving Fred Archer, had been illegal in England. Sloan's defence, though reasonable, was unavailing. He argued that his bet (for £2,000) was placed on his own account, which was quite legal in America: he also added that he knew of no jockey, on either side of the Atlantic, who did not bet. Little sympathy need be wasted on Sloan, who was also shown to have accepted a present from a professional gambler after winning the Cambridgeshire, but his crimes were different only in their scale and brash execution from the normal practice. Nor were those of Lester Rieff, who was warned off the following year for not trying to win a race at Manchester.

Soon, with British jockeys learning the American style of riding, and adapting it to English conditions, and assisted by the removal of this unfair competition, there were hopes of an early end to this particular transatlantic invasion. Soon, too, the Prince of Wales's rumoured offer to Sloan was forgotten as his appearances at the racecourse became occasions for expressing the intense patriotic emotions aroused by the Boer War. The popular fervour reached its height in 1900. At Aintree in April the Prince (wearing a brown bowler which thereafter became the latest fashion) was cheered wildly as his horse Ambush II won the Grand National. The news must have gladdened the heart of Queen Victoria, who, spurred by the presence of so many Irish soldiers in South Africa and reassured by the relative quiescence of this turbulent part of her realm, was paying a visit to Ireland for the first time in almost forty years. Carefully screened from protesters, the old Queen was able to enjoy the cheers of loyalists and, in a last attempt at pacification, was encouraged to take up the cause of Catholic education. Her return home also brought better news from the war. Mafeking was relieved from siege by the Boers in May, five days before her eighty-first birthday, and a new word, 'mafficking', was coined to describe the celebrations: six extra men were hired to deal with the congratulatory telegrams. There was further occasion for rejoicing in June when the Prince's colt, Diamond Jubilee, foaled in the year of that memorable event, won the Derby. The excited emotions of the crowd were heightened by rumours that Lord Roberts was on the brink of a great victory in South Africa: amid the thunderous applause and prolonged cheering, the crowd, many with tears in their eyes, began to sing 'God Save the Queen'.

Notes

1 W.S. Churchill, *My Early Life*, London, 1930, p. 97.
2 3 September, 1892, quoted in E.S. Turner, *All Heaven in a Rage*, London, 1964, p. 241. In fact carted deer were not killed, merely chased. The Royal Buck Hounds were eventually disbanded in 1902, unlamented, but avowedly as an economy measure, and the sport continued, led by the Rothschilds, and restricted only by the shortage of animals and the money to procure them.
3 For the changes in hunting fashion see D. Birley, *Sport and the Making of Britain*, Manchester 1993.
4 D. Cannadine, *The Decline and Fall of the British Aristocracy*, London, 1992, p. 356.
5 R. Longrigg, *The History of Fox-hunting*, London, 1975, p. 155.
6 *Ibid.*, quoting 'Brooksby' (Capt. E. Pennell-Elmshurst), *The Cream of Leicestershire*, London, 1883.
7 Longrigg, *Fox-hunting*, p. 155.
8 For the views of William Cobbett and of Parson Jack Russell, for example, see Birley, *Sport*, pp. 175 and 207.
9 Longrigg, *Fox-hunting*, p. 154.
10 H.R. Sargent, *Thoughts upon Sport*, London, 1896.
11 *Ibid.*, p. 292.
12 *Ibid.*, p. 80.

13 *Ibid.*, pp. 79–80.

14 Longrigg, *Fox-hunting*, p. 138.

15 Quoted in D. Sutherland, *The Yellow Earl*, London, 1965, p. 135.

16 J. Strutt, *The Sports and Pastimes of the People of England*, London, 1801, reprinted Bath, 1969, p. 8, describing a fourteenth-century illustration, commented that 'the female Nimrods dispensed with the method of riding best suited to the modesty of their sex' adding 'but this indecorous custom, I trust, was never general, nor of long continuance'. He cited also a seventeenth-century fashion adopted by huntresses at Bury in Suffolk for wearing breeches which 'gave rise to many severe and ludicrous sarcasms'.

17 A. Trollope, *Hunting Sketches*, London, n.d.

18 Longrigg, *Fox-hunting*, p. 145, quoting G.E. Collins, *Tales of Pink and Silk*, London, 1900.

19 *Ibid.*

20 E. Longford, *Victoria R.I.*, London, 1964, p. 295.

21 Sutherland, *The Yellow Earl*, p. 112.

22 *Ibid.*, pp. 115–6.

23 Sargent, *Thoughts*, p. 247.

24 *Ibid.*, p. 261.

25 *Ibid.*, p. 242.

26 *Land and Water*, 24 December, 1892.

27 Cannadine, *Decline*, p. 365.

28 For the Prince at Sandringham see C. Hibbert, *Edward VII: a Portrait*, Harmondsworth, 1982, pp. 94–5.

29 Sargent, *Thoughts*, pp. 242–3.

30 *The Treatyse of Fyshinge wyth an Angle*, added to *The Boke of St Albans*, 1496.

31 H. Davy, *Salmonia or Days of Fly-fishing*, London, 1828.

32 E. Grey, *Fly Fishing*, London, 1899.

33 *Fishing Gazette*, 10 March, 1900, quoted by J. Lowerson, 'Coarse Fishing and Working Class Culture', in *Pleasure, Profit and Proselytism*, ed J. Mangan, London, 1988.

34 *Newcastle Daily Journal*, 29 May, 1890.

35 Anthologised in *Hardy's Book of Fishing*, ed. P. Annesley, London, 1974, from which the extracts in this section are drawn.

36 A. Lang, *Angling Sketches*, London, 1891.

37 For early horse-racing see Birley, *Sport*, *passim*, esp. for the Victorian period, pp. 224–5, 228–304. For fuller treatment see W. Vamplew, *The Turf*, London, 1976, 'Horse-racing' in T. Mason, *Sport in Britain*, Cambridge, 1989, pp. 215–42 and *Pay Up and Play the Game*, Cambridge, 1988, *passim*; and D. Craig, *Horse-racing*, London, 1982.

38 Sir Alexander Cockburn, *Hansard*, 11 July, 1853.

39 K. Chesney, *The Victorian Underworld*, Harmondsworth, 1972, pp. 334–5.

40 M. Seth-Smith, *A Classic Connection*, London, 1983, p. 261.

41 Charles Greville, *Diaries*, pub. 1875–87, quoted in R. Mortimer, *The Jockey Club*, London, 1958, p. 74.

42 He was the son of the 1st Earl, the celebrated 'Mad Jack' Durham whose report on Canada had upset early imperialists.

43 Ellesmere, 'Concerning Stewards, *Badminton Magazine*, vol. 12, 1901.

44 Jockeys' and trainers' earnings and their relationships with owners are discussed in Birley, *Sport*, 302–4.

45 Carradine, *Decline*, p. 358.

46 'The American Jockey Invasion', *Badminton Magazine*, April, 1907.

CHAPTER SEVEN

Alien forces

The Prince of Wales's involvement in the Tranby Croft baccarat affair was only the latest of the many times he had outraged the public by his scandalous behaviour. The Queen had grown tired over the years of complaining about his conduct and his choice of friends. His Marlborough Club cronies were a regular source of anxiety. In 1889 one of them, an American, had turned out to be a swindler wanted by the police, prompting *The Times* in a leader on the occasion of his twenty-fifth wedding anniversary to urge him to master 'the unfortunate weakness which has led him to patronise American cattle-drovers and prize-fighters.'[1] The swindler at Tranby Croft was not an American but Sir William Gordon Cumming, a baronet and a Colonel in the Scots Guards. He was cashiered and expelled from all his clubs. 'Thank God! – the Army and Society are now well rid of such a damned blackguard', his former crony sanctimoniously observed. For HRH Cumming's crowning infamy had been to marry, on the very day after the trial, 'an American young lady . . . with money!'[2]

But there was more to link – and divide – Britain and her former colony than money. There was an increasing cultural exchange. America had long attracted vitriolic English writers in search of hair-raising copy; in the other direction had come the novelist Henry James in search of greater sophistication. Now from America came Buffalo Bill Cody's Wild West show, innumerable black-faced minstrel troupes, the evangelists Moody and Sankey and the entrepreneurial Phineas T. Barnum, who made a mega-star of a giant elephant, Jumbo, bought from the London Zoo. In the other direction after Oscar Wilde's lecture tour, expatiating on the aesthetic movement, had come Lillie Langtry, cashing in on her notoriety by appearing on the stage. America was also a tourist attraction for adventurous aristocrats. One was Hugh Lowther, the future Earl of Lonsdale, who claimed to have knocked out the bareknuckle champion, John L. Sullivan, in a private contest with gloves (so as to prove his point that, properly used, they were not the namby-pamby device Sullivan believed them to be). Another – somewhat less successful in his attempts to prove sporting points – was Windham Thomas Wyndham Quin, the fourth Earl of Dunraven, an Anglo-Irish peer, politician, race-horse breeder and yachtsman, who made almost annual visits between 1869 and 1896.

Yachting and the foreigners

Yachting was not like the Turf: it was much more elitist, an alternative summer recreation away from the crowds and the bookmakers. Indeed the purists, exemplified by the exclusive Royal Yacht Squadron, had in its early years turned up their noses at yacht racing, especially when it involved handicapping that threatened the in-built advantages of the bigger boats. However there had inevitably been a gradual increase in organised competition, the distinctive feature of the age, showing itself in the multiplication of regattas at every socially conscious resort and a proliferation of lesser clubs, still exclusive and often called 'Royal' but peopled by rich industrialists and other *nouveaux riches*. The RYS itself had been lured, disastrously, into transatlantic competition for the *America's* Cup, which had been held since its inception by the New York Yacht Club.[3]

These challenges in the biggest class of racing yacht had gone wrong for the British partly through inferior design but mainly because of the gentleman and players relationship between the owners and their professional crews. In 1887, with the RYS affecting lofty indifference – it was a long trip over and it meant forgoing a whole racing season at home – the challenge had been taken up by a Glasgow businessman James Bell of the Royal Clyde. The atmosphere before the race was soured by the efforts of his designer, G. L. Watson, to keep his plans secret and the subsequent discovery that the finished boat *Thistle* did not exactly conform to specification. And after the customary British defeat the slanderous rumours that John Barr, the professional skipper, had sold the race led to his taking up permanent residence in the States. *Thistle* continued to be highly successful in British waters, an ominous sign that was ignored or misread by the patriots. The quest was for bigger and better yachts that would – incidentally, of course – overshadow the Americans.

No fewer than four new Big Class yachts built to a controversial new design, featuring a 'spoon' or 'Viking' bow, came out in 1893. They were thought likely to set new standards, and one of them, *Britannia*, owned by the Prince of Wales was, on his own reckoning, 'the first yacht afloat'. He greatly enjoyed presiding over the annual festivities at Cowes of the RYS, of which he was Commodore, and now looked forward to cutting an even bigger dash. His hopes were rudely shattered, however, by his nephew, the egregious Kaiser Wilhelm II, whom the Prince himself had graciously proposed for membership but who had so far abused the privilege as to set out to become what HRH irritatedly called 'the boss of Cowes'. In this the Kaiser was mischievously assisted by the Earl of Lonsdale, who many thought something of an inter-loper at Cowes anyway.

No great yachtsman himself, Lonsdale had inherited his brother's yachts and in 1893 determined to use them to return the Kaiser's hospitality during his now annual visits to Cowes. By then even the indulgent Queen Victoria was tiring of her grandson's attentions, indicating that, since such frequent visits were 'not quite desirable', the Kaiser could not stay with her at Osborne House.[4] He stayed instead on his official yacht, the *Hohenzollern*, giving occasion to much Germanic naval display. Lonsdale was not a member of the RYS, and he was disinclined to put himself forward in the usual way (and run the risk of being black-balled by HRH). So, in effect, he assumed it. Admirals were automatically entitled to membership and his brother had been honorary Vice-Admiral of the Cumberland Coast. Lonsdale affected to believe the title was hereditary. It was not, and indeed had passed to someone else, but the assertion created sufficient confusion for Lonsdale to install himself at the Regatta on such a lavish scale that there could be no question of not giving him membership. To HRH's further chagrin the Kaiser's boat *Meteor* beat *Britannia* for the Queen's Cup.

That *Meteor* was in fact *Thistle* modified and re-named was not only a painful irony for the Prince but a further ominous sign for that year's *America's* Cup challenge. This, after protracted debate about the rules, was being mounted in earnest on behalf of the RYS by the erstwhile Under-Secretary for the Colonies, Lord Dunraven, an intellectual not to say pedantic fellow, with theories on horse-breeding as well as yachting. It was Dunraven's *Valkyrie II* that had set the new fashion and much now depended on her. She was defeated, but so narrowly that Dunraven was encouraged to try again. His hopes of success were bolstered when *Vigilant*, his 1893 conqueror, came over to Britain the following summer and in seventeen races against *Britannia* was beaten twelve times. One of the occasions, recorded in late 1894 by *The Field*, indicates the inordinate nationalistic importance attached to the outcome. 'Yacht-racing,' the report read, 'caught on in the South of England last season more than ever before, but it is doubtful if a match of any sort would ever attract such a multitude of people as lined the shores on Saturday last from Kirn to Dunoon and filled the steamboats to view the contest between *Vigilant* and *Britannia* for Her Majesty's Cup. It is true that the racing was stirring enough to have galvanised a mud engine into life, but such unbounded delirious enthusiasm as was displayed when *Britannia* won we should never have expected from the sober Scots folk. There were many reasons, however, for this. *Britannia* is a Scottish boat owned by the Prince of Wales and the Scots are nothing if not loyal: further she had defeated the representative yacht of America'.

The Americans, unfortunately, had a new representative, the *Defender*, which proved too good for Dunraven's *Valkyrie III* in the 1895 races. This was the year Dunraven fell out of love with America. He became convinced that the syndicate who owned *Defender* were out to do him down. Certainly C. Oliver Iselin, the designer and syndicate manager, had a reputation for acuity, but on this occasion at least he had attempted nothing untoward and Dunraven was completely nonplussed. He had not endeared himself to the organising committee by extreme fussiness about small points: he was particularly insistent on the re-calculation of time allowances if any alterations were made to the published dimensions of the boats; yet when the committee came to inspect *Valkyrie III,* he was not available to show them over. Having lost the first race he complained that the course had been crowded with pleasure boats. This was accepted, but Dunraven then made the mistake of accusing Iselin of having additional ballast illicitly stored on board overnight. This, of course, was a serious charge, equivalent to cheating at cards, but when it was refuted Dunraven, instead of apologising, drifted off into paranoiac, wild assertions. The second race began with a collision: Dunraven careered off to the finish as if he were the innocent victim but the committee found him to blame. Iselin sportingly offered him a re-run, but Dunraven refused in highly offensive terms. Finally he withdrew from the race amid accusations of fraud and returned home. When Dunraven repeated his allegations in *The Field,* the New York Yacht Club protested and asked the RYS to take up the matter. The RYS, cocooned in suspicion and xenophobic hostility, declined. The New Yorkers, left with no alternative, held their own inquiry, during which Dunraven grew angrier and more abusive, eventually resigning just before his membership was withdrawn.

The affair had become a matter of national honour and pride. Diplomatic relations were already strained. Politically the USA was as ambivalent towards Britain as the British were towards their former colony: anti-British feeling was still a good way to demonstrate independence and a Freudian cloak for the USA's own imperialist urges. It surfaced during Grover Cleveland's second Administration when, in July 1895, he invoked the Monroe doctrine (separation of European and Continental American interests) and intervened in a dispute between Britain and Venezuela over the boundaries of British Guiana. Kipling, who was living in the United States at the time, believed that war was near. He had been received at the White House, finding Cleveland and his circle 'reeking bounders', and torn between anger and fear made plans to evacuate to Canada in the event of trouble.[5] An alarming wave of jingoism swept the USA. The rumpus in the Press over Dunraven did not help. Not everyone took the matter entirely seriously. An English yachtsman cabled a friend on the New York Stock Exchange, 'If we come and bombard New York will you make sure your pleasure steamers don't get in the way?': the reply expressed the hope that in the interests of a well-fought contest the British warships were better than their yachts. But the general tenor of the editorials and correspondence columns was aggressive in the extreme.[6]

Equally, most loyal Britishers thought it high time the Americans were put in their place. Then with the RYS in a state of righteous indignation an unwelcome olive branch was offered to the NYYC by Mr Charles Rose, of the Royal Victoria YC, Ryde. Rose, the *nouveau riche* owner of *Satanita,* another of the 1893 Big Class yachts, proposed to build a new cutter to take up the America's Cup challenge. *The Field* described Rose's behaviour as 'off-hand' and likely to offend British yachtsmen. The rumour spread that the Prince of Wales, known for his love of moneyed Americans and his pretensions as peace-maker and arbiter, was behind the move.[7] Rose wrote to *The Times* denying it but few believed him. Finally Dunraven, in an interview, described the challenge as offensive – did not the American Press contend that it was a mark of censure on himself and a vindication of the NYYC? – and declared that Rose was not even British but an American. His shameful (Canadian) ancestry thus revealed, Rose prudentially withdrew his challenge.

The political crisis passed. Britain could not afford to quarrel with America: she already had enough trouble with the Boers in Transvaal and with Turkey (whose massacres in Armenia outraged civilised opinion in Britain, France and Russia but which was cynically supported by the Kaiser's Germany). Tactful statesmanship by Lord Salisbury saved the immediate situation. Chamberlain, who had an American wife, was active behind the scenes. Cleveland lost office and his successor, McKinley, took the safer route of tariff protection to safeguard American interests. The storm-tossed waves of the yachting world gradually subsided, but it was undoubtedly just as well that there were to be no more challenges for the America's Cup until 1899, by which time Dunraven was off the scene. The USA had by then found other outlets for her aggression in Cuba and Mexico. Chamberlain and Kipling resumed their pursuit of the somewhat romantic notion of an Anglo-Saxon transatlantic alliance. And having found triumphant satisfaction in Kitchener's methodical, devastating revenge for General Gordon's death at Khartoum Britain was focusing her attention on the coming war against the Boers and the attitude Germany might take towards it.

HRH had been suffering considerably from the Kaiser's increasingly arrogant behaviour. The beginning of the 1895 Cowes Regatta had been marked by his arrival in his official yacht accompanied by the German Fleet's two latest destroyers, *Wörth* and *Weissenburg,* named after victories in the Franco-

Prussian War, and on the twenty – fifth anniversary of the battle of Wörth he had addressed his sailors in such boastful terms that the Prince pronounced it an insult and a battle of words was launched in the newspapers of the two countries. Yet the Kaiser was entertained on such a lavish scale by the Earl of Lonsdale on his yacht *Verena* that many other yachts crowded near to try to catch a glimpse of the proceedings. The Kaiser added further insult by withdrawing *Meteor* from the Queen's Cup on the grounds that the handicappers were biased against him. Before leaving Cowes he approached G.L. Watson, *Britannia's* designer, and ordered a new yacht that was to be bigger and better than the Royal yacht. All of this was too much for HRH. He sold *Britannia* to John Lawson-Johnston, the Bovril millionaire, and withdrew from yacht-racing. 'The regatta at Cowes,' he complained, 'was once a pleasant holiday for me, but now that the Kaiser has taken command it is nothing but a nuisance . . . perpetual firing of salutes, cheering and other tiresome disturbances.'[8]

That winter British patience was further tried when the Kaiser (with whom Lonsdale was staying at the time) sent a telegram of congratulation to Kruger, the leader of the Boers, on thwarting the pre-emptive strike attempted by Dr Starr Jameson of Cecil Rhodes's British South Africa Company. Jingoist opinion had been roused and HRH suggested to his mother that Wilhelm needed 'a good snubbing'. [9] She counselled caution, rebuking HRH for his tendency to make sharp, cutting remarks which only caused irritation and did harm. Even she, however, was so upset by the Kaiser's attitude to Turkey that she declined to invite him to the Diamond Jubilee celebrations in 1897.[10] But nothing could stop his visits to Cowes. In 1899, in fact, his visit, which HRH had feared might be ruined, as in the past, by his overbearing Junker aides, had gone surprisingly well. The Kaiser did his best to charm everyone, he won much praise for coming to England at a time when anti-British feelings were running high in Germany, and his ostentatiously friendly intent was taken as an indication that he would not side with the Boers when it came to the point. It was unfortunate, however, that, although *Meteor II* proved irresistible, he should once again repeat his complaints about the 'perfectly appalling' system of handicapping.[11] HRH manfully bit the bullet and tried to overcome his scepticism as talk of an Anglo-German alliance was renewed.

He was much more enthusiastic about the renewal of diplomatic relations with the American yachtsmen signalled by a fresh challenge for *America's Cup*. The new challenger was his friend Sir Thomas Lipton, knighted the previous year with his strong support. Lipton was a typical product of the new mercantile Britain. Born in Glasgow of Ulster Catholic stock he had been a cabin boy on the Belfast boats at the age of thirteen, and spent five years in the States before returning to Glasgow to start the chain of grocery shops with

which by 1880, aged thirty, he had made his first million. He was an enthusiastic yachtsman – though his first notable boat, the giant steam yacht *Erin* of
1,240 tons was not the sort to please sailing purists – and his American
connections led him to turn his attention to *America's Cup*. In 1888 he had
offered to finance a challenge if a yacht could be designed, built and manned
by Irishmen, but as there was no suitable Irish designer, the idea fell through,
and the opportunity, for reasons already discussed, did not arise again until
1898, when the dust had begun to settle on the Dunraven affair.

Lipton was not, in spite of the support of HRH, a member of the RYS. He
was in trade, no matter on how grand a scale: "Why does the Prince of Wales
go yachting with his grocer?' the Kaiser asked. Other unkind people reckoned
his America's Cup venture was just a device to sell more tea, and Lipton
certainly made a point of saying that he hoped to benefit his shareholders by
the publicity. He also still hoped to bring work to his parents' native city of
Belfast, and when Harland and Wolff regretfully decided they lacked the
necessary experience to build the projected *Shamrock* gave the job to his own
native Clydeside instead. It was through the Royal Ulster Yacht Club that
Lipton conducted his negotiations with the NYYC. His challenge the following year, ending in cheerful defeat, did much to repair the damage done by the
patrician Dunraven, and left the RYS purists, rather like the MCC con-
templating Shaw and Shrewsbury's encounters with the Australians, not
quite sure which set of vulgarians to deplore most.

Lipton's rejection by the RYS emphasises that, according to the complex
rules of British snobbery, owning a big yacht was not in itself a guarantee of
entry. On the other hand it was no use applying if you did not own at least
one. The Squadron's motto was said to be:

> Nothing less than 40T
> May ever race with our burgee.

Happily they were not entirely typical. There had always been a few enthusiasts along the coasts who were prepared to rig up a mast and sail a converted
rowing boat, but hitherto the smallest manufactured yacht had been 17 to 19
feet, costing up to £75. It was in Ireland that regatta organisers first began to
recognise smaller craft for competition purposes and boat-builders to respond
to the commercial opportunity. In 1887 in Dublin Bay the Water Wags took to
the water – unballasted centreboard dinghies 14 ft 3 in long and costing, at
first, no more than £15 (demand later pushed up the price to £20.) Even in
England there were changes. On the Itchen at Southampton fishing or ferry
boats between 22 and 28 feet were converted for racing and manufacturers
later used these as models for purpose-built yachts. The Solent Club soon had
three regular racing classes up to 21, 25, and 30 feet. The Corinthian Clubs,

pioneers of the rare kind of amateur yachting in which the owners actually took the wheel themselves, were increasingly active, and the Royal Albert of London and the Royal Victoria of Ryde were two senior clubs that encouraged smaller class racing.

By 1888 10-, 5-, and 2.5-rated classes were fairly generally accepted and by 1895 the young Duke of York, the future George V, a former naval officer and a keen yachtsman, was racing in a new 1.5-rated class. Soon there was even a 0.5-rated class. This was the specialism of the Minima Club, London, which in 1895 challenged the Seawanahaka Corinthian Yacht Club of Canada to a series of contests. These were a great success. The Seawanahaka not only presented a trophy but raised a fleet of small boats specially for the purpose. At this level at least where the prestige of nations and the *amour propre* of great men was not at stake, it was possible to regard sport as an ambassador of good will.

The not quite noble art

One of the earliest British cultural exports to America was boxing. Cricket was introduced about the same time, but notwithstanding remarkable achievements amongst Philadelphian gentlemen in the nineties took root less strongly.[12] In boxing Americans had taken up the old bareknuckle London Prize Ring rules with such enthusiasm and success that the world champion, John L. Sullivan, the 'Boston Strong Boy' was reluctant to give them up in favour of the Marquess of Queensberry's marginally politer gloved convention. His view, which he endured repeated prosecution to sustain, still had followers in Britain. The Queensberry rules had two sections, one for amateurs and another for professional 'contests of endurance', and the latter had been much more controversial, especially amongst existing veterans. Rounds of fixed (three-minute) duration, followed by a minute's rest, replacing the conventions of the Prize Ring, where time could be called by one of the contestants dropping on one knee, required skilful footwork rather than brute force and gamesmanship, at which some old 'pugs' excelled. The prohibition on 'wrestling or hugging' was another unwelcome change for some. Few old campaigners liked the ten seconds recovery time allowed after a knockdown compared with the half-minute of the Prize Ring rules.

Most of all they disliked the use of gloves, which they associated with the 'mufflers' devised for the protection of gentlemen noviciates to the noble art of earlier days. Amongst the gentry innocent traditionalists such as Harry R. Sargent thought them an incitement to 'hammer-and-tongs' aggression in which a man could repeatedly batter an opponent's face without the restraining fear of breaking his knuckles. But a more typical opponent of gloves was the uncouth George Baird, the Scottish heir to an industrial fortune who liked to be known as 'Squire Abingdon'. Taking up with Lillie Langtry in the early 1890s he consoled her for occasional beatings-up and other humiliations with money, race-horses and a 220-ft yacht. A talented amateur rider who 'wasted' in time-honoured fashion on brandy and soda, a patron of the Turf and a lover of cock-fighting and ratting, the anachronistic and profligate Baird showed another side of British nostalgia.

Baird was an admirer of the shifty Cockney Charley Mitchell who had once taken advantage of Sullivan's casual and boozy approach to knock him out of the ring. In 1888 there was great excitement at the prospect of a return match under Prize Ring rules. The requirements of the law meant that it had to take place on Baron (Nathan) Rothschild's estate at Chantilly in France. There was only a handful of spectators – thirty or forty according to some accounts – no gate money, no purse, only side-bets. But the atmosphere was tense. Amongst the spectators, a reporter friend of Sullivan recalled, 'was Billy Porter, the bank burglar, who afterward died in the German salt mines. He had a revolver in each overcoat pocket, and notified those in Mitchell's corner that Sullivan was to have fair play. Sullivan got it.'[13] Mitchell's second was his father-in-law, 'Pony' Moore, the famous Christy minstrel,[14] who had bet everything he had on the fight. Mitchell preserved the family fortunes, if not its honour, by retreating rapidly throughout the fight, waiting for the champion to falter through exhaustion. After thirty-nine futile rounds, with icy rain falling, a draw was declared. The French police, lurking in the bushes, arrested both men immediately the contest ended.

Both Charley Mitchell and Jem Smith, the current British Champion, fought bareknuckle if they could but were obliged by the changing times to operate with gloves as well. Advocates of gloved contests, amongst whom the Earl of Lonsdale was prominent, maintained that as well as being legal they could offer just as good sport as bareknuckle. Their cause was helped by loopholes in the Queensberry rules. They specified 'fair-sized' gloves, and 'skin-tight' was sometimes deemed sufficient to meet the letter of the law. Furthermore the Queensberry rules did not specify the number of rounds to be fought in a professional contest, nor provide for a decision 'on points' to be decided by the referee or judges as they did for amateur competition. Consequently 'fight to a finish' was the usual arrangement, and there were some gruelling affairs.

Queensberry rules satisfied most members of the Pelican Club, the current arbiters of pugilistic taste. Their contests, staged after dinner, over brandy and cigars, for an all-male coterie were the height of fashion. Queensberry himself was a founder member, and Lonsdale was a leading light. Baird had joined, faute de mieux, but found it all rather tame. The club's finest hour came in 1889. Lonsdale had discovered a West Indian Negro, Peter Jackson, who had begun his boxing career in Australia, instructing at the San Francisco Athletic Club.[15]

Jackson's opportunities in the American ring had been limited by his colour[16] but Lonsdale persuaded the Pelican Committee to match him against Jem Smith. He was motivated less by a passion for racial equality than the desire to make a betting coup. Smith was the idol of the Fancy, and few could imagine him losing to this unknown. Lonsdale lengthened the odds by allowing no-one to see his protégé in training, keeping him secluded on his mother's estate at Cottesmore, and sparring with him himself in secret. The result was an easy two-round victory for Jackson. Smith's backers blamed the new rules for his defeat, but like it or not he had to get used to them.

Earlier that year Baird and a few other bareknuckle enthusiasts had matched Smith against a young Australian, Frank Slavin. The fight had to be held abroad – this time in Bruges – and two groups of rival patrons travelled across from England. From the outset the Smith-Baird camp, some armed with coshes and knives and even revolvers, did their best to intimidate both Slavin and the referee. Nevertheless after fifteen rounds Smith was clearly in trouble, and Baird, apoplectic with drink and frustration, gave the word for his men to 'do in the Australian bastard'; they swarmed into the ring, and one of them clubbed Slavin over the head. A Slavin man, Lord Mandeville, waving a bowie knife, kept them at bay long enough for the Australian to make his escape, but Smith's backers had achieved their purpose. The abandoned fight was declared a draw and they saved their money. Indeed the smart gamblers, some of whom had backed Smith 'not to lose', managed to make a profit.

This sordid episode marked the end of the London Prize Ring, but it also irreparably damaged the Pelican Club. Baird was expelled and soon afterwards took himself and Charley Mitchell off to America for a proposed bout for the heavyweight championship. But Mitchell, recently released from jail, was arrested on landing and Baird set out on a monumental binge, as a result of which he caught a fatal dose of pneumonia. A more serious loss for the Pelican Club was its boxing manager, John Fleming, who was caught up in the scandal. Efforts were made to start afresh, but the club was split down the middle and never recovered. Lonsdale, however, emerged as the upholder of 'clean sport' and set about protecting it from the attempts of the bourgeoisie to ban professional boxing altogether. An American promoter had brought over the Irish-born lightweight champion, Jack McAuliffe, to fight Slavin at the Ormonde Club. The police moved in and the magistrates set bail for both boxers. Slavin's backers hesitated, but, whilst they were dithering, Lonsdale not only put up bail for him but took over his defence. The Treasury solicitors withdrew the charges, and Lonsdale was the hero of the hour.

Lonsdale was the natural choice as President of the new National Sporting Club set up to replace the moribund Pelican in 1891, on the initiative of Fleming and the stern, uncompromising A.F. 'Peggy' Bettinson, who ensured high standards inside and outside the ring. Admission tickets, limited to 1,500, were priced in guineas not pounds. Dinner jackets were de rigueur for the members and their guests; they did not applaud during the contests (the term 'fight' was discouraged); they clarified and strictly applied the Queensberry rules, bringing in points' verdicts; and they did everything possible to ensure honest boxing – a tall order. The venture got off to a good start, and its success was assured by a spell-binding contest between Peter Jackson and Frank Slavin in which the excitement was heightened by the hushed appreciation of the spectators. The NSC became an institution and boxing gradually came out of the shadows.

The Marquis of Queensberry added a second string to his reputation for upholding the British tradition of decency and fair play when his denunciation of Oscar Wilde's 'posing as a somdomite' (sic) led to Wilde's prosecution in 1895 after lurid trials that made Lonsdale and HRH's heterosexual affairs seem harmless frolics. Poor Wilde had committed the ultimate Victorian sin of getting caught; Lord Arthur Somerset and Prince Eddy were more fortunate. Decadence was out: Kipling (or if you were Lord Salisbury, Alfred Austin) was in. And Kipling's belief in breaking rules for a noble cause was yet to send him beyond the pale.[17] Boxing was no longer the favourite form of institutionalised violence amongst the gentry. It had been supplanted by team games: but Thomas Hughes himself had deplored its fall from favour and many modern muscular Christians thought it bred in boys the admired British virtues of courage, self-control, and dogged endurance of pain. Its cause had been assisted by the Queensberry rules and their distinction between professional bouts and the three two-minute round amateur affairs with points awarded for style and disapproval of fighting. The Amateur Boxing Association (1880) had had an easy task in preserving purity: there were no 'shamateurs' in boxing.

At first many of the new amateur boxing clubs were socially restricted, but the sport in its modern guise admirably suited the purpose of those muscular Christians whose mission took them amongst the deserving poor. Amateur boxing was a splendid outlet for the educational and social ideals of Quintin Hogg's Regent Street Polytechnic and its several imitators, with their essentially lower middle-class clientèle, while for the university settlements in urban working-class areas boxing was an obvious way of canalising aggressions that might otherwise have found outlets in street violence and other anti-social activities. Church and other charitable boys' clubs took it up with enthusiasm, and found it an excellent source of new members, as did the YMCA, as it developed beyond its earlier interest in spiritual to corporeal matters. Works sporting clubs became keen supporters. Working men's clubs, especially in London, also formed boxing sections, and though their federal body, the Club and Institute Union, were cool about the idea, for ethical reasons, boxing contests had an enormous appeal to the run-of-the-mill membership and were a good way of raising money: a crowd of a thousand watched a contest at the United Radical Club in Hackney in 1891, for instance.

Amateur boxing spread from London in a similar pattern of social and regional diffusion to other sports. The public school and university men preferred to conduct their contests in private rather than in open competition, but the clear and natural Queensberry division and the consequent probity of the emerging clubs enabled the ABA to build up an organisation that devotees of all classes could join without sacrifice of the principles that had so clearly been put at risk in the other competitive sports with a mass appeal. There was soon, nevertheless, a plebeian cast to the proceedings. A polytechnic club member became an ABA champion as early as 1890, and in 1898 five of the finalists came from two polytechnics (Goldsmith's Institute and Finsbury). The first winner of an ABA title from outside England, also in 1898, was H. Marks of Cardiff Harlequin Harriers. It was very much a British enthusiasm. An American Amateur Athletic Union for boxing had been formed in 1888 but outside the English-speaking countries it was held in low esteem. De Coubertin and his aristocratic Continental associates would not countenance its inclusion in the 1896 Olympics, regarding it as ungentlemanly, dangerous and 'practised only by the dregs of the population', nor did it find a place in the Paris Games of 1900.

The fact had to be faced, furthermore, that amateur enthusiasm for boxing was inspired by the professional sport, which in its new legalised form was beginning to flourish with the greater urban prosperity of the nineties. Small local halls offered weekly shows and the sporting press gave wide coverage to bigger contests. Even the more fashionable end was not yet free of trouble, however. In 1897 the NSC found themselves in court again. Indeed they had to defend four cases of manslaughter in the next four years. Whether because, as the die-hards had argued, hitting with gloves inflicted more damage than hitting with bare fists, especially without the relief of bowing the knee, or whether from mischance, four boxers died from injuries inflicted in NSC rings between 1897 and 1901. On the first occasion both Lonsdale and Sir George Chetwynd appeared as expert witnesses. 'There is no brutality whatever in boxing when it is properly conducted', Lonsdale testified, 'and this one was properly conducted.'[18] The magistrate agreed with him. A year later a Grand Jury of the Criminal Court acquitted the NSC authorities in a similar case. When yet another death occurred in 1900 public opinion was both thoroughly aroused and thoroughly divided, and the NSC officials' appearances were alternately booed and cheered. The Grand Jury, reflecting this division, failed to return a true bill, leaving the issue unresolved.

By 1901 and the fourth death drastic measures were required, and the NSC engaged the great Marshall Hall to conduct their defence. His task was made no easier by the blood-curdling testimony of one of the defence's own witnesses, John Douglas, a former amateur champion, a noted referee and later President of the ABA. Still, with the help of more moderate evidence from Bettinson and the rest, Marshall Hall demolished the opposition and professional boxing, though still not declared legal, was allowed to continue. The Treasury solicitors had achieved little by their forays into court and they decided to let the matter drop. What the outcome would have been had the defendants been one of the small promoters in the provinces, unable to afford the services of a great advocate, must be a matter of speculation, but if boxing was no longer the 'noble art' it still had powerful backing and a firm place in British mythology.

Sadly for the nostalgic, it was across the Atlantic that the realities lay. The American authorities had clamped down on bareknuckle contests in 1890 and three years later Sullivan was knocked out in a gloved contest by 'Gentleman' Jim Corbett, and thereafter Queensberry held sway. Corbett spent most of his time as champion appearing on the stage but he had returned to the ring to brush aside Charley Mitchell in three rounds in 1894 and one of the abiding legends of the ring for British enthusiasts was the feat of the 'Cornishman' Bob Fitzsimmons in winning the heavyweight title from Corbett three years later. The British never tired of the stories, in the long years of American domination that followed, of how the bald, spindle-shanked veteran survived a tremendous battering for fourteen rounds before sinking his famous left-hand punch into the champion's solar plexus. But Fitzsimmons, although born in Cornwall, had left it as a child, and did all his boxing in New Zealand and Australia before sailing to California in search of fame and fortune. He never fought in Britain and by the time he beat Corbett his best days were over, as, in boxing terms at least, were those of his native land.

Notes

1 J. Brough, *The Prince and the Lily*, London, 1975, p. 285.
2 *Ibid.*, p. 293.
3 See D. Birley, *Sport and the Making of Britain*, Manchester, 1993, pp. 225–7, 292–4.
4 E. Longford, *Victoria R.I.*, London, 1964, p. 655.
5 A. Wilson, *The Strange Ride of Rudyard Kipling*, London, 1977, p. 259.
6 See I. Dear, *The America's Cup*, London, 1980.
7 Rose's late father was a Scot who had emigrated to Canada, where he had been a finance minister before retiring to England and becoming a banker. His many services to the Crown earned him a knighthood, as well as the post of receiver-general to HRH's Duchy of Lancaster estates.
8 C. Hibbert, *Edward VII: a Portrait*, Harmondsworth, 1982, p. 269.
9 *Ibid.*, p. 149.

10 Longford, p. 686.

11 Hibbert, *Edward VII*, p. 269.

12 For the story of US cricket, including the Philadelphian tours and the great bowler, J. Barton King, see J. Marder in E.W. Swanton (ed.), *Barclay's World of Cricket*, London, 1986, pp. 127–9. For early boxing links see Birley, *Sport*, p. 165 and *passim*.

13 A. Brisbane, *New York American*, 21 September 1927, reproduced in S. Andre and N. Fleischer, *A Pictorial History of Boxing*, revised edition, New York, 1987, p. 56.

14 The best-known of the black-faced minstrel troupes; organised by the Christy brothers of New York.

15 Lonsdale had been temporarily exiled in 1888 by the trustees of his estate, to give themselves a little financial respite and to allow his latest sexual scandal time to blow over. He had embarked, improbably, on an expedition into the Arctic Circle on behalf of the Scottish Naturalists' Society and had returned a year later by way of San Francisco.

16 Sullivan, who set the tone, openly boasted that his standing offer to fight anyone did not extend to blacks: 'I have never fought a Negro and I never will.' D. Batchelor, *Big Fight*, London, 1954, p. 70.

17 The discriminating first noticed the trend in *Stalky & Co.* in 1899.

18 D. Sutherland, *The Yellow Earl*, London, 1965, p. 171.

CHAPTER EIGHT

Home and colonial

Bob Fitzsimmons was part of an increasing trend. Between 1881 and 1901 nearly 5 million people left the United Kingdom to start a new life abroad – over 3 million from England and Wales, 1.3 million from Ireland and half a million from Scotland. The great magnet was the USA: over 60 per cent of the total and over 80 per cent of the Irish went there. Canada, despite assiduous attempts to attract settlers, though second, was a long way behind. Australia, even after the stigma of penal colonisation had faded, was a poor third. The flow to the 'white' colonies was to double in the new century but meanwhile their doings were much less familiar in Britain than those of the USA. For the rest of Britain's possessions there was a new rhetoric of imperialism. Joseph Chamberlain began his long spell in the important new office of Colonial Secretary by declaring idealistically, 'It is not enough to occupy certain great spaces of the world's surface unless you can make the best of them – unless you are willing to develop them.' The reality was that defending and consolidating the great spaces became the principal concern.[1]

Suspicion of Russian intentions towards India had led Britain into secret alliance with the Austro-Hungarian Empire and Italy for the defence of the Balkans and the Straits. All the European powers were engaged in grabbing and exploiting territories throughout Africa. Growing British domination of Egypt to protect the Suez Canal, the quickest sea-route to India, led to tensions with Russia's ally, France, the creator of the Canal, and was the background to General Gordon's troubles in Sudan. Similarly the strategic importance of the Cape of Good Hope. a longer but safer alternative route, made it important to keep a hold on Southern Africa. Fear of being attacked on two fronts by the Franco-Russian alliance led Germany into fitful attempts to strike accord with Britain, but the Kaiser also aspired to world-power status. Germany made a bargain with Britain in East Africa, (which sealed off Suez from the Indian Ocean) in return for Heligoland, strategically important for the development of her naval strength, but she also encouraged French ambitions to penetrate Sudan from the Upper Congo.

Britain's policy, involving no fixed alliances, had left her potentially isolated (so that she was temporarily disconcerted, for instance, by the Venezuelan affair) but she was strong enough to defend her interests if necessary and relaxed enough to be content, most of the time, with Lord Salisbury's shrewd policy of preserving the status quo. Above all she was convinced that British control was greatly to the benefit of all the inhabitants of the vast territories for which she was responsible despite their markedly different racial and cultural characteristics. This reassuring thought encouraged a sense of superiority in the British that found crude expression in the triumphalism of the Diamond Jubilee celebrations. This so offended Kipling, who saw the Empire as a serious responsibility not a toy, that he sent a poem to *The Times* about it. Humility not pride, awe rather than arrogance ought to be the keynotes of an imperial festival:[2]

> If, drunk with sight of power, we loose
>   Wild tongues that have not Thee in awe'
> Such boastings as the Gentiles use,
>   Or lesser breeds without the Law –
> Lord God of Hosts, be with us yet,
> Lest we forget – lest we forget!

The hymn-like cadences and Old Testament imagery admirably suited this stern message, and the poem struck a chord that impressed all but the most mindlessly jingoistic. Some radical intellectuals, indeed, misread Kipling's plea as a recantation of imperial conviction, but he made his point more clearly the following year in his appeal to the Americans to share in the task of development:

> Take up the White Man's burden –
>   And reap his old reward:
> The blame of those ye better,
>   The hate of those ye guard –

The white man's burden

The burden was greatly lightened by the games the white man took with him. This was initially nothing to do with imperialism. Victorian Britishers played games for their own recreational purposes wherever they happened to find themselves. Badminton was devised by Indian Army officers with time on their hands. Cricket, much earlier, had been the first export. The Navy played it against British residents in Chile and Buenos Aires and against the garrison in Gibraltar. Merchants and missionaries played it everywhere from Portugal to Shanghai.[3] That it could have a civilising influence on native populations in colonial territories was an incidental, later, discovery. In Fiji, acquired in 1874, the first governor believed that the involvement of locals in the improvised matches of transient mariners had led to a decline in head-hunting; and by 1895, the Attorney-General, J.S. Udal (MCC and Somerset) was able to tour New Zealand, with a racially mixed team including six Fijians – all chiefs, of course.[4]

Kipling, a more sophisticated imperialist, had less faith in cricket's magic. Kitchener, having avenged General Gordon's death, was raising money from the British to build a school for the Sudanese at Khartoum – and teach them cricket. Kipling depicted the reaction of a Muslim schoolmaster serving with the Bengal Infantry:

> How is this reason (which is their reason) to judge a scholar's worth,
> By casting a ball at three straight sticks and defending the same with a fourth?
> But this they do (which is doubtless a spell) and other matters more strange,
> Until, by the operation of years, the hearts of their scholars change:[5]

But what better to teach them than games? The fortunate pupils of Gordon College, Khartoum were taught not only cricket but Winchester's own variety of football.[6]

However, though the ethos of Empire-building through games was soon to be taken up in earnest, notably by the middle-class career civil servants who constituted the proliferating imperial bureaucracy, older traditions survived. The Army overseas, for instance, were mainly concerned with their own recreation and training, and they were just as interested in taking home the games they discovered in foreign parts as in spreading British culture abroad. The most prized discovery was the ancient Persian game of polo which they had come across in north-east India being played by the native aristocracy and the tea-merchants of Calcutta visiting their up-country plantations. Inter-regimental tournaments had begun out there in the 1870s but just as quickly the game also became the latest and most exclusive craze at home.

It took some time to spread beyond the elite regiments at the Hurlingham Club. Then things began to stir. As the 1891 *Badminton Library* volume put it, 'Many regiments took up the game; the Universities did the same; Hurlingham awoke to the fact that polo was becoming a popular amusement; the International Gun and Polo Club started operations at Brighton, and soon all chance of the game falling into obscurity was provided against.'[7] Its arrival in Dublin was recorded with suitable facetiousness. 'In Ireland polo rapidly advanced to a prominent position, while the "horseyness" of the game and the "scrimmage" so dear to the Milesian[8] mind caused it to be extremely popular amongst the masses who came "in their thousands" to look on in the Phoenix Park and pass their remarks on players and ponies – often perhaps in uncomplimentary language, but generally very much to the point.'[9] It had also been taken to America by James Gordon Bennett, Senior, who imported the neces- sary equipment and plutocratic enthusiasm, and by 1886 the Hurlingham Club was sending over the first of many visiting teams.

Polo, the *Badminton* author reckoned, was the queen of sports. For one thing it had 'the advantage of being devoid of the element of gambling which has tended so much to degrade many of our other sports. For it is a sport that induces men to run personal risks for mere honour and glory, a refreshing reflection in these days, when the widely different terms of "sportsman" and "sporting man" are so frequently confused by the ignorant.'[10] It was also the best preparation for life: 'no sport . . . makes a man more a man than this entrancing game, none fits him more for the sterner joys of war or enables him better to bear his part in the battles of life.'[11] Its place in the military scheme of things emerges clearly from Winston Churchill's memoirs. Churchill had learned the game at Sandhurst, and took it up seriously on being commis- sioned in the 4th Hussars, where it was a natural recreative offshoot of the cavalry training manoeuvres and equitation skills that were still considered essential to military success. Polo was the principal consolation of his service in India. Military duties were completed in the morning. In the heat of the day came six hours of siesta punctuated by lunch. Then at five o'clock 'the station begins to live again. It is the hour of Polo. It is the hour for which we have been living all day long'.[12] This daily routine was enlivened by regular competi- tions, sometimes regimental tournaments and sometimes even grander affairs involving native regiments as well. 'Tournaments in Hyderabad were a striking spectacle', Churchill recalled. 'The whole ground was packed with enormous masses of Indian spectators of all classes, watching the game with keen and instructed attention. The tents and canopies were thronged with the British community and the Indian rank and fashion of the Deccan.'[13]

Nevertheless it was inevitable that the Indian sporting scene in general should be as Anglicised as were the history and geography curricula of the leading schools. A good example was Calcutta, which we have already noted as an early centre of rugger and of hockey as well as polo. Calcutta, which had been the headquarters of the East India Company, was a big city, with well over a million inhabitants, and it was of great commercial importance. It had a correspondingly large garrison, together with hundreds of civilian admini- strators, educators and the like. There were scores of sporting clubs. Many were private, often exclusively European, with their own grounds. Even the less favoured had access to the Maidan. This was a huge open space in front of Fort William in the centre of the city, originally intended to provide a clear field of fire for the defensive guns. By the 1890s it had developed into a vast, sprawling sporting complex with golf courses, lawn tennis courts, bicycle tracks, riding paths and cricket, hockey and football pitches. Spectators could be accommodated, though charges usually went to charity.[14] Here was the missionary spread of British sport in action and here the social distinctions of the British sporting scene could be observed with native involvement complicating the situation.

When the Calcutta Football Club, temporarily eclipsed by the vogue for polo, was revived in 1884 it still tried to keep up rugby (considered superior, the official history makes clear, both in the Army and the Navy: 'Dartmouth, Sandhurst and Woolwich recruited potential officers from the Rugby playing schools').[15] After a few years, however, they were obliged to concentrate on soccer. This involved some social sacrifice. The Dalhousie, the earliest soccer club, had been founded by young business men and traces of this commercial origin remained in the Trades Cup, which was open to both European and native teams. In 1892 a Bengali team actually beat a British regimental side. When the Indian Football Association was formed (also in Calcutta) in 1893 its Shield knock-out competition was restricted to whites as was the Calcutta League in 1898. This was to be amended a decade later but the clubs themselves remained racially distinct and it was to be many years before the Indians achieved appropriate representation on the governing body.

Imperial values: the Harris years

Racial separation seemed natural to Lord Harris, who in 1890, after a short period in Lord Salisbury's government, became Governor of Bombay. Family tradition (Indian Army and colonial service) led Harris to a greater than normal interest in Britain's overseas possessions: his father was governor of Trinidad and of Madras. For him cricket was a matter for reverence, he had long believed in its power as an educative and unifying force and despite his early disappointment in New South Wales looked forward to the opportunity to put his ideals into practice amongst the Indians. As early as 1885 when the new-style imperialism was in its infancy he had affirmed the British undertaking 'to educate oriental people on western lines, to imbue them with western modes of thought and to strive at western systems of government'.[16] Now on the eve of his departure for Bombay he told his friends that 'he had done his best to further the interests of the noble game (in England) . . . and that he intended to extend his patronage to the promotion of cricket in India'.[17] He had mixed success. In his zeal for westernising the natives he swept aside questions of religion and caste in the cricket competitions he organised between Hindu, Muslim and Parsee. They played against white teams, though the resident British kept their own exclusive clubs free of native invasion. Not all Indians liked being westernised in this fashion and the rising

Congress party were highly critical of the Governor wasting his time on cricket when more important matters cried out for attention. Yet throughout his life Harris was to maintain that cricket had 'done more to consolidate the Empire than any other influence'.[18]

On his return to England Harris became President of MCC which he later described as 'perhaps the most venerated institution in the British Empire'.[19] He distinguished himself in 1896 by fiercely opposing the selection for England of the Indian Prince, Ranjitsinjhi, recently down from Cambridge University, and was frustrated only by the independent-minded Lancashire selectors who picked the team for the third Test on their own Old Trafford ground. (Ranji made 62 and 154 not out.) It was at this time, a contemporary recalled, that an MCC member told him he would try to get him expelled for 'having the disgusting degeneracy to praise a dirty black'.[20] Ranji himself was nevertheless a fervent imperialist. His book the following year, auspiciously called *The Jubilee Book of Cricket*, was dedicated in fulsome terms to the Queen Empress and in later years he described cricket as 'certainly amongst the most powerful links which keep our Empire together . . . one of the greatest contributions which the British people have made to the cause of humanity'.[21]

West Indians had no native Princes to blaze the trail for them. Their torch was carried by white men, like the young P.F. Warner, son of the Attorney-General of Trinidad and a follower of Lord Harris. Slavery had been abolished only in 1833, and the black man took up the game as best he could with clubs developing on socially distinct lines, graduated according to skin colour. It was the white clubs that entertained the English teams led by R.S. Lucas, Sir Arthur Priestley, Lord Hawke and P.F. Warner that visited the Caribbean in the 1890s. Priestley's team were reminded by the (white) Solicitor-General of Barbados of 'a strong filial feeling . . . the natural outcome of the relationship that exists between us and the Mother Country. We are Sons of Old England'.[22] On the field of play black men were more prominent. For the first tour of England, led by Warner's older brother, several were chosen, mostly to do the bowling chores. One who was chosen as a batsman, L.S. Constantine, discovered disconsolately standing on the quay as the team's boat prepared to leave, was only enabled to afford the trip by a last-minute whip round. He went on to make the first century by a West Indian in England.

The sporting brotherhood envisaged by Harris and the like was not always so easy to establish even in the white colonies where the task of maintaining the links between expatriates and the home country could be quite difficult. Sometimes, of course, these links became less meaningful to newer generations of the colonists themselves. Canada, the oldest and therefore ripest for independent thinking and also corrupted by French and American influence, not only showed depressingly little interest in cricket but had

1 Miss Blanche Bingley was the Wimbledon ladies champion in 1886 and, as Mrs G.W.
Hillyard, five more times between 1889 and 1900. Neither she nor her dignified
successors resorted to 'rational dress' or anything like it.

4 'Aren't women as good as men?' This was the highly disturbing question asked by the British Ladies Football Club seen here playing its first match on Saturday 30 March 1895.

Facing page
2 King Edward VII inspects a day's 'bag' at Sandringham during the 'Great pheasant era'.

3 W.G. Grace took up bowls (and its organisation) when his cricketing days were numbered. Here he is seen, on 8 June 1901, watching the more formally dressed John Young, President of the New South Wales Bowling Assocation.

5 Yorkshire were the rugby giants before the 'split' of 1893. This team, which beat the best of England in February 1890, included nine international players.

6 Soccer supporters already had a bad name, and this group of Everton supporters, up for the Cup in 1906, are obviously enjoying themselves too much for the gentleman in the trilby hat.

7 The fashionable vogue for cycling began in 1895 and, though brief, left a legacy of controversy. Those who favoured the kind of garb shown in the advertisement were an embarrassment to many suffragists and serious sportswomen.

8 Jack Hobbs, England's finest opening batsmen, was a
model professional in the golden age of the amateur.

9 The Welsh featherweight 'Peerless' Jim Driscoll, seen here wearing his Lonsdale Belt, was the idol of the National Sporting Club in the Edwardian era.

developed as national sport a game that had no comparable standing at home. The Governor-General, Baron Stanley, later the sixteenth Earl of Derby, assiduously patronised sports designed to foster links with the old country – cricket, yachting, rifle-shooting – but he achieved immortality by donating in 1893 the Stanley Cup for ice hockey. Scottish links had more success. The fifth Marquis of Aberdeen not only gave his imprimatur to golf and urged the Ottawa Cricket club to diversify into other sports – tennis, bowls and quoits – but revived the fortunes of curling. Even so it was a long time before Canadian curlers, amongst whom Scottish emigrant families were prominent, were able to persuade the Royal Caledonian club to visit them.[23]

Anglophile Australians, of whom there were still very many, were also distressed by the apparent indifference of home sporting authorities towards them. MCC's aloofness and the reasons for it have already been noted. It was not until 1893 that they were prepared to accord even an official welcome to Australian cricketers touring England. It was longer still before they began sponsoring English tours to Australia. The tours of 1894–5 and 1897–8 were led by the 'amateur' A.E. Stoddart and financial responsibility was shared by Melbourne CC and their rivals, the trustees of Sydney Cricket Ground. (There was as yet no Australian Board of Control. Indeed there was not yet, officially, an Australia: federation of the six colonies came only in 1901.) The cult of the dashing amateur had sufficient credibility in the upper reaches of Australian society for the tours to be deemed a success, though the more nationalistic sections of their press, still complaining of the 'everlasting snobbery' of the gaudier 'Hinglish' amateurs, marked down Stoddart on the first tour as a better winner than a loser and became derisive on the second at the excuses offered by his team for their failures. A particular source of ribald comment was A.C. MacLaren's claim that a fly in the eye had got him out in the fourth Test. The Australian tourists to England continued, of course, with their distressingly egalitarian financial arrangements, ignoring the conventions. Furthermore the manager of the 1899 tourists told *Cricket* magazine that their success stemmed from their more democratic approach to the choice of captain and their rejection of the debilitating philosophy of 'gentlemen and players'.

It was a somewhat different story in South Africa, where cricket, first played by the Army, had been enthusiastically taken up by the British settlers. There were no 'non-white' members of their clubs. The first English touring team (1888–9), recruited on a visit to England by Major R.G. Warton of the General Staff in Cape Town, was led by the enterprising 'amateur' C. Aubrey Smith who liked it so much that he settled there and went on the stage. Two years later, Walter Read, Oxonian captain of Surrey and a regular tourist – twice to Australia – took out a team. The Currie Cup, initially donated for the best performance by a local team against Read's tourists, was afterwards retained as a trophy for inter-provincial competition. Lord Hawke, who led the first official MCC tour in 1895–6, so enjoyed the experience that he volunteered to lead another in 1897–8.

Though sharing Harris's political views and his authoritarian outlook, Lord Hawke was a very different animal, basically a self-indulgent idler. He was categorised by the *DNB* simply as a 'cricketer', and he did little else with his life but play as long as he could and then become a committee man. He had developed the taste for travel with Vernon's teams to Australia in 1887–8 and a minor tour of India and Ceylon in 1888–9, and he made no fewer than four tours in the 1890s.[24] Hawke's imperialism was of a sentimental and self-centred kind – no share of the White Man's Burden for him. His attitude to India may be judged from a set of verses retrieved from his scrapbook which he thought 'too beautiful not to see the light of print' in his autobiography:

> A land that we've conquered and have to hold
> Though it costs us millions of lives and gold,
> Shall we call her the jewel of England's fame?
> Or throw our curse at her vampire name?
> But whether we bless her, or damn her, or deride her,
> We are bound by our honour to stand fast beside her.[25]

He was less ambivalent about South Africa. During his first visit there he was entertained by Cecil Rhodes, still under a cloud for his complicity in the Jameson raid: Hawke recalled afterwards that he never had a 'merrier meal'.[26] Conversely he declined to visit President Kruger and disapproved of the attempts of some of his team to invite the Boer leader to watch the team play.[27]

Cricket was not the only game to follow the flag to South Africa. The Rugby Union organised a tour in 1891 – with Cecil Rhodes guaranteeing the Western Province Rugby Board against financial loss – and they went again in 1896. The RFU was very proud of its contribution to the recreative well-being of the colonies, beginning with a successful mission to Australia and New Zealand in 1888 by a combined team from England, Scotland and Wales, no doubt a very different affair from Shrewsbury's commercial venture. As the Centenary History put it, 'In those glorious days when Britain was proud to have an Empire, it was the Dominions and the Colonies who received the first fruits of what the Rugby Union had done in gathering together the threads of a game that was gaining popularity at great speed.'[28] This was something of an exaggeration. There had indeed been a great spread of the game in all kinds of remote foreign parts, particularly through the armed services, but by the nineties the controllers of both football codes were too preoccupied with domestic problems – popularisation, commercialism and professionalism – to concern themselves greatly with overseas development. The year 1893 was one of crisis and schism for the Rugby Union and in the rest of the decade they managed only the 1896 South African visit and a tour of Australia by a British Isles team in 1899.

In soccer, with the FA locked in combat with the rapidly growing monster of the Football League, things were even worse. The professional clubs were interested chiefly in their own profits and success and took little enough interest even in home internationals let alone missionary work. That it was the game of all British games that took firmest hold throughout the world owed little or nothing to the FA. True the soccer authorities took a paternalistic, and often offensively patronising pride in the spread of this British creation, but they virtually ignored its organised development in other countries, eventually to their cost. Internationals meant games between England and Scotland with the Welsh and Irish fixtures as added, minor attractions. The Cup and the League Championship were the things that really mattered.

But the soccer men were only a bad example of the self-regarding, tunnel vision of sporting authorities generally. The notion of a Pan-Britannic Festival demonstrating the industrial, cultural and athletic achievements of the British race, with the aim of strengthening imperial links, might have been expected to achieve a warm welcome when it was propounded in 1891, not least amongst those who believed that the strongest links came through sport. John Astley Cooper, the Anglo-Australian who first suggested it, calling for 'actions for the benefit of mankind, which may make the name of England to be sung for all times as an example to races yet to come', had no doubt that sport should play a central part: 'Athletic exercises should have a place', he wrote, 'for before we are a political, or even a commercial and military people, we are a race of keen sportsmen.'[29] And when, before long, the industrial and cultural side of the project had dwindled to a single conference the idea of an athletic festival continued to attract declarations of support from people of consequence and the press. Indeed the scale of the project grew bigger and bigger whenever it was discussed.

Yet the more it did so, the less likely it became that it would actually happen. The governing bodies of the various sports at first gave the idea a cautious welcome and awaited details. Cooper got off to a bad start by first suggesting athletics, rowing and cricket as appropriate sports – fair enough – but then suggesting that 'the prizes should be in sums of money of great value'.[30] This was in July, 1891. By October he was writing to *The Times* proposing instead that the winners should receive purely symbolic recognition, but by then it was too late. In April 1892, the AAA made it clear that they could not sanction any competition involving both professionals and amateurs. Another unfortunate result of his well-meaning enthusiasm was that some Americans got the idea that he intended an Anglophone festival including them. In

September Cooper received a letter of support from J.E. Sullivan, secretary of the US Amateur Athletic Union, who thought the Chicago World's Fair of 1893 would be an ideal opportunity to try out the plan. When Cooper replied that he wanted his Festival to be in England and that he saw it as an imperial venture, negotiations came to an end.

But within the Empire itself he was no more successful. He had written to various sporting bodies in the (white) colonies and received some support in principle, but the idea got no further, not least because Cooper did not see it as his place to go into the tiresome details of suggesting how to put principle into practice. Thus when MCC got a letter from the 'Australasian conference' on 8 January 1894 asking whether they had considered the scheme and what they proposed to do about it , they replied that 'at present they had seen no scheme but would be prepared to consider the same when submitted'.[31] Similarly on 3 March 1894 the AAA, exasperated by newspaper enquiries as to their views on the matter, issued a statement saying they had 'been unable to consider the project as no scheme has been laid before them by its promoters'.[32] Cooper protested that this was not his function, but his moment had come and gone. Even genuine supporters of the idea had hoped any Festival would not occur too often lest it interfere with domestic sporting programmes; and this was a criterion any attempts at organised overseas competition had to meet.

The great game

Sportsmen were nevertheless doing a good deal in their own way to spread the games they loved throughout the Empire. The assumption was that the British gift for games was an essential part of their unique capacity to govern their vast domains. It was also assumed that proficiency at games equipped young men for the Empire's defence. The particular military virtues claimed for polo have already been noted. But everyone could not be a cavalry officer. At the other end of the social scale soccer had its place, too. As the *Football World* of Sheffield explained in 1895, 'It does not make trained soldiers of our men, it is true, but it enhances in them the spirit of competition, never-know-when-you-are-beaten, never-say-die.' These were followers, not leaders. In 1897 Lord Rosebery, presenting the FA Cup, declared that soccer encouraged those 'splendid characteristics of the British race – stamina and indomitable pluck'.[33] He might have been describing a good horse. There was no intrinsic reason why Dartmouth, Sandhurst and Woolwich should prefer rugger: it was simply that they thought soccer was no longer a game for gentlemen and thence for officers.

Similarly it was not cricket, as such, but the gentlemanly spirit in which it was supposed to be played, the honour code that it embodied, that made it such a potent symbol. Newbolt's *Vitaï Lampada*, written as Kitchener was recapturing the Sudanese desert from the dervishes, is the classic text:

> And it's not for the sake of a ribboned coat,
> > Or the selfish hope of a season's fame
> But his captain's hand on his shoulder smote –
> > 'Play up! play up! and play the game!'

The sequel makes the application explicit:

> The sand of the desert is sodden red –
> > Red with the wreck of a square that broke:
> The Gatling's jammed and the Colonel's dead.
> > And the regiment blind with dust and smoke.
> The river of death has brimmed his banks,
> > And England's far and honour a name;
> But the voice of a schoolboy rallies the ranks:
> > 'Play up! play up! and play the game.'

In practice the Gatling carried a message of its own. For Kitchener in crushing the natives had demonstrated the devastating power of the new machine guns, which the Germans had in plenty.

There was still, however, one more war of the old-fashioned kind to be fought. When the British took up arms against the Boers in 1899 in support of the Outlanders, the only question seemed to be the propriety of attacking a small, weak opponent, and they were not whole-hearted about it. But the nation's pride was stung when the Boers hit back hard, and after the humiliating early defeats the re-action to the relief of Ladysmith and Mafeking was near-hysterical. There followed a long period of frustrating guerrilla warfare. Peace was not finally to be concluded until May, 1902 – the old Queen did not live to see it – but long before then Kipling was clear that there could be no real victory. He only hoped that the lesson would be learned. In July, 1901, he ferociously satirised the complacent, 'commonsense', balance sheet attitude to things imperial:

> Let us admit it fairly, as a business people should,
> We have had no end of a lesson: it will do us no end of good.

Not only the out-moded army leadership but the whole establishment had been exposed:

> Not our mere astonied camps, but Council and Creed and College –
> All the obese, unchallenged old things that stifle and overlie us –
> Have felt the effects of the lesson we got – an advantage no money could buy
> us.[34]

No one was listening, and he sharpened his pen.

Notes

1 W.S. *Churchill, A History of the English-speaking Peoples,* in A. Briggs (ed.), *Our Island Heritage,* London, 1981, p. 121.
2 See C. Carrington, *Rudyard Kipling: His Life and Work,* Harmondsworth, 1970, pp. 321–6, for a discussion of the origins and reception of the poem.
3 E.W. Swanton (ed.), *Barclay's World of Cricket,* London, 1986, pp. 60–146, gives a survey of how cricket started everywhere from Argentina to Zimbabwe.
4 A. Kirk-Greene, 'Sport and His Excellency in the British Empire', *IJHS,* September, 1989, p. 227; P.A. Snow, in Swanton, *Barclay's,* p. 83.
5 *Kitchener's School,* 1898.
6 Kirk-Greene, 'Sport and his Excellency', p. 225.
7 J. Moray Brown, 'Polo', in *Riding and Polo,* Badminton Library, London, 1891, p. 256.
8 From Milesius, a fabulous Spanish king said to have settled in Ireland: hence jocularly Milesian = Irish.
9 Brown, 'Polo', pp. 257–8. G. Vigne (*Travels in Kashmir, Ladakh and Thibet,* London, 1842) had memorably described polo as 'hockey on horseback' and this is what it was popularly called in its early years in England. A contemporary Dublin magazine staked a claim for the revived Irish national game, calling polo 'hurling on horseback'.
10 *Ibid.,* p. 286.
11 *Ibid.,* p. 235.
12 *Ibid.,* p. 113.
13 *Ibid.,* p. 126.
14 See T. Mason, 'Football on the Maidan', *IJHS,* May. 1990, esp pp 85–8 on which this passage is largely based.
15 Titley and McWhirter, *Centenary History,* p. 93.
16 Cricket, vol. 4, 1885, p. 454, quoted in J. Bradley, 'The MCC, Society and Empire, *IJHS,* May 1990, p. 13.
17 Bradley, 'The MCC'.
18 G.R.C. Harris, *A Few Short Runs,* London, 1921.
19 G.R.C. Harris and F.S. Ashley-Cooper, *Lord's and the MCC,* London, 1924, p. 209.
20 Sir Hume Gordon, *Background of Cricket,* London, 1939, p. 157.
21 In a speech quoted in *The Charm of Cricket Past and Present,* C.H.B. Pridham, London, 1949.
22 Bradley, 'The MCC', p. 18.
23 See G. Redmond, 'The Governors-General of Canada and Sport, 1867–1909, *IJHS,* September 1989, pp. 193–214.
24 Even then his appetite was not sated: he went back to Australia in 1902–3 and, astonishingly, to Argentina in 1912–13 when he was fifty-two years old.
25 Redmond, pp. 274–5. See also J. Bradley, 'The MCC', *IJHS,* May. 1990, pp. 3–21.
26 Lord Hawke, *Recollections and Reminiscences,* London, 1924, p. 153.
27 *Ibid.,* p. 158.
28 U.A. Titley and R. McWhirter, *Centenary History of the Rugby Football Union,* London, 1970, p. 93.
29 J.A. Cooper, 'Many Lands – One People. A Criticism and a Suggestion', *Greater Britain,* 9, 15 July 1891, quoted in K. Moore, 'The Pan-Britannic Festival', in *Pleasure, Profit, Proselytism,* ed. J.A. Mangan, London, 1988, p. 146.
30 *Ibid.*
31 Bradley, 'The MCC', p. 17.

32 K. Moore, 'Pan-Britannic Festival', p. 157.
33 T. Mason, *Association Football and English Society*, Brighton, 1980.
34 For the full text see R. Kipling, *Collected Works*, London, 1940, pp. 299–300.

PART II

The Islanders
1901–1910

CHAPTER NINE

An age of contrasts

Kipling returned to the attack in the autumn of 1901. *The Islanders* excoriated the politicians:

> Arid, aloof, incurious, unthinking, unthanking, gelt

and poured scorn on the hedonistic upper classes. They had sent a pitifully inadequate army to South Africa:

> Because of your witless learning and your beasts of warren and chase
> Ye grudged your sons to their service and your fields for their camping place.

Britain had been saved from humiliation by volunteers from the other colonies, 'the Younger Nations':

> Then ye returned to your trinkets, then ye contented your souls
> With the flannelled fools at the wicket or the muddied oafs at the goals.

What use would sport be when the real test came?:

> Will the rabbit war with your foemen – the red deer horn them for hire?
> Will ye pitch some white pavilion and hastily even the odds
>   With nets and hoops and mallets, with rackets and balls and rods?[1]

The state of the nation

If it was not entirely certain that Britain would shortly face a showdown with Germany, as Kipling believed, it seemed highly likely that she would soon be at war with one or other of the major European powers. Whilst Britain herself had no clear policy for developing her overseas territories, merely assuming that British rule was best, she had inevitably been caught up in the competition amongst the Europeans for colonial spoils. She took precautions against a Russian challenge in the East by forming an alliance with Japan. Nearer home the time had come to seek an accommodation with either France or Germany. The Kaiser's bombast and Germany's formidable industrial challenge turned the scale. France, the historic enemy, now seemed a better prospective friend, despite her alliance with Russia. The main achievement of the Unionist government, now under Balfour's leadership, was to conclude the Anglo-French Entente of 1904.

They faced difficult problems at home. Victorian progress had bred confident expectations of a growing prosperity for all. Since 1 per cent of the population owned over 60 per cent of the nation's capital and 11 per cent enjoyed 50 per cent of total earnings, there was evident scope for change, and as much individual wealth came from land ownership and investments there was an obvious need to increase manufacture and the employment it brought. With growing foreign competition it seemed doubly important to turn the empire to economic advantage. In return for preferential tariffs in the more advanced 'white' colonies, Britain had renounced commercial treaties with foreign countries that would undermine imperial trade. This was a limited success: trade restrictions were of greater advantage to the 'haves' than the 'have nots'. Exports continued to rise, keeping ahead of imports, but this, though good for the balance of trade, did little for the poor. The population was still growing – it reached 45 million by 1911 – and low-price imports would have helped them more.

The arguments of reformers who looked for redistribution of wealth were strengthened by a succession of investigations into the plight of the poor, such as Charles Booth's *Life and Labour of the People of London* (1889–1903) and Seebohm Rowntree's study of conditions in York. These for the first time attempted a definition of poverty – as distinct from the old legalistic Poor Law concept of pauperism – and the reports made a correspondingly greater impact. Rowntree[2] found that 28 per cent of families had incomes below subsistence level and that 48 per cent of children were going hungry in order to help sustain bread-winners in working order. This contrasted sharply with the conspicuous wealth and extravagance of the aristocracy and the infiltrating plutocrats, and the ever-rising fortunes of the middle classes who now had electricity in their houses, telephones, motor cars, gramophones and other evidences of progress. As the Liberal economist Sir Leo Chiozza Money put it, half the country's wealth went to some 5 million people, while the remaining 39 million had to make do with the other half.[3] To earn £5,000 a year was to be one of a tiny elite: the average adult male industrial worker's wage was some £70 a year. Nearly a third of the working population were women and they were paid even less than men – the lowest type of adult worker, the charwoman, got as little as £30 a year.

Housing naturally reflected these inequalities. Britain had become the most urbanised country in the world – nearly 80 per cent of the population had become town-dwellers – and supply could not keep up with demand. This was particularly so in London, which now had a population of over 7 million (compared with 5 million in Scotland and 4 million in Ireland) but everywhere the urban sprawl continued. For the middle classes £2,000 or even £1,500 would buy a superior family house even in London: £1,000 would buy a magnificent suburban property in the provinces and £500 a very decent one. But there was no need to buy and most people preferred to rent. Mrs Beeton's *Household Management* in 1906 recommended setting aside one-eighth of annual income for housing. And the typical working man's home, 'a brick or stone terrace house with a kitchen, a parlour in the front with perhaps a bay window, a lean-to scullery opening to a backyard or small garden, and three bedrooms above', though little enough, was probably the highest national standard of housing of anywhere in the world.[4]

Yet conditions varied greatly in different parts of the country. Rents in England for workers' houses ranged from 4s to 7s and more a week (£10 to £17-plus a year). In Ireland and Scotland they were generally somewhat lower, but, in London, Dublin and the other great cities, working-class families often could not afford to rent a complete house. Hence the tenement solution: 4s 6d a week was the 'fair' London rent for a single room.[5] And not all the problems were in the towns. The grim reality of living conditions in the West of Ireland or the Highlands of Scotland made a nonsense of the romantic myths of nationalist intellectuals, and in rural England 'leaking roofs and damp brick or earth floors were common, and even in model villages there was no drainage, no refuse collection and no running water. A candle or oil lamp was the only light.'[6]

The government was not unaware of the need for change. 'National efficiency' demanded the belated reform of state education that came in the Act of 1902, Balfour's finest achievement, which extended and improved elementary education with opportunites for transfer to a linked system of secondary grammar and technical schools. The Irish Land Purchase Act, 1903, and the Unemployed Workmen Act, 1905, were lesser and pragmatic but not insignificant recognitions of deep-seated problems. The government came to grief, however, in trying to find a cure for the nation's economic ills. Chamberlain's conversion to the cause of tariffs and imperial preference split the Unionists and gave the grateful Liberals fresh heart. Balfour's valiant attempts at compromise baffled even his supporters and signally failed to save a policy that, put to the country, proved less appealing to the British electorate than importing cheap foreign food and mass-produced clothes. Renewed enthusiasm for free trade brought the Liberals a landslide victory in 1906.

Despite their electorally prudent assurances of continuity in defending and maintaining the Empire the new government of Sir Henry Campbell-Bannerman was nevertheless suspected not only of radical leanings but of softness on imperial matters – the fiery Welsh demagogue, David Lloyd

George, was a notorious pro-Boer. Another worrying sign of the times for traditionalists was the election of fifty-three Labour members to the new Parliament. In practice they were far from radical: the spirit of trades unionism from which they drew their main support was by no means egalitarian but biased towards the more highly skilled and better paid, and the unions themselves were held in check by restrictive legislation. And whatever the Commons's reforming zeal they had to contend with the House of Lords.

The in-built contradictions of the situation developed further as the task of leadership fell to the enigmatic Asquith, a bourgeois academic lawyer, a Yorkshireman with a shrewd brain and a tough character, a non-conformist but with an appetite for high life. The tax proposals of his Chancellor of the Exchequer, Lloyd George, in 1909 – an increase in death duties, raising the standard rate of income tax from 1s (5p) to 1s 2d in the pound and introducing supertax on incomes over £3,000 a year – were denounced by Rosebery as 'not Liberalism, but Socialism, the negation of faith, of family, of property, of monarchy, of Empire'.[7] But in truth they were brought in as much to finance naval rearmament as to fund the new old-age pension of 5s (25p) a week for needy and worthy citizens over seventy.

Life and leisure

Whatever the plight of the poor they spent less and less time on seeking the consolations of religion. In 1851 a survey had indicated that only 40 per cent of the population were regular churchgoers. Fifty years later 25 per cent was nearer the mark and 20 per cent in the cities. Even this attendance was often formal: the better sort, especially in rural areas, went to church to set a good example. There were regional and ethnic variations. In Ireland, where religious, cultural and ethnic identity were interwoven, church attendance was something of a contest. Elsewhere the Catholics were more observant, outwardly at least, than members of the Established Church, as were the non-conformists in such strongholds as Welsh mining villages and Scottish crofting communities. In less God-fearing districts, where the by-laws were correspondingly lax, the great counter-attraction for the working man was the public house. The working-class Sabbath was taking on its modern role as rest and recuperation not so much from six days' labour as from five days' labour followed by a bout of hectic pleasure. Saturday mornings still had to be spent at the factory or office but afterwards came sport and then, depending on age and inclination, an evening at a dance or music hall or in the pub.

In cultural matters the middle classes continued to make the running. There were signs, however, of widening horizons. The first commissioned work of the controversial sculptor Jacob Epstein appeared in 1907, and social realism was the core of the Camden group of painters, led by W.R. Sickert, who found inspiration in the music hall. Writers, too, extended their range. Conrad's *Nostromo* showed the effect of western industrial and commercial mores on an undeveloped part of the world. Galsworthy's *The Man of Property* explored the workings of conscience in upper middle-class society. E.M. Forster contrasted English gentility and fear of vulgarity with Italian vitality in *Where Angels Fear to Tread* and *A Room with a View*. And for the first time the emerging classes below found their laureates: H.G. Wells for London and Arnold Bennett for the industrial midlands. There was also a mass of less serious fiction: crime stories from G.K. Chesterton's Father Brown and E.W. Hornung's cricket-playing 'gentleman cracksman' Raffles, to Sax Rohmer's evil Dr Fu Manchu, the adventure novels of Baroness Orczy, P.G. Wodehouse's Psmith and the popular racing stories of Nat Gould.

It was a great age for music. Elgar provided the assurance that England not only had a truly first-rate composer but could inspire great music. Sir Thomas Beecham, son of the pill-manufacturer and music patron, began his career as an impresario of opera and ballet as well as a notable champion of the country's other great Edwardian composer, Delius. Ralph Vaughan Williams successfully married folk song with choral tradition. Undeniably, classical music was a middle-class taste, and the gramophone records which helped its spread in the 1900s were at first costly, but in the days before wireless and television there was correspondingly more 'live' music for working-class people to enjoy, particularly, of course, in the towns.

It was the better sort, too, who first discovered the new American syncopated music, ragtime. It was not vulgar like its successor, jazz, but a gentler, more charming affair. The Duchess of Westminster hired Vic Filmer to play 'Temptation Rag' in the nursery for a children's party.[8] American influence, since the minstrel shows, was widespread – on, for instance, the English composer Leslie Stuart who wrote 'Little Dolly Daydream, Pride of Idaho' and the immortal 'Lily of Laguna'. It spread through the music halls, then in their heyday, and G.H. Elliott, 'the Chocolate-Coloured Coon', singing 'I used to sigh for the silvery moon' and performing a soft-shoe shuffle, took his place with the rest: George Robey, Nellie Wallace, Harry Tate, Wilkie Bard, Florrie Forde, Harry Lauder and Little Tich with his preposterous boots.

The music hall had enormous appeal and every town of any size now had one. The 'legitimate' theatre had also spread as railway travel had allowed touring companies to take replicas of London successes to the provinces. Most of what was offered, and wanted, was pure escapism, but Victorian melodrama had already been infused with naturalism and, as in the novel, social issues now came to the fore. Shaw scattered his anarchic ideas like a machine gun. Galsworhy's *The Silver Box* was about inequality before the law between rich and poor, his *Strife* dealt with the effects of a strike and *Justice* showed up prison conditions. J.M. Barrie's *The Admirable Crichton*, however, made a Gilbertian joke of social inequality and the whimsical *Peter Pan* was ineffably middle-class.

Miss Annie Horniman, daughter of the tea merchant, helped shift the focus from London, using her money to build the Abbey Theatre in Dublin (putting up with many nationalistic excesses before finally withdrawing her subsidy) and founding the Gaiety Theatre Repertory Company, Manchester, which bred a school of dramatists much influenced by Ibsen. For all the earnestness of such concern with social issues, however, the theatre was essentially for the middle classes and the middle aged. The Regent Street Bioscope, which opened in 1906, was the forerunner of a new theatre for the working classes and the young. Cinemas all over the country were soon displaying Mack Sennett's bathing beauties, the Keystone Cops and the fascinating sagas of the Wild West to rapt audiences.

The cinema was to be a useful new way for young working-class men and women to meet together. The most popular outdoor recreation, walking, was also often a shared activity, having its roots in courtship rituals. Dancing, in village halls or the new urban saloons, was another. Sex apart, however, the working man's chosen hobbies characteristically did not include offering relief from household drudgery for his womenfolk. The effects of urbanisation and industrialisation were evident but the older, rural past had a powerful appeal, often harking back to an agricultural or even earlier, hunting, existence. Men gardened, perhaps on an allotment rented from the local council. They kept dogs, sometimes for sporting purposes, or pigeons for racing. They went fishing, on rivers when they could get to them, or on the crowded banks of canals or reservoirs. And their distinctively modern pleasure was in organised sport, playing, spectating or weighing up form and prospects through the columns of the daily newspaper.

The judicious weighing up of form often related to the Turf and hence involved gambling, an age-old British addiction to which Edward VII himself was given but which moralists thought particularly debilitating to the lower classes. Betting was now thoroughly organised big business, using the latest technology. At the Doncaster races in 1901 30,000 telegrams were sent out by the special telegraphists provided by the Post Office. Football, too, was not only the leading spectator sport, attracting crowds of 20,000 or more every week in the bigger towns, but, through the burgeoning coupon system – the 'pools' – a leading source of gambling.

All this was very worrying, but in fact the Edwardians spent twenty times more on alcohol than on gambling. Drink was cheap and the public houses were open all day, until as late as midnight in London. Every week there were over 4,000 prosecutions for drunkenness and the average consumption of beer per adult was six pints a week. There was one public house for every 300 people. Some no doubt were foul dens of iniquity and all were notoriously lively on Saturday nights and Bank Holidays. But most were well conducted and fairly quiet – music, even singing, needed a licence – and above all they were warm and friendly. The atmosphere was likely to be smoke-filled, for tobacco was also cheap and widely used. Cigarettes were not yet suspected of being cancerous, though they were thought bad for the wind if you were an athlete. They were also thought a sign of degeneracy amongst the young, an indication of street corner loutishness inducing hollow chests and curvature of the spine. There was growing concern about the nation's physique, corrupted like its psyche, many believed, by town-dwelling. The answer was more exercise – playing games, not watching them.

Royal sports: Edwardian style

The new King himself was, of course, a sporting man, but scarcely of the new model: Edward VII had not had a public school education and thus had missed the benefits of communal muscular Christianity. The long hours of private tuition had also proved useless intellectually, and a certain proficiency in foreign languages, especially French, was his best asset. He warmly welcomed the Entente Cordiale: the culture of Paris and Biarritz was much more congenial to him than that of Berlin and his nephew, Wilhelm. His visit to Paris in 1903 was a great success. At home, too, the King's manifest enjoyment of his new role communicated itself to his subjects, many of whose sporting tastes and social habits – the Turf, gambling, smoking and drinking – he shared.

They could also appreciate, if they could not be there to see, his pleasure in buying back *Britannia* and resuming his now unquestioned place of honour at Cowes. Edward had been irritated by the Kaiser's officious behaviour before Victoria's funeral and by his ostentatious expressions of grief and affection at the actual ceremony. But he bit his lip and did the honours. conferring the Garter on Crown Prince Willy. The Kaiser's apparently renewed Anglophilia extended to proposing an Anglo-German alliance, with England watching over the seas and Germany the land. His Chancellor, von Bülow, was less enthusiastic about the idea, especially since Lonsdale was making the most of the fact that the Kaiser had replaced *Meteor* by a Scottish boat: German shipbuilders did not find this amusing. And relations between uncle and nephew grew steadily worse, not least because of the Kaiser's habit of gossiping about the King's relationship with Mrs Keppel.[9]

Edward found more agreeable occupation in supervising Sir Thomas Lipton's preparations for a new America's Cup challenge with a specially-built *Shamrock II*. Sadly, however, the 1901 encounter was, despite disagreements amongst the Americans, another British failure. Still it gave Lipton further practice in the role of sporting loser, one for which he was greatly admired, especially in the USA. The year 1903 gave him yet more. *Shamrock III* was his biggest boat so far, but she came up against an even bigger one. The American *Reliance* was 143 ft long and had more than 16,000 square feet of canvas, about eight times the size of a modern 12-metre yacht. By this time Lipton was almost the only British yachtsman sailing boats of this size, and some of his shareholders began to question whether the publicity he was getting was worth the money. Most owners, however wealthy, were turning to slightly smaller boats. The new one-design South Coast class (24 tons, 57 ft overall) introduced in 1903 attracted many aristocratic owners. Lower down the scale a 6-metre cruiser-racer cost £200–£250. *Yachting Monthly*, launched in 1906, soon enlarged its title to *Yachting and Boating Monthly*, in pursuit of dinghy sailors. This wider readership was greatly interested in boat design and competitions for a £5 prize brought out several young men who went on to prominence.

As King, Edward had even greater opportunity to preside over the social side of sport and to set standards in those matters of protocol and correctness of dress by which he had always set such store. The Kaiser came in for special treatment. When he visited England in 1902 Edward asked him to travel to Sandringham in plain clothes, informing him that it was 'not customary to wear uniform in the country in England'. The visit was an abject failure, though the entertainment included not only music and a company of actors from London but the great cockney music hall artiste Albert Chevalier. The Emperor seems to have been unimpressed by the delights of 'Knocked 'em in the Old Kent Road' and 'My Old Dutch'. Indeed nothing seemed to please him and his know-all attitude and supercilious manner got on Edward's nerves. His clothes for duck-shooting in the Fens were an olive-green Norfolk jacket, with matching trousers tucked into bright leather boots, an armless shooting cape and a green cap – correct but ostentatious and bizarrely cut. Annoyingly enough, the Kaiser shot well, especially considering that he was obliged to use a light gun because of a withered arm. But fellow-guests were appalled when his officers began shooting hares with their revolvers. As the Kaiser boarded his official yacht to depart his uncle was heard to mutter, 'Thank God he's gone.'

It had not helped that Lonsdale had up-staged the King with the lavish week of sport and pageantry he laid on at Lowther. Edward liked to be the centre of attention, whether host or guest, and he expected to be humoured. His favourite hosts, like Sir Ernest Cassel, knew, for instance, that when the King played croquet he liked to be matched against ladies like the Duchess of Sermoneta, who was not only very pretty but an extremely bad player. (Even she could falter. When she once, by a fluke, played a shot that knocked his ball into a rose bush the atmosphere was icy.) Edward also liked his little jokes. When a neighbour, Sir Somerville Gurney, inadvertently shot one of his hen pheasants at a stage in the season when only cocks were supposed to be killed, his rebuke was heavily jocular, 'Ah Gurney, what a one you are for the ladies!' He was so pleased with his witticism and the laughter it evoked that he elaborated to the point of tedium, and worse. And Sir Felix Semon, who had already earned a sarcastic rebuke for wearing a decoration on the wrong lapel, never heard the last of it when he shot a stag below the accepted size.[10]

Size and antler-count were of great moment to stag-shooters, though beauty and symmetry were also admired, in death if not in life. Bird shooters were more interested in quantity. An inordinate and gruesome pride was taken in the record 'bags' obtained. Grouse-shooters did best. A total of 2,748 birds was shot in a day by nine 'guns' at Broomshead in Yorkshire in 1904.[11] Readers of *Baily's Magazine* were invited to send in to the editor the names of the best shots they knew. They were a small but lethal group – such men as the Marquess of Granby, Earl de Grey, Lord Walsingham, Lord Ashburton, Lord Westbury, Prince Victor Duleep Singh, the Hon. A.E. Gathorne-Hardy, the Hon. Harry Stonor, Major Arthur Acland-Hood. They were known familiarly as 'the professionals', not because they did anything so vulgar as shoot for money, but because they spent most of their lives at the sport. In April 1905 the *Badminton Magazine* printed the views of fifteen of these experts on what was the most difficult shot, stirring accounts of high pheasants coming into a wind, dropping with a curl and so forth. Fourteen of the fifteen picked pheasants as the hardest to kill. Yet Lord Ripon dispatched 222,976 of them during his long shooting career (1867–1913), an average of 4,774 a season. Daily bags of a thousand and more were common in what was known as the 'great pheasant era'.

In his later years Edward VII had come to enjoy racing even more than shooting: he liked the company of racing people and what he called, with less than sparkling originality, 'the glorious uncertainty of the turf'.[12] There was the added pleasure of not being bothered by the tiresome Kaiser or his friend Lonsdale, who after an early and distressing gambling debacle[13] had steered clear of the Turf. And, though Edward's private fortune was spent, and his mother had prudently left hers to her younger children, the generosity of Parliament, which provided him with an annual income of £470,000 to add to his Duchy of Lancaster revenue of £60,000, left him well able to indulge his whims. His race-going, in fact, was an opportunity to combine pleasure with royal duty, for his visits, especially to great events like the Derby, had become occasions for national celebration, bringing King and people together in a warm glow of mutual delight in being British.

Ascot, especially, became Royal Ascot again. It was an irony in view of the old Queen's attitude to the Turf that the grief of so many illustrious subjects at her passing should find expression in the 'Black Ascot' of 1901. The fashion writers revelled in the elaborate display of mourning inspired by Edward VII's highly developed sense of the language of clothes. Thereafter Ascot was a gay annual extravaganza emblematic of the Edwardian age. The cost of entry to the Royal Enclosure went up from £1 to £4 a day: reserved seats in the grandstand were £1 10s and £1. Irish loyalists, too, basked in the sunshine of the Edwardian style. The King made a state visit with the charming Queen Alexandra in 1903 spending a day at the new flat race course in Phoenix Park.

On this occasion he was advised that a visit to Punchestown would be beneath the royal dignity. This reflected the change in fashionable Irish taste, following the English pattern, in which the old 'natural' courses were tending to be superseded by park courses. Punchestown had suffered somewhat since the death of the Marquess of Drogheda. Nevertheless Edward revived fond memories the following year when he spent two days at Punchestown, drawing the biggest crowds since 1868. But he received a truly royal reception at Leopardstown. This new course (1888), modelled on Sandown Park, conveniently near to Dublin and served by a branch railway line, now held six meetings a year and had become the leading centre for steeplechasing, the old Irish specialism, as well as the Flat. When he paid a quick visit to Dublin in 1907 for the Irish International Exhibition everyone who was anyone went to the special meeting arranged in his honour at Leopardstown. 'A leading characteristic', the *Irish Times* observed, 'was the wealth of ostrich feathers which adorned at least nine out of every ten hats worn by ladies in the Members' Enclosure.'[14]

Sadly Edward had enjoyed little success as an owner since becoming King. By 1904 he had twenty horses in training but still scarcely won a race. His total winnings in 1905 were a mere £970. In desperation he turned back to steeplechasing, instructing Lord Marcus Beresford to buy the 1904 Grand National winner, Moifaa, but under the royal colours it fell at Becher's Brook. All of this was bad for the national morale, as well as Edward's own, and things looked even blacker after two more disastrous seasons in 1906 and 1907. It seemed to symbolise the state of British racing as a whole. Foreign invaders, notably American, were sweeping the board. Though the dubious Tod Sloan and Lester Rieff were gone, American jockeys won the Derby in 1901 and four out of the following five years.

American or not, Danny Maher, the 1903 winner, who won again in 1905 and 1906 and was champion jockey in 1908, was not only very popular but known to be straight: Lord Durham, no less, had pronounced him 'a most respectable boy'. In this respect he compared favourably with many of the natives. Morals apart, the English jockeys responded well to the challenge and were by now using a modified 'Americano' crouch to good effect. The real threat was from American trainers and breeders. The irrepressible John Huggins, when asked by *faux-naif* journalists if there were many crooks on the American Turf, replied 'Not a one, they've all migrated over here.' Huggins himself was, however, honest as well as successful. Leading trainer in 1901, he produced 102 winners with a prize-money value of £87,000 during his time in England, through hard work, superior techniques and the kind of skilful professionalism that aroused spiteful comment from some effete and amateurish Britishers.

Doping was the chief source of rumour and controversy Interfering with horses was not, of course, an American invention, and the simplest way of 'stopping' a fancied horse – a bucket of water just before a race – required no cunning use of chemicals. The new phenomenon, the capacity to improve the performance of a horse had, however, been perfected in the United States and was part of the armoury of the more sophisticated trainers. The Jockey Club, for whatever reason, were not disposed to try to do anything about the rumours. Most owners were more interested in results than in the methods used to get them. It was left to the independent-minded George Lambton to arouse their attention. He got the permission of his brother, Lord Durham, to conduct an experiment, with the stipulation that no bets were to be laid. He doped half a dozen moderate horses to bring in five winners and a second. Such evidence from such a source could not be ignored. In 1903 it became a 'warning off' offence to administer, cause or allow drugs to be used. This did not, of course, solve the problem of how to detect them. A saliva test introduced in 1910 assisted detection of the crime but not the criminal. The Jockey Club's solution, to hold the horse's trainer responsible whether he knew anything about the offence or not was rough justice, and in later years deemed to contravene principles of natural justice, but meanwhile it was an advance.

American breeders were also depressingly successful, and this could hardly be attributable to crookery. However it was observed that in 1901 the Jockey Club had relaxed its rules to admit certain bloodstock lines not previously included in Weatherby's Stud Book, and that afterwards large-scale American breeding methods and the closure of many tracks of dubious reputation in the United States had flooded the British market. A single breeder, James Ben Ali Haggin, had a catalogue of 2,000 horses at keen prices. Rubio, bought from Haggin for $75, had gone on to win the Grand National. When New York State introduced anti-gambling legislation in 1909 the Jockey Club took fright and restored its original definition. Even so hundreds of horses had been admitted to the elite circle and the prospect of thousands of their coarsely bred descendants alarmed the purists and terrified British breeders.

Patriotism, unless it could be combined with self-interest, was a secondary consideration with serious racing men, from top to bottom of the sport, but to the average sport-loving Britisher who liked an occasional flutter and a day at the races it was important for British jockeys to do well and particularly distressing that the royal fortunes were at such a low ebb. The situation was saved by Irish bloodstock and a great patriotic gesture from a loyal, if eccentric subject, Colonel Hall-Walker, a Liverpool gentleman who kept a stud at Tully in Co. Kildare. Despite Hall-Walker's breeding methods, which were based on astrology, it was a remarkably fine one. He now offered, in response to the national emergency, to lease six horses to the King. There was great rejoicing when one of these, Minoru, proved good enough to win the Derby in 1909, ridden by a thoroughly British jockey, Herbert Jones.

And that same year, despite Lloyd George's Budget, society ladies made a brave show at Ascot. *The Times'* fashion correspondent's account of Gold Cup Day, 1909, was a tone poem:

> Such fragile materials as muslin, laces, nets and soft silk were the only wear . . . white – including dead white, Ivory and ficelle – predominated, while black achieved an extraordinary success in millinery. A delicate, subtle mauve appeared in equally delicate materials. Fine net or ninons, embroidered in ficelle, very handsomely worked in bold raised patterns and long coats were among the successes of the day.[15]

Horse-power

Even Ascot could not escape all the inroads of modernity. There had been a car park since 1905. That year also the King had himself broken with tradition, arriving in a black Mercedes before transferring to the Royal Coach for the traditional procession along the course. Edward had bought his first car, a Daimler, in 1902, but his simple pleasure had been spoiled by the Kaiser's characteristic and patronising display of omniscience. 'What petrol does it use?' Wilhelm had asked. The King did not know. Potato spirit was the best, he was informed: poor Edward, who had not even heard of it, was further chagrined to be given a demonstration of its manufacture.[16] Lonsdale was better at handling the problem of German technology. The Kaiser had made a Mercedes available to him during his visit to Berlin the previous year and Lonsdale had ordered one, complete with driver-mechanic. When it arrived, however, he sent it back to have the chrome replaced by silver and he had a second Mercedes follow the first in case of breakdowns.

The magnificent horse-drawn coach in which Lonsdale continued to drive to Ascot and in the procession was greatly admired, and he had the body work painted – eighteen coats – in the same gaudy yellow livery on his motor cars. (When he became President of the Automobile Association he graciously permitted it to be used on its official vehicles.) Lonsdale was thus conspicuously arrayed in July 1907 at the ceremonial parade that marked the opening of the new Brooklands motor-racing stadium. Brooklands was built for Mr H.F. Locke King on his estate in Surrey and organised on the model of the Turf: the riders wore colours like jockeys and its official starter was a member of the Jockey Club. Its vertically banked track was the finest in the world and it soon became another great British sporting citadel. Brooklands was also used for motor-cycle racing. In car-racing the Germans, French and Italians were superior in everything but driving, but motor-cycles were a British specialism. The French, as with the bicycle itself, had pioneered the notion, but British enthusiasts, using the Isle of Man and Northern Ireland to by-pass the legal difficulties, took over the organisation of road-racing. The Ulster and Manx Tourist Trophy races brought to the fore not only British riders but British machines – Matchless, Norton, Triumph, Scott, Rudge and Dot, short for 'devoid of trouble'.

Motor vehicles further lowered the status of the bicycle. True it had become an accepted part of the lives of modern young women who now used it for everything from posting a letter to taking a spin in the country. At Girton students were allowed to ride into Cambridge after 1903 and a year later were allowed to cycle to lectures after dark provided that at least three went together;[17] and at Westfield College in 1905 girls won permission to cycle alone and to make the journey into London.[18] But the bicycle in some of its cheaper manifestations was also the vehicle of the working man, the key to mobility in the quest for jobs. Technically its evolution was nearing completion: the free wheel came in at the turn of the century with stronger brakes to compensate for the loss of back-pedalling, quickly followed by the three-speed gears of Sturmey and Archer. In sporting terms, the Continentals were forging ahead in road-racing and track-racing, though more popular in Britain, retained its dubious reputation as somewhat lower than athletics.

For Lonsdale the motor-car was always second-best to the horse. He had been mortified at having to give up his position in the hunting world, and in 1904, when funds once more allowed, he determined to recapture his former glory. What he really would have liked was the post of Master of the King's horse, but he obviously had no chance of this as long as Edward VII was alive.[19] He turned instead to an old ambition, seizing the opportunity in 1906 when the Mastership of his father's old Hunt, the Cottesmore, became vacant. Lonsdale was not a popular choice. Older members recalled with distaste his crude efforts to force himself on them in the 1880s when he had first succeeded to the title. Everyone knew of his bullying techniques at the Quorn.

They succumbed to the lure of his money, but soon regretted it. He drove away the huntsman Thatcher, a controversial figure, even before he started, writing him a 3,000-word letter, full of searingly brutal criticism. Thatcher's successor Gillson received an even longer letter at the end of his first season, mercilessly laying bare his weaknesses.[20] Lonsdale's tyrannical approach also drove members away, subscriptions dwindled and the £2,000 he had been guaranteed was not forthcoming. After three seasons Lonsdale called for a vote of confidence from the remaining members. This was narrowly achieved with the aid of the farmers and landowners who, of course, felt the benefit of his fanatical concern for discipline. Then a disaster occurred at one of his coal-mines, Whitehaven. A total of 134 lives were lost, but Lonsdale also lost a lot of money, and the necessary retrenchment included giving up the Cottesmore.

He enjoyed greater success as President of the first International Horse Show, sponsored by the Olympia Company, newly formed with a capital of £20,000, in June 1907. *Horse and Hound* was lyrical about the project: 'All nations have sent the best of their kind and the Olympia Company has spared neither trouble nor expense in their reception. The arrangements were most elaborate, the prizes princely, and the decorations highly artistic, hence a large and fashionable attendance, which included a goodly proportion of ladies.'[21] Indeed nearly 140,000 visited the show over the six days. The prizes, including one of £375, attracted 600 horses – 2,000 entries – to 124 classes. Neither profit nor competition, perish the thought, were avowed objectives. At the inaugural luncheon Lonsdale adverted to the expected improvements in horse-breeding, other speakers suggested that 'the amity of nations must necessarily be promoted and increased' and the treasurer, Mr Euren, secretary of the Hackney Horse Society, specifically disavowed interest in large profits. Yet the takings were over £37,000 and a lucrative future lay ahead. Lonsdale was in his element as the show developed year by year. He presented the prizes for popular events such as a turn-out of costermongers' donkeys with decorated carts driven by Pearly Kings and Queens. One year, to the horror of the officials, a Cockney Donah threw her arms around his neck and gave him a kiss: Lonsdale delighted the crowd by dancing round the ring with her as the band played 'If You Were the Only Girl in the World'.[22]

There were some among the younger generation who showed more signs of coming to terms with modern technology, demonstrating how sport of a newer kind could be related to the sterner challenges ahead. The Hon. C.S. Rolls, that rare bird an aristocratic engineer, had broken the record for the journey from Monte Carlo to London in 1906 in a car he had built in partnership with Henry Royce at Derby. He had also distinguished himself in the

Gordon Bennett Balloon race that same year and was one of the first to fly the new heavier-than-air machines pioneered by the Wright brothers. In 1910, the year after Blériot's cross-channel flight, he won great acclaim by flying there and back without touching down. Rolls's potential talents as an aircraft designer were lost the following month when he was killed in a tournament at Bournemouth, but he was to be followed by the young T.O.M. Sopwith who that year won a prize for the longest flight on the continent and went on to design and manufacture a series of innovatory war-planes. There were many more, however, who remained addicted to the horse.

Hunting and National Hunt racing

A good example of the type was Siegfried Sassoon, author of *Memoirs of a Fox-hunting Man*. Sassoon was of the country gentleman class, in comfortable circumstances and under no pressure to do more with his life after Marlborough and Cambridge, which he left without a degree, than to hunt, play cricket and – reflecting the artistic leanings of his mother's family – collect books and write poetry. The *Memoirs* is lightly fictionalised autobiography, authentic in its detail and superbly evoking the period and the philosophy of the young men who were to be sent into the trenches in 1914. George Sherston, Sassoon's hero, is an orphan with a substantial private income, living in the care of an amiable but class-conscious aunt. His introduction to the values of a hunt-loving elite in a 'thoroughly unsporting neighbourhood' where the farmers made no secret of shooting the few foxes that there were, was at the hands of Dixon, a groom 'deeply imbued with sporting instincts' who had worked in stables, racing or hunt, from the age of fourteen. It was Dixon who first taught him how to play cricket and proudly watched his first appearance in the village Flower Show match. Sassoon's celebrated description has all the cricket stereotypes, but is sharply etched with affectionate irony. The village team has all classes – small farmers and yokels, visiting 'cracks', a public schoolboy on holiday, a wicket-keeping vicar with an MCC tie who needed to be watched, and is led by a local saddler. The umpire calls 'hout', the 'unofficial mayor' doffs his hat to the gentry, the band plays 'Soldiers of the Queen' and the officer home from the Boer War is splendidly reticent about his gallant deeds.[23]

Sherston progressed, under Dixon's supervision, from child's pony to full-grown horse, quickly developing an awareness of social nuances. Cosmo Gaffikin, the hunting and steeplechasing blood who sold him his first horse, was over-dressed. Likewise Bill Jaggett 'a hulking coarse-featured thruster, newly rich, ill-conditioned and foul-mouthed' – 'What with the vulgarly horsey cut and colour of his clothes and the bumptious and bullying manners which matched them, he was no ornament to the Dumborough Hunt.'[24] Sherston, of course, took himself to a good London tailor and bootmaker. The ostentation and vulgarity of the Dumborough was at one extreme: at the other was the nearby Potford whose new Master 'hunted the hounds himself and did everything as cheaply as possible. He bought the most awful old screws at Tattersall's, made his stablemen ride them all the way down from London to save the expense of a horse-box, and brought them out hunting the next day.'[25]

A Hunt's character was also revealed in its end-of season races. Each Easter Monday the Dumborough held a Hunt Steeplechase that was thoroughly up-to-date – crowds, jockeys in coloured jackets, lots of bookmakers and keen competition to win. Sherston, eating into his financial resources, was soon hunting on average five days a fortnight with a splendid new horse, Cockbird. (His old one had been pensioned off to the Coshford Vale Stag Hunt, a mid-Victorian relic 'kept on its legs by the devoted efforts of a group of prosperous hop-farmers and a family of brewers' chasing imported beasts released from a van.[26]) Cockbird, hunting regularly, qualified for the Colonel's Cup at Dumborough Races, and Sherston, having won, went to sleep murmuring to himself, 'Next season I'll come out in a pink coat.'

This, after a season's cricket, he duly did, but he transferred his allegiance to the Ringwood, an old hunt now under a new Master, Denis Milden, an Oxford man who had acquired a whiff of the brogue while learning to hunt in Ireland.[27] Milden hunted his own pack, not merely for economy, but because he was a perfectionist and he enjoyed it. Sherston was also impressed by Milden's efficiency in dealing with correspondence, mostly complaints or requests for compensation from farmers, and by the patient and methodical way he built up what was to become a great pack.

The Ringwood Hunt's Point-to-Point, in contrast to the Dumborough's modernity, was, as Dixon put it 'a real old-fashioned affair': the old natural type of course was slower, more unpredictable for the riders and less attractive to the modern spectator but it had the true country flavour – and the riders were genuine amateurs. Steeplechasing, though of mixed ancestry, was, because of its unpredictability, relatively honest. The Grand National, assisted by Edward VII's long-standing interest, had become a great national festival but its dominance was not altogether good for the sport. The public found the lesser races attractive enough, especially when well-known riders like 'Tich' Mason Arthur Nightingall, Ernie Pigott or Jack Anthony were involved, but the prizes were pathetically small, so that owners and trainers tended to regard the season as a build-up for the one big race. And lesser meetings, with a handful of runners in many races, were wide open to manipulation for gambling purposes. Even worse was the hybrid, hurdle-racing, dominated by converted flat race horses, which, because there was much less risk of falls, was much more attractive to the gamblers; it was open to all the abuses of the flat but without its social cachet. There remained point-to-point meetings, in which amongst many rough rustic affairs there were some of impeccable breeding that preserved the all-important links with hunting. The need was to prevent point-to-points from becoming replicas of steeplechasing, keeping to the old-style open-country courses, and restricting entries to genuine hunters.

In 1902 the NH Committee had appointed Thomas Pickernell – the former gentleman rider 'Mr Thomas' – as Inspector of Courses. The standards he set were objective enough but were obviously more easily met by promoters with ample resources. The bias towards the affluent was even more obvious in the matter of discipline. Hunt certificates were easier to obtain for the well con-nected, and the gentlemanly code did not allow too many questions being asked. This was bad enough but there were even cases of switching horses. In 1904 the committee sought the help of the MFH Association to which almost all Masters now belonged. They were not an easy body to deal with, being resistant on principle to being told what they could and could not do. Influential Masters like Lord Portman saw no reason why Hunts should not regulate for themselves the local farmers' races that were included in most NH programmes and many saw nothing wrong in accepting entries from puppy-walkers and others on the fringes of hunts.

The extension of NHC control was a slow business. Meanwhile its social reputation was enhanced by the highly superior point-to-point meetings that studded the calendar. The Stock Exchange's annual event was a splendid affair. The members of the Bar had their own club, the Pegasus, which staged prestigious events. The House of Commons had an annual point-to-point in Epping Forest. (Colonel Hall-Walker's victory in 1910 was marred somewhat by the death of the Member for Crewe after a fall.) The better regiments and the better colleges at Oxford and Cambridge held their own meetings. The Cottesmore held regimental races for the officers of the Coldstream, Grena-diers, Scots and Royal Horse Guards, the Pytchley for the Life Guards. The Whaddon Chase and Lord Rothschild's Staghounds held annual events.

A modern aristocrat

That neither social eminence nor sporting prowess was any guarantee of probity was demonstrated by the early career of Lord Dalmeny, heir to the fifth Earl of Rosebery, now in disgruntled retirement. Rosebery was renowned for his acerbic tongue and he was not particularly fond of his son. On first seeing the product of his marriage to the Rothschild heiress, he is said to have remarked, 'Le Jew est fait; rien ne va plus.'[28] But Dalmeny, though unbeautiful and unintellectual was strong and athletic and he became a great sporting figure at Eton before going on to Sandhurst. In 1902 a sycophantic newspaper, describing him as 'a handsome young soldier, tall, athletic and deservedly popular', suggested that though he had the family love of horseflesh on the whole he preferred cricket, football and rackets to horse-racing ('a desire to take a share in sports that require a personal exertion . . . that was curiously absent in his father as a young man') and that he was even less interested in betting than Rosebery.[29] That the writer was wide of the mark in this last particular did not emerge for some time.

In 1903 in order to please his father – a difficult task – Dalmeny left the Grenadiers to become the prospective Liberal candidate for Midlothian. To occupy his time between constituency-warming duties, he hunted, shot and played polo and registered his colours under both Jockey Club and National Hunt regulations. But his chief interest in the summer was cricket, and in 1904 he became Captain of the Surrey County Cricket Club and, indeed made a success of it. Surrey, which had famous players like Tom Hayward, Bobby Abel, J.N. Crawford and, from 1905, the young Jack Hobbs, had under-performed through poor leadership, and they now began to do better. Dalmeny himself averaged over twenty in the dashing style that characterised the age, earning the praise of the weekly magazine, *Cricket*: 'A really first class bat with a variety of strokes which betoken the master.'[30] His election to Parliament when the Liberals swept to power in January, 1906, led to a sarcastic comment from a gossip columnist the following season: 'Lord Dalmeny is very anxious that his Parliamentary career shall not interfere with his prowess as a cricketer. At the same time he is laudably desirous that his devotion to cricket shall not prevent him from doing his duty to the electors of Midlothian . . . Quite recently when playing for Surrey at the Oval he had to hunt about for a substitute to field for him as he was anxious to speak and vote for the Second Reading of the Coal Mines Eight Hour Bill.'[31]

After the 1907 season Dalmeny made the supreme sacrifice, leaving Surrey, but unfortunately without corresponding benefit to his constituents. On 3 April 1908 the *Glasgow Herald* reported on a 'regrettable incident' in a steeplechase. In a two-horse race Dalmeny's opponent, Lord Gort, who had fallen, was able to remount and haul back a long lead to win. This provoked a hostile demonstration from the crowd. There was worse to come. In October 1905 he had figured in a sordid episode at Sandown Park, when after a two-horse race between two amateur riders the loser, West Fenton de Wend-Fenton, was warned off by the Jockey Club. Dalmeny had backed the winner at long odds and was widely rumoured to have been in on the deception, but nothing could be proved and the gossip had died down.[32] Now in 1908 the resentful de Wend-Fenton published a *roman-à-clef*, with the unmistakable punning reference to Dalmeny's family name in its title, *The Primrose Path*, showing an unscrupulous 'Earl' as the villain in a highly coloured account of the 1905 affair.

As before, Dalmeny withstood the gossip, and there was no question of the National Hunt Committee taking any action. Rosebery is said to have told his friends 'that Dalmeny ought not to be allowed to have anything to do with racing' but it was the 1909 Budget, on which father and son reached rare agreement, that led to his resigning his seat in Parliament.[33] His wedding that year brought him back into the headlines. It was the social event of the season, attracting much laudatory attention. The Socialist weekly *Justice* spoke only for a depraved minority when it condemned the nuptials as a 'Scotch-Jewish-English aristocratic plutocratic combination' and predicted that 'years before Lord Dalmeny has reached the age of his talkative and useless father the system of capitalist plunder on which his fortunes are built will have received a very ugly shock'.[34]

Notes

1 For the full text see *Definitive Verse of Rudyard Kipling*, London, 1940, pp. 301–4.
2 S. Rowntree, *Poverty: a Study of Town Life*, London, 1901.
3 A. Marwick, *The Deluge*, London, 1965, p. 23. A compensation was that no one with less than £160 a year paid income tax.
4 P. Thompson, *The Edwardians*, St Albans, 1977, p. 35.
5 So claimed by Sartorius, the landlord in Shaw's first play *Widowers' Houses* (1892) and for this he could not afford to carry out repairs.
6 Thompson, *The Edwardians*, p. 40.
7 K. Young, *Harry, Lord Rosebery*, London, 1974, p. 44.
8 I. Whitcome, *After the Ball*, Harmondsworth, 1973, p. 153.
9 The Hon. Mrs George Keppel, a 29-year-old, cigarette-smoking fashionable beauty, was married to the Duke of Albemarle's seventh son, for whom Sir Thomas Lipton had obligingly found work at Edward's request.
10 C. Hibbert, *Edward VII: a Portrait*, Harmondsworth, 1982, pp. 225–6.
11 Even more, 2843, were shot on the same moor in 1913. For the various records see E. Parker, *The Shooting Weekend Book*, London, 1952.
12 Hibbert, *Edward VII*, p. 199.
13 He had lost £18,000 in a card game against Captain Machell, his brother's racing manager: see D. Birley, *Sport and the Making of Britain*, Manchester, 1993, p. 302.
14 *Irish Times*, 12 July, 1907.
15 D. Laird, *Royal Ascot*, London, 1976, pp. 169–70.
16 Hibbert, *Edward VII*, p. 272.
17 K.E. McCrone, 'The Lady Blue', *IJHS*, Spetember 1986, p. 199.
18 K.E. McCrone, 'Women's Sport at the University of London', *IJHS*, September, 1990, p. 213.
19 George V is said to have remarked, 'I should really like to have Hugh, but I could not possibly afford him'.
20 Both letters are printed in full in Sutherland, *Yellow Earl*, Appendix 1, pp. 240–246, appendix 2, pp. 241–53.

21 8 June 1907.
22 D. Sutherland, *The Yellow Earl*, p. 169.
23 S. Sassoon, *Memoirs of a Fox-hunting Man*, London, 1928, pp. 53–79.
24 *Ibid.*, p. 29.
25 *Ibid.*, p. 132.
26 *Ibid.*, p. 175.
27 Like most of Sassoon's characters Milden was based on a real person, Norman Loder. Ireland was the traditional place to start for a serious intending Master of the modern sort, with limited means and relying on guaranteed subscriptions.
28 Young, *Rosebery*, p. 17.
29 *Ibid.*, pp. 31–2.
30 *Cricket: a Weekly Record*, 17 May, 1906.
31 24 May, 1906, quoted in Young, *Rosebery*, pp. 43–4.
32 Young, *Rosebery*, pp. 47–9.
33 *Ibid.*, p. 49.
34 *Ibid.*, pp. 65–6.

CHAPTER TEN

The pleasure-seekers

The 'system of capitalist plunder' and the 'aristocratic, plutocratic combination' were unlikely to be shaken by sport. Indeed the alliance had helped to build it up in the first place, and was still in good repair. Blatant on the Turf, it flourished more discreetly in exclusive sporting clubs like the metropolitan Queen's and Prince's and their regional counterparts. Real tennis and racquets were the truly prestigious activities but both lawn tennis and golf had Balfour's imprimatur, and each had its social niche. In such sports the clubs' purpose of catering for their individual members was not submerged in the frenzied hiring of teams to compete against each other for gate-money. Nevertheless tournaments and championships had already brought their own temptations.

Golf: paradise at a price

It took a little longer than usual for the skilled working-class golfer to reap the rewards that come from the curious human pleasure in vicarious achievement. Yet there were signs of what was to come. Gate-money forced itself on the attention of clubs that staged the bigger tournaments, if only to seek reparation from spectators who rampaged over courses willy-nilly. Professionals were growing restive at the hands of club members who did not appreciate their gallivanting off to play in competitions, secretaries who reported on their diligence and sobriety and amateurs who encroached on their traditional preserves.

A golf club secretary might be paid £150 or £200 a year for his administrative duties yet still retain his amateur status. One such was A.E. Stoddart, who left first-class cricket in 1901 aged thirty-eight with no settled profession and soon became secretary of Neasden Golf Club. This brought a big improvement in his handicap – he reached Colonel Bogey's standard in a year – but the life was more congenial than was good for him.[1] A more purposeful 'shamateur' was the lawyer H.S. Colt, formerly golf captain at Cambridge, who was not only paid secretary of the illustrious Sunningdale but a leading golf architect. The professionals, mostly of working-class origin, accepted the anomalous status of the middle-class secretaries much as their counterparts in cricket did, and malcontents were even more isolated. Colt's incursion into course design, a hitherto professional domain, was a more controversial matter and though he airily brushed criticism aside it added to a growing sense of grievance. There were great variations in conditions of employment, and the golfing boom did not always seem to be working to the professionals' advantage. Proper remuneration for teaching, for instance, might have made restrictions on playing in tournaments easier to bear, but tuition fees were too often regarded as gratuities rather than business arrangements. Similarly the old idea of '£40 a year and a shop' instead of a decent guaranteed wage was even less attractive if pros could not, or were not allowed to, take advantage of new commercial opportunities. In the early days professionals had made the clubs they sold to the members. Now mass-produced hickory shafts, club-heads or finished clubs were replacing the old hand-crafted type. Most professionals still did repairs, but they more and more had to look for profit from retail sales. These could be plentiful enough; but some club committees preferred to manage retail outlets themselves and if professionals lacked flair, persuasive powers or commercial drive their incomes might be greatly reduced. It was such anxieties that led to the formation in 1902 of the Professional Golfers' Association. The idea had been first mooted publicly by an anonymous letter to the press from a North Wales professional. Controlling bodies of sports were not noted for their enthusiasm for trades unions: nor, indeed were sportsmen themselves. In golf, their trade and servicing functions, together with their relative isolation and consequent vulnerability, gave club professionals a greater incentive towards unionisation than most sportsmen, and a broader basis for it. Nevertheless the more successful they were in the competitive end of the sport the less likely they were to interest themselves in the greatest good of the greatest number. The humbler sort were fortunate in that their cause was taken up by a leading tournament player, J.H. Taylor, who took a personal interest in the formation of the PGA, persuading other great players like Harry Vardon, James Braid and Sandy Herd to join, and also by his tactful approach winning the backing of enlightened amateurs. Harold Hilton, the editor of *Golf Illustrated*, wrote a supportive article, for instance. So the PGA received a fair welcome.

No sooner had it got going, however, than the inherent tensions between the tournament players and the rest began to show. Two years earlier an American pharmacist, Osburn Haskell, had invented a new golf ball, which had now found its way to Britain. It was made by winding elastic at tension around a rubber core – a mechanical process – and it was easier to control and went further than the 'guttie'. Both aspects presented problems for the professionals as a body: first it threatened one of their traditional trades, making and re-moulding gutties; second by reducing the skill requirement it seemed likely to narrow the gap between amateur and professional, removing some of the mystique.[2]

So dramatic a challenge so early in the organisation's life was too much for the PGA, and their resistance collapsed almost as soon as it began. Whatever hope there might have been of a united front disappeared when Sandy Herd, a prominent member, tried out the Haskell ball in practice, decided to use it in the 1902 Open Championship – and won. When the Amateur Championship was also won by a player using a Haskell that was the end of the argument. Everyone switched to the new ball within a year or so – leaving only a few Scottish purists muttering that it took all the real skill out of the game. It certainly made golf an easier game. It also became an even more popular one, to the great advantage of everyone, including the rank-and-file PGA members, though this was not immediately apparent.

Internal tensions, indeed, increased as the PGA, unsuccessful in its protests over the architectural activities of amateurs like Colt, did better in furthering the interests of the handful of tournament players. Even before the national organisation was fully under way the London and Home Counties Association had held its own closed competition for a £15 prize. This was not an attempt to challenge the authority of the amateurs – indeed a Cup was presented to the winner by the Tooting Bec Golf Club – or take over the organisation of competitions, but an early bit of self-help. What it did do, however, was sharpen interest in professional competition amongst potential sponsors, notably the popular newspapers and ball and equipment makers, a move towards commercialisation that was not generally welcomed in amateur circles. The PGA made a spectacular breakthrough in 1903 when the *News of the World* sponsored a professional match play championship. The prize-money, £200, was more than twice that of the Open.

Golf's rapidly increasing popularity did not mean that it cost less. Even the new balls, mass produced and with companies competing to get a share of the market, were hard to find at less than half-a-crown, which had been the going rate before the introduction of the guttie in 1845. There was also a snobbery surrounding the type of balls people used, with their distinctive little markings and endorsements by great players. The popularity showed itself rather in the growth of club membership, controlled both socially and financially, and in the appearance of new clubs, including many of an even more exclusive kind. The biggest expansion took place in Greater London. The fifty or so clubs grew to eighty-nine between 1900 and 1910.

The railways and property and land developers were now regular partners.

Golf courses sometimes followed housing as at Ellesborough (1906) whilst the accidental discovery of an expanse of suitable soil led to the creation of Sandy Lodge (1910), a fine course whose construction was supervised by Harry Vardon, and the railway and property development followed. It was a happy chance that land was so readily available from owners, increasingly fearful of Liberal government policies, at the time the Haskell ball created a demand for bigger courses. Tree-lovers were not always so delighted. N.L. Jackson played a leading part in an enterprise at Stoke Poges, Berkshire, in 1908. The syndicate leased 600 acres at Stoke Park and cut down 3000 trees to make a course designed by H.S. Colt and constructed under the supervision of its secretary, Hugh Alison, a former Oxford player, also a golf architect.[3] 'It is a spot to suggest rather the loved solitudes of the dryads but to Mr Colt it also suggested a very charming mashie shot', commented *The Times*.[4] Nevertheless six members of the Royal Family attended its opening along with a large selection of the peerage. Alfred Harmsworth, who had become Lord Northcliffe in 1905, was one of the first members.

There were occasional attempts to extend golf to the less wealthy, but belonging to an artisan club was still the best way for working-class amateur players. Such opportunities were of course restricted by geographical accident and the inclinations of the members proper. Nor was this neo-feudal relationship likely to suit everyone. There was a growing demand among the urban lower middle classes. The London County Council caused great controversy in 1908 when they took over responsibility for the Royal Epping Forest course and turned it into a public course. The following year they created headlines again by building a new course at Hainault Forest, designed by J.H. Taylor and his partner. Green fees were a shilling and a season ticket cost two guineas. This was a considerable success, especially at weekends, but not every rate-payer thought it a justifiable use for their contributions: the more affluent saw no reason to pamper the lower orders and the more socialistic thought nothing of this pastime of bloated capitalists.

In amateur competition British domination lasted slightly longer in golf than in other games, largely because its mysteries, and the skills of club manufacture and golf course construction took longer to disseminate. American technology was a potent force, as the Haskell ball had shown, but innovations were generally kept in check by the R&A. A good example occurred in 1904 when an Australian-born American, Walter J. Travis, used a centre-shafted putter to win the British Amateur Championship. Travis was an aggressive fellow, outspoken in his criticism of the gentlemanly organisers of the competition, the Royal St George's, Sandwich, whom he thought a snobbish and patronising bunch. The R&A banned the new putter, a prohibition that remained in force for fifty years, and would doubtless have liked to ban Travis himself. Happily he was a temporary phenomenon and British complacency remained largely undisturbed.

In women's golf there was even less trouble from the Americans. After the outstanding Irish players Rhoda Adair and May Hezlet and a brief Lottie Dod intervention came the Scot, Dorothy Campbell, who in 1909 set new standards on both sides of the Atlantic. All were to be eclipsed by Miss Cecilia Leitch, generally known as Cecil, a 17-year-old semi-finalist in the women's championship in 1908. She hit the ball tremendously hard and caused even the die-hards to revise their opinion of women's golf. In 1910 Miss Leitch played Harold Hilton in a match over 72 holes at the fashionable Walton Heath (1904) and Sunningdale courses, playing off the men's tees. The match, highly publicised, was billed as 'the battle of the sexes', always a good line and particularly eye-catching at a time of great suffragette activity. It was of greater sporting than political significance. Given half a stroke a hole Miss Leitch narrowly won, but civilisation managed to survive. Feminist politics rarely interested women golfers, who were engaged in a more traditional battle. Their progress in competitive golf and in ordinary club play was a great fillip to middle-class women's self-esteem, but this did not cause them to question their subordinate status within the game, let alone outside it. When the R&A emblematically recognised women's golf by allowing the 1908 ladies' championship to be played at St Andrews, the ladies were most courteously treated and even taken on a tour of the clubhouse to see its historic trophies; and though the competitors had not only to change but to eat at their hotels this was progress enough.[5]

Lawn tennis and the quest for manliness

Cecil Leitch further endangered convention by preferring a hair-ribbon to a hat and wearing skirts a foot above the ground. Such tomboyish aberrations were not usual, however, and most women paid more attention to the demands of femininity, even in golf in which thick boots were the serious woman's choice for foot and ankle wear. In lawn tennis, which potentially exposed limbs to more frantic and more public gaze, the customary high standards of decorum were maintained. The trend-setters, the Wimbledon champions, were still the petticoated married ladies of the 1890s. Mrs Hillyard, now well advanced in years, still graced the scene. Mrs Sterry, who returned to take the title again in 1901 and 1908 , saw no need for skirts any shorter than two or three inches above the ground. And their successor over the next twenty years, Dorothea Douglass, who became Mrs Lambert Chambers in 1907, was from the same mould.

The daughter of a clergyman, who had encouraged her athleticism, she became a fine all-rounder – an Ealing badminton and Middlesex hockey player and a fine golfer. Her tennis was methodical rather than brilliant or flashy, qualities alien to her nature. This emerges clearly from her remarks on dress in her highly influential book, appropriately entitled *Lawn Tennis for Ladies*.[6] She defended women's right to take exercise and thought the idea that sport spoiled their appearance was ludicrous. A lady tennis player ought to look neat and attractive, but it was impossible to be 'just so every second' and in any event women were more interesting in lively action than observing the sort of fashion that required immobility to keep every hair in place. She commended the example of experienced players who increasingly avoided trailing skirts, dressy blouses and trimmed hats. She advised abandoning hats altogether and recommended a plain, white gored skirt four or five inches above the ground, a plain white shirt with collar and tie, and white shoes and stockings.

As a girl Mrs Lambert Chambers had been encouraged to play against men but though this had helped greatly to develop her defensive game, she was not a forceful player. This reflected the limits of her feminism which though rejecting the 'shrinking violet' school of thought was based on complementing, not attempting to rival, male muscularity. It also exposed a weakness. Her initial run of Wimbledon victories in 1903 and 1904 was interrupted when she was beaten twice in the next three finals by the strapping May Sutton from California. It is hard to imagine that Mrs Lambert Chambers would ever, as Miss Sutton had done in the heat of their 1905 encounter, roll back her cuffs to reveal bare wrists. This was some comfort for chauvinists, as were Miss Sutton's Devonian origins, but they were doubtless relieved that she did not compete in the 1908 London Olympic Games in which Mrs Lambert Chambers gave a suitably ladylike exhibition.[7] Now over thirty she returned to take the Wimbledon title in 1910.

In the men's game the first seven years of the century belonged entirely to the Dohertys. Their 1901 doubles victory over the Americans Dwight Davis and Holcombe Ward in the exemplary conditions of Wimbledon put the first Davis Cup debacle into perspective, and the Americans showed proper respect in defeat. Alas, even the Dohertys could not prevent a second Cup defeat in New York in 1902 – the Irishman, Dr Pym, was not in good form – but normality was restored at Boston in 1903. British dominance was further demonstrated in 1904 by the subjugation of Belgium (admitted along with France to the competition that year) and again in 1905 and 1906 when the Americans felt the lash.

Reggie Doherty, the star of the 1890s, was in poor health and in 1901 he lost his Wimbledon singles title to A.W. Gore, son of the first winner, Spencer Gore. Laurie Doherty at once assumed Reggie's mantle, taking Gore's covered court title at the illustrious Queen's Club, holding it for the next six years, and in 1902 beginning a series of Wimbledon victories that ended only with his retirement five years later. Reggie, meanwhile, recovered sufficiently to take the doubles title with Laurie between 1903 and 1905 (they won it eight times in all) before his health failed again. The following year Laurie, having reached thirty, gave up tennis at the height of his fame, taking up golf (and becoming good enough to compete in several Amateur championships). When he died in 1919 a long leading article in The *Times* gave him – and lawn tennis – a place in the pantheon: 'He played an English game in the spirit in which Englishmen think games should be played. He was a typical Englishman, and it is a source of legitimate pride to his countrymen that we can think him so.'[8]

Back in 1907, however, lawn tennis had not risen so far above its dubious claims to virility as to be regarded as a source of national vigour rather than a threat to it. Few public schools played it and, though the universities did, its status was somewhat ambivalent. In 1906 Cambridge's Regius Professor of Medicine told the pupils of Leeds Grammar School, a northern citadel of rugger and cricket, that undergraduate enthusiasm for lawn tennis was 'a moral waste'.[9] Real tennis had a better reputation. It had been the first game at which Oxford had played Cambridge and it was they, MCC, the exclusive Queen's and Prince's Clubs that had led its recent revival. This was limited by the need for elaborate and highly expensive courts. There were nevertheless some thirty clubs, including two in Ireland and one in Scotland, and a new club in Manchester good enough to attract the leading professional, Peter Latham, from Queen's Club. Unfortunately, however, many British professionals who had served the exclusive clubs, often in family tradition, had emigrated to the United States to work in the country clubs of the East Coast elite. Their teaching bore fruit and when real tennis appeared on the Olympic programme, for the only time, at London in 1908 the American amateur Jay Gould beat the English champion and advocate of athleticism, Eustace Miles of Rugby and Cambridge, for the Gold Medal.

Real tennis's simpler variant, rackets, also played with a hard ball, in which courts were a more affordable proposition, was much esteemed and highly popular in the public schools.[10] Competition amongst Old Boys continued in the exclusive clubs and the universities. H.K. Foster, of Malvern and Oxford, one of a great cricketing family, was the amateur champion in the early years of the century, and rackets, fortified by the MCC and university tradition, was to remain a recognised training sport for gentlemen cricketers. Of its high status there was no doubt. One of the semi-finalists in the 1903 Olympics was John Jacob Astor, son of William Waldorf, a naturalised Briton, future Baron and owner of *The Times*, currently serving in the Life Guards after leaving Eton and Oxford. The amateur champion, was E.M. Baerlein, of Eton, Cambridge and the Manchester club.

There was also a (fairly) soft ball version, squash rackets, which had begun at Harrow as a quieter, less destructive means of passing the time for boys queuing up to use the rackets court – banging the ball against a gable end of the school buildings – and was developing as a country house sport. Quite a few of the great houses in Britain and Ireland now had purpose-built courts, as had the Bath Club in Dover Street. There was as yet no uniformity of rules, though the Americans, who used a larger ball, had an amateur championship from 1906, and in Britain rackets players like J.E. Palmer-Tomkinson and the young Irishman T.O. Jameson were increasingly taken with the potentialities of squash. In the public schools, however, another hard ball variant, fives, played with the hand (as real tennis, *jeu de paume*, had originally been) was taken more seriously. Fives, too, had started from improvised beginnings – it was first played on the chapel steps at Eton – and its purpose-built courts reproduced the idiosyncratic features of its early origins. It had retained its tribal characteristics and there were three different types, called after their originators, Eton, Winchester and Rugby. Though played by limited numbers, fives was the badge of hardihood amongst schoolboys, fitness fanatics and nostalgic schoolmasters, all highly important contributors to the Edwardian games cult.

The image of lawn tennis, by contrast, was as 'a game that has so majestically received the hall-mark of suburban gentility'.[11] It conspicuously lacked, furthermore, not only public school muscular Christian but popular support. In 1899 the sporting journalist F.G. Aflalo had placed it 'among the pastimes that cannot be easily made the pretext for heavy expenditure'.[12] But his analysis of what it actually tended to cost was discouraging to egalitarians. Such widening of the circle as there had been had come from the sports facilities of the better business houses and a few industrial firms. Similarly the defensively vague claims of Mrs Lambert Chambers that it was 'more or less within the reach of all, rich or poor', and could be 'played on one's own lawn . . . or even some of the public parks' did not bear close examination.[13] Under the 1905 Unemployed Workmen's Act, inspired by the depression of the previous year, local councils had been able to extend and improve their parks and one or two places had built lawn tennis courts, on a modest scale in Bristol and a spectacular one at Platt Fields, Manchester. But municipal provision was patchy at best and there is little evidence that the populace were falling over themselves to play this toffs' game.

Beyond suburbia, and beyond Mrs Lambert Chambers's indomitably bourgeois respectability, there was, in fact, a more glamorous lawn tennis world. The royal flavour of the ancestor game had been re-captured by such early enthusiasts as King Gustav V of Sweden and Carlos I of Portugal and a new younger royal set was graced by Alfonso XIII of Spain and the Crown Princes Gustav of Sweden and Wilhelm of Germany. Theodore Roosevelt built a court at the White House on his accession in 1904. Covered and asphalt courts added to the attractions of the Swiss winter sports resorts. Grand Duke Michael presided over the tournament at Baden-Baden, which had enjoyed the organising talents of N.L. Jackson, who had also been responsible for the first tournament at St Malo and in 1903 advised the syndicate behind the sports complex at Le Touquet.

The growing international tournament circuit accelerated a trend, naturally much deplored by British purists, towards 'pot-hunting' and worse. The foreigners were, of course, the worst offenders. (The most celebrated case was that of Max Decugis, the French Davis Cup player, temporarily suspended in 1910 for converting prizes into fruit and vegetables which he sold for cash. When he lost a tournament in England Decugis joked that he was trying to win the second prize as he already had too many gold cigarette cases.) There was much criticism, too, of what were called 'manufacturer's players': the tournament idols, suggested one muscular moralist, would 'go down to posterity as little, if anything, above tradesmen's touts'.[14] Competition amongst equipment manufacturers, inseparable from any sport, was particularly strong in lawn tennis, which had been born in a welter of disputes about patents.[15] In fact the corruption was just as evident in the game's authorities as the players. The biggest scandal of the time, indeed, surrounded the All-England Club itself.

It stemmed from the determined efforts of the firm of Slazenger, making themselves over from mid-Victorian gentility to exploiters of the mass-market in sporting goods, to win the Wimbledon tennis ball concession from their rivals, F.H. Ayres, who had enjoyed the privilege of donating the balls used at the tournament since 1881. Slazengers' chosen instrument was Archdale Palmer, a business man whose affability and contacts had led him to the position of Secretary of All-England, a troubled post in a club born in controversy and still regarded as a stumbling block by the LTA. The LTA, resentful of the AELTC's pretensions to a status akin to that of MCC, particularly objected to a private club running the Wimbledon tournament and taking the lion's share of its profits. It was manna from heaven to them, therefore, when after the 1905 championships a referee, a journalist called Eveleigh, resigned in protest at AELTC's conniving at the use of illegally sized balls supplied by Slazenger, and let it be known to his friends in the press that he had also been offered £100 by the firm as a sweetener.

Palmer, according to the account of George Hillyard, a later and more upright secretary of All-England, had contrived a round robin from the leading players urging the committee to switch to Slazenger balls: they, though preferring the customary Ayres' variety, had agreed, whereupon, Palmer, with the concession secured, had actually joined Slazenger as general manager whilst still remaining secretary of the AELTC.[16] In the rumpus that followed the LTA, who led the attack, were strongly supported by those like C.B. Fry, currently campaigning against the 'thraldom of trade influence' at Queen's Club as well as the AELTC, who saw it as the inevitable consequence of appointing a secretary from the world of commerce, a thing to which MCC would never have stooped.[17] Others, however, argued that standards as high as Wimbledon's could hardly be maintained in an amateur sport without trade support, that Ayres themselves had achieved the initial concession, and those they still held at Bournemouth and Eastbourne, in similar fashion, and, most telling of all, that the journal of the self-righteous LTA was subsidised by Slazenger.

Palmer was obliged to resign as AELTC secretary and the club eventually decided to buy the balls for the championship in future. The LTA, meanwhile, was fortified in its hostility to All-England, and in 1906 proposed an alternative national championship. This the AELTC easily resisted; Wimbledon might not be the biggest tournament – that honour could now be claimed by Eastbourne – but it was undoubtedly the best and in its snobbish fashion, the least tainted by professionalism. In any attempt to 'democratise' it on LTA lines, its defenders argued, 'something of the spirit that has hitherto pervaded it, will probably be lost. It is not a sport for the masses.'[18]

Since lawn tennis's moral obliquity was seen as one of the causes of the British physical decline that had troubled the nation since the Boer War, international failure in such an effete activity was not widely considered an overwhelming disaster. There were others far greater, as we shall see. Nevertheless when the Dohertys retired in 1906 and the newcomers Australasia and the Americans began to dominate the Davis Cup it did not help the nation's morale. If Wimbledon did not present such a black picture, at least on the surface, it was because the Australian, N.E. (later Sir Norman) Brookes, who won the singles title in 1907 did not re-appear for seven years because of the ties of his career. This allowed the veteran Gore back into the picture and he won in 1908 and 1909, but it was ominous for British tennis that at the age of forty-one he was now the best player. Similarly in the minor tournament at the London Olympics in 1908 veterans were to the fore The doubles final was won by the unlikely combination of George Hillyard, now forty-four years old and Reggie Doherty, emerging briefly from retirement. The outstanding player on the British circuit was Brookes's young doubles partner A.F. Wilding, a New Zealander who had gone up to Cambridge in 1902, qualifying for the law in the intervals of travelling round the world, whenever possible on his motorcycle, playing tennis. Wilding, after winning the Wimbledon doubles twice with different partners, had so far advanced by 1910 as to begin a string of singles victories as well.

Fashions, indoor and outdoor

Limits of space (rather than philosophical nicety or even personal prejudice) preclude exploration of the vast range of pastimes, particularly indoor ones, that occupied enthusiasts and manufacturers alike in the quest for the attention of leisured Edwardians. Thus billiards, of ancient lineage professionalised in Victorian times and still considered superior to snooker, can be given no more than a respectful nod. Similarly we can merely note the brief appearance of table tennis (or Gossima or Ping-Pong as two of its patentees called it) as a commercial and competitive phenomenon in 1902. Even Badminton, in which the number of clubs affiliated to the Association shot up from 69 in 1901 to 190 in 1907, and which induced a speculator to put up its first purpose-built hall in Kensington in 1908, can only be noted as still up and coming and still resolutely amateur.

Bowls can command a little more attention if only because of its contribution to the 'north–south divide' and because, in the absence of continental, or American, interest, it was, and was to remain, a British and white colonial idiosyncrasy. The colonials, furthermore, had to fend for themselves. The Imperial Bowling Association, never much more than an optimistic name, was soon to be absorbed by its replacement, and the International Bowling Board, which W.G. Grace fathered, was a British Isles affair. In 1903 the English Bowling Association was formed when W.G., fortified by access to the Scottish Association's rules, contacted English clubs putting forward the idea of a single governing body. The incentive was the prospect not only of better-organised competition within England but of international matches against Scotland. The IBA were sidelined as W.G., under the cloak of discussions about affiliation, conducted separate negotiations for a home international tournament (at Crystal Palace, of course). Irish and Welsh Associations were formed and came together with the Scots and English in an International Bowling Board in 1904. The IBA, caught flat-footed, now found themselves being offered the opportunity to disband and allow their English member clubs, many of whom were seceding anyway, to join the EBA 'in return for a fair and just representation'. The 'merger' followed in 1905 and in the subsequent expansion W.G.'s London Counties did conspicuously well.[19]

London Counties also successfully exploited the possibilities of indoor play. Alley bowls, once a notorious ale-house sport and vehicle for gambling, had remained popular in various regional forms, notably in London and the West country (where it was known as skittles). Bowlers, particularly in Scotland, had also been trying to devise an indoor, winter version of the game proper. Eventually after years of experiment with floorboards strewn with sand and so forth, more suitable floor surfaces – bata-weave, coconut matting, baize, felt, jute – were discovered and the first club, the Edinburgh Winter Bowling Association, was formed in 1905. But the galleries of Crystal Palace offered really attractive surroundings and the indoor club formed there in 1906 under the presidency of W.G.'s brother, R.P. Grace, was the making of the game.

Outdoors the gambling fervour and the starkly competitive tendencies of the brasher elements of the population found their best expression in crown green bowling. In the industrial north of England – and in the parts of North Wales influenced by Lancashire mores – they played bowls on greens which were higher in the middle than at the edges, an arrangement that added to the scope for cunning variations and use of the bowls' bias. Crown green bowling had a style and a following all of its own, and every northern public house worth its salt had its green. By the turn of the century open tournaments, with handicaps for professionals and attendant bookmakers, were well established. Blackpool, the north-country answer to Brighton, was the main centre. Its Talbot Handicap (started in 1873 and called after a Hotel) had over 1,000 entries by 1910 and a second, the Waterloo, had been started in 1907. There were leagues, usually based on public houses, in most of the surrounding industrial areas. Not surprisingly, perhaps, it was the professionals who first formed themselves into an association, in 1905, joining three years later with the owners of the greens they played on to form the Lancashire Professional Bowlers' Association. This introduced its own elitism, strictly controlling admission by invitation only. In southern eyes it also further diminished the credentials of the British Crown Green Amateur Bowling Association (1907), and this anticipation of the modern relationship between amateur and professional sport was some way ahead of its time.

Both kinds of bowls were played by women – there were no problems of decorum or dress involved – but, of course, on sufferance, and they were more prominent in the south where the game was preponderantly middle-class and club-based. Women bowlers were sufficiently numerous in the capital for the London County Council, ever to the fore, to require one of the rinks in each of its seventy-six parks to be set aside for female use in 1906. A few clubs had women's sections and their early competitions were arranged by male clubs – the first, in 1908, was for the wives of members of the Southey BC, Wimbledon. Though mixed play was not common neither were there many exclusively female clubs. The first was founded at Kingston Canonbury, Surrey, in 1910, and it was not long before it was playing challenge matches against other ladies' teams.

Women were also prominent on the burgeoning winter sports scene – the ubiquitous Lottie Dod, for instance, was a gifted figure-skater – but it was the formation of the Public Schools Alpine Sports Club in 1902, an offshoot of Henry Lunn's flourishing travel agency, that really conferred the seal of approval on winter sports. Though not a public school man himself Lunn made sure his son Arnold was, and with his enthusiastic participation brought the spirit of organised competition to the snow and ice. The Sports Club's annual trophy event was a social as well as a sporting success. Lord Roberts of Kandahar was a Vice-President and he and other dignitaries like the Earl of Lytton, the former Viceroy of India, presented the awards. Until 1910 there was one cup for the combined results in ski-ing, tobogganing and skating competitions.

It was an unnatural coalition, however. British skaters were still very con-scious of their dignity, standing aloof from Continental initiatives such as the Northern Games in Stockholm in 1901 with its speed skating races and other vulgarities. They were equally appalled by the excesses of Continental figure-skating, exemplified by the liberal 'free-style' antics of the 'Viennese' school. When figure-skating was introduced to the Olympics at London in 1908 the men's final was won by a Swede, Salchow, who included a spectacular leap in his performance. Dignity and British standards were better preserved in the ladies' final won by Mrs Madge Syres, a veteran of earlier championships at Davos who came out of retirement to win the day. But there were alarming prospects in store.

Nor had the skaters much in common with the reckless young men who were in the process of transforming tobogganing from a family frolic into a highly organised sport. When the St Moritz Bobsleigh Club opened its first run in 1903 it began to oust the individual contests by introducing a team element. Its British public school ethos proved congenial to the international set who now thronged the Swiss hotels. Crown Prince Willy, who became Honorary President, took it up with annoying German efficiency. The sort of Britisher who loved tobogganing was J.C.T. Moore-Brabazon, later Lord Brabazon of Tara, a Harrovian and Cambridge engineer and pioneer of both aviation and motoring. From 1907 he was to go down the Cresta Run each year until his death in 1964 and in his youth he three times won its coveted Curzon Cup.

The skiers were also regarded as somewhat unorthodox modernists. Ski-ing had hitherto been chiefly known as a means of transport in Norway, whence it had been taken to the USA, and as a technique developed by the Austrian Army. The Ski Club formed at Davos in 1903, seven strong, were the first serious British students of ski-ing for sporting and mountaineering pur-poses.[20] The crudities of racing was not for them, but they introduced tests and standards, for speed as well as style, laying the foundation for the next age when racing took hold. Mountaineering on skis was thought outlandish by the prestigious Alpine Club, and it was the young Arnold Lunn who pioneered this new manifestation of muscular Christianity. After Harrow he had gone, in 1906, to Oxford, where he failed to take a degree but as well as such distinctions as editing *Isis* and becoming President of the Union, founded both the University's Mountaineering Club and its Alpine Ski Club. When he and his university friends went into action they did the thing thoroughly, producing the first good ski guide to the Alps and the first comprehensive study of snowcraft for skiers.

At home, meanwhile, the National Skating Association had so far been infected by the democratic spirit as to propose the inclusion of roller-skating[21] (of which it had had a branch since 1893) in the London Olympics. This was not to be. The chief success of roller-skating, which had come with the technical improvement of the skate in America, was as a companionable mixed sport, and it had a particular appeal to the lower middle classes. It was easier to learn than ice-skating and its costs to both commerical providers and performers was less. By 1910, when the craze was at its height, most towns in Britain had at least one rink, even if it was only a flat roof. C.B. Cochrane, in charge of Olympia at the time, had a flourishing rink there. All it lacked was grace – and prestige.

Notes

1 Stoddart came to a sad end, probably hastened by money problems, drink, the war news and, above all, gloomy contemplation of how little of substance he had made of a life, in which games came easily to him and brought him public adulation in his youth. He shot himself in 1915, aged 52.

2 Cf. G.B. Shaw, *The Doctor's Dilemma* (1906), 'All professions are a conspiracy against the laity.'

3 Looking back N.L. Jackson, *Sporting Days and Sporting Ways*, pp. 179 ff., appears to have forgotten Colt and to have exaggerated the number of trees felled.

4 15 December, 1908, quoted in J. Lowerson, *Sport and the English Middle Classes*, 1870–1914, Manchester, 1993, p. 136.

5 For the main sources used in this section, other than those specifically referenced, see Chapter Five, note 28. K.E. McCrone, *Sport and the Physical Emancipation of Women, 1870–1914*, London, 1988, is the main modern source on women's golf and lawn tennis.

6 London, 1910: summarised more fully in McCrone, *Physical Emancipation*.

7 Charlotte Cooper had won at Paris in 1900: see Chapter Four note 29. There was no women's competition at St Louis. In London Mrs Lambert Chambers beat an all British field on grass and Miss Gwendolen Eastlake-Smith beat Miss Angela Greene indoors.

8 12 August, 1919. This might have served as an epitaph for both Dohertys. Both died young, Reggie in 1911 aged 39, Laurie in 1919 aged 43.

9 *Truth*, 9 August, 1906, quoted by Lowerson, *Sport and the English Middle Classes*, p. 280.

10 For the early history of tennis and rackets see D. Birley, *Sport and the Making of Britain, passim*.

11 *Baily's Magazine*, November, 1907, quoted by Lowerson, *Sport and the English Middle Classes*, p. 104.
12 F.G. Aflalo, *The Cost of Sport*, London, 1899, quoted by H. Walker in T. Mason, *Sport in Britain*, p. 256.
13 Lambert Chambers, *Lawn Tennis for Ladies*, p. 5.
14 P.A. Vaile, *Wake up, England*, London, 1907, p. 99, quoted in Lowerson, *Sport and the English Middle Classes*, p. 178.
15 See Birley, *Sport*, pp. 313–14.
16 G.W. Hillyard, *Forty Years of First-Class Lawn Tennis*, London, 1924, p. 43.
17 *C.B. Fry's Magazine*, no. 7, 1907, pp. 324 ff., quoted in Lowerson, *Sport and the English Middle Classes*, p. 177.
18 'E.M.', [Eustace Miles], *Baily's Magazine*, February, 1907.
19 P. Sullivan, *Bowls the Records*, pp. 22–3. The 95 affiliations of 1907 reached 237 by 1914.
20 William Slingsby (1849–1929), an enthusiast for Norway and things Norwegian, was the first, and practically the only early notable mountaineer to use skis for the purpose.
21 Roller skating's first successful club, the Aldwych, was formed in 1908. As a competitive sport its spearhead was speed skating. There were also off-shoots like roller-hockey, which had an appeal to nations outside Canada and the northern USA which made the running in ice-hockey. Competition was fierce amongst its devotees but they were never numerous, nor did they have the prestige needed to impress the IOC.

CHAPTER ELEVEN

Stern endeavour

Edwardian sport was more than simply part of the growing entertainment industry. The British had invested games with social and moral values and given them a central role in developing the nation's leaders. A propagandist for the public schools in 1901 wrote 'If asked what our muscular Christianity has done we point to the British Empire. Our Empire would never have been built up by a nation of scholars and logicians.'[1] Such noble ideals apart, games are manifestly not merely played for fun, even by amateurs: they are survival mechanisms with a vital function as preparation or as surrogate for serious conflict. As Swift succinctly put it, 'Most sorts of diversions in men, children and animals, are an imitation of fighting.'[2]

Boxing: the Lonsdale Belt

The Earl of Lonsdale drew cheers from the crowds at the International Horse Show when he dealt with a rough fellow who disagreed with one of his decisions by knocking him down. That was the truly British way to settle an argument, particularly if you shook hands afterwards. Lonsdale liked nothing better than an evening at the National Sporting Club and the members adored him. There was tumultuous applause as he arrived, immaculate in white tie and tails and smoking an enormous cigar, to take his ring-side seat. The NSC was now well established. 'Peggy' Bettinson, a stern but benevolent dictator, imposed standards of honesty and of conduct that had never been known in the annals of the 'noble science'. Purses were modest, but the spectators knew they could expect good clean, honest fights.

The Coronation Tournament of 1902, however, showed where the balance of power now lay: American heavyweights, middleweights and welterweights were in a class of their own. The heavyweight champion, James J. Jeffries, a 16-stone Ohio boiler-maker, had crushed the veteran Bob Fitzsimmons, 52 pounds lighter, in 1899 and after that no British challenger had a look in. When the Canadian Tommy Burns came to the NSC in 1907 he toyed with the British champion, Gunner Moir, for nine rounds and then knocked him out – 'more as an act of grace than anything else' as Viscount Knebworth, author of the Lonsdale Library *Boxing*, put it. Yet Burns only held on to the title because of the prejudice against black men, and when Jack Johnson finally managed to pin him down to a contest he was crushed with contemptuous ferocity. The series of American 'white hopes' now produced, from Gunboat Smith to Frank Moran, though markedly inferior to Johnson, were all better than the British champions. The difference showed when Sam Langford, a smaller black man than Johnson, came to the NSC in 1909 to fight – and beat – Iron Hague of Mexborough.

By then the British boxing public were beginning to learn to settle for gallant defeat rather than mere victory. In this they were greatly assisted by the stylish but fragile Bombardier Billy Wells, who was discovered in, and bought out of, the Army. His first purse, in 1909, was for £8, but he was soon receiving £100 a fight from the Australian promoter Hugh D. McIntosh, then trying to attract the fashionable dinner-jacketed set to his contests at Olympia. Young and handsome, Wells was a great attraction, to women as well as men. In Britain he disposed elegantly of several minor opponents – Porky Flynn, Sergeant Sunshine, Private Voyles and Seaman Parsons – and before his unfortunate vulnerability to relatively light blows on the jaw was exposed seemed like the white champion everyone was seeking. So far he had only boxed in Britain. American referees and rules were thought deplorably lax, if not biased towards local men. Chauvinists pointed to the victory of the bantamweight Joe Bowker over the Californian champion, Frankie Neal, at the NSC in 1904, and contrasted it with the notorious 'no decision' outcome of the contest between the British featherweight, 'Peerless Jim' Driscoll, and the American champion Abe Attell in New York in 1906. Shrewder operators, like the lightweight Freddie Welsh, stayed at home until the Americans could be induced, by a large enough share of the purse, to come to London.

Welsh, for all his sagacity, was not universally admired amongst the London aficionados. Uncomplicated battling was what the traditionalists preferred, especially from the Celtic fringe – he was Welsh by birth as well as name. Viscount Knebworth was particularly censorious: 'Welsh', he recalled in the 1930s, 'introduced the modern craze of a pugilist being everything in the world except a pugilist, and talking about everything except pugilism. He knew the value of publicity and courted it, never a likeable trait in anyone. He was a vegetarian and made a cult of physical training. He was a clever man after his lights . . . But this cold, callous attitude of making boxing not a grand fight so much as a paying proposition, if it is wise, is certainly not attractive.'[3] Jim Driscoll was more to Knebworth's liking. Born of Irish parents in Cardiff's dockland, where he learned to fight as a newsboy, Driscoll had fought bareknuckle in his early days. 'Out of the ring', wrote Knebworth, 'Driscoll was erratic, quick-tempered, excitable and generally Welsh. Inside the ring he was as cool as ice.'[4] He had made his name at the NSC in 1907 with an epic win over Joe Bowker, who had risen to lightweight in his later years. Unlike Bowker Driscoll had taken his chance in America: the unfortunate results have been described, but he remained the darling of the NSC, epitomising all it stood for.

As well as the slums of Cardiff, Glasgow, Belfast and the English industrial cities, the pits and steelworks were other fruitful sources of recruitment. Lads battled away for pitiful sums but great local renown in the backstreet boxing halls. For rural youth, fairground booths were often the first stage in progress up the professional ladder. One such graduate was Digger Stanley, who succeeded Joe Bowker as bantamweight champion in 1910. London was the great magnet. Most of the regular venues were sleazy affairs. The Ring at Blackfriars was a converted warehouse, originally a non-conformist chapel, founded by Dick Burge, a former lightweight champion who was rehabilitating himself after a spell in prison for fraud. At Premierland (admission 6d to 3s 6d on Thursdays; 1s 2d to 5s on Saturdays) a little group of bookmakers gathered around pillars bearing posters that read 'Betting strictly prohibited'. Wonderland, in the Whitechapel Road, was a former Music Hall which offered the Greatest Boxing Show on Earth for 2s 6d, standing room 1s. There Monty, the jellied eel man, sold his wares in 3d basins 'which when empty could be thrown at the police, who had the unsporting habit of intervening to protect the referee from rowdies who disapproved of his decisions'.[5] But there were bigger promotions at Olympia and White City, or in the open-air at football grounds.

This commercial challenge put the NSC on their mettle. They were not disposed to compete with the new promoters in the matter of purses, which were becoming alarmingly high, but they were in danger of losing ground if they did nothing. They produced a master-stroke, offering, in addition to prize-money on their usual modest scale, a Championship Belt at each of seven weights: a boxer who won the title and retained it three times kept the Belt and received a pension of £50 a year for life. Lord Lonsdale, after whom the Belts were called, provided the first one himself. (It cost £250 from Mappin and Webb.) The contest, in November 1909, was for the lightweight title, between Johnny Summers, the reigning champion, and Freddy Welsh; and Lonsdale was given a standing ovation when he buckled the Belt around Welsh's waist at the end.

Amateurs and wrestlers

For those who preferred more active ways of canalising the primal urges beneath the veneer of civilisation, the Lonsdale spirit imbued the amateurs as well as the professionals. Fighting was still the acknowledged way to settle arguments everywhere from the public house to the public school and putting on the gloves gave the encounter its sporting credentials. Even public schoolboys admired the American professionals: P.G. Wodehouse, an enthusiastic boxer in his youth, took with him a letter of introduction to Corbett on his first trip to the States;[6] and, as he testified, being able to box was a useful asset in the daily life at Dulwich. Its status in the public schools inevitably fell short of that of team games, but though it was frowned on in a few progressive, modern places, they had their own exclusive annual championships at Aldershot (Wodehouse reported on the 1901 encounters for *Sandow's Magazine of Physical Culture.*)

After school it had fewer participants amongst the middle classes. Competitive interest at the Universities lay almost entirely in the annual 'Varsity match, which merited only a half-Blue. And though there were socially superior clubs, like the Belsize Park in St John's Wood and the Stock Exchange Boxing Club, the laurels in open competition increasingly went to the Lads' Clubs run by churches and similar philanthropic organisations, which were generally in the poorer areas of the big cities. Indeed the ABA, founded by middle-class enthusiasts, now presided over an increasingly democratic movement. The number of its affiliated clubs had increased from the dozen founder members of 1881 only to 46 in 1906, but in that year Mr John Douglas, the erstwhile fiery defender of the NSC, became President, and began a vigorous and highly successful expansionist policy.

Its basis – and the secret of its success – was competition. These were held at every weight offering a ladder of achievement for boys from the moment they joined a club. Very few amateur boxers made the transition to the professional ring, and even fewer achieved success in what was a very different, much tougher world. Those who ran amateur clubs were vigilant in their efforts to keep their sport free of undesirable influences, such as betting, and there was no question of any payment to the boxers. The dour, relentless Jewish fighter Matt Wells, amateur lightweight champion from 1904 was one of the first to use amateur prowess as a stepping-stone to success in the professional ring. Conversely the old 'professors' hired by the gentlemen's clubs of the 1880s were giving way to amateur coaches or men like W. Childs, the 1908–9 amateur middleweight champion who became an instructor at Cambridge University.

Though the ABA championships were open to clubs throughout the United

Kingdom, so far English lads, particularly Londoners, had predominated. In the winter of 1910–11 Scotland, Ireland and Wales began holding their own national championships, and 'home' international matches soon followed. Wales, so strong in professional boxing, especially at lighter weights, lagged behind the other three in the amateur game, mainly because so many of the more talented young Welsh boxers – 'mountain fighters' – tended to fight for money from an early age. Scotland, by contrast, had as well as a Glasgow-dominated professional tradition, an Edinburgh amateur one: two of the five titles at the ABA championships of 1902 were won by Scots, both from the Edinburgh Harriers club. Scottish enthusiasm for the amateur side of the sport spilled over into acrimony in 1909 when there was a heated argument between rival governing bodies. Ireland, rich in natural talent, had little professional boxing outside Belfast (and so no spur to higher achievement) and relatively little Catholic involvement in the ABA-dominated amateur sport.

The more violent excitements of boxing had long relegated the older sport, of wrestling, to relative obscurity in Britain. The classical Graeco-Roman style[7] was still much admired on the continent, but its practitioners, if they came to Britain in search of sporting fortune were likely to have to find it in strong man acts on the music hall circuit, as did the German champion, Frederick Muller, known professionally as Eugene Sandow, before setting up his Institute of Physical Culture in St James's Street. Wrestling contests, in a variety of bucolic styles, had a certain residual attraction in Cornwall (in spite of Methodist disapproval), Lancashire and the Lake District, and at Highland gatherings, and a hybrid style known as 'catch-as-catch-can', livelier and more sophisticated than most, had a minority appeal both as a professional spectacle and as a manly diversion for the members of the elite Amateur Athletic Club.[8] The Americans had their own more theatrical 'free-style' and champions who wrestled all-comers, any style.

Professional wrestling, though fascinating, belonged even then to the world of show business rather than sport. As the strong man acts lost their novelty, exhibition wrestling and all-comers' challenges, rarely genuine, took their place. The first of these in London, at the Alhambra, Leicester Square, featuring a returning emigrant to America, Jack Carkeek, sparked off a vogue for matches against exotic foreign opponents like Ali Hassan, the Turkish Giant, and Mabul Khan from the mystic orient. The remarkable Russian, George Hackenschmidt, taken up by the theatrical agent C.B. Cochrane, only became popular when he learned how to toy with opponents long enough to make things interesting and when his innocent desire to wrestle honestly (and thus boringly) was off-set by a German stage-villain, Schackman, who fouled incessantly, abused the referee and got up to all manner of tricks before Hackenschmidt finally nailed him. When this palled there followed Yousouf, the Terrible Turk, actually a Marseilles dock-labourer, and his successor, Madrali, both imports from America. Attempts to stage straightforward contests in Graeco-Roman style, which involved long spells of immobility, failed miserably. When Pederson the Dane defended his world title against Aberg of Russia at the Theatre Royal, Holborn, the crowd started singing 'Dear Old Pals' and the manager stopped the contest.

By contrast the organisers of the revived Olympic Games, who did not countenance boxing at all and disapproved of free-style wrestling, gave an honoured place to Graeco-Roman. The single event of 1896 was followed by three at Athens in 1906. Paris had ignored it and St Louis in 1904, Games from which de Coubertin stayed away, was characteristically given over to free-style and suspect amateurs. The British Olympics Committee, at London in 1908, offered three events in Graeco-Roman, all won by continentals, and five in catch-as-catch-can, in which they won three gold medals and the Americans two. For Britain, whose star, the Cumberland middleweight Stanley Bacon, was one of four brothers who dominated the scene for many years, this alas was the zenith of wrestling achievement. Even then the boxers did better. Spurned until St Louis and contested there only in Yankee hugger-mugger, boxing was naturally featured at the London Olympics and British competitors duly won at all five weights. A notable success was that at middleweight of Mr J.W.H.T. Douglas, an England cricketer and future captain, a public school man and son of the ABA President. The official report was suitably charitable to the opposition: 'For the most part our visitors were not of sufficiently high class to have a real sporting chance of victory, which made their presence even more meritorious.' But in truth there were very few foreign competitors – and no Americans.

Rowing: Henley and the foreigners

Americans did not meet the exacting social standards required for entry to the London Olympics in rowing either. Five years earlier R.H. Lyttelton[9] had blamed the troubles in British rowing on 'the fact that in America there do not appear to be the same regulations as in England – and the American invasion of England includes the chief prizes of Henley as well as the tube railways of London'.[10] This was serious: the prestige of British rowing was at its height. The staunch refusal of the ARA and the Henley Stewards to relax their definition of amateurism took care of its social standing, which was further enhanced by the reverence for rowing and rowing men in the public schools and universities. They were a very special breed, not only coming from the most elite schools, but embodying above all others the spirit of muscular Christianity. They worked like voluntary galley-slaves to perfect their art.

And, as we have seen, they even accepted the need for coaching (provided it was not done by professionals) and for rigorous training (provided it was for the sake of the team). Eights were the thing and the gruelling encounter between Oxford and Cambridge was the ultimate test.

Not unnaturally – because as well as their dedication they had plenty of talent to pick from and also plenty of time at their disposal – the Boat Race crews reached a high standard, as did the college crews and the clubs like the great Leander who competed at Henley. This strengthened the British belief that their way of running the sport had to be jealously guarded. They remained aloof from the emergent European organisation, the Fédération des Sociétés d'Aviron, and early Olympic rowing had done nothing to suggest that lesser nations were fit to be entrusted with the responsibilities of international competition. Only one Briton, a solitary sculler had taken part in the chaotic and commercialised affair in Paris in 1900. The Grand Challenge Cup at Henley was the pinnacle of rowing competition and it had become clear that it needed to be protected against the dangers of unbridled internationalism.

It caused a stir when an overseas crew reached the final of the Grand in 1901. The intruders, the University of Pennsylvania were known to have a professional coach. Fortunately they were beaten – by Leander, of course – but Dr Warre, the Headmaster of Eton and a leading figure in the sport, spoke for many when, in a motion to the Henley Committee, he expressed the fear 'that the good nature of the stewards of Henley Regatta, in permitting the rowing trophies intrusted to them to be contended for by all the world, will endanger the best interests of amateur rowing, for the encouragement of which they were originally presented'. He had powerful supporters, including Willie Grenfell, the future Lord Desborough, and R.C. Lehmann. A majority of clubs in membership, when polled on the issue, thought total exclusion of overseas crews too extreme, but there was a widespread call for greater safeguards against concealed professionalism.

The consequent tightening of the rules, after the 1902 Regatta, excluding crews coached or 'controlled' by professionals, reduced the number of undesirable entries to the Grand, and Leander duly prevailed for the next three years. The Americans continued to give trouble, however, in the sculls. Two United States scullers were refused entry in 1903, and the following year L.F. Scholes of Canada, who had beaten the previously invincible British oarsman, F.S. Kelly, was much criticised when he allowed the Diamond Sculls trophy to be displayed in his father's bar in Toronto. Furthermore problems with the eights soon returned. The winners of the 1904 St Louis affair – which no British oarsmen attended – were the Vesper Boat Club of Philadelphia. Their entry had been accepted for the Henley Grand in 1905, but an enquiry afterwards revealed that their expenses had been met from public subscription, that all the crew had taken money payments and some had made false statements. Vesper were banned from Henley for life and the clamour resumed for a ban on all foreigners.

Instead the Stewards again did the gentlemanly thing, in effect inviting the lesser breeds to come within the law. Entries would be allowed only if their national governing bodies were prepared to certify that they conformed to ARA ideas of amateurism. In 1906 only Belgium, Germany, Holland and Canada felt able to do this. It was a considerable shock, therefore, when a Belgian club won the Grand, reinforcing their point the following year when they came back to beat Leander themselves. In this context the Henley Stewards faced a challenge when the British Olympic committee decided to include rowing in the 1908 Olympics. They did not come out of it very well, causing considerable dismay even amongst their admirers by banning foreign crews from Henley in order to help British preparations for the Olympics. This was too much even for the chauvinistic British Press, especially since it meant that the Belgian club would not be able to defend their title. The Belgians won many friends by their sportsmanship in indicating that they would not have contemplated appearing at Henley so soon before the Olympics anyway, a slap in the face for the Stewards by its implication of which was the more important competition.

The Stewards had also presumed too much by taking it for granted that they, as of right, would be staging the Olympic Regatta at Henley, and they were dismayed to learn that the BOC had plans to hold it nearer London. Much internal wrangling and manoeuvring within the ARA ensued, spilling over into the sporting Press. The Stewards fought a spirited campaign, in the course of which their secretary wrote pseudonymously to *The Field* suggesting that nobody had ever heard of Putney, before they got their way. The international range was not much enlarged – only Britain, Canada, Germany, Holland, Norway and Hungary were eligible, or wanted, to compete. However the result was a suitable triumph for British standards. Britain provided seven of the eight finalists in the four events. Leander appeared in three and won two, providing both finalists in the coxless pairs, and the crowning satisfaction was when they beat the Belgians in the eights. The Belgians' subsequent victory in 1909 at the Henley Grand must have given them a deal of pleasure.

Ironically the University Boat Race, the most elite event of all, was by far the most popular one in rowing, for thousands of Londoners annually thronged the Towpath enjoying the spectacle – free. There were plenty of people who had been to Oxford and Cambridge cheering on their crew, but many more who had not, and everyone from Dukes to dustmen took sides. Boat Race night tended to encourage young rowdies 'of the Upper Class [who] liked the sound of broken glass',[11] or stole policemen's helmets as trophies, but it was all highly enjoyable. Apart from this impeccably amateur and idiosyncratically British event only sculling had any great appeal for the average man and woman, however, and sculling was ideologically suspect. Furthermore the ARA's socially restrictive policies had greatly encouraged this aspect of professional rowing.

In his heyday and in the riverside districts where rowing was popular, Ernest Barry, the professional champion sculler, was given the sort of idolatry associated with mass spectator sports. Sculling was heavily dependent on gambling and much of his popularity was because he could be relied upon to try to win, and very often did so. Barry was of waterman stock, having won Doggett's Cap and Badge in 1903, and he came to the fore in 1908 when he won the British championship in record time from the veteran Australian, Towns, later beating another great Australian, Dick Arnst for the world championship. There was nothing of the rude mechanical about Barry, and his immaculate clothes and dignified bearing raised the standing of the professional in public esteem as much as his rowing raised its standards of performance and of honesty. This made it all the more unfortunate that the ARA's rules prevented his using his coaching skills to the benefit of British amateurs. Along with many other fine professionals he had to go abroad, when the time came for him to give up competitive rowing, to find a coaching job. America, Australia and Germany were the chief beneficiaries, seemingly having fewer inhibitions about the corrupting effect of professional coaching on the amateur performer.

Boating and swimming

The manliness that was so much admired in rowing was naturally a grave handicap to its spread amongst women. This apart rowing had a special place in the bachelor-dominated muscular Christian world of the public schools, where boys were brought up to regard young females chiefly as a source of temptation. If cold baths were the proverbial prophylactic rowing was an organised subjugation of the flesh that served the same purpose. We have noted the limited extent to which boating had commended itself to the authorities of Oxbridge women's colleges and the care they took not to trespass upon a treasured male preserve. Competition was not to be contemplated. There was greater freedom, however, in the women's colleges of the University of London where the Thames was somewhat different from the Isis or the Granta.

Bedford College, unhampered by concern for the susceptibilities of proprietorial male neighbours, had developed by the early years of the new century an impressive array of competitions in canoeing, skiffs and sculling as well as team-rowing. Westfield College students had also enjoyed boating since the 1890s and from 1908 rowed competitively against other colleges and, occasionally, against outside ladies' clubs. By contrast at the socially superior Royal Holloway College the atmosphere was nearer to that of Oxbridge: there was no boat club until 1905, and racing was not encouraged. The women in mixed colleges were not so aloof but showed less initiative: at University College there was no Boat Club until 1912; at King's College the sport languished in spite of helpful co-operation from Dr Furnivall's Hammersmith Club.[12]

Perhaps the greatest benefit that rowing conferred on women's sport at this time was its incidental encouragement to swimming: the authorities of the Oxbridge women's colleges insisted on girls who wanted to go boating taking a swimming proficiency test. This seems at first to have been a disincentive to boat club membership rather than an encouragement to swimming sport. The situation gradually changed, however, in part because of the girls' own inclination towards competition and inter-college rivalry, in part because having a private pool was both a status symbol and a great incentive to practice. An important turning point was the acquisition of a pool by Girton in 1900. Girton, which was some distance from the river, had not much interest in rowing, but the pool now became a great attraction: from 1907 there were matches against Newnham and they combined to race against Oxford.

At London University the aspirant Royal Holloway now began to compete. The college had had its own heated pool since 1894 and the staff included a teacher who gave regular instruction in swimming and life-saving; there had been annual swimming sports since 1899, with badges for diving and mastering difficult strokes; and there was a club from 1903, but serious competition did not begin until 1908 when matches against other London colleges and against Oxford and Cambridge started. Thereafter Royal Holloway, which was the instigator of the first London University championships (1910) was at the forefront of competitive swimming. The humbler, more independent-minded Bedford College on the other hand formed a club in 1897, using the nearby Marylebone Baths. (There were separate times for women's use at public baths, and often separate entrances, and special arrangements could be made with colleges and clubs to hold their sessions in private.) There was 'a great spirit of unity' amongst these pioneers and they arranged life-saving classes, swimming sports days and competitions in racing and diving not only within the college but against other colleges and local high schools. When organised University competitions and the Oxbridge matches began, Bedford students did exceptionally well.[13]

The women's advance was eased because they threatened no entrenched public school-dominated male coterie. Competitive swimming conspicuously lacked social lustre. Though of great antiquity and military utility, and though commended in recent times by progressive physicians, it had never been a fashionable recreation. The main provision of covered pools – highly desirable in the British climate – had come under the early Victorian Baths and Public Washhouses Act, which in itself gave them a social stigma: they were called baths rather than pools. So far as the public schools were concerned swimming instruction might be given for safety reasons and was a standard requirement for rowing, but expenditure on pools was rare and swimming competition rarely encouraged.

The needs of adult swimmers with more than casual but less than pecuniary interest were catered for by the Amateur Swimming Association which had risen from the ashes of the Metropolitan Swimming Association in 1896 and had immediately set about ensuring its amateur purity. The social level of its concerns may be judged from its first regulations which excluded people who swam for money or took more than third-class rail expenses, sold prizes or worked as bath attendants, but allowed in professional footballers, schoolteachers and baths managers and life-saving instructors. As *Truth* commented in 1902, 'as a body swimmers are scarcely so well up the social scale as the leading tennis players'.[14] Even so, questions were raised when one of the amateur championships of 1905 went to a baths attendant. Swimming suffered also in having no great spectator appeal, so that the professional might be admired as a splendid specimen, but could not expect substantial rewards from racing. The glamorous end of the sport was cross-channel swimming in which the name of the entrepreneurial Captain Webb still resounded. Men's swimming had been part of the Olympics since the beginning but, lacking public school support, it was not a British strong point. Hungarians and Americans dominated at first but in the 1908 Games in London the Briton Henry Taylor, a breaststroke and middle-distance swimmer from Oldham, won three gold medals and his team mate Frederic Holman broke the world record in the 200-metre breaststroke. Britain also established a reputation in the boisterous sport of water polo.

Athletics and the Olympic spirit

Neither women's swimming nor rowing were, of course, among the sports the British Olympic Association included in the programme of the 1908 Olympics. Nor was athletics itself. Watching women running in their drawers had been an occasional salacious male pleasure of an earlier, less refined age, and even in Edwardian times no lady amateur would have been prepared to display herself scantily clad in public even if the IOC had been prepared to countenance it, which they were not. De Coubertin was renowned for his pronounced anti-feminist views. Lawn tennis, as we have seen, was considered suitably decorous even in 1900, archery events for women as well as men were held in 1904 and 1908 and Mrs Frances Clytie Rivett-Carnac was part of her husband's team – the only entry – in the 1908 7-metre London–Ryde yachting event. Otherwise the Olympic ideal, true to its classical Greek original, did not extend to women.

Domestically, the world of amateur athletics was not only exclusively masculine but, despite the elevated ideals of its governing body, socially suspect and deeply divided. Oxford and Cambridge were the soul if not the spearhead: their interest in open competition was lessened by social constraints which frowned on the idea of training and coaching and by the public school preference for team games. Relay-racing was heavily emphasised in the annual inter-Varsity meetings and in joint matches against Harvard and Yale. In most public schools there was an annual sports day, basically an occasion for entertaining parents, but of little further interest. London AC held an annual Public Schools Sports Meeting, but there were virtually no inter-school contests, and in much of the country public school boys or old boys would not dream of entering local meetings. If they did they had to be prepared for squalid dressing room conditions and atmosphere. 'Northern' urban parts were the worst. Even if there was no actual betting, the prizes, convertible into currency, brought excessive keenness amongst the largely artisan competitors, and the system of handicapping encouraged 'running for a mark' even amongst the very young.[15]

The AAA's control over the outer 'northern' fringes of its empire was far from complete. Its main concern was the continued success and integrity of its own annual championships. In the early days Oxford and Cambridge and London AC had been the mainstays with regional specialisms for the field events – Ireland for the weight, the hammer and often the high and long jumps, Ulverston or Windermere for the pole-vault – and the less exclusive Harrier Clubs for the longer track distances. Now the pattern had changed somewhat, with more Harrier and 'northern' clubs in evidence and the American world record holder Arthur Duffey winning the 100 yards four times in a row from 1900 to 1903.

(Happily not many of the great Irish field events men had been lost to the Gaelic Athletic Association. This resulted not from any loss of nationalist fervour in the GAA – on the contrary it was revitalised by Anti-Boer War feeling – but from its waning interest in athletics, in which many obstinate Dublin clubs saw no point in separate rules, and its concentration on the more politically fruitful hurling and Gaelic football. Individual athletes such as Maurice Davin's nephew, Tom Kiely, five times AAA hammer-throwing champion, threw off the British shackles but many remained within the Unionist-controlled Irish AAA. The GAA made a clean break from them in 1906 but tunnel vision, lack of funds and the drain of promising athletes to America or to the professional circuit in Britain inhibited progress.[16])

The Americans' tiresomely consistent success and distinctly un-British approach was another cross the AAA had to bear. American values were starkly exposed by the 1904 Olympic Games at St Louis. De Coubertin had initially been enthusiastic about the Games crossing to the New World, but the IOC, even before the precise location was agreed, realised the dangers and took the precaution of asking, modestly enough, that any professional events be given less prominence than amateur ones. But they found themselves in a minor trade and publicity war and glumly had to accept that, as in Paris, the Olympics could only be held on schedule if they were part of a commercial event. De Coubertin could not bring himself to attend, and he was particularly appalled at reports of 'Anthropological Days' in which imported 'savages' performed tests of speed and endurance.[17] The Games proper were poorly contested numerically and in international terms.[18] The British stayed away but were mildly irritated when the GAA's Keily, who had paid his own fare to St Louis, won the 'All-round Championship' (Decathlon). In the other track and field events all but one gold medals were won by Americans, sometimes very impressively, but a number of races were obviously professional and presented with a mixture of showmanship, stage-management and incompetence.

The IOC were greatly upset: they determined to carry on but vowed never to allow contact with commercial sponsors again. There was a growing feeling in Britain that it was time to show the foreigners how to run things. In 1905 a group of enthusiasts for various sports set themselves up as a British Olympic Committee with the intention of staging an international event of their own. Willie Grenfell, now Baron Desborough, became its President. Ironically the IOC's hegemony was saved by the success of an 'alternative' event held in Athens in 1906 which despite its unofficial status achieved fair success, and was near enough for Europeans to be able to afford to attend – and for ten British and Anglo-Irish to win gold medals. De Coubertin laid plans for the next Games in Italy in 1908.

Meanwhile the AAA, still cool about the Olympic idea, moved into action domestically on the all-important question of amateurism. The Harrier Clubs, where cross-country running had largely replaced the old jolly hare-and-hounds affairs, and where hard training was de rigueur, were the chief culprits, as their social composition might lead one to expect. The immediate concern was an outstanding distance runner called Alf Shrubb. Shrubb had been a manual worker when he first joined Horsham (Sussex) Blue Star

Harriers in 1898 at the age of eighteen. Six years later, having joined South London Harriers (and become a tobacconist) he had won the AAA championships at ten miles and four miles four times in a row and the mile title twice. That same year at Ibrox Park football ground, Glasgow, where he had earlier set the two mile record, he broke the world's records for an hour's running, ten miles and six, and at the end the crowd carried him from the track singing 'Will Ye No' Come Back Again?' He was to do so, but only as a professional, for the AAA banned him shortly afterwards.

The professional circuit had been going through a bad patch after a few years of revival. One of their recent heroes had been Beauchamp R. Day, an Irish prodigy who became one of the great sprinters of the era. At sixteen Day had joined the Scottish club Haddington Harriers, then one of the foremost in Britain, and at eighteen was competing successfully in national championships and home internationals before turning professional in 1901 and winning the Powderhall sprint the following year. He then spent long spells in South Africa, New Zealand and Australia, where the sport was thriving and whose graduates were soon to add spice again to the British scene. Meanwhile the interest of soccer and Rugby League clubs in staging athletics meetings – many professional footballers were also sprinters, which helped their training and gave them another string to their bow – enlarged the home circuit. The grounds of Glasgow Rangers, Celtic, Broughton Rangers and Rochdale joined Powderhall and the rest as important centres. In 1903 a Welsh syndicate introduced an annual handicap at Pontypridd which became known as the 'Welsh Powderhall'.

Day had gone into professionalism openly, but many of his contemporaries went to inordinate lengths to conceal their amateur form before launching themselves onto the professional scene. 'J.A. Garside of Edinburgh Harriers' who succeeded Day as Powderhall champion in 1902 had been given a generous handicap of 13 yards (in 120). He turned out to be a Leeds man. The deception led to heated protests, but he got away with it, for once bets had been paid revelations about the winner were not welcome. The trick was to discover the fraud before the damage was done; and this happened in 1905 when a mysterious 'H.J. Scott, Edinburgh' was discovered, after much careful detective work, to be M.J. Sheehan, one of the many up-and-coming Welsh athletes.

Shrubb's expulsion was only a temporary fillip to professional athletics. To tickle the jaded palates of the public some promoters turned their thoughts to a new attraction, greyhound and whippet racing, which was catching on in many industrial areas as a cheaper more accessible, alternative to horse-racing. The first to take it up was Powderhall, in 1905, in mixed programmes with athletic events, and there as in other places the dogs usually took precedence. Before long poor Shrubb found himself having to share the limelight with greyhounds and to perform in novelty events such as competing against horses, and he soon took himself off to the Dominions and America. An international circuit was developing, and Britain seemed temporarily to be losing its central position.

Things were looking correspondingly better for the amateurs. Italy had dropped out of the Olympic reckoning in 1907 and the BOC had been asked to step into the breach. Though there was little time left, the emergency offered a chance to show British organising ability and established an appropriate relationship with the IOC which gave the British plenty of leverage in policy matters. They were fortunate in another respect: the organisers of the forthcoming Franco-British Exhibition offered to provide – without commercial strings – a stadium where most of the planned sports could be staged in a suitable setting. This was the White City, at Shepherd's Bush, costing £40,000, the most advanced in the world at the time. The London Games of 1908 were undoubtedly a great feat of organisation which probably no other nation had the experience and expertise to perform and in this respect they more than equalled de Coubertin's expectation. The British naturally enjoyed success in the team games they brought into the Olympic programme.[19] Financially, too, the Games did well. High prices kept the numbers at the athletics events at the White City down initially but some 80,000 people attended the final day of the athletics. The events were also generally well presented. Henley was, of course, a model and the swimming events were better-staged than ever before.

What was less pleasing, and indeed somewhat embarrassing for those who believed in the British reputation for fair play, was the standard of judging in the athletics. The British had been allowed the unique privilege of providing their own judges, with 'foreign assistants' in subordinate roles. They proved unworthy of the honour. There had been some eyebrows raised in the cycling. In the sprint the British favourite got a puncture early on and the rest crawled around until near the end a Frenchman shot forward to win by inches: the NCU officials declared the race void because everyone had exceeded the time allowance and refused to permit a re-run. However, the main problem arose in the athletics in which British and American antagonism came to the fore. The Americans showed themselves both vulgar – some of their competitors turned up for the steeplechase in white shorts which was against AAA regulations – and triumphalist. After a victory in the long jump one newspaper commented disdainfully, 'They were entertained then from the American stand by the singing of "There'll be a hot time in the old town to-night", by the fluttering of United States flags, and by the blowing of a new instrument of torture such as is employed at country fairs. The Americans made themselves a nuisance and behaved in a manner which is happily quite foreign to British athletic grounds.'[20]

They were also thought prone to dubious tactics. This appears to have been the root cause of the fracas that disfigured the 440 yards race. The British favourite, a 26-year-old Anglo-Scottish Boer War veteran, Lt Wyndham Halswelle, faced three Americans in the final, and, fearing team tactics, officials stationed themselves at 20-yard intervals round the track. When Halswelle tried to overtake on the outside and an opponent ran wide to prevent him, the officials shouted 'foul' and 'no race' and broke the tape before the American could get there. One runner was removed from the track physically, a great row broke loose between British and American partisans and it was half-an-hour before order was restored. The offending American was disqualified and the race was ordered to be re-run but the other Americans refused to take part and Halswelle had a walk-over victory.

There were other deplorable episodes, of which perhaps the most bizarre was in the tug-of-war, a survival of old rustic sports, nowadays thought too unsophisticated for serious competition but a popular and exciting event in 1908. In one of the heats the American entry found themselves up against a team of Liverpool policemen wearing their heavy regulation boots. The Americans took exception and the headlines of the *New York Times* next day read 'English unfair in Olympic Games . . . Liverpool Team wears Monstrous Shoes that arouse ire of Americans who kick in vain'.[21] One way and another the British judges fell some way short of perfection. James Sullivan the Secretary of the American Athletic Union wrote of them, 'They were unfair to the Americans, they were unfair to every athlete except the British, but their real aim was to beat the Americans. Their conduct was unsportsmanlike and absolutely unfair.'[22] The BOC afterwards had to devote much of a 60-page report to defending their honour.[23]

The British venture into internationalism was unfortunate in other ways. Her own athletes had not done well, with victories only in unfashionable events like walking and the steeplechase, and at unfashionable distances afterwards discontinued, and none of the winners were from the gentlemanly clubs. Worse, the world record-holder and AAA champion in the mile, Harold Wilson, from Sheffield Hallamshire Harriers, not only lost to an American but immediately turned professional. The awful possibility of what was supposed to be a show-case for amateur purity turning into a breeding ground for 'pedestrianism' loomed ahead. Nor was the Empire any help. On the contrary the 19-year-old South African R.E. Walker, who had achieved a surprise victory over the American favourites in the 100 yards also turned professional.

Walker's home town of Johannesburg was an important – and rich – new professional centre, especially in sprinting, with athletes like Beauchamp Day and the Australian Arthur Postle, 'the Crimson Flash', another Powderhall winner, settling there. Day, who was something of a barometer of fashion, had come back to Britain in 1907 and for the next few years the professional scene was enlivened by regular contests between overseas stars like Walker, the black Canadian E. Eastman, the American, C.E. Holway, the great Australian Jack Donaldson and British champions like W. Growcott of Banbury and the Irishman W. Campbell (also known as W. Dales of Houghton). Another sinister sign was that Walker's Olympic victory owed much to last-minute tuition from a British professional coach. This was Sam Mussabini, employed by the Harrier Club of the Polytechnic, supporters of the NARA against the ARA and now the spearhead of the Harrier Club movement.

The Olympics had also demonstrated the power of publicity and commercially based, spectator-dominated competition. The Marathon – at which the Oxo Company had supplied the competitors with flasks full of drinks made from their celebrated beef extract – had provided a dramatic climax to the Games. After the disappointment of the home competitors falling out early the Italian Dorando Pietri had won British hearts by entering the stadium first and falling and getting up again four times before staggering to within yards of the tape and collapsing. To tumultuous cheers he was helped across the line in front of the second man, John Hayes of America. Alas the Americans lodged a protest and this, for once, was upheld. Honour was served, however, when next day a special gold cup was presented to Pietri by Queen Alexandra herself and the rafters rang.

The Press were quick to exploit the possibilities. That October the *Evening News* sponsored a marathon over the Olympic course for a £100 prize. Powderhall held a Marathon in their New Year Gala. Both were won by unknown Frenchmen, one a London waiter. Meanwhile both Pietri and Hayes had taken up lucrative American offers to turn professional and in January, 1909, Pietri was matched against Alf Shrubb at the Polo Grounds New York. Soon these two, Hayes, the Frenchmen and a Canadian, Tom Longboat, were part of a regular circus which drew big crowds wherever they went. The *Sporting Life's* 1909 Marathon – again over the Olympic course – attracted 40,000 to the White City. The winner, at last an Englishman, C.W. Gardiner, also won again the following year when he beat Pietri for a £100 prize on an indoor track specially laid with coconut matting at the Albert Hall.

The marathon craze faded almost as quickly as it had begun but meanwhile professional long-distance running was back in the public eye, providing future Olympic champions from the working classes with another incentive than simply honour and glory for all the months of self-denial it took to get into condition. This apart, commercial links with the Harrier end of amateur athletics were strengthened. The *Sporting Life*, for instance, sponsored Polytechnic Harriers in organising an annual race from Windsor to the Chelsea Football Ground at Stamford Bridge. Long-distance running was not normally attractive to the Oxford and Cambridge men and the idea of arduous training with its aura of professionalism, was anathema to them. But by then talent, even for those with ample leisure, was rarely enough unless it was backed up by hard training – and coaching – in short events as well as long, and it was the Harrier clubs that came more and more into the reckoning.

Notes

1 J. Cotton Minchin, *Our Public Schools: Their Influence on English History*, London, 1901, p. 113, quoted in J.A. Mangan, *Athleticism and the Victorian Public School*, Cambridge, 1981, p. 108.
2 J. Swift, *Thoughts on Various Subjects*, 1711.
3 Viscount Knebworth, *Boxing*, London, n.d. p. 88.
4 *Ibid.*, p. 91.
5 D. Batchelor, *Big Fight*, London, 1954, p. 86.
6 Over Seventy, in *Wodehouse on Wodehouse*, Harmondsworth, 1981, p. 488.
7 'Graeco-Roman' wrestling had little or no resemblance to any specific Greek or Roman classical style, but was so called for its imagined similarity to the more restrained forms of ancient wrestling as distinct from the Greek pankration or 'all-in' kind and its modern Anglo-Saxon variants.
8 W. Armstrong, *Wrestling*, London, 1889, introduction, p. iv.
9 One of six famous Cambridge cricketing brothers, from a leading aristocratic, sporting, political, intellectual and fashionable family, Robert was better-known for his criticism than his play.
10 R.H. Lyttelton, 'Amateur and Professional', chapter in H. Hutchinson (ed.), *Cricket*, London, 1903, p. 194.
11 H. Belloc, 'John', *New Cautionary Tales*, London, 1930.
12 K.E. McCrone,' The Development of Women's Sport at the University of London', *IJHS*, September, 1990, pp. 204–5.
13 *Ibid.*
14 6 February, 1902, quoted by J. Lowerson, *Sport and the English Middle Classes, 1870–1914*, Manchester, 1993, p. 169.
15 For a searing condemnation of the 'northern' athletics scene see the writings of F.A.M. Webster, e.g. *Athletics of To-day*, London, 1929.
16 The GAA's neglect of cycling, which had no place in Irish history, was even worse and it led in 1903 to the formation of an independent Gaelic Cyclists' Association in opposition to the IAAA-dominated Irish Amateur Cycling Association.
17 For a balanced account see M. Gøksyr, 'The Anthropology Days at St Louis', *IJHS*, September, 1990, pp. 297–306.
18 Only 617 competitors entered (compared with 1319 in Paris) including entries for exhibitions of out-of-the-way sports like basket-ball, baseball, lacrosse, roque and motor-boating, and of these 525 were from the USA and 41 from Canada.
19 In some, like hockey, only British teams were involved. There was a somewhat muted triumph in soccer when a British team, weakened by disagreements within the FA, took the gold medal, not without difficulty, defeating Denmark in the Final. See Chapter Twelve below. In rugger, in true amateur style Cornwall, the reigning

English county champions, were entrusted with the British honour against the Australian tourists: they lost heavily but gallantly.

20 D. Wallechinsky, *The Complete Book of the Olympics*, London, 1988, p. 90.
21 18 July, 1908. All the British teams, who came first, second and third, were from the police.
22 Lord Killanin and J. Rodda, *The Olympic Games*, London, 1984, p. 37.
23 T.A. Cook, *The Olympic Games of 1908 in London*, London, 1908.

CHAPTER TWELVE

Muddied oafs: the populists

For most Edwardians sport meant cricket and football. In urbanised Britain the natural cycle of the year had become the succession of the cricket and football seasons. Football, 'the winter game', suited both the climate and the mass of the people better – half a million and more regularly took part in organised soccer, quite apart from countless schoolboy and casual encounters. On the face of it this was an achievement of which the muscular Christians who had made public school football their emblem could be proud. Certainly the masses had been diverted from baser pursuits, but had they not in the process debauched the game beyond recognition? 'Only a quarter of a century ago', wrote one despairing critic, H.F. Abell, in 1903, 'if any one had dared to hint that a hearty, wholesome national pastime might be an indirect source of national danger, he would have been ridiculed', but since then had come the debilitating 'Football Fever' whose principal characteristics were the 'infection of the working classes . . . and the part played in it by money.'[1]

Soccer: football fever

The earnest idealists who sought to fit soccer into the concept of 'rational recreation' were trying to build on a shaky foundation. The young workers they were attempting to reach evinced an entrepreneurial spirit of their own. The status of the teams they played for depended on success in the local leagues and cup competitions that had sprung up all over Britain, and success depended on collecting gate-money. This was bad enough, but many able-bodied young men preferred to watch the professional clubs that had reached the summit of this pyramid rather than play themselves. For the urban masses football was often the supreme social experience, and the success of their team a vicarious glory nothing else in life could supply. The growth in crowds watching matches in the Football League and its Scottish and Irish equivalents – from a weekly two millions or so in 1895 to six millions a decade later – was the most remarkable phenomenon in sport.

The context was one of mounting anxiety about the military inadequacies revealed by the Boer War. Whilst Kipling saw the preoccupation of the public school 'muddied oafs' as culpable frivolity, establishment opinion deplored the effect of its commercialised debasement on the physical and moral fibre of the masses. If Football Fever and its emphasis on spectatorism continued to grow, Abell reckoned, 'a startlingly large mass of the very sort of material required (in the hour of need) will not merely get useless and unworkable itself, but will be sowing the seeds of such a crop of weeds as the most elaborate treatment in the future will be unable to eradicate'.[2] When in 1901 the Board of Education issued its first 'Model Course of Physical Training for Use in the Upper Departments of Public Elementary Schools' it was after consultation with the War Office and it consisted mainly of drill and callisthenic exercises.[3] An official syllabus, based broadly on the Swedish system of educational gymnastics, was issued in 1904. That same year an Inter-Departmental Committee on Physical Deterioration reported unfavourably on the health and physique of Army recruits. Attention was drawn to the poor condition of children in city elementary schools, and a widespread campaign to encourage healthy exercise was mounted. By 1906 games began to find a place in the more liberal curricula of the enlarged elementary school system of the 1902 Act.[4]

Some influential military men shared Kipling's doubts about whether games were an adequate means of character development for the task in hand. The Boy Scout movement started by Sir Robert Baden-Powell, the hero of Mafeking, emphasised camping, woodcraft and similar functional activities rather than games. 'B.-P.' had particular worries about soccer:

> Football in itself is a grand game for developing a lad physically and morally, for he learns to play with good temper and unselfishness, to play in his place and 'play the game' and these are the best of training for any game of life. But it is a vicious game when it draws crowds of lads away from playing the game themselves to be merely onlookers at a few paid performers . . . Thousands of boys and young men, pale, narrow-chested, hunched up, miserable specimens, smoking endless cigarettes, numbers of them betting, all of them learning to be hysterical as they groan and cheer in panic in unison with their neighbours.[5]

The moralists were up against not only a social phenomenon but the commercial interests that fed it. 'Don't let people talk of abolishing football, or this country will suffer industrially as well as physically', wrote William Shilcock of Birmingham in 1905.[6] Shilcock was himself a successful manufacturer of football boots and balls, and a host of clothing manufacturers, firms supplying tickets, turnstiles, fencing, pavilions, baths, cups, medals and other paraphernalia gave work to thousands. So did gambling. The postal credit football coupon scheme had been a great success, and since it had been declared legal the Anti-Gambling League were reduced, from 1905, to campaigning not for its abolition but for limitation of its prize-money. They were fighting a losing battle. A contemporary estimate suggested that at least 25,000 coupons were circulating every week in the Liverpool St Helens area alone.[7] And the pools bred all sorts of parasitic trades. Newspapers were now employing tipsters for football as well as the Turf. Catering, historically one of the earliest sources of profit from sport, also flourished mightily. Several tons of comestibles, and a prodigious amount of drink were supplied to the estimated 110,000 who attended the 1901 Cup Final to see Tottenham Hotspurs play Sheffield United. This massive crowd was a freak occurrence occasioned by the involvement after so many years of a London club.

London's delayed and fitful entry into professionalism was not the fault of the entrepreneurs. Its best football grounds had not grown up around distinguished teams. Crystal Palace, which had succeeded the Oval in 1895 as the venue for the FA Cup Final, had been developed as a general sporting centre: its own soccer team, founded only in 1905, was not in the Football League. Stamford Bridge, Chelsea, which had seats for 5,000 and standing room for 95,000, was the creation of H.A. Mears, a building contractor who bought and adapted the London Athletic Club's historic stadium. Chelsea Football Club was started in a hurry in the close season of 1905, with a former Glasgow Rangers player as manager and a lot of imported Scottish players, in order to try to fill it. Chelsea started in the Second Division, won promotion after two years, but soon dropped down again, acquiring a reputation for inconsistency that made it something of a music-hall joke.

London now had a dozen senior professional teams, but none were outstanding. Arsenal had an inaccessible ground and were in serious financial trouble by 1910. Of the rest only Chelsea and Tottenham Hotspurs, promoted in 1909, achieved First Division status. Fulham and Clapton Orient were in the Second. Most – Brentford, Crystal Palace, Millwall, Queen's Park Rangers, Watford, West Ham and newcomers Charlton – were in the Southern League. By contrast the First Division championship in the decade up to 1910 went to Newcastle (three times), Liverpool and Sheffield Wednesday (twice each), Manchester United, Sunderland and Aston Villa. The dominant soccer ethos was not just commercial – it was Northern. Even in the chancier FA Cup, after Tottenham's triumph in 1901, only Southampton (1902) and Bristol City (1908) amongst the southerners managed to reach the Final and both were unsuccessful.

The Times's report on the 1907 final between Sheffield Wednesday and Everton found even its style unsatisfactory: it was 'professional football of the commonplace type: there was much pace, the kicking was hard, the ball was much in the air, and fouls were plentiful'.[8] But it got results, which was what the supporters wanted. In 1907 J.H. Gettins of Millwall, a club not subsequently renowned for the cool detachment of its spectators, told the readers of one of the many handbooks on soccer that 'the old vehement and one-sided attitude of partisanship' was 'giving way to higher notions of the game.'[9] The wish was father to the thought. Apart from 'Derby' matches, cup-ties and crucial League encounters the crowds were rarely seriously disorderly. But if pitch invasions grew fewer this owed more to better crowd control than lessening fervour: few clubs had the massive iron railings Sheffield Wednesday had prudently erected at Hillsborough in 1887, but most had some form of restrictive barriers.

The FA kept a monitorial eye cocked for negligence by clubs particularly those which occasionally connived at timely interruptions or protests at referee's decisions. Referees themselves were given greater powers and ordered, for instance, not to speak to players before matches or to bet on the outcome. The Football League, whose collective morality was loftier then that of its member clubs, shared the FA's disapproval of gambling and its effects on the 'hooligan behaviour of the minority'. William McGregor, the League's founder, claimed in 1907 that there had been 'a steady increase in the respectability of the gate' – a suitably detached way of referring to the patrons.[10] They certainly seem, from photographs, to have been infinitely more respectable than their modern counterparts, soberly dressed, with a fair number of bowler hats amongst the flat caps, and collars and ties in place even in stressful situations. They were mostly male, although the leading clubs had their female supporters. When Newcastle United played Aston Villa in the Cup final of 1905 at Crystal Palace they were cheered on by members of the Newcastle Ladies' Final Outing Club, whose intrepidity was thought remarkable by a contemporary male writer, not so much for braving rough conditions as for initiative: 'they had their own lady secretary, paid their own subscriptions, and with the latter-day independence of the sex, came to London in their own saloon without the assistance of a single mere male'.[11] In some places there were footwarmers for ladies in the primitive grandstands.

The mass market did not, however, lend itself to refinement. Standards of accommodation were low – seats, covered stands and toilets were in short supply. Most grounds were built cheaply and shoddily, and older building materials and technology were sometimes not up to the demands of the new era. It was the collapse of newly enlarged wooden terracing at Ibrox Park, Glasgow, that led to the disaster at the England–Scotland game in 1902, when 26 spectators crashed to their deaths and over 500 others were injured. After this the building regulations were altered, and steel and concrete came into use. Great earth banks were used as the foundation for terracing. Many grounds had mounds – known as Spion Kop after a battle in the Boer war – on which spectators could crowd at cheap rates. There was, conversely, not much demand for luxury and its attendant higher prices. An enterprising businessman, James Grant, built a stand at Celtic Park, Glasgow, in 1905 in return for a share of the profits. It had two storeys, with padded tip-up seats and sliding windows that could be closed in rainy weather. Unfortunately it turned out to be badly ventilated and the windows had to be removed. Either way it was not very popular and Grant lost money on the transaction.[12]

Scotland's 'Football Fever' was renowned, particularly in Glasgow where the intense rivalry between Rangers and Celtic had added sectarian spice. There were smaller-scale parallels in Edinburgh, with its Hearts and Hibernians clashes, and between the two Dundee clubs. Glasgow's Third Lanark were also capable of heading the Scottish League in 1904 and winning the Cup the following year, but Rangers and Celtic, who could better afford to keep their players from the fleshpots of the English League, were generally ahead of the rest. For Celtic in particular this was a glorious era, in which they won the League six years running from 1905 to 1910. For Rangers, it followed, it was a time of great frustration, not helped by the triumphalism of Celtic supporters.

The climax came in 1909. Rangers had achieved nothing since winning the League in 1902 and the Cup the year after. Celtic had piled on the agony by adding to their League dominance Cup victories in 1907 and 1908. The two rivals met in the Final in 1909 and the issue was still undecided after two replays. The crowd, frustrated by the stalemate, had hoped extra time was to be played and when the players left the field about six thousand people swarmed on to the pitch, tore up the goal-posts and broke down fences, turnstiles and payboxes, starting a fire in the middle of the pitch and dancing round it. Policemen, firemen and even ambulance men were stoned. The police, who began by throwing stones back at the rioters, got the ground clear by seven o'clock, suffering fifty-four casualties and there was a good deal of damage in the surrounding streets. The Cup was not awarded that year.

It was a sad irony that this sordid affair took place at Hampden Park, the home of Queen's Park, whose amateur tradition had been translated into greater celebrity and greater profit from its ground than from its team. Hampden, built in 1903, was bigger and better than even Ibrox and Celtic Park, both of which had also been enlarged. As well as a neutral venue for Cup Finals Hampden also provided a fitting setting for the periodic visits of the England team which were the highlights of the 'home' international championship. These were closely contested – only once was there more than a goal in it, home or away – and though the championship itself was somewhat unreal because of the relative weakness of the Irish and Welsh teams it represented a higher standard of organisation (and the British thought a self-evidently higher standard of play) than the occasional matches between neighbouring European countries that began in 1902.[13]

In the championship England's greater population and resources usually tipped the scales in her favour. On the occasions when it did not they found it easy to take refuge in the wider assumptions of superiority that made the terms 'English' and 'British' interchangeable. Conversely the Celtic nations not only had greater fervour – a quality that was jocularly accepted by the English – but sometimes an extra edge of resentment at their historic over-lords, which showed itself particularly in soccer, the game of the 'have-nots'. For the Scots even the week-by-week enmity of Rangers and Celtic was forgotten once a year in the tussles against the English. It was an added source of resentment that so many Scots had been lured south to play for English clubs. Some indeed would have excluded these 'Anglos' from the national team. The Lord Provost of Glasgow speaking after the 1904 international drew applause when he regretted 'that when Scotland pits herself against the sister part of the kingdom . . . we have to bring to our aid those who are without the realm of Scotland'.[14] But pragmatism prevailed, and English fans had no difficulty in taking Scots, Irish and Welsh players to their hearts if they wore the shirts of Liverpool, Newcastle or any other town where the Football League held sway.

Wage slaves and Corinthians

The League may have sought respectability, but the ethos it had bred was abhorrent to the FA. A particular source of chagrin was that the £4 maximum wage rule was being subverted by under-the-counter payments. The FA took action when they could get evidence, which was not very often, although the practice was widespread. Matters came to a head in 1904 in a series of scandals centring on Manchester City and their gifted but turbulent star, Billy Meredith. Meredith was thought a socialist radical by the authorities, but he entirely embraced the free enterprise principle, frequently proclaiming it in his newspaper articles. 'They congratulate me and give me caps', he complained, 'but they will not give me a penny more than men are earning in the reserve team.'[15] Years later he was to attribute Manchester City's success to 'the fact that the club put aside the rule that no player should receive more than £4 a week. From 1902 I had been paid £6 a week and Livingstone was paid ten shillings more than that . . . I don't believe any member of the team was paid less than I was, and the season we carried off the Cup (1904) I also received £53 in bonuses . . . The team delivered the goods and the club paid for the goods delivered, and both sides were satisfied'.[16]

At the time the FA, though it had ordered an investigation of the club's books, had found no evidence of these illegal wage-payments, but they did discover two cases in which signing-on fees of more than the permitted £10 had been paid. For this the club was fined £250, the ground was closed for three months, three directors were suspended for three years and the financial director was suspended for life. It was not long before the FA had another chance to probe City's affairs. At the end of the following season, 1904–5, they were contending for the Championship with Newcastle, Aston Villa and Everton, all of them opposed to the maximum wage rule and undoubtedly already evading it. In the overheated atmosphere the City players needed police protection after their match at Everton and there was even worse trouble on and off the pitch when they played Aston Villa. The FA ordered another enquiry, ostensibly into the violence, but actually based on suspicion of something more sinister.

They found indeed that Meredith had offered a Villa player £10 to let City win the match. He was suspended for the 1905–6 season. Though protesting his innocence he went surprisingly quietly – because, it subsequently emerged, he had been assured by the club secretary that he would not lose financially by his suspension. As the winter wore on, however, Meredith received no money and became increasingly belligerent in trying to get it. The Directors, fearing exposure and seeking to get their blow in first, wrote to the FA accusing him of illegally trying to extract payment from them. Another FA enquiry was mounted and this time Meredith decided to come clean. He admitted offering the bribe but claimed that the club secretary had provided it, going on to accuse the club of regularly and systematically flouting the FA rules on wages and bonuses. The players concerned, confronted with Meredith's evidence, for the most part confessed. The directors, beginning with stout denial, also eventually admitted their guilt. The FA's reaction was swift and incisive. The club was fined £250. All the directors were suspended and the chairman and secretary were banned for life. The players involved, several of whom were suspended for a year, were fined a total of £900, and were told they could never play for Manchester City again.

The culture clash was evident from the Press reaction. Even the supporters of professional soccer were divided. The *Athletic News*, which shared the Football League's hopes that the game was gaining in respectability, sought to portray Meredith as an aberration, an ungrateful monster who had not only initiated the affair – 'an offence which ought to have ended his football career' – but, having been 'lavishly paid by the club which ran dreadful risks to give him all they had except the goalposts' had 'dragged everyone else he could into the same mess' with no sense of gratitude to the managers who had cosseted him or of loyalty to 'the comrades who had fought side by side with him'.[17] But the *Bolton Football Field* reflected the view from the terraces:

Meredith was 'no cunning financier or . . . sleek diplomat (but a) village youth, an artist of football and delight to hundreds of thousands of football enthusiasts'. Was it right that the club he had made famous 'should seem to want to be rid of the trouble of him'?[18]

If it did, their rivals were ready to pick up the burden. As Meredith scornfully put it: "The League met and the representatives of each club voted in favour of the punishment meted out to us being enforced. And while their representatives were passing this pious resolution most of them had other representatives busy trying to persuade the "villains whose punishment had been so well deserved" to sign for them under conditions very much better in most cases than the ones we had been ruled by at City.'[19] Meredith himself had every reason for satisfaction at the outcome. He not only improved his lot, but in doing so struck another blow at his old club by signing for their local rivals, Manchester United, newly promoted from the Second Division, under the leadership of an ambitious new manager, Ernest Mangnall. Meredith also contrived to outsmart the authorities and in the process to strike a blow at the retain-and-transfer system which he reckoned treated the player 'as though he were a sensible machine or trained animal'. His views were coloured, no doubt, by the fact that the player was not allowed – officially at least – a share of the fee.

Transfer fees were currently in the news: it caused a sensation when in the spring of 1905 Middlesborough paid Sunderland £1000 for their centre-forward, Alf Common. 'Is this to become a common experience,' asked a correspondent of the *Birmingham Daily Mail*, 'or where will it end . . . There is nothing to prevent a rich club becoming possessors of an international eleven.' The FA, who disliked the system on principle, proposed a limit of £350, but, after three months in which it was patently ignored, the idea was dropped. Its resemblance to a slave-market was increased when in the Manchester City affair the FA ordered the players to be sold to the highest bidder at a public auction in November, 1905. The other players obediently complied, but Meredith protested vigorously on the grounds that he had not cost City a transfer fee in the first place. He also argued that after ten years' service he was entitled to a benefit and produced his contract to prove it. He offered to waive his rights in return for a free transfer to a club of his own choosing, and got his way. If the FA thought that thereby they were saving themselves further trouble, however, they were in for a rude shock. At his new club he joined forces with two players of his own way of thinking, Charlie Roberts, the club captain, and Herbert Broomfield, the reserve goalkeeper. Roberts had been involved in 1903 in a forlorn attempt to form a Players' Union. Now, with Meredith's backing, he began a more serious attempt.

It began promisingly in 1907 with a fund-raising match between Manchester

United and Newcastle. By the following summer it had 1,200 members. J.J. Davies, Chairman of Manchester United, agreed to become the Union's President and J.H. Catton, one of the *Athletic News's* best-known writers, a Vice-President. There were hopes that the FA shared some of its objectives, if only in opposition to the League's sordid way of conducting affairs. In August 1908 the FA's offer of an amnesty if clubs would abide by the maximum wage rule in future had not been taken up and when in December the Union passed a resolution proposing free bargaining, two-year-plus contracts and players sharing in transfer transactions the *Athletic News* noted this as cordial support for 'the FA in their efforts to procure the abolition of the wage rule'.[20]

It was not quite as simple as that. A majority of clubs supported abolition in a FA ballot, but not the requisite two-thirds majority.[21] And whatever their views on the maximum wage rule the authorities were not going to be dictated to by their own servants. C.E. Sutcliffe, a director of Burnley FC and a prominent member of both the FA and the Football League, spoke for many when he reacted indignantly in his weekly column in the *Athletic News*. Sutcliffe wrote more in sorrow than in anger. He had tried to help the players but he could play no part in helping them with 'immoderate and unreasonable demands'. Their ideas of unlimited wages with the right to move from clubs and share in the transfer fees were 'the dreams of visionaries'. Their resolutions were contemptible claptrap' and they were 'committing suicide'. It was no longer 'a fight between one section of the clubs and another, but whether the players have to rule the clubs or the clubs the players'.[22]

In February, 1909, the Football League abruptly changed course and accepted the FA's amnesty. The Union retaliated by threatening legal action to recoup arrears of wages. The clubs reminded the FA and the FA reminded the Union that this was in breach of Rule 48. The Union secretary, Broomfield, replied 'in bombastic fashion', and in March the FA withdrew their recognition of the Union. The classical progression of the dispute continued. With the FA and the League in unlikely but determined alliance the Union began to take soundings about possible affiliation with the General Federation of Trades Unions and Meredith wrote an inflammatory article 'If the Pros Struck'. In three or four years' time, Sutcliffe commented scornfully, 'I reckon the Players' Union will be worth sufficient to pay its members one week's wages . . . If William Meredith thinks the public are with the Players' Union he is sadly mistaken. I come across very few who do not think footballers are amply paid at £4 per week and a £250 benefit after five years' service.'[23]

This was perhaps a partial view, but the militants had lost the support of the many, like the *Athletic News*, who supported some relaxation of the maximum wage limit but regarded the notion of sweeping aside all restrictions as anarchical – the selfish idea of a few rich clubs and a few star players who alone were likely to benefit. It was no coincidence that the leading activists were the league champions, Newcastle, and Meredith's new team, Manchester United, who won the Cup that spring. When during the summer the FA insisted on players signing a 'loyalty clause' in their contracts for the new season, and after further skirmishing, required them to withdraw from the Union or have their registration cancelled, almost all eventually complied. The Manchester United team and a few other militants held out, however, and were duly suspended amid sensational headlines.

It seemed likely that the new season would be disrupted. The Union officers declared themselves affiliated to the GFTU and handed over negotiations with the FA to them. A possible compromise was mooted. The courts had ruled that footballers were covered by the Workmen's Compensation Act of 1906, and the Union agreed to abide by the FA's rules if the FA would recognise the Union and its right to go to law if need be. But the FA flatly refused to pay summer wages of the suspended players – or to allow Charlie Roberts the benefit match he was due. On 31 August, the day before the new season was due to begin a truce was declared: the suspended players were allowed to play, but the FA insisted on the Union disaffiliating from the GFFU as a condition of recognition. In November a ballot of members decisively supported disaffiliation and the Union abandoned the right to strike. Summer wages were paid and Charlie Roberts got his benefit. Even Meredith signed the new contract, though he was the last to do so.

The FA had just as much trouble with amateurs as professionals. Elite clubs like the Corinthians had long been smarting at what N.L. Jackson regarded as their increasingly 'inferior position' within the Association. Even the Amateur Cup launched in 1894 had quickly lost its social cachet and fallen into the clutches of Northern teams like Bishop Auckland, Stockton, West Hartlepool and the like. As the new century began there were still gifted public school amateurs who could hold their own at the highest level. The centre-forward G.O. Smith of Oxford and Old Carthusians was still an automatic choice in 1901 for the full England international side – and its captaincy. He and his Oxonian colleague, W.J. Oakley, had amassed thirty-six caps between them over the previous six years, when international matches were still a rarity. Two other Oxford men, C.B. Fry, that most unusual of amateurs, and R.E. Foster, the only man to captain England at both cricket and soccer, were capped between 1900 and 1902. But thereafter the fountain dried up.

This was largely because professional competition brought higher standards, of effectiveness if not of chivalry, and required a degree of regimentation, rules, punctuality, commitment that did not fit in with the more casual amateur approach. The gulf is clearly visible in G.O. Smith's disdainful recollection: 'The Corinthians of my day never trained, and I can say that the need of it was never felt. We were all fit, and I think could have played on for more than one and a half hours without being any the worse.'[24] But talent was no longer enough. The Corinthians tried to keep the flag flying. Though aloof from organised competition, their occasional forays into the professional jungle still provided the occasional shock. It was an occasion for great celebration when they beat the 1904 FA Cup winners, Burnley, 10–3 in a 'friendly' match. But they were unique and increasingly isolated.

The gentlemanly amateurs, indeed, faced with what John Lewis, a member of the FA Council and Vice-President of the Football League, proudly called the 'revolt of the provinces and the transfer of power to the clubs outside the charmed circle',[25] increasingly withdrew their skirts. When Smith and Oakley retired from the international scene it was to carry on the work of Arthur Dunn, proprietor of a prestigious new preparatory school, Ludgrove, and an advocate of an Old Boys' soccer competition in which the old values would be restored. Dunn had died suddenly and as a memorial his friends initiated the Arthur Dunn Cup. Those select schools who qualified found it a blessed haven. But the exclusiveness had its drawbacks – the schools who did not qualify tended to drift off into the arms of the Rugby Union, for instance – and it did nothing for the strength of amateur soccer generally.

The sordidness of the professional scene, nevertheless, strengthened the belief of the die-hards that they represented something precious that the FA ought to cherish and protect instead of, as it seemed, constantly eroding. During 1905 and 1906 the superior suburban Surrey and Middlesex Associations refused to assume responsibility for clubs which allowed professionalism, suggesting, when the FA demurred, that responsibility for any such clubs or any new ones that might be formed be transferred to the adjoining London FA. The London FA themselves were divided on the issue, which became a rallying cry for the purists. The maverick weekly *Truth* mounted a series of attacks on the FA claiming that it was trying to drive the amateurs out and that the President, Lord Kinnaird, was turning it into the Football Association Limited[26] and an Amateur Football Defence Federation was formed, consisting of the Surrey, Middlesex and like-minded London clubs. They were at once outlawed by the FA, and after months of bitter argument the rebel Associations were expelled.

'The quarrel was not', a later apologist explained, 'with the professional player, who had always commanded the respect and often the admiration of the amateur footballer, but the professionals' myopic administrators'.[27] The Old Boys' Clubs, the universities, and of course the Corinthians now formed a breakaway Amateur Football Association, with an Old Etonian as secretary, and Lord Alverstone, Lord Chief Justice of England, as President. *The Times* greeted the new body with enthusiasm and was soon able to report that it had led to 'such a recrudescence of zeal for the purely recreative side of the winter game as has astonished even the promoters of the new governing body and more its detractors'.[28] The joy was premature.

Such success as the AFA had was in the south, again reflecting the geographical dimension of the social divide. By 1909 it had some 500 clubs in membership, but even in the south simply being amateur no longer seemed enough, particularly as the professionals were demonstrably better and offered competitive outlets better suited to the needs of ambitious players and clubs. Many stayed with the FA. The AFA started a Cup competition but it aroused little public interest. Even the Corinthians found themselves with nothing to prove: they lost their traditional showpiece match against Queen's Park, and Northern Nomads began to steal something of their thunder. The AFA also found their way to international competition blocked, for the FA was regarded with suitable veneration by the emerging Continental associations.

Despite overtures the FA had stayed away from the inaugural meeting of the Fédération Internationale de Football Associations (FIFA) in 1904. They considered its aspirations ludicrously premature, regarding its early efforts with amused tolerance mingled with exasperation at its incompetence. Before long, however, they were also growing anxious at the way FIFA was interpreting the laws of the game and, ironically, defining amateurism. By 1906 they joined, the other three home associations following suit, and D.B. Woolfall, their treasurer, was elected President. The FA's principal concern was to exercise restraint – 'it appears to be the custom to call as many matches as possible "Internationals"', Woolfall reported[29] – and with this in mind got FIFA to resolve that the term 'international' be reserved for teams selected by National Associations, which, of course excluded the AFA.

The irony deepened since most of the FA's ventures into internationalism beyond the British Isles were amateur. Matches were played against Belgium, Germany and Sweden (1908), Switzerland (1909) and Denmark (1910) but the split naturally weakened their playing strength, the depleted teams did not do well – against opposition in which 'broken time' was often allowed – and interest was fitful. Conversely the AFA were kept out of the first great international showcase for the amateur game, the 1908 London Olympics. In an undistinguished British team one of the star players was Vivian Woodward, who personified the FA's cricket-based notion of an amateur.

Woodward, who was capped twenty-three times for the full England international side, showed that it was still possible for an amateur, and a southern one at that, to reach the heights. He had done so, however, not through the splendid isolation of 'the charmed circle' but in the Leagues: after junior soccer for Chelmsford he had signed for Tottenham Hotspurs in their Southern League days and he was not only a player but a director in 1908 when they were fighting for promotion to the First Division. Woodward was an architectural surveyor, and no public school man, but a true amateur, modest and courteous in demeanour and playing purely for love of the game. There were not many like him in the Leagues. G.O. Smith later wrote: 'I don't remember being asked to play for a League side, and certainly would not have done so, as I had not time except for Corinthian and Old Carthusian games.'[30] But no one could say that any longer if he wanted to be an international.

Neither the FA, the League clubs nor the players showed much interest or saw much profit in professional internationals abroad. Most such encounters were irregular 'friendly' matches between near neighbours: the England team's (naturally victorious) visit to Austria, Hungary and Bohemia in 1908 was a logistically difficult and isolated exception. The four home countries believed themselves – and were believed to be – the best in the world. There was no other international competition like the British one. And it was the excitements of Cup and League, modern versions of the age-old local tribal conflicts, that chiefly interested the common people of Britain.

Northern Union and Rugby League

In some north-country towns the tribal warfare was conducted with an oval ball. All had not gone smoothly for the Northern Union after the split with the RFU. Its controversial new League was a source of internal friction. It suited the fifteen chosen clubs very well, but amid accusations of elitism there was immediate pressure for an extension. Yorkshire Senior Competition clubs, indeed, threatened rebellion and in 1902 two divisions were created, each with eighteen teams. The lower division were particularly vulnerable to the advance of soccer. Founder members of the Northern Union, like Stockport, Tyldesley and Liversedge, were forced to disband at the end of the season. Another, Manningham, changed to soccer as Bradford City in 1903–4. The two division scheme was scrapped, but an experiment with a single big League in 1905–6 still left too many clubs – and their supporters – without interest in competitive honours far too early in the season. In 1907 Bradford Park Avenue, winners of the previous year's Challenge Cup, made a loss of £500 in the new season and joined City in the Association.

This was to be the low point, however. During these years of organisational experiment the Northern Union had also brought in a number of rule changes, of the kind that H.H. Almond had sternly warned against. They were blatantly designed for the benefit of the spectators – weighting the points value of tries as against kicks, abolishing the 'line-out', allowing a player to get up and play the ball after a tackle, relaxing the 'knock-on' law, and finally, in 1907–8 reducing the number of players to thirteen by removing the 'spoiling' wing-forwards. These changes, which made the game more open and less of a free-for-all, pleased the crowds. In 1907 a new club, Bradford Northern, took the place of the defecting Park Avenue and managed to survive. By then the Northern Union's fortunes had begun to improve. The following year they tried a new competitive formula, involving the top four clubs in end-of-season play-offs, and this proved both popular and commercially successful. An equally promising new development was the introduction of a highly lucrative colonial dimension.

This last had the added advantage of discomfiting the RFU. In 1905 the All-Blacks a (white) Rugby Union team from New Zealand had toured Britain, with devastating success. One of the players, G.W. Smith, had seen Rugby League matches during the tour and on his return he and a Wellington businessman, A.H. Baskerville, organised a professional tour of Britain in 1907–8 by a combined team of Australians and New Zealanders. This, to the RFU's chagrin, was a great success, with lasting benefits to the professional code. Several tourists, including Smith himself and a gifted Australian, Lance Todd, joined English clubs, a pattern that was to be repeated in the regular tours by Australian and New Zealand teams that followed. The Northern Union were so heartened and financially strengthened by these developments that they launched a programme of expansion within Britain aimed at what they saw as weak spots in the RFU's empire as well as in soccer strongholds.

Several new clubs were formed, often stimulated by exhibition games. During the innovatory Australasian tour of 1907–8, one of the three Test matches – as their games with the Dominions were brazenly called – was held in Cheltenham on the edge of the West Country and another on Chelsea football ground, drawing 13,000 curious Londoners, by far the biggest gate of the tour. The following year when both amateur and professional Australian sides toured Britain the Welsh were treated to their own 'international' at Aberdare, and Tests were staged in Birmingham and at Newcastle, where there was a record crowd of 22,000. The new clubs stimulated by this missionary drive did not last. One, Liverpool City, came and went in 1906–7, and of the six Welsh clubs enlisted in 1907 and 1908, three lasted only a single season and another only two.[31] Nevertheless there were high hopes of further progress as the decade ended.

In commercial sport, as in business generally, the rewards of success can be great, but no one wants to know about failure. Even in successful clubs professionalism encourages a personality cult not always easy to reconcile with a team game, except through shared success and shared winning bonuses. In the Northern Union the demands of constantly chasing success made their mark on the clubs at all levels. In 1904 they were obliged to abandon their cherished rule requiring players to have a job outside football.

Fortunately this did not make a great deal of difference, since most players kept their week-day jobs anyway. The situation was quite unlike soccer. Though the match fees and winning bonuses might be higher, clubs did not pay regular guaranteed weekly wages or close-season retainers: after the signing on fee it was performance fees only – no play, no pay. Its particular brand of commercialism, offering no security, sharpened the competitive edge on the field of play. Enforcing the rules depended more on the vigilance and strength of character of the referee than the honour code of the players. And since it was a game of fierce physical contact it too often spilled over into violence. But this was all part of the spectacle – not exactly what the crowds came to see, but what they expected at moments of crisis.

Rugby League clubs were smaller-scale enterprises than their counterparts in the Football League. Cup and League finals and Australian tours, home and away, were the great money-spinners for the Northern Union and many clubs depended on the subsidies they received from these ventures. The biggest crowd recorded was 32,509 in 1903 for the Challenge Cup final and ordinary league matches sometimes drew merely a few hundred. It was thus a big undertaking to contemplate overseas signings. Lance Todd's transfer fee when he moved from Wigan to Dewsbury was £450, and the New Zealander Edgar Wrigley got £550 when he left Huddersfield for Hunslet. For clubs that could afford the outlay, however, the money was usually recovered at the turnstiles. At Huddersfield, the local favourite Harold Wagstaff, signed as a 15-year old for five gold sovereigns, held his own with the Colonials, Welshmen and other imports. Billed as 'The Empire Team of Stars and All Talents', Huddersfield offered an early sample of the powerful mixture of the exotic and the home-grown that was to become characteristic of the Rugby League.

Notes

1 H.F. Abell, 'The Football Fever', *Macmillan's Magazine*, no. 89 (1903), p. 276, quoted by J. Maguire, 'Images of Manliness', *BJSH*, December, 1986, p. 276.
2 Abell, 'The Football Fever'.
3 Report of the Ministry of Education, *Education 1900–1950*, HMSO, 1951, p. 70.
4 In his 1909 report the Board of Education's Chief Medical Officer recommended that 'a right system of physical training, designed to develop mind and body simultaneously, should be commenced', a specialist inspectorate was established and all local authorities were urged to appoint organisers of physical training.
5 R. Baden-Powell, *Scouting for Boys*, London, 1908.
6 Quoted in J. Hutchinson, *The Football Industry*, London, 1982, p. 24.
7 A.J. Richardson, 'Football Betting', *Transactions of the Liverpool Economic and Statistical Society, 1906–7*, quoted in further detail by Mason, *Football*, pp. 179–87.
8 22 April 1907 quoted in T. Mason, *Association Football and English Society*, Brighton, 1980, p. 246.

9 In B.A. Corbett *et al.*, *Football*, London, 1907, p. 54, quoted in S. Wagg, *The Football World*, Brighton, 1984, pp. 6–7.

10 Wagg, *The Football World*.

11 Hutchinson, *Football Industry*, p. 55.

12 *Ibid.*, p. 77.

13 Austria beat Hungary 5–0 in October 1902 in the first of these. Belgium and France drew 3–3 in 1904.

14 Quoted in H.F. Moorhouse, 'Scotland against England', *IJHS*, September, 1987, p. 194.

15 Quoted (p. 33) in Dunphy, *Strange Kind of Glory*, which tells Meredith's story from the 'realistic' perspective of present-day football, seeing him as a victim but by no means an innocent one.

16 *Ibid.*, p. 34.

17 *Ibid.*, p. 41.

18 *Ibid.*, p. 43.

19 *Ibid.*, p. 42.

20 *Athletic News*, 21 December, 1908, quoted in B. Dabscheck, 'Man or Puppet?', *IJHS*, September, 1991, p. 224. Dabscheck gives a full account of the dispute which is also discussed in Mason, *Football*, and W. Vamplew, *Pay Up and Play the Game: Professional Sport in Britain, 1875–1914*, Cambridge, 1988.

21 Dabscheck, 'Man or Puppet?', p. 223.

22 'Who Shall Be Masters, Players or Clubs?', *Athletic News*, 11 January, 1909.

23 *Athletic News*, 8 March, 1909.

24 E. Grayson, *Corinthians and Cricketers*, London, 1955, p. 31.

25 *C.B. Fry's Magazine*, no. 6 (1906–7), p. 264 ff., quoted in Lowerson, *Sport and the English Middle Classes, 1870–1914*, Manchester, 1993, p. 185.

26 3 October, 1906, in Lowerson, *Sport and the English Middle Classes*.

27 Grayson, *Corinthians*, p. 146.

28 *Ibid.*, p. 107.

29 J. Arlott, *The Oxford Companion to Sports and Games*, St Albans, 1977, p. 303.

30 Grayson, *Corinthians*, p. 31.

31 Merthyr Tydfil lasted until 1911, and Ebbw Vale, where there was no serious soccer rival, until 1912. No further Welsh clubs joined until Cardiff, who played a single season in 1951/2.

CHAPTER THIRTEEN

Muddied oafs: the purists

Kipling's view of cricket and football was not shared by his friend Cecil Rhodes. When Rhodes died in 1902, his will made prowess 'in manly outdoor sports' an important qualification for the scholarships he bequeathed to enable young men from the Empire to go to Oxford.[1] 'Verily the muddied oafs and flannelled fools have been avenged', commented *Truth*.[2] Of the many sportsmen who took advantage of this bounty those who made the most immediate impact were the rugger men. The Rhodes scholars helped raise the standards of the 'Varsity match which was the centrepiece of the British game – and the British game was in need of stimulus.

Rugby Union: old wounds and new

Even at its 1895 peak, before the debilitating split with the Northerners, the Rugby Football Union had mustered only 481 clubs. Within three years the numbers had dropped to 383 and by 1903 reached rock-bottom with 244. Thereafter the tide turned, but slowly – some forty or so new clubs by the end of the decade.[3] What they lacked in numbers they made up for in prestige: a growing number of public schools and older grammar schools found its physical roughness preferable to the social crudities of soccer, and the services, the London medical schools and the county championship (released from its bondage to Yorkshire and Lancashire) added gentlemanly competition to the staple of friendly club fixtures, arranged on traditional, disorganised lines.

Its home international championship, built up in the early days as a result of the historic rivalry with soccer, was much more satisfactory since national fervour, strong and uncluttered by distracting League and Cup loyalties, was expressed, at least in principle, through the sporting conventions of the better sort. It had certainly become more of a contest since the 1895 split. England, previously dominant, now fared badly. Scotland had three great years and were always hard to beat on their own home ground at Inverleith, Ireland won or shared the Championship three times, and Wales had a 'golden age', losing only 7 of the first 43 matches played in the new century. It was 1910 before England managed to win the title again.

The rampant Welsh, suspected by their opponents of running the game 'on commercial lines' – which they themselves called 'democratic lines' – and certainly guilty of selecting players 'mainly of the artisan class', incurred as much odium as admiration.[4] Welsh commentators complained that Scotland could accept defeat 'by her sister country, Ireland' and 'for the sake of sport . . . by England' but Wales had 'got upon the national nerves'.[5] The Scots responded by sweeping to victory in two Triple Crowns with a fine pack of forwards based on the Edinburgh University team. In 1903 the Irish RFU's treasurer, proposing a rise in admission charges 'to keep out the roughs', made a clear distinction: 'Last year the Welsh fellows broke in all over the ground and smashed up everything they could lay their hands upon.' Over £50 had been paid for a dinner to the Scots and only about £30 for a dinner to the Welsh team. The reason for this was that 'champagne was given to the Scotsmen and beer only (but plenty of it) to the Welshmen. Whiskey and porter were always good enough for Welshmen. The Scotsmen, however, were gentlemen, and appreciated a dinner when it was given to them. Not so the Welshmen.'[6]

Meanwhile the Dominions,[7] apart from Canada which preferred ice-hockey, were advancing apace. New Zealand had been playing Rugby since 1870, when it was introduced by a young man returning from school in England, and had discarded both the 'Australian rules' and soccer alternatives. The Australians themselves were less single-minded, being distracted not only by 'Australian rules' but by professional Rugby, yet highly competitive. In South Africa rugger was an enthusiasm shared by British settlers and Boers. The South Africans won a three-match series against a British touring team in 1903 and the following year toured Australasia, beating the Australians but losing to New Zealand, who had claims to being the best team in the world by then. On their 1905–6 tour of Britain, introducing new tactics and formations, the All-Blacks wrought havoc, scoring a total of 830 points against 39.

The New Zealanders' success, or rather the British defeats, coming so soon after the Report of the Committee on Physical Deterioration, caused alarm and despondency. Here was an example of a decline in the national physique amongst the very group on whom the country's leadership depended. The Press was soon full of critical letters from former players. They began early in the season. On 9 October, after the defeat of Durham, the English county champions, the *Daily Mail*'s headline was 'Is the English Footballer Deteriorating?' and Mr R.G.T. Coventry, an Oxford University player, commented sadly: 'Our national character and physique are nowhere more plainly evidenced than in our games and I am inclined to think that we have lost a good deal of our ancient robustness and sturdy independence.' Two days later a former county captain went further:

> The average Englishman of to-day, becoming more and more a flabby specimen of humanity (in work and in play), avoids, as often as possible, hard knocks, danger and much self-sacrifice. Small wonder the Middlesex team, puffing and blowing before half-time, cut such an amusing figure last Wednesday.
>
> We Englishmen seem to be fast losing our historical grit, allowing 'fat and funk' to take its place. Until the Boer War . . . we used to claim that one Englishman was worth two of any other country.[8]

When the tourists went on to beat Scotland and Ireland and to trounce England before a vast crowd the gloom was profound. The advertising men did well out of it, though: the All-Blacks even endorsed their favourite brand of cigarettes. And interest in the last international, against Wales, hailed as the 'championship of the world', was intense. Wales's narrow victory[9] not only salvaged something of the pride of British rugby, it was an important moment in the expression of a new and more confident sense of Welsh identity. 'What the other nations of these islands has been unable to do has been achieved by these sons of the ancient Britons', wrote 'Ap Idanfryn' of the *South Wales Daily News*, adding, 'To-night is going to be as unforgettable as Mafeking night was.'[10] The imperial reference was important, for this was no secessionist upsurge. The *Western Mail* indeed spoke of Wales 'coming to the rescue of the Empire'.[11]

There was an undoubted air of excess in some of the subsequent fervour, seeking to install Rugby as a centrepiece of indigenous cultural achievement, as in the proposal from the Herald Bard himself for a 'memorial column of simple, massive design, treated in the Celtic style, decorated by discs in bronze'.[12] But this was no simple recrudescence of primal native force. For one thing Welsh rugby was an immigrants' game by origin and its flourishing in this golden age owed much to the new wave of industrial prosperity that had come to South Wales.[13] The Welsh captain, Gwyn Nicholls, had been born in Gloucestershire, the famous 'Boxer' Harding was born in Market Rasen, and H.B. Winfield in Nottingham. The renowned Welsh forwards included men like 'Packer, Watts, Boucher, Hellings and Brice, who won 60 Welsh caps among them during the years 1891–1907, but whose Welshness was geographical only: they had all come to work and live in South Wales from Somerset and Devon'.[14] Conversely, when Lloyd George, from Caernarfon in North Wales, went to Cardiff in 1908 as President of the Board of Trade to receive the Freedom of the city, he performed the ceremonial kick-off in a game between Cardiff and Blackheath, declaring afterwards, 'It's a most extra-ordinary game. I never saw it before and I must say I think it's more exciting than politics.'[15]

North Wales had its rugby outposts, notably around Ruthin and Rydal Schools, but Billy Meredith was the hero of the working man, and the strong links of the region with Merseyside and Manchester intensified the popularity of soccer. Soccer had indeed achieved a strong following in South Wales, too, especially along the urban coastal belt (despite middle-class disapproval of the alien/Northern English/professional newcomer) and rugger, though now sustained by heroic national mythology, had to struggle to retain its hold on the crowds. Victory was all-important in the now-dominant competitive ethos of the time. Wales was beaten by the touring South Africans in 1906–7, but there was some satisfaction in that Cardiff managed one of the only two victories against this powerful side. (The other was by Scotland.) And when the Australians came in 1908–9, demolishing as a curtain-raiser Cornwall, the English county champions fielded against them in the London Olympics, only Wales could beat them. But Welsh rugby now faced a test amongst the very classes from which its recent success had sprung. First, soccer enjoyed a great upsurge in popularity: in 1906 there were 74 clubs in south Wales; by 1910 there were 262 in an array of local leagues.[16] Second, the Northern Union, which had recently developed its own leagues, began a determined hunt for players, especially in Wales where there had been no purge of 'gate-money' clubs.

The Northern Union was tolerable, perhaps even useful, to the Welsh RFU if it remained as a safety-valve for the occasional malcontent who faced ostracism – patriotic as well as purely social – by switching codes. The bigger urban clubs had relatively discreet ways of retaining working-class players. The Swansea team of 1908, for instance, included amongst its predominantly artisan players four publicans, one of them a former boiler-maker. The brewing industry was active in sponsorship of rugby in Wales as it was in the West of England. But in the older industrial areas of the mountains and valleys, where local rivalries thrived in the Glamorgan and Monmouthshire Leagues established in the 1890s, more direct methods were customary – and had led to the expulsion of Aberaman in 1901 and the abandonment for the third time of the Challenge Cup in 1904.[17] There was worse to come. A 1907 enquiry into the 'fixing' of a match between Aberdare and Treorchy revealed a widespread practice of payment to players amongst several clubs and led to the suspension of two club committees and of eight players, including Dai Jones, a collier who had played for Wales against the South Africans. By the following summer six clubs – Aberdare, Barry, Ebbw Vale, Merthyr Tydfil, Mid-Rhondda and Treherbert – had joined Rugby League clubs. Wales were still dominant internationally as the decade ended but fearful that the fierce competition at local level, sharpened by the inroads of soccer and the Northern Union, was becoming counter-productive.

They were certainly taken to task by traditionalists, not only in England (where those advocates of 'public school virtues' who claimed that it was in Wales that 'ill deeds began' could be dismissed as envious snobs[18]) but by more impartial judges. One of these, the respected and objective Scottish critic, Hamish Stuart, declared in 1910 that Welsh club rugby had 'degenerated into as gross a libel on real rugby as the purist ever visioned in a nightmare' with 'unfair and foul play' tolerated by weak referees especially amongst leading clubs and players.[19] The pure flame of amateurism still burned brightly at the Scottish RFU, fanned by such dedicated administrators as J. Aikman Smith, of Edinburgh Royal High School FP who took on the mantle of H.H. Almond, now deceased. In 1903, the year Almond died, the leading Scottish referee, Stirling Crawford, had openly wondered at Wales's selection of miners, steelworkers and policemen who 'really belonged in the Northern Union'.[20] That same year the Scottish RFU had found themselves unable to withstand the pressures to recognise the Border League, an increasingly important source of powerful forwards for the national team but a magnet for Northern Union scouts. Yet the scattered population and rural ambience – which similarly kept professional soccer at bay – contained the menace to manageable proportions. When in 1905 the Scottish international A.W. Little signed for Wigan, the deal was completed in suitably cloak-and-dagger fashion by candlelight at midnight in a Hawick attic.[21]

Religion and politics complicated things in Ireland, but the spread of Gaelic games – mainly in rural areas and mainly in the south – and of soccer – mainly in urban areas and mainly in the north – left rugby less affected by plebeian intrusion and consequently, especially in the south, somewhat above sectarian strife. In 1901 RIC reports included the GAA with the Celtic Literary Society and the Gaelic League as the most active nationalist organisations in the country. The Celtic thrust of the reviving GAA was reflected in its concentration on the distinctive Irish team games. Hurling, the authentic 'national' game, had previously been the mainstay, but now Gaelic football began to flourish both as a playing and a spectator sport. The All-Ireland Finals of 1902 attracted big crowds and the game really arrived in 1905, first in February with a challenge match between Dublin and Tipperary, and then between July and October when over 50,000 people watched one or other of the three matches it took Kerry and Kildare to decide the Final. And as the GAA gained in strength so it flexed its muscles again; the 'foreign ban' was re-introduced in January, 1905.[22] By the 25th anniversary in 1909 Gaelic games were going well.

They did not, however, have a great intrinsic appeal to the politer middle classes, north and south, where the networks, competitive but 'sporting' and socially prestigious, emanating from Trinity College in Dublin and North of Ireland club in Belfast, had gained strength and greatly benefited from rugby's international dimension. And it was soccer, amongst the urban working class generally and in Scotticised areas in particular, that most threatened rugby. In Ballymena, for instance, the rugby club had had an up-and-down existence since its foundation in 1887, more than once being forced to disband because of the counter-attraction of soccer. On the other hand at Dungannon, south-west of Lough Neagh, the rugby club, originally a Trinity offshoot, aroused fierce local pride amongst all classes and all persuasions. And at Derry on the Donegal border, where all three games jostled for supremacy, the rugby team's reception after victory in the Provincial Towns' Cup in 1908 included both Protestant and Catholic flute bands. Such innocent ecumenism was not to last, but rugby's image as a reputable, virile game compared favourably with that of soccer. In Ireland, to be predominantly middle-class meant to be utterly amateur, a point well-taken by socially conscious headmasters not utterly seized with Gaelic fervour who viewed soccer's shortcomings with disdain.

In England the contrast, uncomplicated by the Gaelic dimension, was even more starkly evident and the RFU's future progress was to depend heavily on its esteem in the expanding grammar school sector which generally sought to emulate the public schools. By 1910 Radley, Rossall, Emmanuel and Pocklington had begun to show the way, forsaking soccer's contamination. And meanwhile the revival in England's international fortunes had stemmed primarily from the prestige the game now held in Oxford and Cambridge. England had lost against all three Dominion touring teams, and though she had held her own against Ireland and Scotland she had not beaten Wales since 1897. But the tide was beginning to turn for the Englishmen. The renascence was led by Adrian Stoop, of Rugby School, an Oxford Blue in 1902–3–4, captain of the elite Harlequins, who set out to import some of the 1905 All-Blacks' tactical ideas and give an emphasis to attack. His famous 1910 side included two other Harlequins' backs, J.E.G. Birkett of Haileybury and the glamorous Ronald Poulton-Palmer, also of Rugby and Oxford, with E.L. Chambers of Cambridge University and Blackheath on one wing and F.E. Chapman, a Durham University medical student on the other. Two other Blackheath men, Cambridge medic. H.J.S. Morton and the renowned 'Cherry' Pillman, graced the forwards as did (Sir) Lancelot Barrington-Ward of Oxford and Edinburgh University Medical School. Of the other seven, five were from West country clubs.

The region from Gloucester to Redruth was in rugby terms similar to the Scottish borders, but with sizeable towns to provide crowds, sharpen the edge of competition with soccer, bring in artisan players and customise discreet broken-time payments (and more overt job-finding) for the better ones. There was trouble ahead for the West Country as the RFU sought to purify its depleted but resurgent empire, but it was in the industrial Midlands that tentacles of Northern professionalism first had to be lopped. Leicester was the leading gate-money club remaining in the RFU, and there had been six Leicester players in the England side in 1906. Several of them had been brought to Leicester as part of the club's policy for success in a city whose thriving soccer team reached the First Division in 1908. Amongst the imports were A.L. Kewney and E.J. Jackett, regular England players, one from the Hartlepool shipyard, the other from Cornwall, where he had been a cycling champion and an artist's model.

Investigating complaints, an RFU sub-committee in January 1909, found three less-distinguished players guilty of having previously taken money from Northern Union clubs (and the captain guilty of having signed forms for a Northern Union club without actually playing) but, doubtless highly conscious of the political capital that might be made of a harsher verdict, exonerated the club management and its England stars, concluding 'that the club, having a strong team with a good match list, attracts players who are unable to get such good football in other localities, but that, however undesirable this may be, the players have not benefited pecuniarily thereby'.[23] This remarkable decision so displeased the RFU President, Arnold Crane, who hailed from the Midlands, that he resigned.[24] Nevertheless Leicester were left free to continue their traditional rivalry with Northampton, another club with strong popular support. Coventry, further west, were less fortunate the following year. They were between the Rugby-playing East Midlands and Birmingham, one of soccer's heartlands, and their gates were threatened by the emergent Coventry City soccer team. The rugby club, infiltrated by Northern Union players who had come to work in the burgeoning motor industry, were found to have made illegal payments, concealed in the accounts as the cost of lemons and towels. They were suspended, losing their ground and leading players to a professional group who promptly joined the Northern Union.

It was typical of the RFU's flexible morality that when their Honorary Secretary, Rowland Hill, retired in 1904 they should appoint a paid replacement and at once resolve that the rules concerning professionalism should not apply to him.[25] Unlike the AELTC they wanted no one contaminated by trade. The first holder, Percy Coles, had played for Rugby School, Blackheath and Oxford and was an Eastbourne solicitor, but he lasted only three years before emigrating to Canada as a fruit farmer. The second, C.J.B. Marriott, suited them better. He had captained Cambridge and

Blackheath, and had played several times for England. He was from a Sussex landowning family, and had been Secretary of Queen's Club before coming to the RFU, which he served for seventeen years.

One of Marriott's first tasks was to complete the acquisition and conversion of a market garden at Twickenham into a splendid new ground and headquarters premises. When it was finished there were covered stands for 6,000, terraces for 7,000 and standing for another 24,000. A car-park for 200 vehicles was added. The cost of the conversion was £20,000 on top of the purchase price of more than £5,000. This opulence at its headquarters was another remarkable feature of this amateur game. The RFU shared the ground with Harlequins, who played the inaugural match against Richmond in 1909, before 2,000 spectators. But its main function was as a setting for the internationals,[26] which had begun to attract huge crowds, and for the great fashionable ritual of the season, the Oxford and Cambridge match, which moved there from Queen's Club. Gate-money might be bad for the clubs but it was good for the RFU.

Hockey: amateurs and Amazons

One ball-game that retained Corinthian purity from top to bottom was hockey. The men's game had by now taken on a regular ordered pattern, with Oxford versus Cambridge a highlight of the calendar. There were also annual encounters among the five regions with the South maintaining a marked superiority that reflected the geographical spread of hockey's popularity and also its prevailing social tone. Public school Old Boys and Army officers formed a good proportion of the players. There was little international development and though hockey had taken firm hold in India no one regarded it as a cornerstone of Empire. At home England were overwhelmingly the strongest of the four countries. Annual matches against France began in 1907, but apart from an aberrational draw in Paris in 1908, it was all one-way traffic. The big event of 1908 was the inclusion of hockey in the London Olympics, but it was little more than a home international tournament: England beat Ireland 8–1 in the Final and Scotland beat Wales to take the bronze medal.

Neither the British Olympic Association nor the AEWHA thought it appropriate to introduce women's hockey to the visiting nations – or to the crowds. Indeed the AEWHA had been considerably embarrassed by the publicity attending their early, unexpected success. Commercial exploitation was not part of their preferred scheme of things. The pattern of team competition had grown up on similar lines to that of the men. There were county and Territorial Associations in which the south held sway, England's dominance was just as marked in the 'international' contests and the women did not venture even as far as Paris in search of converts or opposition, though there were enthusiastic players in the Dominions, especially in their English-model public schools.

The separate development of the women's game had left the AEWHA in uneasy balance between preserving a proper feminine etiquette and showing that, in appropriate matters, they were the equal of men. A former pupil of North London Collegiate School later recalled a match in 1902 against Dartford College students when the Collegiate girls were 'given showers and tea after the match, taken for a tour of the college and returned to school with a bouquet of flowers'.[27] On the other hand when the AEWHA, after long deliberation decided in 1907 to follow the lead of the Scottish and Irish Associations by ruling that 'there shall be no hooking or striking of sticks', a great rumpus followed, with some fearing that this was tantamount to admitting that women could not play the same game as men. There were similar arguments about whether the duration of games and the dimensions of pitches should be reduced for women's use. Likewise, although some felt that it might be to women's advantage to develop mixed hockey, hitherto restricted to casual and informal affairs, the AEWHA discouraged the idea, arguing that it was physically dangerous for women to play with men and also that those who did so were likely to be too much concerned with their appearance and their prospects of matrimony.[28]

These latter considerations were both to the fore in the continuing controversy over women's dress, particularly in the matter of skirt length. It was student fashion at Dartford College, where the tunic had become standard wear for hockey and had infiltrated into the adult game, that now caused the biggest stir. In 1910 the AEWHA. although not illiberal on the question of skirt length, reacted sternly when a Dartford student appeared in a county match in her tunic. 'That costume', wrote a correspondent of *The Hockey Field* on 27 January, 'is, without doubt, ideal in that it cannot hamper the movements of the wearer, but at the same time it does not suit itself to public grounds.' And another county player received a brusque warning from her fiancé: 'Please look at page 874 of the *Sporting and Dramatic* and see an awful apparition who plays for Kent. If there is any chance of you wearing kit like that, my foot comes down hard and you have no more hockey.' In the debate that followed, most people were agreed, if not on the need to obey brutal fiancés on all points, that 'every effort should be made to avoid shocking the susceptibilities of their parents or guardians'.

The AEWHA's general principle was that 'every player must maintain a womanly standard' and with this is mind they set the tone with their uniform for the England XI. This was a white canvas shirt, a tie, and a long cardinal serge skirt lined in the front to make running easier and prevent it riding up. What players wore underneath is harder to be sure about. Corsets, it seems, were still the norm. They were discouraged at Dartford, Anstey and the new colleges at Bedford and Liverpool, as well as the leading girls' schools, but the claims of modesty and femininity had to be recognised amongst adults. And, as Edith Head, the editor of *The Hockey Field*, put it 'Many players declare that they cannot wear stays, but there are now so many excellent patterns made especially adapted for athletics that there is no real reason why they should not.'[29] One aspect of the situation that was rarely discussed openly was that some means had to be found to keep up the long, black woollen stockings that were obligatory wear – sometimes two pairs, for added protection. The AEWHA wisely tended to concern itself chiefly with outside appearances and safety, from time to time prohibiting things like heavy boots, unsightly garments and 'unaccustomed cuts'.[30]

Beyond all this there lay the original question about hockey – whether it was a ladylike and seemly game whatever women wore while playing it. There were plenty of male critics, medical and lay, who thought that hockey was responsible for all manner of departures from desirable feminine norms, physical and aesthetic. Many women themselves had similar views – such as that only 'the few square, squat and burly outdoor porter type of girls' should play such a rough, competitive game, which, 'with its muddy field, rush and excitement' was 'surely unadulterated lunacy' for 'the unformed, untrained or nervous girl.'[31] But thousands of young women, mostly of the better sort, took the risk either voluntarily or as part of programmes of physical and moral improvement devised for them by educationalists and other reformers.

These reforms had begun amongst the affluent and it was to be some time before their benefits spread beyond them. The effects of the educational divide on physical education generally have already been noted: neither the exiguous and narrowly utilitarian traditions nor the physical and financial resources of the state elementary schools extended to games-playing on any scale; and, this apart, the challenge to sex stereotypes and conventional public opinion that hockey offered was not the sort of thing these schools normally could, or wished, to go in for. In the adult world the divide continued: hockey clubs were located in superior suburban areas and were correspondingly socially exclusive; practices and matches were held during the week, in the daylight hours of autumn and winter, which put them out of the reach of working girls; there were no businesswomen's, still less works' clubs. The social climate was, of course, changing but the commercial factors that encouraged changes in men's sport were largely missing and, in the wider context, the forces of sexual and of class revolution worked against rather than with each other. In the recent past, a 1907 letter to the *Hockey Field* recalled, an attempt to introduce into a ladies' club a skilled payer whose father was in trade, had failed because several members objected to playing alongside a tradesman's daughter.[32]

The *Hockey Field*, like most sporting publications, was in favour of expansion, and the AEWHA was not without missionary zeal. But it was one thing to talk and write about the power of hockey to bring together women of all sorts by a common interest and quite another to turn it into 'an enterprise, a recreation and an enthusiasm for those working for a living', as the liberal element in the AEWHA wished.[33] The challenge came, as so often, from the North and Midlands. There a few less opulent schools and an occasional factory and office were beginning to play the game and where there were not enough players to form separate clubs the idea of amalgamation was mooted. The *Hockey Field* was in favour, but most of the ladies' clubs were not, despite assurances that they would not have to mingle off the field, and the working-class ventures had to make their own way. Most of these were offshoots of men's clubs, an undesirable connotation in itself for the separatist AEWHA and one which steered the women in the direction of competition, leagues, points and cups and such like Northern habits. In 1910 a Ladies' Hockey League was started in the Oldham district of Lancashire playing regular Saturday afternoon matches on a competitive basis. It was a bad omen for the future.

The really prestigious women's game by this time was lacrosse. Its early, tiny beginnings had resulted by 1905 in the creation of only one adult club, the Southern Ladies. Its founders were former pupils of Roedean, Wycombe Abbey and Prior's Field Schools and its main opponents were the girls of these schools and of a Scottish counterpart, St Leonard's. Unlike hockey it spread upwards from the schools rather than down from the colleges, being thought at first too strenuous for adult young ladies, and it was the physical education colleges rather than Oxbridge that first took it up, but Roedean had given it all the social cachet it needed. Some girls played both games, and the *Hockey Field*, which for a time produced regular reports on lacrosse, campaigned for friendly co-existence, but the different history and nature of the two made rather for rivalry, social as well as athletic. This in turn discouraged both from spreading down the social scale, and it was netball, with its advantages of simplicity and economy of space that made most progress in the state schools, the clubs for working and lower professional class young women and, not least, the YWCA. Happily it had no strongly established male equivalent and hence no commercial perils loomed.

Notes

1 Americans, and, to Kipling's displeasure, Germans were also eligible.
2 10 April, 1902, quoted in J. Lowerson, *Sport and the English Middle Classes, 1870–1914*, Manchester, 1993, p. 75.
3 E. Dunning and K. Sheard, *Barbarians, Gentlemen and Players*, Oxford, 1979, p. 234,

and tables, have extracted and worked up relevant information from the official histories.

4 D. Smith and G. Williams, *Fields of Praise*, Cardiff, 1980, p. 124.

5 *Ibid*.

6 *Ibid*., p. 125

7 The white self-governing colonies, Australia, Canada, New Zealand and the South African group were given this title in 1907.

8 Quoted in J. Nauright, 'Sport, Manhood and Empire', *IJHS*, September 1991, pp. 239–53.

9 It was clouded, slightly, by subsequent controversy over a disallowed New Zealand try': this was fostered by the sensationalist newspapers and does not affect the points at issue. For the match and its social context see Smith and Williams, *Fields of Praise*, pp. 145–75.

10 18 December 1905, quoted by G. Williams, 'Image and Identity in Wales', in Mangan, *Pleasure, Profit*, pp. 128–9.

11 *Ibid*., p. 130.

12 *Ibid*., p. 139.

13 See Smith and Williams, *Fields* and G. Williams in Mangan, *Pleasure, Profit*, pp. 128–42, and in T. Mason (ed.), *Sport in Britain*, Cambridge, 1989, pp. 308–29.

14 Williams, *Pleasure, Profit*, p. 137.

15 *Ibid*., p. 135.

16 Smith and Williams, *Fields*, p. 177.

17 *Ibid*., p. 179.

18 *Ibid*., p. 175.

19 *Ibid*., p. 182.

20 Williams, *Sport in Britain*, p. 320.

21 T.R. Delaney, *The Roots of Rugby League*, Keighley, 1984, p. 108.

22 The Gaelic League's interest in the movement was also growing. It was lady members of the Gaelic League who from around 1902 began, as an alternative to the Anglo-Irish hockey, to play a modified version of hurling. A name for it, camogie, was devised by a leading Celtic scholar and it became formally established as a GAA game in 1904.

23 Delaney, *Roots*, p. 113.

24 Titley and McWhirter, *Centenary History*, biography section, pt 1, p. 4. Kewney and Jackett went on playing for England, though Jackett caused further eye-brow raising when he signed for Dewsbury in the Northern Union in 1911.

25 *Ibid*., p. 120. Described by *The Times* when he died as 'An amateur of amateurs and a Tory of Tories', Hill retired to become President.

26 France, where Rugby had first been played by English residents at Le Havre, and the Captain of the prestigious Racing Club de Paris from 1900 to 1903 and first secretary of the Fédération Française de Rugby was an Anglo-Scot, had reached a high enough standard, with the assistance of imported part-time professional coaches, to join the international circle from 1905 to 1906 when the first game was played against England. These matches were, however, to be something of a relaxing romp for the home countries for some years.

27 R.M. Scrimgeour (ed.), *North London Collegiate School 1850–1950*, Oxford, 1950. The showers were something of an innovation for the prudery that held 'you cannot expect eleven ladies to disrobe in one room' had tended to inhibit the provision of proper changing facilities. M. Pollard, *The Story of the AEWHA*, London, 1965, p. 10.

28 K.E. McCrone, *Sport and the Physical Emancipation of Women, 1870–1914*, London, 1988, p. 133.

29 McCrone, *Physical Emancipation*, p. 246, quoting E. Head, *Hockey as a Game for Women*, London, 1904. Dr Jaeger's knitted and woven woollen corsets, the Royal Worcester Boneless Sports Corset, the Khiva Corslet, the J&B Athletic Girl Corset and Sandow's Corset were all on the market.

30 *Ibid.*, p. 229.

31 *Physical Education*, October, 1904, quoted in McCrone, *Physical Emancipation*, p. 135.

32 *Hockey Field*, 10 January, 1907, quoted by McCrone, *Physical Emancipation*, pp. 133–4.

33 *Women's Hockey from Village Green to Wembley Stadium*, AEWHA, London, 1954, p. 7.

CHAPTER FOURTEEN

Flannelled fools

Cricket, an older, subtler, more cerebral pastime than football, was often called 'the national game'. It was never so merely popular as soccer, but it was more emblematic of what Britain believed she stood for. Its roots were deep in the rural past, its imagery was that of the village green, the blacksmith, the squire and the parson, and its resonances were reassuringly feudal. It was the centrepiece of the compulsory games that now characterised the public schools. In 1900 Dr Warre of Eton had called for an Act of Parliament to make military training compulsory for boys over fifteen. *The Times,* suggesting that this was not the British way, had significantly used cricket to make its point: 'There is no Act of Parliament to compel boys to play cricket yet there is no want of stability in the ordinance that they shall play cricket.'[1]

But it was played enthusiastically, too, by lads in the elementary school system where there were neither ordinances nor proper facilities. 'There was no cricket at the Board school I attended', wrote Sir Neville Cardus describing his childhood in the Manchester slums. 'There were no playing fields attached to this establishment, only a playground made of asphalt.'[2] Yet he was drawn to cricket by a chance visit to the county cricket ground at Old Trafford. Contrary to the moralistic view that spectatorship discouraged participation the 12-year-old Cardus was brought to the game (not just as a leading critic but as a player keen enough to go from local Sunday School league to a job as an assistant 'pro' at Shrewsbury School) by watching A.C. Maclaren. 'This brief sight of Maclaren thrilled my blood, for it gave shape and reality to things I had till then only vaguely felt and dreamed about of romance.'[3]

Romance and reality

The Edwardian years Cardus recalled have a special place in the history of cricket, and its attendant mythology. This was 'the golden age', a time, in particular, of dashing amateur batsmen. The imperious MacLaren, with his opening partner for Lancashire, the graceful Reggie Spooner, scored 368 by tea-time against Gloucestershire in 1903. Gloucestershire's own hero was Gilbert Jessop, 'the Croucher', a whirlwind bowler as well as batsman. Sussex had the magician Ranjitsinjhi and the masterful C.B. Fry, Somerset the stylish L.C.H. Palairet, and Kent the glamorous Kenneth Hutchings. The memory is still treasured of the final Test at the Oval in 1902 when England, with the Ashes already lost, came back from the brink of defeat to win by one wicket. 'Everybody knows', confidently declared A.A. Thomson sixty-five years later, 'how England lost Maclaren, Palairet, Tyldesley, Hayward and Braund for 48; how Jessop . . . played his early overs quietly, and then. . .burst forth in an apocalyptic blend of high art and controlled violence. In an hour his score, enriched by a five and seventeen fours, leaped to 104 out of 139.'[4] And if it was left to George Hirst and Wilfred Rhodes, the last pair, to make the fifteen runs still needed for victory that was made part of a complementary legend, that of the dour, unflinching Yorkshire professional, spiced by Hirst's alleged injunction to his incoming junior partner. 'We'll get 'em in singles.'[5] It was 'Jessop's match' immortalised in newspaper lyricism:

> A Croucher at the wicket took his stand
> And crashed the Cornstalk trundlers to the ropes.[6]

It was also of high significance to the reverential historians that Kent won the championship in 1906. This was in itself a welcome relief from Northern domination: 'Let me record with pride that I was conceived in that great and glorious year wherein Kent for the first time won the County Championship', wrote one addict seventy years later.[7] They had won, furthermore, 'in a manner and by methods practically unparalleled in the history of the competition'[8] They had averaged some 80 runs an hour over the season, day in day out, regardless of the state of the game, always trying to win rather than merely avoid defeat – a triumph for the amateur spirit. It was the county championship that provided the regular diet of excitement for the British public if not in actual attendance then in eager scanning of the scores, the first thing people looked for in the early editions of the evening newspapers.

For those who did go, there was a rich variety of amateur talent: not only stylish batsmen, but all-rounders like B.J.T. Bosanquet of Middlesex, inventor of the googly, and the prodigy J.N. Crawford of Surrey, who abruptly left for Australia when, as substitute captain, the committee refused to give him the team he wanted; fast bowlers like Hesketh Hesketh-Prichard, the blond giant who missed a season with Hampshire to get out his book, *Through the Heart of Patagonia*, and N.A. Knox of Surrey who, unaccountably losing form, decided to take up singing instead; and even G.H.T. Simpson-Hayward who took 68 wickets for Worcestershire in 1908 bowling underarm. Good amateur wicket-keepers were rare but there were the brilliant Gregor MacGregor (captain of

Cambridge University and Middlesex and a Scottish Rugby international) and the entirely remarkable Revd Archdale Palmer Wickham who began keeping wicket for Somerset at the ripe age of thirty-six and was still playing in 1907 aged fifty-two. 'Behind the stumps at the county ground,' we are told, 'his legs wide apart and his gloved hands upon his knees, with a stance so low that his Harlequin cap just appeared above the bails, he chose to wear black-topped pads, grey flannels and a black cummerbund. This dress, combined with a heavy "soup-strainer" moustache and side whiskers, guaranteed comment even in an era when eccentricity was commonplace.'[9]

Yet there were critics even then who complained of drab decline. In 1906 E.V. Lucas, the essayist, one of the many Edwardian *littérateurs* who were besotted by cricket, wrote wistfully, 'not only has cricket lost many of its old simplicities, it has lost its characters, too. In the late process of levelling up, or levelling down, individuality has suffered'.[10] The process was symbolised by the growing interest in 'averages', associated with professionals and their safety-first tactics, but in fact almost as universal as its universal condemnation by the purists. A good tip for a poor speaker at a cricket dinner was to 'let it be understood somehow that you disapprove of keeping a batting average, and every glass on the table will dance and sing to you in sympathy. It does not matter that five minutes before those glasses danced and sang when the young gentleman who won the prize for the possession of the best batting average walked up to the chairman to receive it at his hands'.[11]

It was, in any event, becoming hard to tell the difference between amateurs and professionals. In 1903 R.H. Lyttleton complained that cricket was afflicted by a commercialism so insidious that merely defining the terms 'amateur' and 'professional' which would have been a simple matter forty years before was now almost impossible. 'It is strange that such should be the case', he declared, 'and it is also strange that these difficulties should exist so much more in the case of cricket than any other game.'[12] In cricket, unlike golf, tennis, football or billiards, the boundary line between amateur and professional had been obliterated. There were, he reckoned, two main causes. First, touring Australian cricketers were given the title "Mr" or "Esquire" although they were actually professionals. Second, the lengthening English cricket season had enabled the game to become a full-time occupation. In county cricket, competition and gate-money were the twin evils. 'The winning of matches being the golden key to financial prosperity, the Committees have been driven to adopt a system of paying the amateurs money and what thirty years ago was done in one or two instances is now a matter of universal practice.' Expenses, sinecure posts of club secretary, winter jobs and 'complimentary' matches were the accepted thing. When MCC had been asked to take over the management of Australian tours they could not afford the scale of payment demanded by the amateurs.

There was no need, Lyttleton reckoned, for impoverished amateurs to adopt such underhand methods. They should turn professional. The modern professional, though still drawn from 'the shop, from the factory, from the pit, and from the slum' could nowadays look towards a better and more secure income: some had been known to draw £2,000 from a benefit match. And their dress and deportment made it difficult for the spectator to tell them from the amateur. They could augment their incomes by lending their names to advertising sports equipment or by keeping a shop or public-house. 'The profession of a cricketer, the calling of a professional is in every way an honourable and good one. What puzzles many of us is that, this being the case, so many should adopt the profession but deny the name. . .It is an old proverb that you cannot eat your cake and have it, and if the modern amateur does not care on social grounds to become a professional then let him honestly refuse to play cricket if he cannot afford to play on receipt of his bare expenses.'[13]

A remarkable complement to Lyttleton's argument came three years later in a book by a professional cricketer.[14] Albert Knight certainly testified to the advance made by the professional, in education as well as respectability. His book, *The Complete Cricketer*, was studded with French and Latin aphorisms and included references to William Morris, Matthew Arnold, the *Zeitgeist* and Hardy's *Jude the Obscure*. Knight's criticism of the system displayed remarkable courage, for he was in mid-career, and his forthright condemnation cannot have endeared him to the gentlemanly administrators. His Mandarin style made his strictures even more devastating: 'Many an "amateur", so-termed, playing in county cricket, is more heavily remunerated than an accredited "professional" player. The distinction once had a valid foundation, based essentially on differences of wealth and social station. The reason for that distinction has quite disappeared.'[15] Like Lyttleton he found it extraordinary that cricket alone should try to preserve them. Unlike Lyttleton, however, he was for abolishing the 'exclusive "Mr" or "Esquire"' altogether, rather than trying to make them meaningful. True gentlemen, he reckoned, 'disliked these miserable and most hateful labels and distinctions which sicken honest people by their unfairness.' And in a jibe that must have been as infuriating to the establishment for its parade of learning as for its impertinence he delivered his most devastating thrust: 'I sometimes think. . .that, quite unconsciously, the modern committees have struck upon the great Anarchist Communist's ideal maxim, "Each according to his needs".'[16]

The irony was lost on Lord Harris, now Treasurer and *eminence grise* of MCC. In 1909, in an article in *The Times*, he blandly set out the principles which governed cricket's approach to these matters, manifestly, he reckoned, superior to that in other sports and manifestly acceptable to players on both sides of the social divide. 'Why is it', he asked, 'that in two of the most popular pastimes – football and athletics – so much ire can be roused over the question of amateur and professional, while in a third – cricket – it is viewed with calm indifference?' His answer was that cricket had learned 'the wisdom of experience' – that professionalism was not a matter of whether a cricketer was paid but of 'the daily avocation of the man.' The real distinction was not 'whether A receives £5 or £2 for playing in a match, nor whether B receives £200 and his expenses for representing England in a tour but does he make his livelihood out of playing the game, is it his daily avocation in its season, does he engage himself day in day out to play it from May 1 to August 31? If he does he is a professional, and knows he is a professional'.[17]

As for 'those social regulations which distinguish the amateur and professional at cricket' the professionals readily accepted them and they were trifling anyway. 'From old practice', Harris explained, 'the prefix "Mr" or the affix "Esq." is still used, but no-one sets any particular store by them.' Otherwise the distinctions amounted to 'little more than this, that the rule of the ground should be observed; and that guests should observe the arrangements made by their hosts. For instance, the arrangements as regards dressing rooms are not identical on all grounds.' This humbug concealed the fact that almost everywhere the amateurs had separate dressing rooms and sometimes proceeded from there to the wicket by a separate gate from the professionals. And it was for these 'trifling' distinctions that the whole edifice of deceit and hypocrisy was preserved.

Thus the shamateur tradition of W.G. Grace continued. The Great Cricketer himself, now over fifty, captained the Gentlemen against the Players in 1901 though he was already leading his own team, London County, in his capacity as cricket manager of Crystal Palace. Many other leading amateurs (according to the Harris criterion) also turned out for his team, including C.B. Fry, the archetypal sporting and academic all-rounder, and Gilbert Jessop, who illustrated the degenerative effect of the games cult. Jessop was no scholar. He had left his private school on the death of his father, getting a job as a teacher of sorts and assisting Gloucestershire in the vacations. He then went to Cambridge (assisted by a theological scholarship!) joining in the summer term of 1896, thus including four cricket seasons in his three years of residence before leaving without taking a degree. Jessop played for Gloucestershire in the Cambridge vacations, winning a cap for England in 1899, the year he went down. After a cricket tour of America that Autumn he returned to work for a time on the Stock Exchange, before replacing W.G., on suitably advantageous terms, as captain of Gloucestershire in the summer of 1901. That winter he toured Australia with the team led by A.C. MacLaren – the tour Lyttleton described as too expensive in the way of amateur demands for MCC to sponsor.

When MCC did take over responsibility for the next tour, in 1903–4, and offered 'expenses only' Jessop declined the invitation and wrote about the tour for the *Daily Mail* instead. He also let it be known that he might no longer be able to afford to captain Gloucestershire in future. It would depend, he told the *Daily Express*, on whether the county would support him in his business interests. Later he informed readers of the *Western Daily Press* that his financial problems had been solved and that he was free to play as much cricket as he liked. He had, in fact, been found a job at £500 a year as a director of a tobacco firm, but unfortunately the firm was taken over soon afterwards and he turned more and more to sporting journalism, the favourite recourse of amateur sportsmen.

The tradition of the writer-organiser was well-established: the modern trend was towards the journalist-player. One of best and most prolific was C.B. Fry, who was saved from less dignified ways of upholding his amateur status by marrying money. As well as his regular columns in the daily press, Fry was athletics editor of *The Captain* and later started his own *Fry's Magazine*. Another, less capable and less industrious, was A.C. MacLaren (who also endorsed cricket bats). The most assiduous and influential was P.F. Warner, who, though trained as a lawyer, became the regular cricket correspondent of the *Westminster Gazette* in 1903 and throughout his long career as a player, captain of Middlesex and England, pillar of MCC, and an England selector, earned his living from writing about the game.

On 12 May 1904 a Bernard Partridge drawing in *Punch* showed a cricket match in which all the participants were scribbling away as they played. The lordly F.S. Jackson, whose many business interests included a directorship of the *Yorkshire Post*, thought the new trend irresponsible and said so. Jessop replied with an Open Letter (presumably paid for) to Jackson. 'As a director of an influential newspaper you have some connection with journalism, which makes me wonder why you are unsympathetic to him who wields the willow as well as the pen. The limited income amateur, my dear Jacker, is just as enthusiastic about the game as he who is more fortunately placed. In order to still continue his favourite pastime he has three courses open to him. Firstly, if he is good enough, he may induce the authorities to appoint him to an assistant secretaryship; secondly, if he has any ability whatever in the direction of putting his thoughts on paper, he can accept the opportunity of doing so; and lastly he may become a professional.'[18] To the Harrovian Jackson becoming a professional would have been like taking off his trousers in public. One or two amateurs did make the change, notably E.H.D. Sewell of Essex, who was also a Harlequins rugby player, but he was not only a journalist but a grammar school boy.

Dissidents and defenders

It was taken for granted that the county captains who effectively controlled the day-by-day running of the game would be amateurs. They also had to be full-time cricketers. Not surprisingly the convention produced a fair proportion of former schoolboy heroes reluctant to grow up, gifted wastrels and petty tyrants. For the most part the professionals they led, seeking to exploit the only talent they had to raise them above the level of an unskilled worker, put up with the amateurs with docility. Some, like Knight, who was not only a philosopher but deeply religious, were quietly critical but mannerly enough to keep out of serious trouble. A few were more belligerent – and paid the penalty. Tom Wass, the Nottinghamshire fast bowler, might well have played for England but for his attitude problem. When a distinguished amateur batsman, arriving at the crease, greeted him by his nickname, 'Topsy', Wass replied, 'Tom Wass is my name, but I gi' thee mister and I'll 'ave mister o' thee – if tha must talk.'[19] The most notable professional opponent of the system was Sydney Barnes, the best medium-paced bowler of the era. He was more intelligent than the average, but distinctly spiky and highly resistant to exploitation, like a cricketing version of Billy Meredith. When fate brought Barnes and the equally individualistic Archie MacLaren together on the 1901–2 tour of Australia it was a case of the irresistible force and the immovable object.

The Harrovian MacLaren, from a Manchester business background, was usually at odds with the aristocratic Etonian overlords Harris and Hawke, and his chronic impetuosity made him a constant thorn in the flesh for MCC. His decision to lead the tour, a typical entrepreneurial adventure, was a considerable embarrassment to them and they gave him no help in trying to form a team. By the time Lord Hawke refused to allow *his* two professionals, George Hirst and Wilfred Rhodes, to go on the tour (on the grounds that they might overtire themselves for the following summer) MacLaren was so desperate for bowlers that he turned to Sydney Barnes, a virtual unknown. Barnes was playing in the Lancashire League. He had played one match for Warwickshire in 1895 and later a few times for Lancashire, but he thought it not well enough paid considering the hours and the drudgery involved. MacLaren's offer of a winter tour followed by a season's contract with the county represented settled employment and Barnes accepted.

He brought with him no starry-eyed public school notions of team spirit, which in his experience meant professionals taking second place to amateurs. He was, however, dedicated – to the narrower cause of removing opposing batsmen, for which he had a great talent and from which he took great satisfaction. And he was concerned to secure a just reward for the effort he put in. So far from being overwhelmed by the honour of being selected for his country he strongly asserted his rights as a working man: he took strong exception to not being put on to bowl if the conditions were right and even stronger exception to being asked to bowl when he thought they were wrong. He performed very well in the first Test, and well enough to please everyone but MacLaren in the second, but when called upon to make a big effort in the third he developed an injury. Before long MacLaren's irritation was such that when a storm threatened to sink the ship that was taking the team across to New Zealand he was heard to observe philosophically: 'There's one comfort. If we go down that bugger Barnes will go down with us.'[20]

They survived and returned for the summer with Lancashire. Barnes played in one Test in 1902, and took 6 for 49 in the first innings, but was not picked again. At the end of the season his proneness to injury at critical times led *Wisden* to suggest that he was not a trier. Chosen for the Players against the Gentlemen the following summer he bowled only one over before he 'went lame'. MCC did not select Barnes for the Australian tour of 1903–4. Nor, however, did they offer the captaincy to MacLaren, who had led England throughout the 1902 home series. By this time the early, casual gentlemanly supremacy of MCC and their counterparts in the counties, based on patronage, was being transformed into a self-perpetuating oligarchy dedicated to 'amateurism' and determined to exercise control over the game. They were also becoming aware of their imperial responsibilities under the influence of Harris and Hawke: MCC set great store by having the right sort of amateur to lead their missionary ventures as they took over the responsibility, selectoral and managerial, for all tours as well as home Test matches. Their first choice as captain for the 1903–4 tour was the upright F.S. Jackson, but when his business interests led him to decline they passed over the 'unreliable' MacLaren and controversially selected P.F. Warner, a journalist but a man of discretion *par excellence*. There were no more fears of overtiring Hirst and Rhodes who were both selected. In the tradition of one law for the amateur and another for the professional F.S. Jackson, who never made himself available to tour Australia, was awarded the captaincy of England in the home series of 1905 and then announced his retirement.[21]

Warner, who became the chief disciple of Harris and Hawke in the new century, was eloquent in expressing the virtues of cricket tours in solidifying the Empire and himself toured enthusiastically and with profit to his writing career. The chief beneficiary of MCC's new policy was South Africa which took the centre of the imperial stage in the post-Boer War period. Cecil Rhodes had died in 1902, his memory sweetened by his generous will. A new spirit of goodwill began to be engendered between the Boers and their British fellow-colonists, helped by the conciliatory attitude towards the fallen foe bred by tender consciences in London. When Warner led an MCC tour to South Africa in 1905–6 it was to encourage games which 'had done so much for British manhood' and inculcated 'the spirit of fair play'.[22] His book – there was always a book – described a social highlight of the visit, a meeting with a former Boer Commandant who attested to his great love for both cricket and his conquerors: 'He made no secret of the fact that he liked Englishmen and hinted that South Africa would settle down rapidly and there would be no distinction between Briton and Boer: all would be South Africans – if only, he added, "the newspapers would stop talking".'[23] In fact this new harmony was greatly stimulated by their shared fears that the incoming Liberal government might do something to help the cause of the black majority. They need not have worried. The Liberals were even more sympathetic towards the Boers and they concluded a deal that led to many more years of white supremacy.

One of the most assiduous workers for South African union within the Empire was Abe Bailey, soon to be Sir Abe, a first-generation South African who had made millions in gold share and property speculation. It was his money that sustained much of the touring, home and away. Frank Mitchell, the former Cambridge captain who led the South Africans in England in 1904, was his secretary, and Bailey had also entertained Warner and his men in 1905–6. The idea of 'an Imperial cricket contest between England, South Africa and Australia' that Bailey put forward in 1907 suited everyone's book politically and by 1909 an Imperial Cricket Conference had been set up between the three countries. This grandly-named body's initial task was merely to organise the 1911 triangular tournament (an unhappy experiment never to be repeated) but it had served its purpose for South Africa and was to last for over fifty years as the body controlling international cricket.[24]

Leagues, loyalties, literati and leucocytes

Barnes, meanwhile, was espousing more mundane causes. His relations with Lancashire grew steadily worse, basically because he did not see why when he was called upon to do so much work (he bowled 1,023 overs in the 1903 season) he should only be paid the flat rate. Lancashire's basic terms were then £3 a week in summer and £1 a week over the winter, and when Church, the Lancashire League club, offered him £8 a week to play on Saturdays Barnes tried to use this as a lever to get better terms from Lancashire, including winter employment. He was unsuccessful, and as the end of the season approached Barnes had still not re-signed. In order to put pressure on him MacLaren left him out of the team for the last match. Barnes took exception to this, especially as it meant losing match pay and perhaps a winning bonus, so he turned out anyway. MacLaren, however, was equally determined and had him escorted from the field. So ended Barnes's career with Lancashire, and he spent most of the rest of his very long cricketing life playing in the Leagues and for Staffordshire in the Minor Counties Championship. Nevertheless when many of the leading players refused MCC's terms for the 1907–8 tour of Australia he was again selected and did well, as he did, when fit, in the 1908 home series. But he steadfastly refused to conform, and that for a professional simply would not do.

The Barnes story illustrates the potential loss of talent to the national team through the dominance of county cricket. First-class cricket was conducted, not for the spectators at the turnstiles, but for the members and their committees, and it was run, not by the professionals who were its mainstay, but by the amateurs who were tied by bonds of class, schooling and often of family, to the committees. This effectively froze the upper echelons of the game in the patterns of the past, producing a core of full-time players who performed for the entertainment of the limited number of county members who were able to watch cricket during the week when the great majority of the population were at their work. County players were drawn from two main sources, the public schools and universities on the one hand and the young professionals taken at an early age from club teams on the other.

There were plenty of clubs of course, but especially in the south, which in cricketing terms represented the majority of counties, club cricket was a haphazard affair. An immigrant Australian amateur Dr L.O.S. Poidevin, who played cricket for Lancashire and lawn tennis for Australasia, described the system as 'too magnificently disorganised to do itself justice or reach anything above mediocrity in standard of play'.[25] The League cricket of the industrial North and Midlands, besides being thought by most southerners too competitive and vulgar for amateurs, was seen as a threat to the county clubs. Apart from being a direct counter-attraction they subverted the monopolistic system: as *Wisden* pointed out, 'With the busy scouts of the Lancashire League always on the look out for talent, committees cannot retain their professionals unless they ensure them a large amount of remuneration.'[26]

But there was, like it or not, something in Lord Harris's claim that the gentlemen and players idea suited the British. Jack Hobbs the supreme batsman, was every Englishman's ideal, quiet and unassuming, utterly sportsmanlike in everything he did, and if he exposed the fallacy of the assumptions about the amateur style – he raised batting to a new level, amateur or professional – he pleased the ruling establishment by always knowing his place, always being there as the wise counsellor for every new captain he served under, yet never presuming to seek office himself. Nor was it solely a southern preference. Yorkshire, which had come to exemplify the successful modern side, and whose gifted professionals were distinctly lacking in social polish, were led in feudal style until 1910 by Lord Hawke, who had been born in 1860 and whose average did not bear thinking about.

County pride was the decisive element in this social cement, just as it was in the survival of the championship itself as a spectator sport, long after its hours of play and other obsolete conventions ought to have seen it buried by the urban deluge. It showed itself most strongly, furthermore, in the northern industrial wastes beyond the great divide and strongest of all in the traditional Wars of the Roses rivalry between Yorkshire and Lancashire. Cardus recalled the exquisite agony of watching – or rather not watching – Hirst bowl to Reggie Spooner: 'then would I pretend to be looking on the ground for something while I closed my eyes and prayed that God would make George Hirst drop down dead before bowling the next ball. I loved Spooner so much that I dared not watch him make stroke'.[27] And *The Clarion* columnist might refer in an off-beat account of a Roses match to 'Mister Spoonah', but it was entirely affectionate, and he quoted the comment of a (Lancastrian) spectator, perched on a couple of bricks for a better view, on a characteristic Spooner off-drive: 'Ez yeasy ez shullin' peas.'[28]

Neither county loyalties nor aesthetic appreciation could, of course, persuade the working-class supporter, who paid at the turnstiles, to accept an amateur attitude if that meant regarding winning as relatively unimportant, as purist tradition required. The message from Yorkshire, where this maxim was never held in high regard, was indeed that only actual victory was enough. They were toppled from the championship in 1909 and in a wet summer 'the comparative ill-success of the team brought about a regrettable apathy on the part of the public, especially in Leeds'. By contrast Kent, who won again, 'after a liberal outlay for ground improvements, left off with a net balance for the season of several hundred pounds'.[29] The two metropolitan counties were freest from these pressures, partly because county loyalties, especially in Middlesex, were somewhat artificial but chiefly because there were many more people with weekday leisure. Lord Northcliffe, who could not understand cricket's popularity, asked one of his journalists to find out how these London crowds were made up. He was told that in the capital 'there were members of all classes with little more occupation than counting the hours. Also, folk could snatch a holiday by candour or ingenuity when bat and ball proved an attraction. As to the Oval and how the minor patrons found the money . . . one could only assume that they borrowed from each other'.[30]

Elsewhere, north and south, unsuccessful counties could not look to the turnstiles to improve their financial position, which was usually precarious, nor did they want to. This was no 'profit-maximising cartel'.[31] There was no pooling of receipts, formal subsidisation or transfer fees to help poorer counties: it was Darwinism but of a rather timorous and genteel kind. All counties tried to rid themselves of the tyranny of the turnstiles: even an increase in members' annual subscriptions (which were often no more than a guinea a year) was thought too risky. The consequent hand to mouth existence of the majority of clubs was endured in the consoling knowledge 'that when things get to the worst the money is always forthcoming',[32] if not by the private patronage of individuals, then by appeals for voluntary donations from the membership or general public. There was, in 1909, 'a grave fear early in the autumn that Derbyshire as a first-class county club would cease to exist', but the result of a special appeal was so encouraging that the committee decided to carry on, as had their Somerset counterparts two years before. This was what the Football League had escaped, but at a price the counties were not prepared to pay and that public sentiment helped them avoid.

This sentiment was greatly encouraged by the prevalent Arcadian social and literary values. It was a great age, for instance, for country-house cricket which many had feared would die out with the advent of the county competition. True amateur bliss was still to be had in the itinerant clubs, such as I Zingari, Free Foresters, Grasshoppers and Eton Ramblers, survivors of the great mid-Victorian vogue for such things when Old Clarke and his professional circuses had threatened the decorum of an earlier age. There were still, particularly in the south, plenty of aristocrats and landed gentry, and a few *nouveaux riches*, who were willing and able to open their grounds and great houses to well-bred young fellows, who, daunted by the length and strenuous nature of the county season, were more than content to play their cricket at week-end parties, dressing for dinner in the evening and dancing the night away. True, this kind of cricket was not reported in the evening newspapers, but if the average man cared no more about the results than did the young blades who played in them, he was not immune from their infectious glamour. There was no more dashing hero than E.W. Hornung's Raffles, the gentleman cracksman, who preferred invitations to houses where there were spoons worth stealing.

Literary men, including Hornung and his more orthodox brother-in-law Conan Doyle, had their own idiosyncratic cricketing coteries. J.M. Barrie, who founded the Allahakbarries – a name derived from the Moorish for 'God help us' – was the most devotedly whimsical. The doings of his team, which played a few matches each year against village teams, was lovingly if facetiously recorded. According to Barrie, the more distinguished as authors his men were, the worse they played. 'Conan Doyle was the chief exception to this depressing rule, but . . . the others did occasionally have their day.'[33] A.E.W. Mason, Augustine Birrell, Maurice Hewlett, E.V. Lucas, Owen Seaman, Charles Whibley, F. Anstey, Jerome K. Jerome and Bernard Partridge were amongst those who 'talked so much cricket that it began to be felt among them that they were hidden adepts at the game'.[34] Actors, too, like Rutland Barrington and George Edwardes, with weekday time on their hands, found cricket an ideal pastime, either watching at Lord's or playing their own improvised games.

The big thing about cricket for these urban sophisticates was the sense of getting away from it all into a nobler England: hence the reverence in which village cricket was held. Boys in town and country alike learned to play cricket at school, but the town lads, of the poorer classes at least, usually had to learn on asphalt rather than grass. Of its popularity as a street game there is much evidence in the numerous pictures in the illustrated papers and the humorous drawings in *Punch* and the like of ragged urchins, impersonating their heroes like Hobbs or Jessop, playing with lamp-posts for a wicket, and the many jokes about broken windows and pursuing policemen. In 1908 *The Times* published a long article on 'London's free cricket fields'. On summer Saturdays the parks and open spaces were being put to good use: 'If these patches of green on the map be the "lungs of the metropolis" then one might say that the hundreds of white fleeting figures are the leucocytes of the body municipal. For all the pathetic crudeness of their efforts, these youthful players are actually striving to prevent the physical decay of a nation, far too large a proportion of which is compelled to live and die in huge prison-cities. In these green playing fields of London a greater battle than Waterloo – the battle for the nation's wasted physical force and will-power – is being fought sturdily, steadily, and, let us hope, victoriously.'[35]

It went on to criticise the inadequate royal contribution: 'There is a limited amount of space for cricket in Regent's Park and the other pleasances which are Royal demesnes . . . but I cannot help thinking that more accommodation for so humane a pastime could be and ought to be provided.' Conversely it was warm in its praise of the LCC, which did 'more for the cricketer of very small means than all the other public bodies in metropolis and its suburbs', providing that season 442 reserved match grounds accommodating nearly 10,000 players each week in some 30,000 matches, apart from the unreserved free-for-all areas where thousands thronged in happy confusion. And it lauded the efforts of the university and public school missions in the East End which did 'all in their power to encourage cricket (which was) a salutary discipline for youths who would otherwise spend all their leisure in the sorry-go-round of London street life. . . Unquestionably cricket is the best antidote to Hooliganism'.

Outside London the picture varied: generally urban working-class cricketers were better regarded by the municipalities than footballers (partly because they were less inclined to want to charge gate-money for their matches) but they needed more and better-prepared spaces and these were not often forthcoming. It was certainly easier for them to become spectators than players, though there were many works teams for the more serious, and League clubs encouraged promising players to come and try their hands at the nets. In the country things were vastly better. In September, 1908, E.V. Lucas wrote an enthusiastic article about the revival of the Hambledon club, reminding his readers that there was an older and finer tradition than the county game: 'Any step that can bring sentiment again into first-class cricket is to be welcomed; for a hard utilitarianism and commercialism have far too long controlled it.'[36] Village cricket was thriving and it was a desolate hamlet, indeed, throughout the length and breadth of the kingdom that did not have its team, with a meadow, a roller and perhaps a hut to change in.

Indeed English and Anglophile sentiment about a vanished rural past was enough to keep alive the convention that cricket was the national game. There could hardly be such a thing in the confusing mix of nationalities, political philosophies and traditions that was Britain. Scottish golfers, Welsh rugby men and Irish hurlers were entitled to disagree, and the working-class favourite, soccer, could not be ignored. Bookmakers might also put in a claim for racing, and fishing was not only one of the oldest but the one most practised. There were, in fact, many national sports. Britain was a land of sport-lovers. Flannelled fools and muddied oafs or not, people of all classes sought inspiration or escape in sport. The workers got away from harsh or drab reality. Gilded youth countered boredom. Tired businessmen restored the tissues. Public schoolmasters built an educational philosophy round sport, and schoolmistresses began to follow them. Patriots embraced it as a superior alternative to German regimentation. Progressive young women revelled in its freedoms. Armchair imperialists, gunboat diplomatists and reactionaries of all types took refuge in its committee rooms where a man could still govern without too much interference from democracy. They were to find such solace increasingly necessary in the years ahead. Lord Northcliffe is said to have called Edward VII 'The best King we ever had – on the racecourse', and his death in May, 1910 seemed a fearful portent to the fashionable race-goers clad in mauve and black who foregathered at the Royal meeting three weeks later. 'Those who were not present at Ascot', sombrely observed *The Times*, 'can scarcely realise the gloom of the spectacle.'[37] Things would never be the same again.

Notes

1 The Times, 29 June, 1901, quoted in J.A. Mangan, *Athleticism and the Victorian Public School* Cambridge, 1981, p. 82.
2 N. Cardus, *Autobiography*, London, 1947, p. 29.

3 *Ibid.*, p. 31.
4 Wisden, 1967, p. 122.
5 In fact they did not, and both men subsequently denied the legend. Rhodes said it was 'only a tale'.
6 Recalled by B. Travers, *94 Declared*, London, 1981: his lively account of the match is printed in M. and S. Davie, *The Faber Book of Cricket*, London, 1987.
7 E.W. Swanton, *Follow On*, London, 1977, p. 1.
8 P. Trevor, 'Average Keeping', *The Problems of Cricket*, London, 1907.
9 G. Strong, *The Cricketer*, 1983, reprinted in C. Martin-Jenkins (ed.), *A Cricketer's Companion*, London, 1990, pp. 103–6.
10 E.V. Lucas, 'Cricket, the Backward Look', in *Fireside and Sunshine*, London, 1906, quoted in D. Frith, *The Golden Age of Cricket*, Guildford, 1978, p. 18.
11 Trevor, 'Average Keeping'.
12 'Amateur and Professional', in Hutchinson, *Cricket*, p. 194.
13 *Ibid.*, pp. 205–6.
14 A.E. Knight, *The Complete Cricketer*, London, 1906.
15 *Ibid.*, p. 43.
16 *Ibid.*, p. 44.
17 22 January, 1909. Harris's arguments stood the test of time. The distinction between amateur and professional was not finally ended until 26 November, 1962. Harris himself was so pleased with his rationale that he repeated it in his memoirs, *A Few Short Runs*, London, 1921, pp. 162–7.
18 Quoted in G. Brodribb, *The Croucher*, London, 1974, p. 207.
19 D.R. Allen (ed.), *Arlott on Cricket*, London, 1984, p. 43.
20 B. Hollowood, *Cricket on the Brain*, London, 1970, p. 139. For Barnes see L. Duckworth, *S.F. Barnes – Master Bowler*, London, 1967.
21 There was no question of Jackson's ability: the series, which England won, was a great personal triumph for him.
22 P.F. Warner, *The MCC in South Africa*, London, 1906, p. 218.
23 *Ibid.*, pp. 29–30.
24 Its membership was eventually enlarged to include India, the West Indies and New Zealand in 1926 and when its name was changed to the International Cricket Conference in 1965 it signified that the end of the Empire had come, even for cricketers.
25 Quoted in Frith, *Golden Age*, p. 21.
26 'Notes by the Editor', Wisden, 1910.
27 Cardus, *Autobiography*, p. 151.
28 H. Beswick, 'Our Eli Patronises Cricket', 16 June, 1905.
29 Wisden, 1967.
30 W. Pett Ridge, *I Like to Remember*, London, 1925, in Martin-Jenkins *Companion*, p. 199.
31 See K. Sandiford and W. Vamplew, 'The Peculiar Economics of English cricket before 1914', *British Journal of Sports History*, December, 1986, p. 322.
32 Wisden, 1967.
33 J.M. Barrie, *The Greenwood Hat*, London, 1937, quoted in D.R. Allen, *Peter Pan and Cricket*, London, 1988, pp. 80–1.
34 *Ibid.*, p. 79.
35 7 August, 1908, reprinted in M. Williams (ed.), *Double Century*, London, 1985, pp. 143–5.
36 *The Times*, 4 September, 1908, Williams, *Double Century*, p. 147.
37 15 June, 1910.

INDEX

Coles, Percy 251
collective bargaining 15
Colt, H.S. 195–8
Common, Alf 236
Companies Act 39
companification 25, 39–40, 130
Conan Doyle, Sir Arthur 11, 87, 269
Conrad, Joseph 11
Constantine, L.S. 158
Cook, Thomas 86
Cooper, Charlotte 'Chattie' (Mrs
    Sterry) 83, 199
Cooper, John Astley 168, 169
Corbett, 'Gentleman' Jim 151, 213
Corinthian Football Club 33, 34, 238–9,
    240
Coronation Tournament (boxing) 210
Coubertin, Baron Pierre de 66, 67, 83,
    150, 221, 222, 224
County Cricket Council 25
Coventry R.G.T. 246–7, 251
Cowes Regatta 143
Craig, J. of Inverness 63
Crane, Arnold 251
Crawford, J.N. 192, 259
Crawford, Stirling 249
Cresta Run 87, 207
cricket 16–24, 68, 154, 155, 169, 258–66
    amateur 18–22
    Australia 17, 18, 19, 20, 23, 166, 260–1
    companification 25
    county 18, 19, 24–7
    cups 20, 26
    gamesmanship 22–4
    Gentlemen and Players 18, 262, 265
    in India 157
    laws 17
    leagues 24–7
    one-day 27
    professional 17–19
    spread to colonies 17
    'Test matches' 17, 22, 23, 25
    'Varsity matches 24
    women 98–100
Cricket Ground Company 26
Croke, Archbishop 70, 77
Croke Cups 70
croquet 74, 79, 81
crown green bowling 206
Crump, Charles 33
Crystal Palace FC 231

Cumming, Sir William Gordon 139
Cunard, Sir Bache 122
curling 87, 88, 166
Currie Cup 166
Curzon Cup 207
Cusack, Michael 69, 70
cycling 3, 65, 78–81, 163
    clothing 79–80, 163
    decline in 84–6
    road racing 84–9
    women 79–80, 85, 187
Cyclists' Touring Club 84, 85

Daimler, Gottfried 85
Dales, W. of Houghton 226
Dalhousie 157
Dalmeny, Lord 191–3
dancing 180
Darling, Joe 18, 23, 89
Davies, J.J. 237
Davin, Maurice 69, 70, 221
Davis, Dwight 84, 200
Davis Cup 84, 204
Davitt, Michael 9, 68, 69
Davy, Sir Humphry 127
Day, Beauchamp R. 223, 225, 226
de Grey, Lord (7th Baron Walsingham)
    124, 183
de Wend-Fenton, West Fenton 192
Decugis, Max 203
Deeley, Henry (Henry Mallaby-
    Deeley) 105, 108
deer-hunting 118, 125, 183
Delius, Frederick 179
Derby, 16th Earl of 133, 166
Derby, The 183
Derby County Football Club 25
Derbyshire, cricket 25
Desborough, Lord (Willie Grenfell) 61,
    216, 222
Devonshire, 8th Duke of 104, 117
Dewsbury RFC 44–5
Dial Square FC 41
Diamond Sculls trophy 216
Dod, Lottie 78, 82, 83, 96, 198, 207
dog-fighting 119
Doggett's Cap and Badge 57
Doherty, Laurie ('Little Do') 83–4, 200,
    201
Doherty, Reggie ('Big Do') 83–4, 200,
    201, 204